GENETIC ALGORITHMS AND INVESTMENT STRATEGIES

WILEY FINANCE EDITIONS

GENETIC ALGORITHMS AND INVESTMENT STRATEGIES

Richard J. Bauer, Jr.

John Wiley & Sons, Inc.
New York • Chichester • Brisbane • Toronto • Singapore

To Amy and Mary

Publisher: Karl Weber
Editor: Myles Thompson
Managing Editor: Angela Murphy
Composition: Impressions

This text is printed on acid-free paper.

Library of Congress Cataloging-in-Publication Data:

Bauer, Richard J. Jr.
    Genetic algorithms and investment strategies / Richard J. Bauer, Jr.
      p.   cm. — (Wiley finance editions)
    Includes bibliographical references and index.
    ISBN 0-471-57679-4
      1. Investments—Mathematical models.   2. Investment analysis—
Mathematical models.   3. Genetic algorithms.   I. Title.
   HG4515.2.B38   1994
332.6'01'5118—dc20   93-11984

Printed in the United States of America

10 9 8 7 6 5 4 3

Contents

**PART THREE   GENETIC ALGORITHMS AND INVESTMENT
                STRATEGIES**

Preface

The power of genetic algorithms, and related concepts such as classifier systems, is truly mind-boggling. I am convinced that this software technology will eventually be widely used in the development of trading systems; the methodology is just too powerful for that not to happen. Unlike chaos theory and neural networks, genetic algorithms allow users to explore countless variations of their own trading ideas and philosophy. Markets have always been a battleground of ideas. In the current geopolitical environment, warfare is reverting to the conventional, but today's software developments will cause competition in the investments arena to become the equivalent of nuclear warfare.

This book is intended to be an introduction to genetic algorithms and to show how they might be used to discover attractive trading strategies. It is not a textbook but is meant to be a tutorial. The trading strategies I investigate are merely intended to be provocative; hopefully they will get your wheels turning about how you might use genetic algorithms to develop your own strategies. The results I report are intriguing, but they are certainly not offered as any get-rich scheme. The use of genetic algorithms requires a certain degree of imagination, and I am convinced that some creative person will soon use them to get rich. Hopefully it will be me or you.

My own interest in genetic algorithms has evolved in a fashion somewhat analogous to the way they themselves work. In November 1987, I attended a conference in New York titled "Expert Systems in Business." Gunar Liepins, a mathematician and prominent genetic algorithm researcher, was asked to substitute for another speaker on the program—a chance event, not unlike the random action of a genetic algorithm. I barely understood what Gunar had to say, but I was intrigued. We spoke after his presentation, and he began to send me articles over the next few months. I proposed that we do joint research, trying to apply genetic algorithms to investment strategies. He agreed, and we continued our correspondence via electronic mail. We met again in Ann Arbor in the summer of 1988 at a conference on machine learning.

Our investments-oriented genetic algorithm publishing efforts began in November 1988, when one of our papers, titled "Genetic Algorithms and Computerized Trading Strategies,'' was published in the working paper series of the University of Western Ontario's Business School, where I was on the faculty. This paper was later published as a chapter in *Expert Systems in Finance* (Amsterdam, The Netherlands; North-Holland, 1992). To my knowledge, this was the first published paper linking genetic algorithms to investments. In June 1991, we presented another paper, ''Genetic Algorithms and Stock Market Timing Trading Rules,'' at the 11th International Symposium on Forecasting in New York City, where we also conducted a workshop for IBM's Wall Street customers. By January 1992 I had written a book proposal, and we secured a book contract with John Wiley & Sons. I started working on the manuscript, and Gunar had plans to work on his part during the summer of 1992. Unfortunately, Gunar died suddenly and unexpectedly in February 1992.

I think Gunar would have been pleased with the book. Our association had certain parallels with genetic algorithms. *Crossover* is a term used in genetic algorithms that relates to the exchange of genetic information; Gunar ''crossed over'' some of his knowledge to me. His death was somewhat random, similar to the random elimination of certain individuals in the genetic algorithm population. I thank him for introducing me to the subject and working with me; I wish we could have done more.

There are many people that I would like to thank for their help. My recently departed grandfather, Dajo, taught me great perseverance. He tried for many years to get a manuscript published, and although he did not succeed, his efforts inspired me. My grandmother, Pearl, has always encouraged and supported me in every way. My parents, Dick and Jo-Katherine Bauer, nourished me with love and have blessed me with many opportunities to learn. My cousin, Gwen, gave me constant encouragement and has listened to all of my frustrations. John Wilkerson and Beaty Howard, my business partners, helped me afford to get my Ph.D. I thank RBC Dominion Securities in Toronto for sponsoring my travel to the conference where I first learned of genetic algorithms; special thanks go to Doug Steiner from that organization for his interest and encouragement. For developing my love of mathematics and computing, I thank my former professors Ken-Hsi Wang, Don Hardcastle, Darden Powers, Merle Alexander, and the late Shim Park. For developing my interest in finance, I thank my former finance professors Dave Upton, Richard Peterson, Charles Moyer, and Scott Hein. My colleagues at the University of Western Ontario first heard some of my crazy ideas about genetic algorithms and gave me helpful feedback. They are Ron Wirick, Jim Hatch, Dave Shaw, Larry Wynant, Bob White, and Steve Forrester. My co-workers at Saint Mary's University in sunny San Antonio have also provided great encouragement. They are Dean David Manuel, Julie Dahlquist, Tom Hamilton, Richard Priesmeyer, Jerry Todd, and Connie Abbott. Tom has forced me to answer many tough questions about my experiments. Julie has also asked great questions, provided unending moral support, helped with manuscript preparation, and engaged me in many stimulating discussions. Richard deserves special thanks for our many discussions about chaos theory and genetic algorithms. Connie wages continual battle against my disorganization. I also thank Mei-Lin Lee for helping me get started with John Wiley & Sons. Others in San Antonio have also encouraged me. They are Jeanie Rabke Wyatt, Bill Fries, Harry Miller, David Parsons, David Edwards, and Vince Green.

Finally, I thank my two daughters, Amy Larissa and Mary Elizabeth. They have been the principal source of joy and inspiration in my life. I hope that the best parts of me have crossed over to them.

San Antonio, Texas
June 1993

PART ONE
GENETIC ALGORITHMS, NEURAL NETWORKS, AND CHAOS THEORY

1
An Introduction to Biologically Based Methods

Neural networks. Genetic algorithms. Chaos Theory. Fractals. Expert Systems. Mention those terms to Wall Streeters, and most will likely think you're talking about some high-tech public offerings. In fact, they are new computer tools that could have a far-reaching impact on the Street and finance generally.

From a special report in Business Week, *November 2, 1992, titled "The New Rocket Science: Welcome to the Future of Finance"*

The investments game is changing. Financial markets have always been a battle-ground for competing ideas. There are two sides to every trade. Two competing ideas. Two competing pieces of logic. Both buyers and sellers have what they believe are rational justifications for their actions. In the past, however, this struggle proceeded at human speed because humans were the ones using logic to generate and propagate ideas. We are now moving into a different world.

PCs have been around for only about a decade. In 1983 the PC market was just beginning to take off—RAM was 64K, floppies were 180K, and hard disks were not yet available. These early PCs were expensive by today's standards, with price tags in the $5,000 range. Many of us can remember being amazed by a simple Visicalc spreadsheet and then feeling richly blessed with Lotus 1-2-3. Wordstar was widely used as a word-processing package. It ran neatly on a 64K machine and seemed like almost everything a user could want. Those days are history.

Chaos theory, neural networks, and genetic algorithms are the present—not the future, but the present. These are the tools, the mental swords, used by those who want to do battle in today's financial markets. The best new trading ideas are being developed by computers that rely on computer-generated logic. The battle is being waged at high-tech speed, not human speed. Skirmishes last seconds, battles last minutes, and entire wars are fought in a week.

There are many in the investment community who are resisting this change. Some argue that computerized trading is dangerous and needs to be closely monitored and regulated or that it adds to the volatility of the market and gives the professionals, or those ''in the know,'' an unfair advantage. These are important criticisms and need to be addressed. I offer four main points of rebuttal to those with such concerns.

First, the evidence does not support the theory that computerized trading is the culprit behind market volatility and the crash of 1987. Markets swing back and forth for many reasons and always will. Computers merely speed up adjustments that would have occurred anyway. One can even argue that computers decrease volatility because they bring about many small adjustments by arbitraging minor pricing differentials. In the past, pricing differentials had to get much wider before they attracted someone's attention; now these adjustments occur on a nearly continuous basis. To cap this first part of my rebuttal, computers need data to make decisions. If markets become too chaotic, computers don't get the data they need, and the market reverts solely to human judgment.

Second, what's wrong with making money with the help of computers? Markets have always rewarded clear thinking because they are where ideas come together to be tested and rewarded—or not. Evolution works in markets; the fittest ideas survive. If some people are smart enough to program and use computers to make better decisions, what's wrong with that?

This last point leads directly to the third part of my rebuttal. Computer-driven trading threatens many vested interests. Some professional investors fear they will share the fate of the dinosaurs; they recognize that the world is changing rapidly and they are being left behind. If you can't play the new game, then you try to make sure that the game doesn't change. When people talk disparagingly about computerized trading, look carefully at their motives for doing so. Many who argue against computers ostensibly from some type of philosophical perspective may merely be trying to protect their own jobs.

Fourth, computer trading is thriving whether anyone likes it or not. The technology is here. The genie is out of the bottle, never to be replaced. To blame bad results on computers is like blaming the referees in a football game. Some of you may have been fortunate enough to hear the late Air Force General "Chappy" James, who was an outstanding public speaker. One of his favorite stories was about one of his football games in high school. His team lost, and James was frustrated by many calls by the referees that he and his teammates thought were unfair. When he got home he complained to his father. The conversation went something like this:

"Those referees were unfair. They must have been blind. We actually won that game."
"What color of uniforms does your team wear?" his father asked.
"Blue and gold," James replied.
"What color of uniforms did the other team wear?"
"Red and white."
"What about the referees?"
"Black and white, of course. What's the point, Dad?"
"The point is this. The object of the game is to beat everyone who has on a uniform that's not the same color as your team's."

The point is this: Blaming computers for the current state of affairs is like blaming the referees; it won't do any good. Computers are here to stay. Investors who choose not to use them may be doing so at their own peril.

However, this is not to say that sound investment thinking by humans is fruitless. Computers are only as good as their instructions. They are tools. What is needed is sound human thinking augmented by fast, sophisticated computer logic. There are many different ways this might be done. As a general principle, investors in today's world who do not supplement their own work with at least some computer analysis are operating at a serious disadvantage.

In addition, there are many different investment "games" that can be played on a short-term, medium-term, or long-term basis. The game this book focuses on is more medium-term in duration. You won't learn how to use genetic algorithms to make minute-by-minute decisions; what you will learn is how they can help to guide your monthly trading decisions. As the decision-making time frame is increased, the kind of assistance that computers can provide changes. Many of the criticisms of computerized trading are directed at very short-term strategies.

BUSINESS AND BIOLOGY

Businesses are dynamically evolving groups of humans who are living in a chaotic environment, transforming input into output, and struggling to survive. The fittest survive both internal and external threats. Some businesses efficiently transform input into output, but for others the process is costly and cumbersome. Occasionally even some of the most orderly businesses are overwhelmed by disorder from outside.

The phrasing in the previous paragraph is obviously designed to emphasize similarities at a macro level between the world of biology and the world of business. These similarities seem to be a consequence of our legal and economic system, which was not consciously designed to mimic nature. It is possible that many natural processes traditionally pictured as being strictly in the domain of the physical and biological sciences have many analogs and applications in the social sciences, as the following examples will demonstrate.

Chaos theory, neural networks, and genetic algorithms all have important links to the world of biology. Chaos theory concerns complex patterns that are abundant in nature yet appear to be highly chaotic, or disorderly. Neural networks mimic the web of neurons inside the brain that transforms complicated inputs into meaningful output signals. Genetic algorithms manipulate potential problem solutions, which are represented with chromosome-like structures, in a ''survival of the fittest'' search. These structures are then allowed to evolve into better and better problem solutions.

Chaos theory arose from attempts to explain the natural world. Researchers discovered that simple mathematical expressions often underlie complex, seemingly chaotic natural patterns. The basic equations are quite elementary but require many iterations to generate the intricate patterns.

Neural networks and genetic algorithms differ from chaos theory in that they do not attempt to explain nature; instead, they are software patterned after nature. Neural networks mimic brain functions, and genetic algorithms mimic the process of evolution. The motivation behind both methods is simple: learn from nature's efficiency.

Another common link between these three innovations is the computer. It is no accident that they have attracted increased interest in recent years. All three methods require significant amounts of computing resources. Chaos theory research capitalizes on the computer's suitability for performing repetitive tasks. The equations that govern many chaotic patterns require many iterations to generate the final result, and the pattern's behavior over the second 100 iterations may differ markedly from behavior over the first 100 iterations. A neural network must be trained by presenting it with a test set of data. The network makes predictions, the results are evaluated, and the process is repeated over and over again. Genetic algorithms involve successive generations of a large population. The calculations for each member of the population are similar and are performed repeatedly as the population undergoes successive transformations, generation after generation. None of these techniques would be feasible without the use of computers.

As computing power has become more readily available, research into chaos theory, neural networks, and genetic algorithms has accelerated. Computers already have had an enormous impact on society and business, yet we may have only scratched the surface of their potential. Many applications today are merely computerized versions of traditional paper-and-pencil techniques. Chaos theory, neural networks, and genetic algorithms are in a different league, and they are opening up vast new possibilities for computer applications. Learning about these new fields of study is like learning a foreign language, a process that can alter one's thinking process and view of the world.

BIOLOGICALLY BASED METHODS AND MARKET EFFICIENCY

Financial markets process ideas and information. When new information arrives, traders react and prices change accordingly. If markets process information and news quickly and accurately, then markets are said to be *efficient*. It's hard to get a jump on an efficient market. To do so, you need better information than your competitors have. Market efficiency theory doesn't maintain that stocks are not lucrative investments; it merely says that investing in stocks is a fair bet. You can expect more return only if you bear more risk. There's no easy money to be made.

Over the last quarter century or so, finance academics and practitioners have debated the concept of market efficiency. Some would argue that the application of sophisticated computational methods to investment management has little value because the market is inherently efficient. This is an important criticism that must be addressed. We certainly don't want to waste time on a search that is doomed to failure.

Financial markets are said to be *weak-form efficient* if prices reflect all past price and trading volume history. If the market under consideration is weak-form efficient, then you are probably wasting your time analyzing charts of past price and/or trading volume movements. The market is *semi-strong efficient* if prices reflect all publicly available information. In such a situation you may be wasting your time analyzing annual reports or developing trading rules based on macroeconomic data that is readily available. *Strong-form efficiency* requires that prices reflect all information, including private, "inside" information. Under these circumstances, even inside traders can't make abnormal profits. The type of efficiency that we are concerned with in this book is semi-strong efficiency.

Pretend you are in a debate on the following statement: "Markets are semi-strong efficient; therefore, investors cannot earn abnormal returns using strategies derived from biologically based methods." You disagree with this statement and attack it with four major arguments. The first two arguments are general, whereas the last two are specifically related to the use of biologically based methods.

1. All market efficiency tests are joint tests. For a return to be labeled "abnormal," there must be a definition of what is "normal." Market efficiency tests examine whether the returns from a particular strategy are above and beyond those that would be expected given the strategy's level of risk. Most market efficiency tests use some variation of the Capital Asset Pricing Model (CAPM) or Arbitrage Pricing Theory (APT) to measure risk. If the CAPM or APT are flawed, then the efficiency test results are invalid. Therefore, efficiency tests are joint tests of market efficiency and the validity of the pricing model being used.

This argument is well known in the finance literature. Until asset pricing theory is on firmer ground, the results of market efficiency tests must be viewed with caution.

2. The finance literature uses the term *information* liberally, and although it is used often, it has not been carefully differentiated from related terms such as *data* and *knowledge*. In fact, it is very difficult to find a really careful definition anywhere in the finance literature. The use of this term needs additional refinement, particularly with respect to market efficiency definitions. Does public information include all company-specific information, industry information, macroeconomic data, and knowledge of all mathematical techniques such as chaos theory, neural networks, and genetic algorithms? Descriptions of these biologically based methods are in the public domain, but they are not common knowledge among those in finance. If these methods are not well known, then there is reason to believe that investors may be able to earn abnormal profits by using them.

3. Our ability to process complex sets of information is limited. Psychologists have found that the human mind can only analyze about seven different factors at once. For example, if you try to picture a brick wall in your mind, the maximum number of bricks that can be separately visualized is about seven. Similarly, even chess masters have trouble picturing the board position seven moves ahead. In computer terms, our CPU power is limited. The implication for investment management is that we need sophisticated tools to identify patterns that are beyond our processing capabilities. Biologically based methods may be able to find complex patterns in market activity that we could not normally identify.

4. Because we are biological organisms, our behavioral patterns have a biological basis. Technical analysts have long argued for the existence of a mass psychology or herd mentality that is at least occasionally reflected in the market. Although most technical approaches depend on violations of weak-form efficiency, the notion of a herd mentality may have merit. Biologically based methods may be able to locate these patterns better than other traditional approaches.

ORGANIZATION OF THE BOOK

This book is divided into three parts. Part One explains how genetic algorithms fit into the larger picture of biologically based methods. The basics of chaos theory, neural networks, and genetic algorithms are described and compared. Part One answers the following question: Which method is right for my problem? Part Two explains the nuts and bolts of genetic algorithms. Exactly what is a genetic algorithm? What are the variations? What are some successful applications? In Part Three we move on to specific financial applications. You'll learn how a search for attractive market timing strategies can be conducted using a genetic algorithm. The results, which are intriguing, are described in detail. Finally, we finish with a discussion of additional potential applications and efforts by other researchers.

The three chapters following this one all have a similar structure. Each begins with a description of the biological foundations of the method being discussed. These discussions are not detailed technical descriptions; neural networks and genetic algorithms model biological processes in only a general way, so great detail is not even appropriate. Still, it is helpful to understand the basic rationale behind each method. The major historical developments in the use of each method are recapped, which answers several questions: Who are the founders? Who are the major contributors to the development of each method? When did these developments take place? Because these are all fast-moving fields, it is difficult to pinpoint precisely the current state of the art, but the text will attempt to do so.

Chapter 5 is designed to be a brief, useful reference guide on the use of genetic algorithms versus the use of chaos theory and neural networks. Suppose you have a problem. Would genetic algorithms be more appropriate than the other two methods? This question is addressed by answering many general questions related to chaos theory, neural networks, and genetic algorithms.

The main focus of this book is on genetic algorithms. We will often abbreviate *genetic algorithm* to *GA*, as is done in the research community. The purpose of Part One is to position GAs versus chaos theory and neural networks. Part Two lays out the mechanics of GAs and describes successful applications.

Genetic algorithm methodology is described in Chapters 6, 7, and 9. In Chapter 6 a simple example problem is used to illustrate the basic steps of a GA. The following chapter contains experiments with some of the parameters that control the genetically based operations, showing how they affect both the quality and speed of the solution search. After a discussion of GA applications in Chapter 8, we turn to advanced variations of GA methodology in Chapter 9.

Genetic algorithms have been applied to a diverse array of problems. Because the field was developed principally by computer scientists, mathematicians, and engineers, most of the applications have been in science and engineering. Some of the more interesting nonbusiness and business applications are reviewed in Chapter 8. Investors can benefit from studying GA applications for two reasons. First, applications in one field sometimes trigger the imagination and lead to applications in another field. Second, some of the applications in other fields may be profitably developed by public companies. As investors, we might want to purchase stock in these innovative companies.

Part Three treats a specific investment application: the use of GAs to identify attractive market timing strategies. *Market timing* refers to investment strategies that dictate when to switch back and forth between asset classes. For example, an investor might try to time allocations between a broad-based equity portfolio, such as the S&P 500, and U.S. Treasury Bills. The potential rewards of successful market timing are great, but previous research has documented the difficulty of the task. In Chapter 10 historical data is used to illustrate these rewards, and the major findings of previous market timing research are reviewed.

Chapter 11 presents a discussion of investment philosophy and methodology. The approach outlined here is very general. It could be applied to stocks, bonds, money market securities, currencies, commodities, futures, and options and could be used either for speculation or for hedging.

Chapters 12 through 14 describe some results of applying GAs to searches for attractive market timing rules involving a S&P 500–type portfolio, small-firm stocks, U.S. government bonds, corporate bonds, Treasury bills, and specific stocks. The specific trading rules developed here are based on changes in macroeconomic variables and derived from a large database of publicly available information.

The book closes with two chapters that speculate about areas for further research. This book is more process-oriented than results-oriented, so the method presented in Chapters 11 through 14 is meant to be suggestive of how GAs might be employed to search for attractive trading rules; the results represent only a starting point. Readers who decide to use GAs will probably want to make substantial modifications to the approach taken here, and Chapter 15 examines some of these possible variations. The final chapter outlines how GAs might be used to develop an extremely powerful portfolio management system and also describes experiments being conducted by other researchers.

Also included is a brief glossary of GA terminology and an extensive bibliography, which is divided into four sections: genetic algorithms, chaos theory, neural networks, and market timing. Because our book focuses on genetic algorithms, the GA bibliography is by far the largest. However, readers interested in delving further into chaos theory and neural networks will see plenty of possibilities in the bibliographies for these topics. So are you ready to begin moving past the calculator and spreadsheet into an exciting new world of trading possibilities? If not, you may be left behind in silicon dust.

2
Genetic Algorithms: Survival of the Fittest

Evolution and computation come together in genetic algorithms. Charles Darwin first developed the theory of evolution in the 1830s. Charles Babbage, one of the founders of modern-day computing and a friend of Darwin's, developed his analytical engine computing machine around 1833. They would both probably be surprised and delighted with this linkage of their two fields.

Genetic algorithms are software, procedures modeled after genetics and evolution. GAs are designed to efficiently search for attractive solutions to large, complex problems. The search proceeds in survival-of-the-fittest fashion by gradually manipulating a population of potential problem solutions until the most superior ones dominate the population.

Researchers refer to "genetic algorithms" or "a genetic algorithm," not "the genetic algorithm," because GAs are a broad class of related procedures with many separate steps. Each step has many possible variations, thus leading to a wide range of related procedures.

The purpose of this chapter is to provide a broad overview of genetic algorithms that should be helpful in contrasting them with chaos theory and neural networks, the topics of Chapters 3 and 4. To better understand the biological underpinnings of GAs, we will first briefly review some of the main ideas and terminology from genetics and evolution. Next, the steps in a genetic algorithm will be described in more detail; the final level of detail, however, will be deferred until Chapters 6 and 7. This chapter also recounts the historical development of genetic algorithms as a separate branch of computer science and closes by describing how GA software can be obtained and reviewing some of the major published works in the field.

GENETICS AND EVOLUTION

Genetics is the study of heredity. Geneticists investigate how genes operate and how they are transmitted from parents to offspring. There are many subfields of genetics such as cytogenetics, molecular genetics, behavioral genetics, human genetics, and population genetics.

In humans and other living organisms, cells contain important groupings of special material containing hereditary information. These rodlike structures are called *chromosomes*. Genes are specific factors that are carried by chromosomes. The basic process of coding information within genes and chromosomes is fairly simple, but the possible results are almost limitless in number.

The genetic makeup of each organism is called its *genotype*. The genotype determines and limits many aspects of development and survival. How an organism responds to both normal and abnormal environmental conditions is principally determined by its genotype. The properties of the organism that result from its encounters with the environment are collectively referred to as the *phenotype*.

Genes assert themselves through complex chemical processes that control the production of enzymes and other proteins. Small changes in the production of one enzyme, for example, might produce dramatic effects when combined with other enzymes. Two individuals might have considerable genetic similarity, but minor differences at the microlevel could produce substantial differences at the macrolevel.

Humans normally possess 46 chromosomes arranged in pairs; of these 46, 23 come from the mother's egg cell and 23 from the father's sperm cell. The process by which the number of chromosomes is reduced from 46 to 23 is called *meiosis*. In this process, the members of each chromosome pair move closer together, uncoil, and then exchange genetic material in a process know as *crossover*. Only one of the crossed-over strands is transmitted to the egg or sperm, thus yielding only 23 chromosomes. Crossover does not produce new genes, but it does produce new combinations of genetic material. The number of possible combinations is mind-boggling. Every human is capable of producing over 19 trillion genetically different sperm or egg cells. We all are truly unique individuals!

Living organisms contain extremely reliable, but not perfect, copying machines. Occasionally the copying of genetic material results in slight imperfections, known as *mutations*. The rate of mutation is slow, but it does lead to additional genetic diversity in populations. The short-term effect on a given population is negligible, but mutation can lead to significant changes in a population over longer time periods.

The subfield of genetics that is most closely linked to genetic algorithms is population genetics. Researchers in this field study evolutionary relationships, the mixing of genetic material within and across species, and methods of environmental adaptation.

Most of us nonbiologists probably remember something about the theory of evolution from our high school or college biology classes. Darwin focused heavily on adaptation and the process of natural selection. He realized that most organisms produce more offspring than live to maturity, and yet the number of individuals in a particular species does not vary greatly in the short run. He realized that mortality must play a big role in nature's design. Darwin concluded that nature kills the insufficiently adapted and called this process *natural selection.*

Crossover and mutation produce variations that can be inherited from parent to child. These *heritable variations* permit certain organisms to adapt to their environment. If an organism learns behaviors that allow it to adapt or better survive in its environment, that's nice, but it's not heritable variation—it's phenotype. The genotype is critical to evolution.

Individuals with favorable variations are more likely to survive and produce offspring. Therefore, the characteristics of more highly fit individuals are more likely to be passed on from one generation to the next.

Genetic algorithms are based on some simple notions about evolution, but the theory of evolution was not set in granite when Darwin died. Scientists are still refining ideas about evolution. The process of evolution sounds like a good thing; the world is constantly improving. However, as living organisms in the middle of this process, we might view evolution in a negative light. Eldredge (1991) says "we should see life in a constant struggle not to evolve but to survive," to find a habitat that suits its adaptations. We need to preserve genetic diversity, such as exists in the Brazilian rainforests, not for the future but for the present. We know we can live in our current environment; we may not be able to live in some different, future environment. Genetic algorithms revolve around the simple concept that evolution is good because it leads to improvement. Because GAs are fairly elementary, GA researchers have generally not worried too much about post-Darwinian developments.

GENETIC ALGORITHM PROCEDURES

In the late 1950s and early 1960s, several biologists began experimenting with computer simulations of genetic systems. A.S. Fraser, in particular, engaged in experiments that bore resemblance to genetic algorithms.

However, it was John Holland who began in earnest to develop ideas about adaptive systems theory during the 1960s. He taught courses in adaptive systems theory at the University of Michigan and began to publish many papers on the subject. Gradually he refined his thinking, which culminated in his landmark book, *Adaptation in Natural and Artificial Systems,* published in 1975.

Holland is generally recognized as the founding father of genetic algorithms. All of the early pioneers in this field trace their roots back to the University of Michigan; many Ph.D. dissertations that have explored various aspects of genetic algorithms were written under his supervision.

Because Holland's book is, in many ways, the Bible of genetic algorithms, we feel it is appropriate to include some direct quotes from this pivotal work. Here is a sampling:

The complexity makes discovery of the optimum a long, perhaps never-to-be-completed task, so the best among *tested* options must be exploited at every step. At the same time, the uncertainties must be reduced rapidly, so that knowledge of *available* options increases rapidly. (p. 1)

We can see at once that adaptation, whatever its context, involves a progressive modification of some structure or structures. (p. 3)

Fitness, viewed as a measure of the genotype's influence upon the future, introduces a concept useful through the whole spectrum of adaptation. A good way to see this concept in wider context is to view the testing of genotypes as a sampling procedure. The sample space in this case is the set of all genotypes . . . and the outcome of each sample is the performance . . . of the corresponding phenotype. The general question associated with fitness, then, is: To what extent does the outcome . . . of a sample . . . influence or alter the sampling plan . . . (the kinds of samples to be taken in the future)? Looking backward instead of forward, we encounter a closely related question: How does the history of the outcomes of previous samples influence the current sampling plan? The answers to these questions go far toward determining the basic character of any adaptive process. (p. 12)

Whatever history is retained must be represented in the current population. (p. 13)

. . . an *enumerative* plan exhaustively tests [all the structures]. Enumerative plans are characterized by the fact that the order in which they test structures is unaffected by the outcome of previous tests. [Enumerative plans will eventually find the optimum.] . . . The flaw, and it is a fatal one, asserts itself when we begin to ask, "How long is eventually?" (pp. 16–17)

These concepts provide an important backdrop to the specific procedures employed in genetic algorithms. Descriptions of GA procedures will be accompanied by discussions of how the specifics relate to the general concepts outlined in the above quotes.

In the description of GAs in the second paragraph of this chapter, I purposefully used the phrase "attractive solutions." GAs have been labeled as optimization procedures. They are, but the word *optimization* has some negative connotations, especially in business. Many times in business problems, the word *optimal* is nearly meaningless. It is a highly abstract concept, and given the complexities of the real world, solutions that were optimal in the past may not be optimal in the future. In some of the GA literature, GA procedures are said to be good at finding near-optimal solutions to problems. It is ultimately more accurate to think in terms of attractive or interesting solutions.

The starting point in trying to use GAs as a problem-solving tool is representing the problem in a manner that a GA can work with. Usually this leads to binary representation—representing the parameters of the problem solution using a string of binary digits.

Let's say that our problem is to find a solution to the following problem:

$$X^2 = 64; \text{ solve for } X.$$

For this trivial problem, we only need to remember some basic math; we don't need a computer to tell us that 8 is the solution. But let's see how this problem could be represented in a manner conducive to the use of GAs.

Before going further, however, let's review some binary (base two) arithmetic, which is an alternative to our conventional decimal (base ten) arithmetic. It is actually far simpler because it requires only two digits, 0 and 1, versus our ten (the digits 0 through 9). Binary arithmetic is the backbone of computer software because it lends itself to the on-off nature of electrical circuits. Just as the sequencing of digits is important in decimal notation, it is also important in binary notation. The decimal number 263 is composed of 2×100 plus 6×10 plus 3×1. The three positions (100, 10, 1) correspond to 10^2, 10^1, and 10^0. In a similar fashion, the binary number 110 corresponds (from left to right) to 1×2^2, 1×2^1, and 0×2^0. Or we could rewrite this as 1×4 plus 1×2 plus 0×1. In binary, the three positions correspond to 4, 2, and 1 rather than our conventional 100, 10, and 1. Therefore, the binary number 110 is equivalent to our decimal number 6. Notice that it takes more positions to represent a given number in base two than in base ten.

As an aside, we normally count only from one to ten on our fingers. If we held up four fingers we could count it as four regardless of which four fingers were extended. Consider using binary and counting on your right hand. Hold up your right hand with your thumb to the left and little finger to the right. Extending your index finger and little finger could correspond to a binary 1001. This could be decoded as 1×8 (2^3) plus 0×4 plus 0×2 plus 1×1, which equals the decimal number 9. (In Texas, holding up these fingers would symbolize "Hook 'em horns!" and mean that you are a University of Texas fan.)

Now back to our problem. The potential solutions to our problem can be represented as sequences, or strings, of binary digits. Thus, 10011 could represent a potential solution. However, if this number is decoded into its decimal equivalent, we get 19, which is too high. In our representation, if we allow all combinations of five position binary numbers to be considered as potential solutions, then we would have possibilities ranging from 00000 to 11111. The correct solution, 8, would be represented in binary as 01000.

What we are doing has a biological parallel. The bit string can be viewed as a chromosome-type structure. The 0s and 1s correspond to genes within the chromosome. Just as a chromosome can be decoded to reveal characteristics of an individual organism, a bit string can be decoded to reveal a potential problem solution.

With the problem representation solved, we can move on to the actual steps in a genetic algorithm.

Step 1: Randomly create a population of potential problem solutions. Let's say we use a population size of four. We would use a random number generator to randomly set the bits in our four 5-bit strings of potential solutions. We are effectively proceeding through the four strings, bit by bit, and computationally flipping a coin to see if the bit should be a 0 or 1. As an example, our starting population might consist of the following four individual strings: 00100, 10101, 01010, and 11000. After decoding, the initial guesses at the problem solution would be (in decimal) 4, 21, 10, and 24. With different computer runs, or trials, we would get different starting populations because the bits are being randomly set.

It is important to keep in mind that this is a highly simplified example problem. In real-world applications of genetic algorithms, we would be working with complicated problems having possibly trillions of potential solutions. The bit string would be longer, with a more complex decoding scheme, and the initial population size might be 100 or 200 individuals, not just four.

Step 2: Calculate the performance, or fitness, of each individual in the population. To use genetic algorithms, we must have some means of assigning a fitness value, or score, to each string. In this case, we might use the following:

$$\text{Fitness} = 1000 - \text{the absolute value of (the squared}$$
$$\text{decimal equivalent of the string minus 64).}$$

Don't worry if this sounds rather strange. We need to dissect the logic behind this approach.

GAs are typically implemented in such a way that performance, or fitness, is a value to be maximized. With the above definition, fitness will be maximized when the squared decimal equivalent of the string has a value of 64. In solving the equation, we are really trying to make the difference between X^2 and 64 be zero. Or we could say that we are trying to mimimize the difference between X^2 and 64. Because GAs like maximization, we put the problem in maximization terms by subtracting $(X^2 - 64)$ from 1,000. With a string value of 8, fitness will compute to 1,000; for string values over and under 8, fitness will always be less than 1,000. As an example, let's calculate the fitness values for our four starting strings. They are

(1)	(2)	(3)	(4)
		Column 2	Fitness
Binary	Decimal	Squared	(1000 minus absolute
String	Equivalent	Minus 64	value of Column 3)
00100	4	-48	952
10101	21	377	623
01010	10	36	964
11000	24	512	488

Notice that for decimal equivalents closer to a value of 8, fitness is higher. Clearly the fitness calculation is generally doing what we want it to do. However, this is only one possible means of setting up the fitness calculation for this example problem. There are probably many other possibilities, some of which might be much better.

Step 3: Select individuals to become parents of the next generation. Basically, better-performing individuals should be awarded the privilege of parenthood. Poorly performing individuals may not receive that privilege. There are a variety of schemes for accomplishing this, many of which will be described in later chapters.

Let's consider one possible scheme for selecting parents: throwing away the worst-performing string and replacing it with a second copy of the best-performing string. Because the fourth string in the above list had a fitness of 488, which was the lowest of the four, we will replace it with a second copy of the best-performing string, which had a fitness of 962. Therefore, the parent pool consists of the following strings: 00100, 10101, 01010, and 01010. Notice that we are creating a sampling plan that depends on the outcomes of the performance calculations. The next generation of structures, which will also be sampled by calculating their fitness, is dependent on previous outcomes. The sampling sequence is adaptive.

Step 4: Create a second generation of children from the parent pool. There are a variety of genetic operations that can be performed at this stage. One of the most powerful is known as *crossover* and is inspired by its biological counterpart. First, randomly choose two strings from the parent pool. Let's say the first and third strings, 00100 and 01010, are chosen. Second, randomly choose a point at which the two strings will be cut. Let's say that the point after the third bit is chosen as the cutting point. The two strings now look like this: 001-00 and 010-10, where the dash separates the head from the tail of the string. Third, let a random number indicate whether or not crossover should be performed. As an example, we might tell the computer that we want crossover to happen about 60 percent of the time. If the computer tells us to perform crossover, we then exchange the two tails of the two strings, leaving the head of the first string with the tail of the second string and vice versa. Our strings are now 00110 and 01000, which correspond to decimal values of 6 and 8. Notice that this operation has fortuitously resulted in our finding the optimal string, 01000. This will be further discussed a little later.

At several points in the crossover process, random selections were performed. We randomly chose a pair, we randomly decided where to cut the strings, and we randomly decided whether or not to actually perform the crossover. Randomness, or chance, is one of the distinguishing characteristics of genetic algorithms. It seems counterintuitive that random operations would be fruitful, but they are.

Crossover is a powerful process that extends the search in many directions. The mathematical description of how crossover works is complicated and requires a discussion of how various hyperplanes in the search space are being sampled. To get a feel for the process, picture yourself in a large, dark gymnasium. Somewhere in the gym a large brass bell is suspended in midair from a strong wire. The bell represents the optimal solution. Someone hands you a stack of huge frisbees that you are free to throw in any direction. If you start throwing the frisbees in varying directions at varying angles from various locations, you actually have a reasonable chance of striking the bell or the wire that holds it. If you hit the wire, the bell will probably jingle a bit, giving you some information about where to throw next. Crossover is similar. It cuts through the search space in a highly efficient manner. High fitness values are signals that you may be getting close to the optimal value and should continue sampling in that particular region of the search space.

Mutation is a second possible genetic operation that could be performed. Again, this is a biologically inspired operation. With mutation, a particular bit in a particular string is randomly selected. We then examine the bit and see whether it is a 0 or a 1. If it is a 0, then we mutate it to a 1; if it's a 1, then we do the opposite. Mutation is done with very low frequency; perhaps only one bit in 1,000 will be altered. Mutation gently nudges the search in a slightly different direction.

Crossover and mutation are common genetic operators in genetic algorithms. There are other forms of crossover and other genetic operators that will be discussed in later chapters.

The basic purpose of genetic operators is to transform the population over successive generations, thus extending the search. However, we are not just casting about mindlessly. Certain bit positions in the string may be more critical than others in a particular application. For example, if it is important to have a 010 pattern in bit positions 2 through 4, then strings with high fitness values are likely to have this pattern. Because we consider fitness, or performance, in the selection of the parent pool, we indirectly give special attention to strings with the 010 pattern in positions 2 through 4. Crossover creates the possibility that this attractive pattern will get passed on to other strings and eventually spread throughout the population. So the search is indirectly considering the successes and failures of previous trials. It is not mindless; it has some memory.

Step 5: Return to step 2 and keep repeating steps 2 through 4 until the population converges. Earlier a parent selection scheme was described in which the worst string was replaced with a copy of the best string. This will ensure that good strings will eventually drive out the bad strings. Crossover also spreads pieces of well-performing strings to poor-performing strings. Again, the good is driving out the bad. As these procedures are repeated over and over again, the population will gradually become more homogeneous. When all strings are identical in all bit positions, we would say the population is *fully converged.* If all strings are identical, crossover has no effect. The only possible chance for improvement at that stage is through mutation. However, if the strings are all optimal, then mutation can only worsen the situation, not improve it. So the population will converge. A mathematical method for quantifying the degree of convergence will be described in a later chapter.

In the crossover example we described earlier, there was a fortuitous combination that occurred. Genetic algorithms are guided by random processes that can produce both lucky and unlucky results. Sometimes the population may be hot on the trail of a good string when something happens that diverts the search. Crossover occasionally disrupts good patterns. However, if the GA is properly tuned, the algorithm should eventually pick up the scent of the trail again and close in on the prey.

The fine-tuning of genetic algorithms is an important subject and will be addressed in more detail later. However, it is crucial to understand that there are trade-offs to be made. If the user wants quick convergence, it can be achieved—but at a price. Generally speaking, there is a trade-off between speed of convergence and the quality of the solution. GAs are efficient in that they use limited sampling of very large search spaces to get results that hopefully are attractive. However, a longer search will almost always lead to a better solution. The parent selection scheme is especially critical in determining the length of the search. If some strings quickly drive out all the others, convergence will be rapid, but better strings may have been missed.

MAJOR DEVELOPMENTS IN GENETIC ALGORITHMS

We have already described some of Holland's ideas, but it is important to go into slightly more detail in certain areas. When one first learns about genetic algorithms, it is natural to be somewhat skeptical; many of the concepts seem far-fetched. However, in addition to his broad theoretical ideas about adaptive systems, Holland also mathematically proved several important theorems concerning GAs. We will not go into all the mathematical detail but will attempt to provide an executive-level summary of these theorems.

As background, we must first understand the concept of similarity templates called *schemata*. This requires the use of three symbols: 0, 1, and *. The 0 and 1 are the familiar binary 0 and 1; the asterisk (*) is a "don't care" symbol. Consider the following binary string and two schemata:

Binary String A:	1 1 1 0 0
Schemata 1:	1 * * * 0
Schemata 2:	* * 1 0 *

Schemata 1 is a template that requires a 1 in position 1 and a 0 in position 5, but it is indifferent to the values in other positions. Schemata 2 looks for a 1 in position 3 and a 0 in position 4, but it does not care what comes before or after. Both of these schemata are represented in string A.

Let's say we have a population consisting of 100 five-bit binary strings. Let's also say that schemata 1 fits 25 members of the population and schemata 2 fits 22 of them. Some of these fits are overlapping (that is, they are the exact same strings, just as string A fits both schemata), but most are not. Assume that the average fitness, or performance, of those strings that match schemata 1 is one and one-half times as high as the average fitness of all 100 strings in the population. Further assume that the average fitness of those strings that match schemata 2 is only three-fourths as high as the average fitness of all 100 strings. One of Holland's theorems says (mathematically) that schemata 1 will receive exponentially increasing priority in subsequent generations, while schemata 2 will receive exponentially decreasing priority. Higher fitness is being rewarded; individuals with higher fitness are more likely to parent the subsequent generations. Notice that we are letting the outcomes affect our sampling plan, as suggested in Holland's general principles.

But fitness is not all that matters. Crossover and mutation also affect the course of the search. If we reexamine the two schemata, we can see that schemata 1 is more likely to be disrupted by crossover than schemata 2. Schemata 1 is longer and thus can be severed by crossover more easily, but unless crossover happens between the 1 and 0 in schemata 2, no damage will result. Mutation does occasionally disrupt schemata, but is less likely to do so.

Holland's theorems point to the following general conclusion: Schemata that have a short distance between the outermost 1s and 0s (this is known as *defining length*), have a low total number of 1s and 0s (this is known as *low order*), and have above-average fitness will receive an exponentially increasing number of trials in subsequent generations. These smaller, fitter schemata become important building blocks in the GA's search. The GA concentrates heavily on these building blocks and then pieces them together to find near-optimal problem solutions.

Holland also showed that when a GA is working with a population of n structures, the number of schemata that are being processed is roughly n^3. This makes the GA search procedure highly efficient. Holland called this *implicit parallelism.*

This discussion of schemata and Holland's theorems is intended to make the following point: There are some important mathematical proofs showing that GA search is highly efficient. This is not just something that happens to work; there are sound reasons why it should.

A work that nicely complemented Holland's 1975 book was completed in the same year by one of Holland's doctoral students, Kenneth De Jong. Holland's work was theoretical; De Jong's was pragmatic. De Jong's dissertation was titled "An Analysis of the Behavior of a Class of Adaptive Systems." It was a systematic investigation of GA methodological variations and parameter settings.

De Jong decided to experiment with GAs on a carefully chosen set of problems. He formulated a set of five function optimization problems that have become known as the "De Jong test suite." The set was constructed to include the following properties: continuous, discontinuous, convex, nonconvex, unimodal, multimodal, quadratic, nonquadratic, low-dimensional, high-dimensional, stochastic, and deterministic. It is a rich GA proving ground.

An important part of his dissertation centers on parameter testing. De Jong conducted controlled tests of various crossover rate and mutation rate settings. His recommended settings for crossover at 0.6 and a mutation rate of 0.001 are widely used. (These are also the base settings that we use in Chapters 6 and 7.) The interaction between these parameter settings and GA performance is still not completely understood, but De Jong's work did provide much insight.

In addition, De Jong examined six different reproductive plans; in other words, he studied six different generic GA procedural variations. These tests also yielded important insights into the practical application of GAs.

The importance of De Jong's work can hardly be overstated. It established an important baseline early in the development of the field. His work is widely quoted, and his test suite is still being used for benchmarking of GA innovations.

Another researcher who deserves significant credit in the development of genetic algorithms is David E. Goldberg, who studied under Holland at the University of Michigan. Goldberg's 1983 dissertation was titled "Computer-Aided Gas Pipeline Operation Using Genetic Algorithms and Rule Learning." Goldberg's pipeline application and other GA applications will be described in Chapter 8.

Goldberg has made many important contributions to the GA technical literature; however, his most important contribution to the field may be his 1989 book, *Genetic Algorithms in Search, Optimization & Machine Learning*. Goldberg's writing skill was clearly evident in his dissertation, and his book is also very well written. It was designed for possible use as a textbook for computer science and engineering students and includes sections on the historical development of GAs, detailed explanations of many GA methodological variations, descriptions of applications, exercises, and actual listings of GA software code written in the Pascal language. The thoroughness and lucidity of his book have made it an important reference for those beginning to work with GAs.

Just because we have highlighted the past work of Holland, De Jong, and Goldberg does not mean that they are merely figures from the past. All three have published numerous additional studies, and they continue to be highly active in the field. Their contributions are far from being complete.

GENETIC ALGORITHM SOFTWARE

One of the key advantages of genetic algorithms is that very little of the computer code changes from one problem to another. When writing software, most programmers strive for generality in their programs. They know that it is useful to make software flexible and reusable. GAs work with populations of strings, but all problems do not require the same string length or population size. Therefore, good GA software would probably allow for different string lengths and different population sizes. In addition, selection, crossover, and mutation can all be coded so as to allow for differences in string length and population size. The software routines that perform these routines are merely working with bit strings; they don't care what the strings represent. The only portion of the GA software that is problem-dependent is the fitness calculation, which requires the decoding and interpretation of each string so that a fitness, or performance, value can be assigned to each string. Only the fitness procedure is nongeneric; the other software modules can be used without modification for many different problems.

To use genetic algorithms, you really don't have to know much about the problem. You may have no clue as to how to proceed towards finding an optimal solution. All you really need is a method for assigning fitness to a given string. As long as you can envision how to represent your problem as a bit string (actually

GAs can work with other types of strings—this will be discussed in a later chapter) and can assign a fitness value to every possible string, the GA procedures will take care of the rest. GAs are really fairly simple to use.

To make things even easier, there are several GA software packages available at low cost. The details concerning these packages are described in the following section of this chapter.

GENETIC ALGORITHMS: MAJOR REFERENCES

At the end of the book, you'll find an extensive bibliography of GA references. However, there are three works that we will be referring to frequently throughout this book. Two of these have already been discussed. The three are:

1. Holland, J.H. *Adaptation in Natural and Artificial Systems*. Ann Arbor, MI: The University of Michigan, 1975.

    As stated earlier, this book is in many ways the Bible of genetic algorithms. Holland lays out cornerstones for most of the subsequent work in genetic algorithms. He and his graduate students have done almost all the early work in the field. The book, however, is fairly technical, with many mathematical theorems and proofs aimed at a computer science readership. The books described below are much more readable for a business audience, although they are also fairly technical in many places.

2. Goldberg, D.E. *Genetic Algorithms in Search, Optimization, and Machine Learning*. Reading, MA: Addison-Wesley, 1989.

    This is an excellent overview of the main principles behind genetic algorithms and a detailed description of many GA procedural variations. The book was designed for possible use as an advanced undergraduate or introductory graduate-level textbook for computer science or engineering students. It includes a listing of GA programs written in the Pascal programming language.

3. Davis, L., ed. *Handbook of Genetic Algorithms*. New York: Van Nostrand Reinhold, 1991.

    This book is divided into two major parts. Part One is an excellent GA tutorial written by Lawrence Davis. It is written more concisely than the Goldberg book, probably because it was not expressly designed to be a textbook. Part Two is a collection of application case studies contributed by various researchers in the GA community. The book contains a brief description of two GA software packages, GENESIS and OOGA. GENESIS is a C-based software package written by John Grefenstette that has been widely distributed to the research community since 1985. OOGA is a Lisp-based package that runs in Common Lisp and CLOS (Common Lisp Object System). For further information, refer to pages 374–377 in the book, or contact

TSP—The Software Partnership
P.O. Box 991
Melrose, MA 01276
USA

TEN THINGS TO UNDERSTAND ABOUT GENETIC ALGORITHMS

1. The field is not new. The main developmental work was done in the 1970s. There have been many international conferences devoted strictly to genetic algorithms.
2. There is a large body of GA work in the computer science and engineering fields, but little work has been done concerning business-related applications.
3. Problems must be translated into a form that is suitable for genetic algorithm manipulation. Usually this is done by representing potential problem solutions as a bit string (a sequence of binary numbers—1s and 0s).
4. The problem translation described above can be difficult, requiring some creative leaps of imagination. However, GAs have already been applied to a wide variety of problems.
5. GAs begin their work with a randomly constructed population of initial guesses to the problem solution. Therefore, little knowledge is required to start up a GA procedure.
6. For GAs to work, it must be possible to calculate a performance, or fitness, value for each potential problem solution.
7. Potential solutions that are more fit, or have better performance, receive priority in subsequent generations.
8. Genetically based operations such as crossover and mutation transform the population, extending the search into far-reaching directions. Crossover is similar to mating and is the real power behind the search process.
9. The basic steps described in 6–8 are repeated through subsequent generations. Eventually the population will converge, with the fittest solution(s) surviving.
10. GAs are fast and flexible. They are potentially applicable to many different problems, including investment applications. Their speed and power make them suitable for analyzing complex trading strategies.

3
Neural Networks: Brainware

Neural networks are a form of biologically inspired computing. They are designed to mimic, but not exactly replicate, the functions of the human brain. Researchers essentially said, "Nature seems to have some good ideas; let's see what we can learn," and neural networks are one of the results of their search.

There is considerable difference of opinion about how further development in this field should proceed. Some believe that further study of the human brain would help spur ideas for new advances, while others think that neural network research has taken all it can from biology and is now firmly in the realms of math and computer science.

Neural networks have, at various times and places, been called parallel distributed processing models, adaptive systems, self-organizing systems, neurocomputing, connectivist/connectionism models, and neuromorphic systems. We will use the shortened term *neural nets* for the remainder of the book.

It is difficult to do justice to the history of neural nets in a few paragraphs. Our intention is merely to highlight some of the key players and milestones.

Because neural nets attempt to mimic the human brain, the initial ideas behind them grew out of psychology and physiology. Their roots in these disciplines go back to the 1930s, 1940s, and 1950s with the work of Alan Turing, Warren McCullough, Walter Pitts, Donald Hebb, Nathaniel Rochester, and James von Neumann. In 1957, Frank Rosenblatt at Cornell built a hardware neural net called Perceptron that was capable of character recognition. In 1959 Bernard Widrow and Marcian Hoff of Stanford developed a neural net to be used as an adaptive filter to control noise on telephone lines. This system, now called ADALINE, has a long history of commercial use.

In the 1960s and 1970s, neural net development was hindered by disappointments resulting from inflated expectations and pointed criticisms of some of the earlier research. Although much good work continued to be done, significant interest in neural nets was not revived until 1982, when John Hopfield, a Caltech physicist, mathematically tied together many of the ideas from previous investigations.

Since the early 1980s, interest in neural nets has mushroomed within many different fields and industries. There have been many neural net conferences, both nationally and internationally. Thousands of papers on the subject have been written. Commercial software and applications are now popping up with ever greater frequency.

The remainder of this chapter will describe how neural nets work and how they are being used, including possible financial and investment applications. The intention here is to paint with a broad brush. Interested readers can consult the references for more detail. However, I do want to provide sufficient detail so that a clear distinction can be made between GAs and neural nets; the two techniques have some loose similarities but are really very different.

HOW NEURAL NETS WORK

The fundamental building block of neural nets is based on the nerve cell called a *neuron*. There are many different types and sizes of neurons in the human brain, each of which is like a pencil with many connective strings hanging from both its ends. The connectors on the eraser end, as it were, are the *dendrites,* which carry signals into the neuron, and the *axon* carries signals out via the connectors on the writing end. The point at which these signals are fired from the axon of one neuron to the dendrites of another is called a *synapse.*

Nerve impulses are binary; they are "go" or "no go." However, many different signals pass through the synapses. The neurons "sum up" each incoming signal, and if a signal's sum exceeds a preset threshold value, then the neuron fires it across the synapse to another neuron; if not, nothing happens.

The human nervous system is composed of a complex network of neurons. This enables the human brain to simultaneously perform many computing tasks, otherwise known as *parallel processing,* which is similar to the parallelism present in genetic algorithms. The keys to our behavior and thoughts are embedded in these networks.

This basic structure forms the foundation for neural nets, which can be implemented using either hardware or software. In the hardware mode, electronic circuits mimic neurons and their associated inputs and outputs. In the software mode, linkages of nodes, inputs, and outputs can be programmed; this book will focus on describing neural nets from more of a software perspective.

The term *node* refers to the neural net equivalent of a neuron. Nodes have input signals, which correspond to dendrites, and one output signal, which corresponds to the axon. The input signals are assigned weights and summed at the node before producing output. A simple representation of a node is shown in Figure 3.1.

Inputs

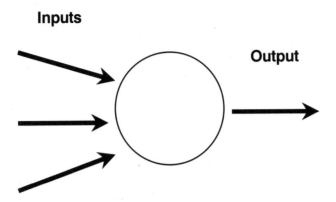

Output

FIGURE 3.1   Neural Network Node

Many steps can occur between input and output within the node. Initially, input signals may be assigned weights randomly; as the network "learns," these weights may be adjusted. There are many methods for making these adjustments, but usually the weights are multiplied by the number of input signals and then summed. This is called the *summation function,* of which there are also many possible variations. The result from the summation function could be passed to an *activation function,* which could alter the summation function result based on a time dependency and then pass its result to a *transfer function,* which controls the firing of output. The threshold of the transfer function could be controlled in a strictly linear fashion (greater input, greater output), or the transfer function could be a nonlinear, sigmoid function, meaning that the output might vary little for a broad range of input but then change significantly over a small range of input values. Finally, a learning function enters into the process. Before discussing these functions in more detail, however, we must consider the typically layered structure of a neural net.

Let's say that a given network has four layers of nodes, as pictured in Figure 3.2. The *input layer* receives inputs and passes them on to the second layer. The output may then be passed along from the second to the third and finally to the fourth layer, which is called the *output layer.* This is where the user finally gets output from the network. The middle layers are called *hidden layers* because they do not directly interface with the outside world. They don't receive direct inputs, and neither do they produce direct output to the outer environment.

The various nodes throughout the network's layers are connected. There are many connectivity options; nodes can receive many input signals but can produce only one output signal. However, the output signal can be transmitted forward to many nodes in the next layer. A given node's output can even be transmitted back to itself or previous nodes as an input. Output that is redirected backwards in the network is called *feedback,* and the network is called a *feedback network.*

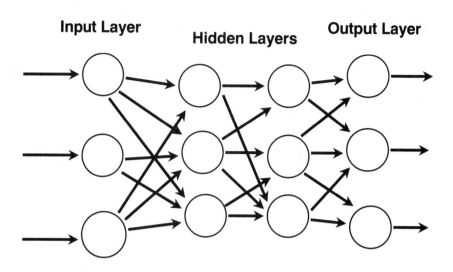

FIGURE 3.2 Neural Network Layers

Networks in which all outputs go forward are called *feedforward networks*. An increase in the number of nodes and layers leads to a greater number of possible connections.

Hidden layers are rather mysterious. They contain much of the knowledge within the network and are therefore vitally important. However, there are no general rules concerning how many hidden layers are appropriate in a given network and no general rules about how they should be connected. In certain applications they act as filters, removing input signal noise as information moves through the network.

Now that we have discussed network layers, let's return to looking at functions. As mentioned previously, a network learns at the node level. The weights at each node are gradually adjusted as the network adapts itself to produce the desired output signal. Many networks use the following weight adjustment method, which is called *back propagation*. First, input is presented to the network and processed, thus producing output. Next, the differences between the desired outputs and the actual outputs are computed. Using these discrepancies, the weights in the output layer are adjusted. Then further adjustments to the hidden layer's nodal weights are made. Finally, the input nodal weights are brought to a more effective level. The system is then ready for new input, and the entire process is repeated.

Learning can be either supervised or unsupervised. In unsupervised learning, the system adjusts itself "on the fly"; it teaches itself. Supervised training, in which a specially designed data set or a human educates the network, is more common. Input data are presented to the network, and the weights are gradually adjusted to produce the desired output. The instructional data set may be repeatedly presented to the network in many training cycles. Because the user is looking for certain desired output, an average error based on the difference between actual and desired output can be computed for each training cycle. When the average error has reached an acceptable level or no further improvement is occurring, the training is complete. The weights present in the network are then locked in, and the system is ready for use with new input data.

The learning process for a neural net is similar to the convergence process with GAs. There is a natural tradeoff between speed and quality. If the network is designed to learn quickly, then the system may reach a "no further improvement" stage very quickly. However, the resulting weights may not prove highly effective when the system encounters new data. Or, if learning is too rapid, the system may oscillate due to the weights having been overcorrected. Training is at the heart of neural net development, and how that training is conducted will greatly affect the quality of the final network.

The rules and models of learning lend their names to much of the jargon used in this field, such as *Hebb's rule, the delta rule,* and the *gradient descent rule.* Other such terms include *Kohonen's learning law, back propagation learning, Grossberg learning,* and *drive-reinforcement theory.* Many of these models are based on work from biology and psychology concerning how humans and animals learn. Neural nets borrow many ideas from nature. As new learning theories are developed, they will probably be applied in neural net systems.

NEURAL NET RESEARCH AND MARKET POTENTIAL

The commercial market for neural net products is rapidly expanding. The market in 1991 was about $140 million; John Stewart, in his article "Can Neurocomputing Live Up to Its Premise?" which appeared in the September 1991 issue of *Credit Card Management,* quotes Schwartz Associates as having estimated that this figure could reach $1 billion by 1995.

Various neural net interest groups and conferences have been formed and are highly active. The Neural Network Society's conference in 1988 featured 527 paper presentations. One worldwide survey polled over 700 neural net researchers.

In 1989, the Department of Defense funded 17 months of neural net research at a cost of $33 million. The military is interested in many possible applications, including target and speech recognition; these uses of neural nets could also prove to be valuable in the marketplace. Target recognition, for example, might be modified for use by commercial airlines.

The Japanese have moved more vigorously than we Americans into neural net research. Their Fifth Generation Computer Project, launched in 1981, is winding down and has had mixed success. Now they are launching the Real-World Computing Project, which focuses on everyday neural net applications. Hitachi and Nippon Telegraph & Telephone (NTT) are both heavily into research and development in this field—in fact, NTT invests more in new equipment and research aimed at expanding the knowledge and use of neural nets than any other country in the world.

The Europeans have joined forces in neural net development with their Esprit, Pygmalion, and Annie projects. The Pygmalion project focuses on software tools, whereas the Annie project is aimed at industrial applications. Siemens Ag, the German electronics firm, is very active in neural net research, participating in Esprit and also working with German and U.S. universities. The Research Initiative in Pattern Recognition (RIPR) in the U.K. is a collaborative effort between government and industry.

Hardware and software companies are in a furious race to develop the best products. Synaptics is hoping to put much of the power of a $10-million Cray supercomputer into a single chip that will act as electronic eyes and ears and might cost only a few hundred dollars. Hecht-Nielsen Neurocomputer has developed a system called the Graded Learning Network (GLN) that allows a robot to train itself. NEC has developed a neural net–based music sound-arranging system. IBM has a neural network utility program that allows users to develop and test networks. Neural net software is now available at low cost and can be used on PCs; packages such as NeuroShell from Ward Systems Group Inc. allow the user to guide the learning process.

NEURAL NET APPLICATIONS

The list of companies that have explored neural net applications is lengthy and prestigious. Over 80 percent of the Fortune 500 corporations currently have investments in neural net research. Many of the results are proprietary, but more details are gradually becoming available. For example, Ford Motor Company is supposedly working on a system to analyze data from the engine computers now being installed in cars. The system could pinpoint problems both on the assembly line and in dealer service departments.

One of the principal application areas for neural nets is image processing. The filtering and pattern recognition capabilities of neural nets make them ideally suited for recognizing images. Many neural net applications have revolved around optical character recognition. The networks can be trained to recognize various fonts and even interpret handwritten data, greatly reducing data entry costs. In 1989, Neurogen, Inc., had developed a production prototype of a system called Inscript for reading handwritten digits. Neural nets can also be used in complete document management systems and can aid in document storage, retrieval, and indexing. The indexing of images is complex and critical to effective retrieval. Neural nets can scan and digitize entire pages of information much faster than is possible using sequential techniques.

Motorola has developed a new chip called Firefly for use in its imaging computer. This is in conjunction with its six-sigma quality (no more than four rejects per million parts) effort. Machine vision systems are expected to yield major quality improvements.

The Japanese have a special interest in the pattern detection capabilities of neural nets. Their intricate Kanji characters have made computerization of language very difficult. Neural nets offer great promise both in written and oral language translation.

Logos Corporation has a neural net system that can categorize words into thousands of linguistic categories. The network functions with a large array of flexible linguistic rules. With better linguistic analysis, computer translation is feasible. Both governments and businesses would welcome faster, less expensive translation services, which are increasingly in demand in today's global economy.

Because neural nets are good at filtering noisy data and recognizing patterns, they are ideally suited for use as sensors, and the factory floor may become much smarter as a result. Machine tool controls are being developed that recognize sound, vibration, pressure, and other conditions. The market for sensors is expected to grow to $1.1 billion by 1994, more than double the 1987 level of $513 million.

Other factory applications include prediction of tool breakage in milling operations, cutting force analysis, ceramic wear analysis in cutting operations, and mechanical equipment fault diagnosis. Neural nets can also be used in the simulation and control of power plants, which require the simultaneous operation of many complex controls.

Process control applications are also well suited for neural net assistance. The lengthy procedures involved in chemical processing, for example, can be modeled by neural net systems, which can be retrained as the plant is modified, unlike expert systems, for which a new rule base might need to be built to accommodate the changes. Rule development in expert systems is notoriously slow.

A system developed by Automation Technology, Inc., has been successfully tested at a pulp-and-paper mill in Arkansas. The system improved uniformity and efficiency in brownstock washer operations. It was designed not to replace existing control systems but to augment them.

Milltech-HOH, Inc., is using a neural net system to control the efficiency of electric arc furnaces in steelmaking, allowing the furnace to operate at peak efficiency without operator intervention.

Neural nets, developed from biological principles, have given back to biology through many medical applications. At the University of California's School of Veterinary Medicine at Davis, they have been used to visually identify blood reactions though microscopes and to examine the genetic heritage of racehorses. A system called PAPNET combines computerized imaging and neural nets to identify clotted blood cells, deformed eggs, and cancerous cells. Other systems are mapping the brains of monkeys and linking the map to behavior patterns. Neural nets are also being used to develop better prosthetic devices, which today are a blend of mechanical, electronic, and computer equipment. Another system has been used in the analysis of electrocardiogram data.

Environmental and geological problems have also been attacked with neural nets. One system has been used to predict salinity in different regions of Chesapeake Bay based on nearly 40,000 observations; it outperformed traditional, linear regression techniques. Texaco has developed a system that offers better predictions of permeability in oil reservoirs.

Airports may be safer places due to neural nets. A bomb detection system based on neural nets analyzes the gamma ray patterns emitted by various objects after being struck with neutrons. The system began field tests in early 1989 at JFK International Airport in New York and is now in everyday use.

Controlling and pricing a hotel's room inventory to maximize profit is a complex process. Walter Relihan, in "The Yield-Management Approach to Hotel-Room Pricing" (*Cornell Hotel and Restaurant Administration Quarterly*, May 1989, 40–45), compares various approaches to this problem, including the use of neural nets. The goal is to adjust room rates on a daily basis based on demand information about future arrival rates.

Marketing offers many potential applications. Neural nets may be able to analyze historical sales data to reveal customer purchasing patterns and identify better merchandising-mix strategies. They may also be used to identify complex demographic relationships in a company's customer base. Their ability to identify nonlinear patterns gives them an edge over traditional regression techniques.

One downside of neural nets is the difficulties they pose for internal auditors. If systems are frequently changing, then they are difficult to audit. Auditors are having to stay abreast of the new technological developments, and firms are having to carefully analyze the controls needed to properly manage this technology.

Many problems that have attracted GA researchers have also attracted neural net researchers; some examples are robot control, database query and retrieval, document clustering, the travelling salesman problem, combinatorial optimization problems, and resource-constrained scheduling.

NEURAL NETS IN FINANCE

Many finance applications of neural nets have already been or are currently being developed. Currency trading, equities trading, image recognition for check processing, and credit approval are a few examples of areas that stand to benefit from these innovations. The insurance industry has found that neural nets greatly assist the procedures involved in rate-making, loss reserve analysis, cost containment, reinsurance, fraud detection, and data entry associated with claims processing.

Banks are finding numerous applications. In 1988 Chase Manhattan Bank began using a neural net that is used to identify fraudulent credit card transactions. The Fraud Detection System, developed by Nestor Corporation, recognizes unusual credit-charge patterns and computes a fraud-potential rating. HNC, Inc., has a system that analyzes a bank's database and past decisions to produce a decision model.

Management, investors, and regulators are all interested in obtaining early warnings of financial distress. In one study, neural nets outperformed traditional multiple-discriminant analysis in correctly categorizing firms as either healthy or distressed. Neural nets have also been used in bank and thrift failure prediction models. In one study, the neural net approach outperformed a traditional logit approach.

Trading systems must be built with care. If the system is over trained on historical data, then it may not work well with future information. Experiments with neural net currency-trading systems indicate that single market analysis is too limited. Neural nets seem ideally suited for technical strategies, which are based on data patterns; however, trading systems may need to incorporate both fundamental and technical information from different markets due to intermarket linkages. One stock selection system combines ideas from neural nets, expert systems, and fuzzy reasoning into a fuzzy neural system. Just as neural nets have filtered noisy visual signals, they have also been used to filter noisy economic data that is then fed into trading systems.

4
Chaos Theory: The Order behind Disorder

It was inevitable that someone would try to apply chaos theory to investment. The intuitive appeal to do so is strong. Any observer of the stock market has watched it undergo numerous, rapid transitions from a strong, steady trend into vibrating confusion. The words *order* and *chaos* are familiar to investors because they are part of the investment experience.

Chaos theory is a young science. Edward Lorenz conducted his computer experiments on weather forecasting in the early 1960s. Later in that decade, Benoit Mandelbrot experimented with fractional Brownian motion and published his groundbreaking work, *The Fractal Geometry of Nature,* in 1977. Mitchell Feigenbaum discovered the universal constant of chaos theory, now known as Feigenbaum's number, in 1975. Popular interest in chaos theory soared in 1987 as James Gleick's excellent book, *Chaos: Making a New Science,* became a national bestseller. Many of the early developers of chaos theory are not only still alive but are still in their forties.

Chaos theory centers more on explanation than prediction, and not necessarily by choice. Lorenz was trying to predict long-range weather patterns when he encountered the problem of sensitive dependence on initial conditions, in which small changes can lead to major changes later on. As researchers learned more about the complicated patterns of chaos, they realized that forecasting is fundamentally more difficult than they previously had imagined, and so their attention was turned more toward explaining nature and its dynamic processes.

It is no accident that chaos theory has grown substantially in recent years. The growth of this science has been closely linked to the growth of computers. Chaotic processes are characterized by repetition; many of the necessary calculations are simple but must be performed over and over again. Computers excel at rapid computation of repetitive functions. Quite a bit can be learned about chaos theory by looking at some simple PC-based examples.

CHAOS THEORY BASICS

The logistic equation is often used to introduce the basic concepts of chaos theory:

$$X_t = k * X_{t-1} * (1 - X_{t-1}), \text{ where } k \text{ is a constant.}$$

This equation can be used to model the spread of an infectious disease. If the infection rate is k, then the spread of infection is proportional to the percentage of the population that is already infected, denoted by X. If X is the percentage infected, then $1 - X$ are not infected. Because infection needs new victims to continue its advance, the spread of infection is also proportional to $1 - X$.

The essence of the logistic equation shows up in other problems. We can extend the lethality of the analogy from the spread of infection to a predator-prey survival situation. For example, the growth of a fox population is roughly proportional to its size. The size of a nearby rabbit population is inversely proportional to the number of foxes. However, as the foxes reduce the number of rabbits, their food supply and survival become threatened. Foxes breed more foxes. The two groups are locked together in a complex iterative loop.

One of the ingredients of a chaotic system is feedback. In the logistic equation, the result from the previous iteration is fed back repeatedly into the next one. This feedback, or *looping,* effect is common in nature and physical phenomena. The squealing of a PA system in an auditorium is the result of noise being amplified and fed back into the microphone. Feedback produces some strange results.

Chaos researchers sometimes take a simple equation and play with its variations. Often, the nature of the results changes markedly with a slight twist of the basic equation. For example, terms can be raised to a power, modified by a trigonometric function, or time lagged. The resulting changes to the original pattern are often dramatic and unpredictable. Chaos research has proceeded more by trial and error than by theory.

Many of the concepts of chaos theory can be illustrated with simple exi mples. To explore some of these concepts, let's focus on a slight variation of the ogistic equation. By adding another term and introducing an extra dependence on preceding values, the resulting patterns will be spiced up a little:

$$X_t = k * X_{t-1} * (1 - X_{t-1} * X_{t-2})$$

This modified equation can be examined easily on a PC with a spreadsheet program. The basic steps are

1. Set up the k value constant in cell A1. Try 1.35)
2. Use cell B1 for the starting x value. Try 0.4.

3. In cell B2, type the following: A1*B1*(1 − B1*B1)
4. Type the following formula into cell B3:
   A1*B2*(1 − B2*B1)   [Note: there is a slight change from the preceding formula.]
5. Type the number 1 into cell A2.
6. Type the following formula into cell A3: A2 + 1
7. Copy the formulas from cells A3 and B3 down through cells A500 and B500 (or further, depending on how much time you are willing to devote to spreadsheet recalculation).

The A column (starting at cell A2) contains the iteration number. Column B contains the result of the iterated modified logistic equation. If your PC has graphics capability, then you may also want to set up columns A2 through A500 and B2 through B500 as ranges in a graph. This will allow you to graph the equation result as a function of the iteration number and see how the resulting X values change over time. We will refer to this graph as the AB graph; a second graph will be discussed later.

Now let's experiment with our modified equation. Different k values produce some widely different behavior. The behavior for different values of k can be summarized as follows:

k value(s)	Behavior of results
0–1.0	The X values converge to 0. Convergence is rapid over most of the range but slows as k approaches 1.0.
1.0–1.495	The X values converge to become greater than 0. Convergence slows as the k value increases. See the AB graph in Figure 4.1. (Note: Figures 4.1–4.7 show the results for seven different increasing k values. The graphs are displayed in ascending k sequence, but our discussion will not always follow this sequence.)
1.495–1.711	The X values begin to oscillate. At first the range of oscillation is narrow, but it increases as k approaches 1.711. The X values are all positive. See the AB graphs in Figures 4.2 and 4.3. (Note: We will discuss Figure 4.4 later).
1.711–2.0	At $k = 1.711$, X begins to take on both positive and negative values. As k approaches 2, the X values bounce around in what appears to be a nearly random fashion. At $k = 2$, the equation becomes unstable, with the X values exploding to infinity. See the AB graphs in Figures 4.5, 4.6, and 4.7.

One commonly cited observation from chaos theory is that systems are sometimes highly dependent on initial conditions. Consider the behavior of our system

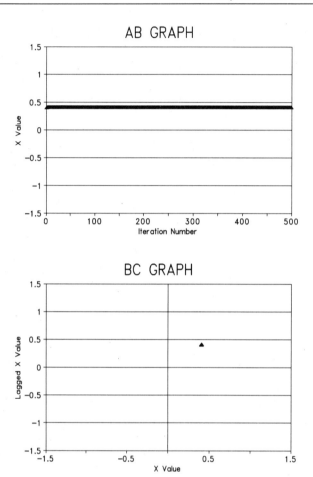

FIGURE 4.1   Modified Logistic Equation: k Value = 1.200

for $k = 1.85$. Using our starting X value of 0.4 in cell B1, the value of X after 20 iterations is $+ 0.0308$. However, if we change our starting value in B1 to 0.401, then X is $- 0.3106$ after 20 iterations. A small change in the initial conditions leads to dramatic differences later on.

Sensitive dependence on initial conditions is also known as the *butterfly effect*. Consider global weather as a complex system of interrelationships. Small changes in one region might create a chain reaction leading to large change in the weather of a distant region. As an extreme example, a butterfly flapping its wings in China might set off a complex series of effects leading to a tornado in Texas—hence, the butterfly effect.

As Lorenz discovered, the possibility of sensitive dependence on initial conditions is bad news for forecasters. Because the initial conditions can never be

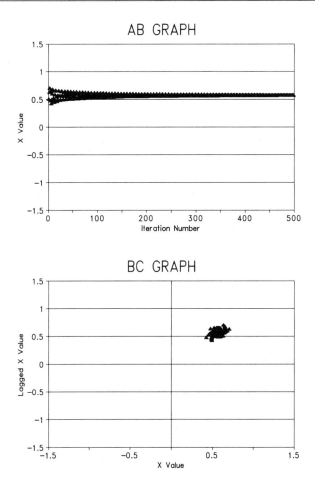

FIGURE 4.2 Modified Logistic Equation: k Value $= 1.495$

known with certainty, long-range forecasting of many systems is impossible. In our simple example we know the underlying equation. However, even that is not much help in forecasting later X values if we don't know the starting point, and in real-life problems we usually don't know either.

A point that is often not emphasized in the chaos theory literature is that some systems are not sensitive to the initial conditions. In our example equation, future values of X are easily predictable for certain k values. If k is 1.1, for example, the system quickly converges to $X = 0.3015$. Small and large changes to the initial value in cell B1 have little impact on X values beyond the fiftieth iteration. A given system may or may not be sensitive to initial conditions—it all depends on the state of the system.

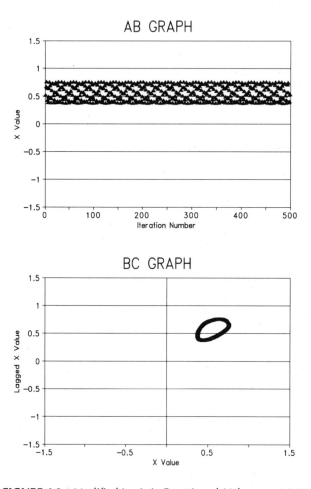

FIGURE 4.3 Modified Logistic Equation: k Value $= 1.540$

Chaotic systems often experience interesting transitions as they move from one state into another. Let's examine the transitions that occur at certain k values. To illustrate these transitions, we will make use of a second graph by creating a third column of data as follows:

1. Type $+B1$ into cell C2.
2. Copy this simple formula down from C2 to cells C3 through C500. Column C is merely a column of lagged values from column B.
3. Create a second graph, using columns B and C. The values from B2 to B500 form the first range, and the values from C2 to C500 make up the second range.

We now have two graphs. We will refer to the first graph, a graph of the X values in column B versus the iteration number in column A, as the AB graph. The second graph, column C versus column B, will be referred to as the BC graph, which will exhibit some dramatic patterns and help us identify changes in the system.

A major transition in our system occurs at $k = 1.495$. At lower values of k, the X values always converge. At first they converge to 0, and then later they converge to values greater than 0. In Figure 4.1, we see in the AB graph that the X values converge to about 0.5. The BC graph shows the X values centering on one point. But as k is increased and approaches 1.495, the BC graph shows the points spiraling into one point. However, at $k = 1.495$, shown in Figure 4.2, the center of the spiral is actually beginning to expand from a single point into an oval. If k is increased to 1.540, as in Figure 4.3, the transition can be clearly seen. Now the X values are oscillating in a curious pattern that appears as a collection of interlocking waves in the AB graph and as a clearly defined oval in the BC graph. The two graphs complement each other; sometimes subtle changes in the AB graph take on a more definite form in the BC graph.

Occasionally, unusual patterns seem to come from nowhere and lead nowhere. As k is increased from 1.540 to 1.711, the AB graph shows an increasingly wider nest of interlocking waves, while the BC pattern is an oval with one end gradually being drawn towards the point 0,0. However, in the vicinity of $k = 1.672$, the patterns change. As seen in the AB graph, Figure 4.4, the X values flatten into a set of parallel lines; simultaneously, the oval in the BC graph becomes fragmented. As k is increased again, the oval in the BC graph is reformed, and the AB graph regains its previous structure. The transition from order to disorder and back to order again can be puzzling and unpredictable.

Chaotic systems can display other misleading behavior. Let's explore what happens to our example equation when $k = 1.711$. (Note: The k values are shown to three decimals; the precise value used was 1.71055.) The AB graph in Figure 4.5 shows the behavior of the X values over the course of 500 iterations. For the first 416 iterations, the X values change in a seemingly random fashion between 0 and 1. However, at iteration number 417 the pattern changes abruptly. Suddenly, X is now between 0 and -1; the X values have flipped from positive to negative. If we had observed only the X values over the first 416 iterations without the benefit of the BC graph or some other analysis and then had been asked about the likelihood of X being negative for iteration 417, we would probably have said, "No way." Does it seem somewhat like an abrupt switch from a bull market to a bear market?

The abrupt transition into negative X values leads to the figure-eight pattern shown in the BC graph of Figure 4.5. If we continue to crank up the k value, we can see a smaller figure eight begin to appear within the larger one, as can be seen in Figure 4.6. Notice that while the BC graph shows a very clear pattern, the AB graph shows what appears to be a nearly random scattering of positive

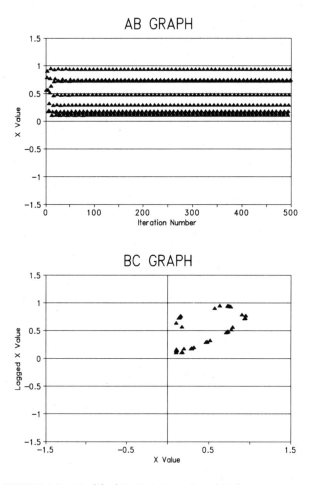

FIGURE 4.4   Modified Logistic Equation: k Value $= 1.672$

and negative values. The X values have an amazingly complex structure that is certainly not evident in the AB graph.

Digressing for a moment to think about the stock market might perhaps make chaos theory seem more intriguing. Are complex patterns lurking in stock prices and returns? The picture in Figure 4.5 could bring joy to the hearts of most technical analysts. Chaos theory advocates might argue that there are many similar patterns right in front of us every day—it's all in the way that you look at the data.

One of the ideas to emerge from chaos theory is the notion of an *attractor*. Attractors show up frequently in the preceding examples. For lower values of k, we can say that the X values are attracted to a certain value. At $k = 1.350$, the system is attracted to $X = 0.5092$. Looking at the BC graph, we say that the

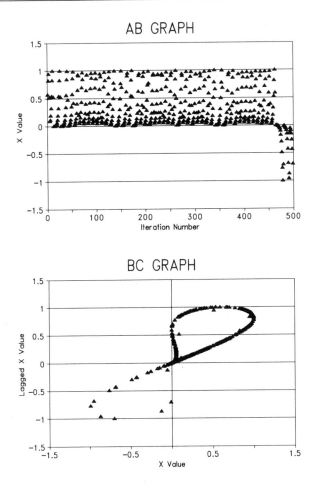

FIGURE 4.5 Modified Logistic Equation: k Value $= 1.711$

system is attracted to a certain point. At higher values of k, the attractor in the BC graph is either an oval, a figure eight, or a double figure eight. At the transition points, one attractor loses out in a tug-of-war with another, stronger attractor.

If we increase k sufficiently, the system finally becomes unstable and is attracted to infinity. Figure 4.7 shows the system at $k = 1.999$. The AB graph shows wildly fluctuating positive and negative X values. In the BC graph, the figure eight has become fuzzier, more upright, and both taller and fatter. If we watch the system as k approaches 2.000, we may have the sense that it is getting more and more out of control. It's as if the system were covered with gasoline, waiting to explode. Going from $k = 1.999$ to $k = 2.000$ is like lighting a match—*poooooooff!* Perhaps the transition is similar to the transition that occurred from

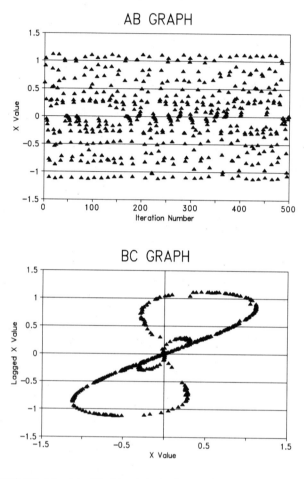

FIGURE 4.6   Modified Logistic Equation: *k* Value = 1.800

Friday, October 16, 1987, to Monday, October 19, 1987. Seen in this light, chaos theory can be tantalizing.

CHAOS THEORY RESEARCH

As would be expected of any new science, chaos theory has numerous roots in other disciplines, for example, mathematics, physics, biology, chemistry, engineering, economics, philosophy, and computer science. Articles on chaos theory appear in publications such as *Water Resources Research, Journal of Atmospheric Science,* and *Communications in Mathematical Physics.* The basic patterns described and explained by chaos theory appear in tree leaves, coastlines, and cigarette smoke; the breadth of the field makes it difficult to grasp. There are still

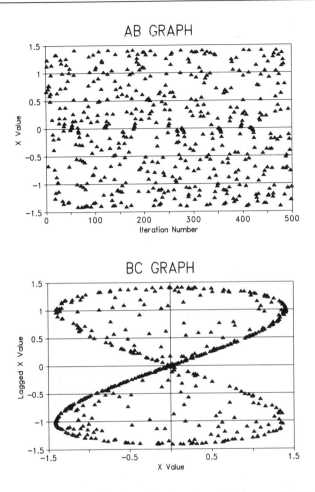

FIGURE 4.7 Modified Logistic Equation: k Value = 1.999

few books that offer a comprehensive view of the science, and those that do are immediately outdated due to the time it takes to bring a book to market.

Some of the early advances in chaos theory were connected to the problem of turbulence. Physical systems undergoing transitions often exhibit turbulent behavior. Smoke rising from a cigarette starts off in lazy curls and then gradually twists and turns; a small breeze can violently disrupt whatever pattern is discernible; the surface of boiling water changes from a glassy isolated pond to a storm-tossed sea. Simple transitions had defied an easy explanation, even by the likes of Einstein and Heisenberg. But the scientific world experienced some turbulence of its own in 1971, when David Ruelle and Floris Takens published ''On the Problem of Turbulence,'' laying one of the cornerstones of chaos theory.

Chaotic systems often seem drawn to certain values or patterns. In Figure 4.6, the attractor is a double figure eight, as seen in the BC graph. Ruelle and Takens explained turbulence using the concept of a *strange attractor*. The formal definition of this term relies on topology, the mathematics of stretched and twisted shapes. However, a strange attractor can be easily visualized. Imagine a physical system and that we are measuring and plotting two of its parameters. As we plot them on a graph, the system seems to be tracing out a figure eight. However, upon close examination we see something very odd; each eight is in a slightly different place. All the eights are close, but they are never exactly the same. Never. We can plot an infinite number of figure eights in this same finite space, and they never exactly repeat. The system has a strange attractor, but the behavior never completely stabilizes.

Benoit Mandelbrot is probably the person most closely linked to the development of chaos theory. A capsule description of Mandelbrot might include the following: Polish-born, French-educated, mathematician, Jewish survivor of the Holocaust, researcher for IBM, and creator of the term *fractal*. This word is derived from Latin roots meaning "breaking," as are the words "fracture" and "fraction." Mandelbrot's *The Fractal Geometry of Nature*, published in 1977, is the unofficial Bible of chaos theory. But fractals themselves are not easily defined; Mandelbrot himself has wrestled with two different definitions. He first defined fractals in topological terms, relying on a concept known as the *Hausdorff-Besicovitch dimension*. Later he switched to the following simpler definition:

A fractal is a shape made of parts similar to the whole in some way.
The latter part of this definition refers to the *self-similar* feature of fractals, meaning that they repeat themselves with many variations on the same underlying pattern.

In addition to fractals, Mandelbrot is known for the discovery of the *Mandelbrot set*. Complex numbers, which have two parts, one real and one imaginary, are often plotted in a two-dimensional graph called the *complex plane*. Every complex number is either in or out of the Mandelbrot set, and the calculation used to decide this is quite simple. But if we plot the Mandelbrot set by placing a black dot at all points in the complex plane that are in the set, we get an amazing picture: snowflake-like objects with many ins and outs on their edges, reminiscent of the Norwegian coast. We also notice a certain self-similarity; the objects appear to contain smaller copies of themselves. But when we magnify the picture, everything gets stranger still. The intricate detail of the objects never ends, no matter how precisely we refine our calculations. Let's start out with a certain graph scale, for example, one having -2.0 to $+0.5$ on the real axis and $-1.25i$ to $+1.25i$ on the imaginary axis (the Mandelbrot set is actually contained within these boundaries). If we were to take some portion of this graph and then blow it up to $100,000 \times$ magnification, we would still find objects with beautiful intricate detail. Repeating the magnification again and again would continue to reveal these fascinating objects.

The complex patterns evident in the Mandelbrot set and other figures all point towards a geometry different than traditional, Euclidean geometry, in which geometric lines and shapes are described as either one- , two- , or three-dimensional. With fractals, the measurement and dimensionality of objects becomes complex. The classic fractal measurement problem is the length of a coastline like Norway's, which consists of many jagged ins and outs linking fjords and rivers to the ocean. What is the length of Norway's coastline? This sounds like a simple question; however, the answer depends on the size of your ruler. Smaller rulers allow more precise measurement of the many turns in and out, thus increasing the measured length of the coastline. Problems like this led to the concept of *fractal dimension*. The dimensions of fractal objects can be mathematically defined with precision, but the answers are not the clean, whole numbers of Euclidean geometry. The fractal dimension of Norway's coast is 1.52. It is neither one-dimensional nor two-dimensional; the dimensionality is somewhere in between.

If the fractal dimension of a figure seems odd, then try thinking about the fractal dimension of a time series. Actually, this isn't too big of a mind-bender due to its similarity to the coastline problem. Graphing a "noisy" time series, such as monthly stock returns, will result in a very erratic line with many ups and downs similar to the ins and outs of the Norwegian coast, and if the Norwegian coast has a fractal dimension, then one can probably be calculated for a time series. The work of H.E. Hurst has centered on this concept.

Hurst, a hydrologist working on the Nile River Dam project, experimented with different calculations concerning reservoirs. In his 1951 paper, "Long-Term Storage of Reservoirs," he describes his statistical methods. Let's assume that over a five-year period a reservoir receives 100 units of water. The average influx is 20 units per year, and the average outflow should be 20 units per year. However, suppose the inflows on a year-by-year basis are 35, 30, 5, 0, and 30. The year-by-year cumulative amounts are 35, 65, 70, 70, and 100. If the inflow had been spread smoothly over the five years, then our cumulative amounts would have been 20, 40, 60, 80, and 100. In our case the cumulative deviations from a smooth average inflow are $+15$, $+25$, $+10$, -10, and 0. The maximum cumulative deviation is $+25$, and the minimum is -10. Hurst would have described this series as having a *range* of 35 units, the difference between the cumulative maximum and minimum. He also defined the *rescaled range,* which he designated *R/S,* as the range divided by the standard deviation of the original observations.

Hurst performed his rescaled range analysis on many naturally observed time series, such as the flows of the Nile river. From these observations he also developed the following empirical law:

$$R/S = (a * N)^H$$

where R/S = rescaled range
                              N = number of observations
                              a = a constant
                              H = the Hurst exponent

We will bypass some of the details and jump straight to the most important things to understand about rescaled range analysis, which are

1. For a given time series, the Hurst exponent may be estimated using the above equation. For more details, refer to E. E. Peters, *Chaos and Order in the Capital Markets* (New York: John Wiley & Sons, 1991).
2. The Hurst exponent will range in value from 0 to 1. If the time series is purely a random walk, then the Hurst exponent will be equal to 0.5. Values greater than 0.5 indicate a persistent, or trend-reinforcing, series.
3. The inverse of the H value is the fractal dimension of the series.

INVESTING AND CHAOS THEORY

Many people are talking about the possible application of chaos theory to investing, but there is a limited amount of published work on this topic, which is possibly due to the proprietary trading nature of any interesting findings. Edgar Peters has been the major pioneer in this area, publishing the only book on the topic. We will save a description of his work until later in this section.

In his article "Testing Chaos and Nonlinearities in T-Bill Rates," printed in 1991, M. Larrain merges ideas from both technical and fundamental analysis into an overall equation containing both linear and nonlinear terms. The technical nonlinear component is referred to as the *K-map*, while the behavioral fundamental component is called the *Z-map*. Larrain proposes that erratic, or chaotic, interest rate patterns develop when the K-map overpowers the Z-map. But the market can be driven by a well-behaved fundamental macroeconomic structure for significant periods of time and also experience chaotic periods. Chaos theory may explain an important portion of market behavior, but not all of it. Thus, technical and fundamental approaches are both valid.

The idea that markets can switch back and forth between chaotic and non-chaotic periods is also discussed by T. Vaga in "The Coherent Market Hypothesis" (1990). His ideas draw on those of E. Callan and D. Shapiro in "A Theory of Social Imitation" (*Physics Today,* 1974, vol. 27), which deals with the polarization of opinion in social groups. In coherent bull markets the risk-return trade-off becomes highly attractive; return is high, risk is low. Markets emerge from coherent phases into chaotic periods where risk dominates rewards. His work provides hope to those who believe that it may be possible to time movements in and out of markets. Investors who can successfully identify coherent markets stand to earn substantial profits.

S.C. Blank, in "Chaos in Futures Markets? A Nonlinear Dynamical Analysis" (1991), investigates the futures prices of the Standard and Poor's 500 index and soybeans. He finds that both markets show nonlinearities that are partially deterministic. The results are consistent with an underlying structure of deterministic chaos.

Edgar Peters has published more about chaos and investing than anyone else. His first (and previously mentioned) book, *Chaos and Order in the Capital Markets*, has been very successful. He is currently finishing a second book titled *Fractal Market Analysis*. He has also written several articles for the *Financial Analysts Journal*.

One of the main methods that Peters uses is R/S *analysis*. He has used this technique to examine the characteristics of many different series of returns and has found evidence of persistence in market returns; the past *does* influence the present. Market returns are not normally distributed; they have a fractal distribution with infinite variance. Peters calculated the Hurst exponent and a cycle length for various series using market data from January 1950 through July 1988. He concluded that technologically-driven industries like the computer industry have a high level of persistence but tend to have short cycle periods, which suggests that returns in these industries may be somewhat predictable, but only for one- to two-year periods. Returns for industries that are more mature and stable, such as the utility industry, may be less persistent, but the underlying cycle does not change as frequently. We will report some of these results in more detail in Chapter 14, because we use Peters's results as a starting point for our investigations of market timing rules for individual stocks.

ORGANIZATIONS AND CHAOS THEORY

It is not surprising that researchers have been trying to apply chaos theory to the analysis of various organizational issues. Humans interact in organizations in a complex manner involving multiple feedback loops, which helps explain why organizations can sometimes go from calm stability to turbulence with little advance warning. Some researchers have examined the links to chaos theory in a qualitative fashion, whereas others have been more quantitative.

In "Discovering the Patterns of Chaos" (1989), R.H. Priesmeyer and K. Baik look at the quarterly performance of twenty publicly traded companies using "limit cycle" graphs, in which changes in sales are plotted on one axis against changes in earnings on the other axis. The authors find that some companies show stable repetitive patterns that seem to revolve around some type of underlying attractor, while other companies experience transitions into more chaotic states. They conclude that management can inadvertently disrupt stable performance with some common decisions. Priesmeyer and J. Davis expand on the concept of limit cycles and their relevance to major strategic decisions in "Chaos Theory: A Tool for Predicting the Unpredictable" (1991). Management should be particularly attentive to stabilizing corporate performance after major strategic decisions such as divestitures or acquisitions.

T. Bahlmann's article, "The Learning Organization in a Turbulent Environment" (1990), applies some of the ideas from chaos theory to six major companies in the Netherlands that went through periods of severe crisis. The author compares such periods to chaotic turbulence and urges organizations undergoing such transitions to focus on how they can learn to survive.

"Planning and Chaos Theory" (1991), by T.J. Cartwright, examines the implications of chaos theory to planning and finds both good news and bad news. The good news is that complex behavior such as that seen in chaotic city environments may be governed by some fairly simple underlying principles. However, determining those principles is extremely difficult, thus making prediction nearly impossible. Planners may need to focus on incremental and adaptive planning.

Because chaos theory places emphasis on the importance of initial conditions, several researchers have examined the connection between chaos theory and the early stages of new companies. In a study published in 1990, Eisenhardt and Schoonhoven examined 90 U.S. semiconductor firms that were founded between 1978 and 1985. They found that growth depended critically on the founding top management team and initial conditions. Smilor and Feeser's work of 1991 examines the factors governing the birth and growth of entrepreneurial companies and the link between those factors and chaos theory. They suggest that chaos theory may help explain the nature of risk in these new ventures.

Priesmeyer offers insights into many different areas with his book, *Organizations and Chaos,* published in 1992. He presents 34 different propositions that he divides into the following topic areas: marketing management, financial management, production management, human resource issues, forecasting and visioning, and strategic management. Many of the propositions revolve around the concepts of *phase plane* and *limit cycle.* The phase plane is the two-dimensional plane for plotting the changes in two variables of interest. For example, we might plot changes in sales versus changes in earnings. The time trajectory of the points plotted in the phase plane is called the *limit cycle* of the entity under investigation. Limit cycles could plot as just a point, an oval, a figure eight, or some more complex pattern. We will focus on the finance-related propositions, although many of the ideas have investment implications.

Priesmeyer's finance-related propositions, numbered 8 through 10 in his book, are as follows:

8. Financial analysis requires more than simply a study of the current relationships between various financial measures. Understanding and prudent intervention require an awareness of the chronological patterns in the activities those measures represent.

9. Phase plane diagrams provide a way to express the current state of an income statement's relationships. Because certain zones on the phase plane can be related to specific conditions, appropriate intervention strat-

egies are prescribed directly by observing the current position of the limit cycle and phase plane.

10. Phase plane diagrams report financial information that is often used for ratio analysis in a way that much more effectively displays the behavior of the contributing measures.

Most financial analysts would not take issue with proposition 8. Analysts often examine ratio trends, thus considering chronological patterns. However, in Priesmeyer's phase plane plots, the horizontal x-axis does not represent time. For example, he may plot the change in net profit on the vertical, or y-axis, versus change in sales on the horizontal, or x-axis. Changes in the limit cycle thus obtained may signal important changes that are occurring in the financial condition of the company. Using this technique allows the analyst to get an overview of the chronological patterns that wouldn't be possible with traditional techniques.

Proposition 9 and 10 essentially argue for the use of phase plane diagrams to analyze financial statements and ratios. Priesmeyer contends that phase plane diagrams can be useful in guiding managers towards better operational decisions; the patterns in a sales/profit-related limit cycle might point to the need for a focus on pricing strategy and greater profit margins. Phase plane analysis may also help investors make better investment decisions. For example, if investors spot disturbing changes in the limit cycles of certain relationships, then they may want to bail out of their investment.

CONCLUSIONS

Chaos theory is a complex topic, covering many different issues. However, from an investment standpoint, we think the following points are the most important:

1. Chaos theory explains why predictions are nearly impossible in many situations. Unless the initial conditions are known with a high degree of accuracy, prediction is difficult. And even if the initial conditions are known, prediction may be impossible without knowing the underlying equations that govern subsequent behavior.

2. Financial markets may experience periods of relative stability punctuated by periods of erratic behavior.

3. Industries and individual stocks may differ substantially in their underlying patterns. Stock returns may be more persistent in certain industries or for certain companies.

4. Systems can display seemingly stable behavior just prior to abrupt transitions. Investors must be alert to the possibility of rapid transitions.

5. Traditional financial analysis may be lacking because insufficient attention has been devoted to the time trajectory of various financial ratios and financial relationships. Chaos theory may provide some techniques for improved analysis.

5

Questions and Answers about Using GAs

The purpose of this chapter is to provide a brief reference guide to using GAs versus chaos theory or neural networks. A question and answer format is provided, allowing the reader to quickly find and focus on particular areas of interest.

1. What type of problem is most suitable for using GAs?

The main word to consider is optimization; however, that term can be misleading. GAs are optimization procedures. If you want to either maximize or minimize something, then you have an optimization problem, and GAs are probably appropriate. However, GAs don't necessarily find an optimal solution; they may only find near optimal solutions, which may be acceptable for most business applications. In the investments business, performance is often relative; the "highest" return is great, but "high" may be quite acceptable.

Another word to consider is *search*. If you have a problem that involves a large search space—that is, a large set of possible solutions—then it is a good candidate for a GA. Searching can take large amounts of time for two reasons. First, the sheer size of search space means that there are many possible answers to the basic problem. Second, if the problem is extremely complex, then the calculation time associated with each potential answer may be lengthy. As you will see in later chapters, in our case we face a large search and lengthy calculations associated with each potential solution.

2. How do you set up the problem in a way that a GA can use?

This can be the trickiest part of using GAs. Somehow you must find a way of representing your problem as a string of values. Usually binary coding is used, with the string being a sequence of 0s and 1s. GA researchers have invented many clever techniques for structuring problems as strings. The best starting point is probably to read about other applications and see some of the ideas that have been used. Basically, the string will represent variables or relationships that can take on a wide range of values.

Problem representation can be both the most enjoyable part of using GAs and the most frustrating. It can be fun testing different problem representations. There are usually many creative possibilities. However, the process of finding a suitable representation can be time consuming and vexing. You might have a gut feeling that there must be a way to represent the problem as a string, but it may take considerable thought before the light bulb of ingenuity turns on.

3. When GAs optimize, what gets optimized?

You need to remember that the GA is trying to find an optimal string—in other words, the GA is trying to make your string as good as possible. If the string represents parameter settings, then the GA is trying to find the best parameter settings for the problem at hand, the parameter values that lead to maximum fitness, or performance.

The preceding paragraph seems simple enough, but there are some subtleties involved. The string representation and performance calculation are critical. GAs are good at finding an answer, but you need to make sure that you are asking the right question. "What do I really want to optimize?" is a question worthy of careful deliberation. The old computer adage, "garbage in, garbage out" (GIGO), applies. If the performance calculation is not structured properly, then you will be disappointed with the results. A computer is great at following commands. You just need to make sure that you are giving it proper marching orders.

4. What if you want to minimize, not maximize?

A simple transformation is usually all that is required. In some of the later chapters we focus on two different sides of a similar problem. In one instance, we try to develop attractive trading rules that maximize returns. In the way that we had the problem formulated, this yielded fitness values in the range of roughly 1.7 to 2.2. We also looked at the flip side of the problem, which involving finding trading rules that consistently did poorly (a consistently poor rule can be valuable if you do the opposite of what it recommends!). For this aspect of the problem, the fitness values were small positive values or negative values ranging from −2.1 to +0.5. To transform this second set of values that we were trying to minimize, we subtracted the fitness value of 10.0 (an arbitrary number chosen to be larger than the largest positive fitness value). This resulted in transformed fitness values between 9.5 and 12.1. If all of the fitness values had been negative, we could have transformed the fitness by just using absolute values and trying to maximize. These simple techniques can always transform a minimization problem into a maximization problem. By doing this, possible revisions to the GA computer code are avoided. Alternatively, the GA software could be adjusted to accomplish minimization.

5. How do you calculate string fitness, or performance?

The fitness calculation is critical. As stated earlier, GAs will try to optimize what you tell them to optimize, so the fitness calculation should have a strong link to the problem you want to solve. Fitness calculations can be very simple or extremely complex. For investment problems, fitness could be the return that might have been earned if a particular investment strategy had been used in the past, and the return could be just the annual compound return calculated over some time period. However, there could be many additional refinements. For example, the return might be a time-weighted average that places greater emphasis on more recent results. The time-weighting could be a simple linear weighting or some type of exponential weighting.

The fitness calculation is directly linked to the string. For every possible string pattern, you must be able to assign a fitness value to a given string, which might somehow represent four possible parameter settings of a given function. The parameter values might have a binary representation in the string. The fitness calculation would break the string into four binary pieces, convert the binary values to their real equivalents, and then plug these parameters into the function to compute fitness.

There are endless variations of how problems can be represented as strings and how fitness can be calculated. Reviewing other applications is probably the best way to get ideas about how the fitness calculation might be handled in your particular application.

6. When would chaos theory be better than a GA?

This is a difficult question. In general, chaos theory techniques are geared more toward explanation and description than forecasting. Indeed, chaos theory recognizes the extreme difficulty of forecasting chaotic systems due to sensitive dependence on initial conditions. Some chaos theory techniques, such as rescaled range analysis, are designed to identify the presence of chaos but do not uncover the underlying mathematical formulas that would facilitate forecasting. If the goal is mostly to describe behavior and understand the system in a general way, then chaos theory may be more appropriate. GAs optimize and as such require at least some beginning structure or hypothesis from which to work. Chaos theory techniques may lead to a better understanding of the system without requiring any starting assumptions.

In later chapters, we will develop some ideas about using both chaos theory and GAs to tackle investment problems. For example, chaos theory might be used to determine whether or not the current state of the market was conducive to forecasting or not. If the investor decided that the market seemed to be in a more predictable state, then using GAs to develop trading strategies might prove lucrative. If the market were in a more chaotic unpredictable state, then such efforts might be futile.

7. What is the main drawback to chaos theory?

The reaction of some people to chaos theory is "This is interesting, but so what?" Learning that a system exhibits chaotic behavior is enlightening but can leave you feeling stuck. There are many equations, such as the modified logistic equation we used in Chapter 4, that demonstrate chaotic behavior and allow you to generate complex data patterns. However, researchers have found the reverse task to be virtually impossible. There is no clear-cut procedure for taking chaotic data patterns and working backwards to the underlying mathematical relationship. So if chaotic patterns appear in financial market data, it may mean that future prices could be predicted if the underlying equation was known, but finding that equation may be impossible for now.

8. What lessons from chaos theory may apply to GAs?

Some of Peters's research indicates that stock market cycles may be approximately five years in length. Prices within the five-year window are related to each other; older prices have no bearing on present prices. If this is true, then using historical data more than five years in the past to build trading systems for current use may be fruitless.

In addition, Vaga's coherent market hypothesis posits that there are certain phases of the market cycle in which prices may be more predictable than in other phases. Identifying the current market phase would allow one to have some sense of whether or not prediction efforts might be worthwhile. There may be periods of time when market timing and prediction are just not possible.

9. When would neural networks be better than a GA?

Again, this is a difficult question. Although some might disagree, it seems that neural networks rely more on empiricism than theory. Neural nets operate much like a black box. You describe inputs and desired output, take a guess at a network structure and possible functional relationships, and then experiment. Therefore, little knowledge of the underlying relationships is required. With GAs, you do need some starting framework or hypothesis.

The distinction concerning prior knowledge of the problem is subtle. GAs require a string, an interpretation of each possible string, and a way of calculating fitness. However, you don't need to have any strategy for how to accomplish the optimization; the GA handles that part in somewhat of a black box fashion. You don't have to know much, but you do need to have some understanding of how the pieces interrelate. With neural nets, less beginning knowledge is necessary.

10. What are the main drawbacks to neural networks?

The black box nature of neural nets is probably the aspect that bothers people the most. To some, neural nets appear to be sophisticated voodoo. Linking inputs to outputs through a loosely defined network can be perplexing because networks are difficult to interpret. You may know that something works, but you really don't know why it works; you don't end up with an equation that you can point to and perhaps interpret.

In addition, considerable experimentation (and possibly some luck) may be required to develop a useful network model. There are many variations of neural nets that can be attempted. The number and type of node connections, the number of hidden layers, and the possible variations of learning mechanisms are essentially infinite. Testing can be extremely time consuming. A test is conducted, the results are reviewed, a new approach is formulated, and a new test is conducted. This basic cycle may need many repetitions.

11. What are the main advantages of GAs, compared to chaos theory and neural networks?

The main advantage of GAs, especially for investment applications, is that it allows you to directly test a general hypothesis or theory about financial markets. You have to start with some premise. For example, we started by supposing that macroeconomic data are related to security returns and further postulated a form of the relationship. We then set up a system to test literally billions of possible trading rules based on a general structure. Because you, as the user, define the relationship, at least in an overall sense, then you have some feel for how to interpret the results. With neural nets, interpretation of the resulting system can be difficult; with chaos theory, you identify only the presence of a relationship, not its nature. The requirement of a starting premise can be viewed either positively or negatively. We see it as a distinct advantage.

12. How much computer programming is required to use GAs?

Some, but not much. Most of a GA software package is generic. GAs work on strings, performing crossover and mutation. The GA procedure does not care what the strings represent, except for the fitness calculation, so the only computer code that must be altered from one application to the next is the fitness calculation and data interface. The modules of GA code that control selection, crossover, mutation, convergence calculations, and so on do not change from one application to the next—or at least they don't have to change. If you are doing sophisticated tinkering to your algorithm, then modifications may be necessary; otherwise, no. The standard GA implementations have been written in C, Pascal, and Lisp. Therefore, some knowledge of one of these computer languages will probably be necessary, unless you have access to a package with a sophisticated user-friendly shell that circumvents the need for direct programming.

The need for some programming is a drawback compared to neural nets. There are many commercially available neural net packages that shield the user from programming. The same will probably be true in the future for GAs, although due to the infinite possible variations of string interpretation and fitness calculation, designing a generic user interface will be more difficult.

13. Where do you get GA software?

The main sources are listed at the end of Chapter 2. Interest in GAs is growing rapidly, so additional software options should be available in the future.

14. Are GAs only good for very large problems?

The speed of GAs makes them ideal for ill-defined problems with a large search space. They are especially good at attacking problems that cannot be addressed by other methods. However, GAs can also be good for smaller problems, particularly a set of related small problems. If the string size is small enough, all possible combinations can be examined using enumerative search. However, even if this is possible, it may still be advantageous to use GAs. When computing time is a constraint, a GA may be useful even though other methods might have been possible if time were not a constraint.

In addition, as mentioned earlier, GAs can be good for smaller problems for which the time required to evaluate a potential solution is lengthy. If calculations are long and tedious, then even a small search space is difficult to explore. GAs are good at quickly focusing in on the most attractive points in the search space.

15. How do you know that the GA solution is optimal or near optimal?

You probably don't. If you already knew the optimal solution, why would you be using a GA? Because you don't know the optimal solution, there is probably no way to determine whether the solution is or is not optimal. One method to determine possible optimal values is to perform multiple trials of the GA. Let's assume you run 25 trials. If 10 trials all result in the same highest fitness value, then it is likely that the optimal solution has been found. However, if the best result of the 25 trials is never duplicated, then you are always left wondering, "Would more trials possibly lead to a higher value?" If it seems unclear that the optimal string has been found, then you just have to decide whether or not the results are acceptable. If they are not, then either more trials or some change to the algorithm is needed.

However, for most business problems this is not a major drawback. This is especially true in the investments field. The relevant concern is not "Do I have the best of all possible trading strategies?" but rather "Do I have a profitable trading strategy?" If you can outperform most of the competition, then you're in pretty good shape. In the social sciences, "optimal" is a fleeting and elusive concept, because what is optimal today may not be optimal tomorrow.

16. Can a GA converge to a poor solution?

Yes. There are several possible reasons. First, the GA may be converging prematurely. If, for example, the selection procedure forces rapid convergence, then the search may be ending too quickly. A short search may find only poor solutions. Second, the problem representation or performance calculation may not be functioning as intended. GAs, as computer programs, essentially do what they are told to do, so a poor solution may be the result of poor instructions. Third, it may simply be bad luck. GAs begin from a random starting point. Sometimes they get off to a bad start and never quite recover. Additional trials may lead to a much better solution.

17. How critical are the GA settings, such as crossover rate?

These settings do make a difference, but there is a fairly broad range of settings that will all result in roughly the same performance. We investigate the impact of various parameter settings in Chapter 7. We would advise beginning with commonly used parameter settings and focusing more attention on problem representation and performance calculation than the GA settings.

18. How fast are GAs?

As Einstein pointed out, speed is relative. In our research, we were using a Pascal-based version of GAs implemented on a 386 PC with a math coprocessor. Our performance calculation required extensive data access and computations. Running 120 trials of our GA required approximately four to five hours of computer time, which means that each trial took roughly two minutes, with convergence occurring after about 100 generations. We have found that data analysis and the development of creative new approaches to problem representation or fitness calculation are much more of a bottleneck than computer time.

19. Are GAs theoretically sound?

Yes. The work of John Holland and others has provided a solid theoretical foundation. The implicit parallelism of GAs makes them highly efficient search procedures. However, there have been many ad hoc modifications that lack theoretical justification. The mathematics that underlies GAs is complex, making mathematical proof difficult. The most basic proofs demonstrating that GAs are theoretically solid are in place, but much work is still needed.

20. Will interest in GAs eventually overtake chaos theory and neural nets?

We see current interest in GAs being where chaos theory was probably five or more years ago. Chaos theory is probably more understandable at an intuitive level and has the distinct advantage of being visually appealing. Gleick's book, *Chaos,* was well written and easily understood by a lay readership. GAs will probably never develop the same mass appeal; but we think their behind-the-scenes use will skyrocket. The potential applications are limited only by the imagination. Even though GAs are fast, additional increases in computer speed will accelerate the development of GA applications. With even faster computers, extremely complex optimization problems can be tackled with PCs.

The interest in GAs is also probably behind interest in neural nets by two or three years. The commercial availability of neural net software has spurred the development of its applications. Neural nets offer a black box approach that in some ways requires less thought than using GAs.

However, we believe that in the long run the power offered by GAs will prove virtually unbeatable. They are just too good not to eventually gain greater acceptance. Ironically, the fittest of the three methods will eventually win out—or some combined approach that is a conceptual crossover. Remember, crossover is very powerful!

PART TWO
GENETIC ALGORITHM METHODOLOGY

6

A Genetic Algorithm: Step by Step

In this chapter we use a simple example to illustrate the basic components of a genetic algorithm. In the next chapter, we will show how some of the basic genetic operations introduced in this chapter can be fine-tuned. Additional example applications, which are more sophisticated, are discussed in Chapter 8, and advanced variations of GA methodology are covered in Chapter 9.

EXAMPLE PROBLEM

Consider the problem of a book publisher, JWI, trying to minimize costs. Annual sales for one title, *Avoiding Extinction,* are forecasted to be 20,000 copies; the rate of sales is expected to be fairly constant throughout the year, without significant seasonal variation. In the past, JWI has done quarterly printings in similar situations. Therefore, one alternative is to run four quarterly printings of 5,000 copies each, but management is greatly concerned about rising printing and distribution costs.

JWI's costs have both fixed and variable components. Each printing requires a new setup of equipment, which mainly entails cleaning up from the previous run and typesetting for the new run. The total cost of each setup is $6,000, which is a fixed cost for each new printing. Once printed, books must be stored before they are shipped. Larger printings reduce the number of printings needed per year but require more warehousing space. Warehousing and distribution costs are roughly proportional to the average level of inventory, which, on average, will be one-half the size of each printing. Management wants to know how many books to print in each run so that costs will be minimized and profit maximized.

There are several methods for solving this type of optimization problem, a classic economic order quantity (EOQ) problem. Therefore, one solution method is to use the appropriate EOQ formula and directly calculate the optimal size of each printing. A second possible solution method is trial and error. Total costs could be computed using various estimates of the optimal printing size. Larger printings reduce total setup costs but increase the warehousing and distribution costs, whereas small printings do just the opposite. Successive trial-and-error guesses could be used to zero in on the optimal level, which balances these two cost components. A third approach would be to let a genetic algorithm find an attractive solution. The phrase ''attractive solution'' is used purposely; GAs will often find optimal solutions but may find only near optimal solutions.

Of the three possible problem-solving methods just described, the EOQ formula is clearly the best for this situation (assuming you remember the formula or can look it up quickly). The trial-and-error approach works fairly well, especially with the use of a spreadsheet program's what-if capabilities. Of the three methods, using a GA is probably the worst because GAs are generally better suited for larger, more complex problems. But it will be much easier to learn about GAs using a small problem with a known solution.

The EOQ formula for the example problem is as follows:

$$Q^* = \sqrt{\frac{2\,F\,D}{V}}$$

where
F = fixed setup cost ($6,000)
V = variable cost ($6 per unit)
D = annual demand (20,000 units)

The variable cost primarily represents the cost of warehousing printed books. The solution is 6,325 books per print run.

The selling price of *Avoiding Extinction* is $30. In addition to the costs already described, JWI must consider office overhead, ink, paper, and royalties. These other costs will total $350,000 for the year. Using this additional information, we can create the trial-and-error table shown in Table 6.1. Scanning down the profit column, we find that profit will be maximized with a production run of between 6,200 and 6,400 books. Figure 6.1 is a graph depicting the setup and variable

Table 6.1 EOQ Example Problem—Trial and Error Solution

Quantity Printed (per run)	Printing Costs Fixed Costs	Variable Costs	Total Costs	Other Costs	Total Revenue	Total Profit
4,000	30,000	12,000	42,000	350,000	600,000	208,000
4,100	29,268	12,300	41,568	350,000	600,000	208,432
4,200	28,571	12,600	41,171	350,000	600,000	208,829
4,300	27,907	12,900	40,807	350,000	600,000	209,193
4,400	27,273	13,200	40,473	350,000	600,000	209,527
4,500	26,667	13,500	40,167	350,000	600,000	209,833
4,600	26,087	13,800	39,887	350,000	600,000	210,113
4,700	25,532	14,100	39,632	350,000	600,000	210,368
4,800	25,000	14,400	39,400	350,000	600,000	210,600
4,900	24,490	14,700	39,190	350,000	600,000	210,810
5,000	24,000	15,000	39,000	350,000	600,000	211,000
5,100	23,529	15,300	38,829	350,000	600,000	211,171
5,200	23,077	15,600	38,677	350,000	600,000	211,323
5,300	22,642	15,900	38,542	350,000	600,000	211,458
5,400	22,222	16,200	38,422	350,000	600,000	211,578
5,500	21,818	16,500	38,318	350,000	600,000	211,682
5,600	21,429	16,800	38,229	350,000	600,000	211,771
5,700	21,053	17,100	38,153	350,000	600,000	211,847
5,800	20,690	17,400	38,090	350,000	600,000	211,910
5,900	20,339	17,700	38,039	350,000	600,000	211,961
6,000	20,000	18,000	38,000	350,000	600,000	212,000
6,100	19,672	18,300	37,972	350,000	600,000	212,028
6,200	19,355	18,600	37,955	350,000	600,000	212,045
6,300	19,048	18,900	37,948	350,000	600,000	212,052
6,400	18,750	19,200	37,950	350,000	600,000	212,050
6,500	18,462	19,500	37,962	350,000	600,000	212,038
6,600	18,182	19,800	37,982	350,000	600,000	212,018
6,700	17,910	20,100	38,010	350,000	600,000	211,990
6,800	17,647	20,400	38,047	350,000	600,000	211,953
6,900	17,391	20,700	38,091	350,000	600,000	211,909
7,000	17,143	21,000	38,143	350,000	600,000	211,857
7,100	16,901	21,300	38,201	350,000	600,000	211,799
7,200	16,667	21,600	38,267	350,000	600,000	211,733
7,300	16,438	21,900	38,338	350,000	600,000	211,662
7,400	16,216	22,200	38,416	350,000	600,000	211,584
7,500	16,000	22,500	38,500	350,000	600,000	211,500
7,600	15,789	22,800	38,589	350,000	600,000	211,411
7,700	15,584	23,100	38,684	350,000	600,000	211,316
7,800	15,385	23,400	38,785	350,000	600,000	211,215
7,900	15,190	23,700	38,890	350,000	600,000	211,110
8,000	15,000	24,000	39,000	350,000	600,000	211,000
8,100	14,815	24,300	39,115	350,000	600,000	210,885
8,200	14,634	24,600	39,234	350,000	600,000	210,766

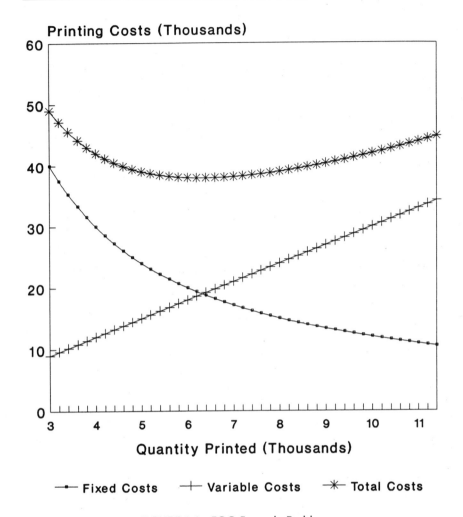

FIGURE 6.1 EOQ Example Problem

costs. Small printings increase fixed setup costs, whereas large printings increase warehousing costs. Total fixed setup and variable warehousing costs reach a minimum with a printing run of about 6,300 books, as shown in Table 6.1. We know from earlier calculations that the optimal printing run is 6,325 books.

A GENETIC ALGORITHM SOLUTION

We refer here to *a* genetic algorithm solution, not *the* GA solution, for two reasons. First, there are many methodological variations of genetic algorithms that could be used. Second, there are other problem representations that could be used to attack the example given.

The following steps below describe a "plain vanilla" GA, the basic features of which can be found in most other GAs.

1. Choose the problem representation

The first hurdle to overcome in using GAs is *problem representation*—we must represent our problem in a way that is suitable for handling by a GA, which works with strings of symbols that in structure resemble chromosomes. The representation often relies on binary coding; a typical example looks like this: 0010101011. The ten bit positions each contain either 0 or 1. The string must in some fashion stand for a potential problem solution.

GAs work with a population of competing strings, each of which represents a potential solution for the problem under investigation. The individual strings within the population are gradually transformed using biologically based operations. For example, two strings might "mate" and produce an offspring that combines the best features of its parents. In accordance with the law of survival of the fittest, the best-performing individual in the population will eventually dominate the population.

In our example problem, we are trying to optimize the size of the printing run. Let's call this variable S. Our goal is to find the value of S that minimizes the total setup and warehousing costs, which in turn will maximize our profits. Annually, the maximum value of S is 20,000. This would correspond to printing all 20,000 books in a single large run. S is the only variable in our optimization problem.

The most straightforward binary coding of this problem is to represent the value of S as a binary string. For example, the binary number 110 has a decimal equivalent of 6 ($1 \times 2^2 + 1 \times 2^1 + 0 \times 2^0$). Because the maximum value of S is 20,000, the binary representation will require many bits. If we were to use 14 bits, the maximum binary number would be a string of 14 ones: 11111111111111. To find the decimal equivalent of this binary number, raise 2 to the fourteenth power and then subtract 1. This yields the number 16,384. With 15 bits, the maximum decimal equivalent would be 2 to the fifteenth power minus 1, or 32,768. We now have a choice to make: If we use 14 bits, then we don't capture the full possible range of S values, but if we use 15 bits, we go beyond the maximum value. To keep things slightly more manageable, let's go with 14. Also, it probably would be reasonable in this problem to expect the optimal value to fall within the range of 1 to 16,384 (we have already calculated the optimal value and know it is 6,325, but we are pretending we don't know that).

2. Initialize the population

There are no strict rules for determining the population size. Population sizes of 100–200 are common in GA research. Eventually, through the steps described below, the population will converge. *Convergence* means that all or most of the strings in the population are identical. Definitions of convergence will be discussed later. Users often experiment with population size, seeing how different values affect convergence and the quality of results. We will experiment with various population sizes in the next chapter.

Larger populations ensure greater diversity but require more computer resources. In our example problem we will use a population size of 20. This is very small, but this helps to simplify our examination of the GA's performance from one generation to the next.

Once the population size is chosen, then the initial population must be randomly generated. Random selections, needed for various steps in genetic algorithms, are easily performed by using computers. Because the population has 20 strings of 14 bits, 280 bits must be set to either 0 or 1. The computer sets the value of 280 bit positions with a simulated coin toss. We expect approximately 140 bits to be set to 1 and 140 to be set to 0. The actual results of such a process are shown in Table 6.2.

The initial population is usually formed as we just described, but there are some exceptions. Sometimes it may be desirable to "seed" the initial population; this GA variation will be discussed in Chapter 9. Problem constraints can also be addressed during the initialization step. For example, if we had chosen a 15-bit representation, then the decimal equivalent of some strings would have exceeded 20,000, the annual demand. These values would not have caused a problem, because the GA quickly rules out unattractive solutions. However, we could have constrained the string values during the initialization step. Any strings with dec-

Table 6.2   Initial Population

String Number	String
1	00100010011010
2	00101011001000
3	00000010100011
4	00110001010100
5	00111100110101
6	10111001101001
7	10011011001111
8	01100101001100
9	11001010111000
10	11001111101100
11	00010011000001
12	11011010101010
13	10010011010010
14	10001100000000
15	11011001000111
16	11010001011111
17	00001000111011
18	11100011011000
19	11001111110010
20	11000011111011

imal equivalents greater than 20,000 could have been discarded and replaced with a randomly chosen string that met the constraint.

3. Calculate fitness

Now that we have a population of potential problem solutions, we need to see how good they are. Therefore, we calculate a fitness, or performance, for each string. Doing so can be simple and fast, as it will be in our example problem, or it can be complex and time-consuming. In Chapter 11, when we apply GAs to a search for stock market-timing trading rules, the fitness calculation will be very complicated and require considerable CPU time.

For our printing cost problem, the fitness calculation is straightforward. Each string is decoded into its decimal equivalent. This gives us a candidate value for the optimal size of the printing run. Next, the total costs and resulting profit are calculated using the values discussed earlier. The profit figure is the fitness value for the string under consideration. The results for the initial population are shown in Table 6.3. We will return to fitness calculation in subsequent generations of the population.

4. Perform selection

Genetic algorithms work with a population of competing problem solutions that gradually evolve over successive generations. Survival of the fittest means that only the best-performing members of the population will survive in the long run. In the short run we merely tip the odds in favor of the better performers; we do not eliminate all the poor performers. This can be done in a variety of ways.

We will use a simple selection scheme. The first step is to generate a ranking of the competing strings based upon their fitness, which was calculated in the previous step. We then replace the poorest performing string, the worst of the 20, with a copy of the best performing string. We are left with a population that, for now, is identical with the preceding generation except for one string; there are now two copies of the best string in our population of 20.

Assume that during the creation of the initial population, our random initialization gets lucky and generates a string that corresponds to the optimal solution. Let's give this optimal string a name—OPTIE. As we will see in subsequent steps, OPTIE could be altered through crossover or mutation. But if OPTIE continues to survive intact, then it will always be replacing the worst-performing string in each generation. Because we are only replacing one string per generation, we know it will take at least 20 generations for the population to converge.

A more likely scenario is that convergence will take far more than 20 generations. For example, one string may dominate the population for 10 generations only to be overtaken as number one by another string. The ultimate winner must survive at least 20 generations of competition before it has replaced all other members of the population.

If selection is done in a heavy-handed fashion, then the population will converge quickly. We could eliminate the five worst-performing strings and replace them with five copies of the best-performing string. With this approach, and an initial population that included OPTIE, we could reach convergence in four generations. Yet, as we know in finance, there is no free lunch. We may sacrifice solution quality when the population converges quickly. This is known as the *premature convergence* problem; with rapid convergence, the GA may not have adequate time to explore the search space.

5. Perform crossover

Crossover is the step that really powers the GA. It allows the search to fan out in diverse directions looking for attractive solutions and permits two strings to "mate." This may result in offspring that are more fit than the parents.

Crossover is accomplished in four small steps. First, two potential parents are randomly chosen from the population. Second, we perform a weighted, computerized "coin toss" to determine whether to actually perform crossover. The "coin" is biased so that it tells us "Yes, perform crossover" with a 6-out-of-10 probability. Third, assuming the answer is Yes, we randomly choose a splicing point. Fourth, we then cut each string at the splicing point. For example, we might cut between bits 6 and 7, creating two pieces for each string. The first piece would contain bits 1 through 6, while the second piece would contain bits 7 through 14. Finally, we exchange the two tails of the strings and then reconnect the pieces. String A now has the tail from string B, and vice versa. Crossover is illustrated in Figure 6.2.

Earlier research has shown that a crossover rate of 0.6 is usually effective, but there is no proof that this value is best for all possible GA applications. In the next chapter we will experiment with the crossover rate.

Again, crossover is the real driving power behind the GA because it leads to a very efficient combing of the search space. This may be difficult to picture; the following analogy should help.

Consider a large square of land that we are almost certain covers an underground oil reservoir. We can drill a well to explore any point in the square. Initially, all drilling points appear equally attractive. Now consider an exploratory well-drilling program that creates four wells simultaneously. There are endless possible patterns of four wells; if we were going to drill four sets of four wells, then we might proceed in the ABCD or EFGH patterns shown in Figure 6.3. Most of us probably would proceed according to some "logical" pattern, and countless other possibilities exist. Crossover, however, scrambles the solution search back and forth between various logical patterns. In the oil well example, the GA crossover approach might choose the sequences BHED or ABEG. These might appear to be haphazard and illogical, but there is a high probability that extensive experimentation with different patterns is likely to be fruitful.

Crossover also gains much of its power through the selection procedure. Selection, described in step 4, tilts survival odds in favor of the better-performing members of the population. Let's say that in a particular problem, the pattern 1011 in bit positions 5 through 8 leads to highly effective solutions. Let's also

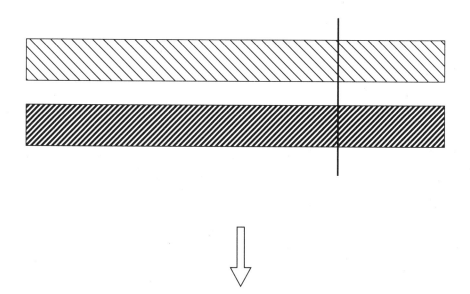

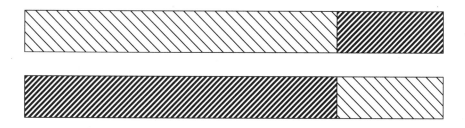

FIGURE 6.2   Crossover Diagram

assume that a 1100 pattern in bits 1 through 4 is effective. If a particular string, string Y, has the 1011 pattern in bits 5 through 8, then it will have a high degree of fitness, and its chances for reproduction are therefore higher. If string Z has the 1100 pattern in bits 1 through 4, then similar arguments would apply to it. If both strings have been reproduced, then there is an increased chance that a child of Y and Z, created by crossover, will have a 10111100 pattern in bits 1 through 8 (the bit position numbering here is from right to left). This child may be superfit, having inherited good characteristics from each parent.

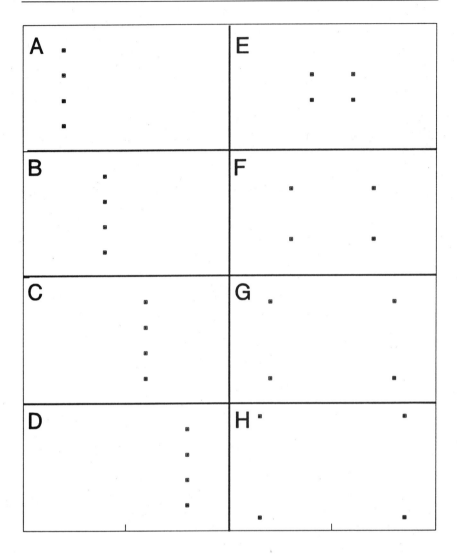

FIGURE 6.3   Oil Well–Drilling Patterns

6. Perform mutation

   Mutation introduces random deviations into the population. Mutation zaps a 0 to a 1 and vice versa. Each bit position for every member of the population is examined. The computer randomly decides whether mutation should occur. Mutation is usually performed with low probability, otherwise it would defeat the order building being generated through selection and crossover. Mutation attempts to bump the population gently onto a slightly better course. Figure 6.4 illustrates this process.

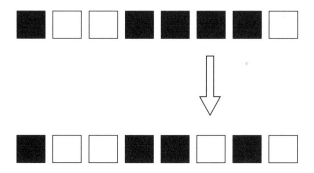

FIGURE 6.4 Mutation Diagram

In our example problem, we will mutate with a 0.001 probability (1 out of 1,000). The consequences of higher mutation rates will be examined in the next chapter. In some advanced GA variations, the mutation rate is allowed to vary over successive generations.

7. Check convergence

Convergence is often measured using the concept of *bias*, which is defined as a measure of agreement among the population. Bias assumes values between 50 and 100 percent. As an example, consider bit position 9 for all 20 members of the population. If 10 of the members have a 1 in position 9 and the other 10 have 0s, then the split is 50–50, and the bit bias is 50 percent. If the split is 75–25 (15 1s and 5 0s), then bit bias is 75 percent. If the split is 25–75, then bit bias is still 75 percent; it is the greater of two percentage split numbers. From bit bias we go to string bias. In our example, there are 14 bits in each string; the string bias is the average of the 14 bit bias values. From now on, all references to bias will mean string bias, which will serve as a summary measure of convergence for the entire population.

The convergence rate is greatly affected by the selection procedure. If selection is heavy handed, then the population will converge quickly. For most GA variations, the rate of convergence will gradually diminish from one generation to the next. Generally, there are diminishing returns to the GA search.

Convergence is, to some degree, in the eye of the beholder. A population with a bias of 95 percent is fairly uniform. Because mutation disturbs the existing order, higher mutation rates will make it difficult for the population to converge completely. Different users may have different opinions about what constitutes convergence.

We have now reached the end of the basic steps. After calculating a convergence measure, such as bias, then we have two possible courses of action. We can stop the GA or continue by returning to step 3. If we have reached convergence, then we examine the population, which is in general agreement concerning the ''solution'' to our problem. If we have not reached convergence, then we permit continued evolution of the population by returning to step 3.

What if the GA seems to be taking forever to converge? An alternate termination criterion is a maximum number of generations. For example, we could stop the GA if bias is greater than 95 percent or if the GA has been running for more than 1,000 generations. If convergence is too slow, then we may need to adjust the selection procedure, crossover rate, mutation rate, or some combination of the three.

The price of premature convergence may be a problem solution that is far from optimal. Large difficult problems usually require some compromise. The user who desires a quick answer may have to settle for a nonoptimal solution; the user who desires a high-quality solution must be more patient.

GA RESULTS FOR THE EXAMPLE PROBLEM

Now let's see what happens when we run the GA described above. Table 6.3 shows the initial population with the decimal equivalent of each string value, which, as you'll recall represents a guess at the optimal value of S. The fitness number is the profit associated with each attempted S value. The initial population contains guesses that range from 163 to 14,552. String 8 reprents the best guess, with a value of 6,476.

Table 6.4 shows the results of the transition from generation 1 to generation 2. The gradual improvement in the population can be seen in some of the details. The guesses in this generation range from 560 to 15,943. String 8 from the first generation has been duplicated and appears twice, with new string numbers of 13 and 14. Therefore, this pattern is poised to exert increased influence on the population. Strings 11 and 16 from generation 1, which represented guesses of 1,217 and 13,407, respectively, have been crossed to create strings 15 and 16 in generation 2. The resulting string patterns represent guesses of 5,215 and 9,409, which are both closer to the optimal value of 6,325.

However, crossover also can send some of the population searching in the wrong direction. For example, strings 5 and 20 from the first generation cross, and both get further from the optimum value. String 5 is modified from a guess of 3,893 to 3,827, while string 20 goes from 12,539 to 12,597. If you examine the workings of a GA at this level of detail, you need to remember that this is good, not bad. We know that the optimal value is 6,325; the GA does not know this. It is searching for the optimal value, casting nets in various directions and trying to land the big catch. It will probably succeed, but that will take some time.

The particular search we have been describing did not find the optimal value of S, but it came very close. By generation 24 it had identified a good guess of 6,328. After 50 generations, the population bias was 95 percent; after 74 generations, the population converged to a bias greater than 99.5 percent. The result from one trial can be lucky, unlucky, or somewhere in between. The average performance of many trials may be much different than the result of only one trial.

Table 6.3 Initial Population (with Fitness Calculation)

String Number	String	Decimal Value	Fitness
1	00100010011010	2,202	188,898
2	00101011001000	2,760	198,242
3	00000010100011	163	−486,685
4	00110001010100	3,156	202,509
5	00111100110101	3,893	207,496
6	10111001101001	11,881	204,257
7	10011011001111	9,935	208,116
8	01100101001100	6,476	212,042
9	11001010111000	12,984	201,806
10	11001111101100	13,292	201,096
11	00010011000001	1,217	147,746
12	11011010101010	13,994	199,443
13	10010011010010	9,426	208,991
14	10001100000000	8,960	209,727
15	11011001000111	13,895	199,679
16	11010001011111	13,407	200,828
17	00001000111011	571	38,129
18	11100011011000	14,552	198,098
19	11001111110010	13,298	201,082
20	11000011111011	12,539	202,813

Table 6.4 Population—Generation 2

String Number	Parents		Crossover Site	String	Decimal Value	Fitness
1	14	17	4	00001000110000	560	34,034
2	14	17	4	10001100001011	8,971	209,711
3	18	15	11	11000011011000	12,504	202,891
4	18	15	11	11111001000111	15,943	194,644
5	7	10	1	11001111101101	13,293	201,094
6	7	10	1	10011011001110	9,934	208,118
7	20	5	9	00111011110011	3,827	207,163
8	20	5	9	11000100110101	12,597	202,683
9	12	9	4	11001010111010	12,986	201,801
10	12	9	4	11011010101000	13,992	199,448
11	19	2	14	11001111110010	13,298	201,082
12	19	2	14	00101011001000	2,760	198,242
13	8	8	6	01100101001100	6,476	212,042
14	8	8	6	01100101001100	6,476	212,042
15	16	11	13	01010001011111	5,215	211,344
16	16	11	13	10010011000001	9,409	209,019
17	6	4	2	00110001010101	3,157	202,518
18	6	4	2	10111001101000	11,880	204,259
19	13	1	14	10010011010010	9,426	208,991
20	13	1	14	00100010011010	2,202	188,898

Table 6.5   Summary of 100 Trials

Average solution: 6,297
Maximum value: 6,656
Minimum value: 6,111
Average number of generations: 56
Number of times optimal solution found: 29

Table 6.5 summarizes the results from 50 trials; the GA found the optimal solution in 29 of them. The average solution value, 6,297, was extremely close to the optimal value. The GA also worked quickly, reaching 99.5 percent convergence in 56 trials, on average. In short, the GA performed exceedingly well. With a larger population, we might have achieved better results. We will experiment with population size and other GA parameters in the next chapter.

The performance of the various trials is also summarized in Figures 6.5 and 6.6. Figure 6.5 shows that near optimal fitness values were approached quite quickly. Of course, this is partially due to the shallow nature of the curve around the optimal point. Small to medium deviations from the optimal value of S do not have a great impact on total profit. Figure 6.6 illustrates bias as a function of generation number. In most cases, the population bias was over 90 percent by the fortieth generation.

LESSONS FROM THE EXAMPLE PROBLEM

1. **The basic steps of a GA are simple.** The idea of using genetic operations as a model for software sounds complex, but the procedure breaks down into a series of simple steps that can be carried out in many different programming languages.

2. **The only step in the GA that is problem-specific is the performance calculation.** Crossover, mutation, and selection all work the same for every problem under investigation. These operations work blindly on a population of strings; they do not care what the strings represent. The only link between the GA and the problem is the performance calculation, which is one of the major advantages of the GA approach. If you can represent important aspects of your problem as a string and have a method for assigning performance to each unique string, then the GA approach may be appropriate. All the steps, except for the performance calculation, are generic.

3. **The GA marches efficiently toward near optimal solutions.** If you are going to use a GA, then you must be prepared to accept a near optimal solution. For many problems, especially business problems, this may be easily acceptable. The GA search procedure probes here and there in the search space looking for good solutions but quickly closes in on attractive possibilities.

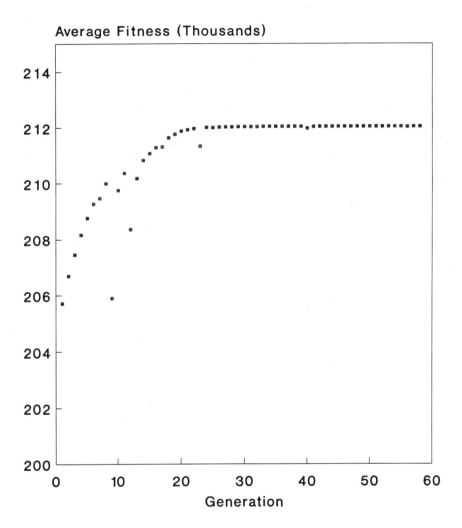

FIGURE 6.5   Average Fitness by Generation

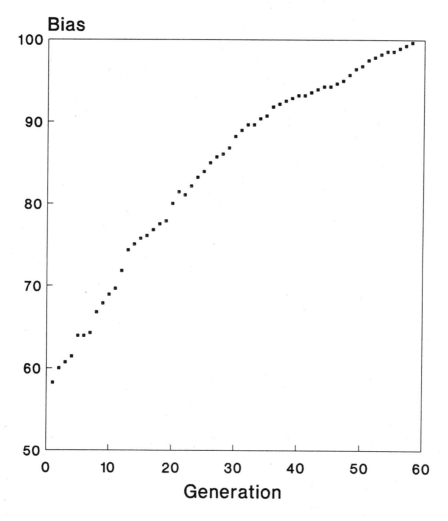

FIGURE 6.6 Bias by Generation

4. **GAs are especially well suited to function optimization problems.** The example problem involves optimizing a profit function; in this instance profit depends on only one parameter, or variable. Many similar business problems may require more than one parameter, a contingency that is easily accommodated in the GA approach.

7
Fine-Tuning the Genetic Algorithm

In Chapter 6, we demonstrated the basic operations in a genetic algorithm by stepping through a simple example problem. However, as mentioned previously, genetic algorithms are a class, or family, of related procedures; there are many possible variations, and the choice of which variation to use will affect the speed of convergence and the quality of the solution(s). In this chapter, we explore the impact of varying some of the basic GA parameter settings.

We could continue to use the example problem from Chapter 6. However, we prefer instead to move to a larger, more realistic problem that will better demonstrate the true power of genetic algorithms and also offer a preview of what will come in Part 3 of this book. Consider the possibility of a numerical rule that would signal to us on a monthly basis whether to be fully invested in a broad-based common stock portfolio, such as an S&P 500 index fund, or to be fully invested in Treasury bills. We call this a *market-timing trading rule*. In Chapter 10 we discuss our definition of market timing and how it relates to the concept of tactical asset allocation.

Clearly, relative opportunities are important in this decision. For example, if Treasury bill rates are exceptionally high, then it might be preferable to keep money parked in T-bills rather than risk equity exposure. Other interest rate relationships, such as the long-term versus short-term yield spread and the corporate versus Treasury yield spread, might also be important factors to consider. For now, let's not worry about the exact nature of the relationship between these factors and our "stocks or T-bills" decision; let's just assume that these relationships might somehow be relevant.

We are moving towards the development of a market-timing trading rule of this general form:

IF the Treasury bill rate is LESS THAN X, AND the yield spread between long-term Treasury bonds and Treasury bills is LESS THAN Y, AND the yield spread between corporate bonds and Treasury bonds is LESS THAN Z, THEN invest in common stocks.

IF NOT, THEN invest in Treasury bills.

Later we will consider additional flexibility regarding the LESS THAN and the AND components of this rule structure. Now we want to focus on the X, Y, and Z values, which largely determine the success or failure of the rule.

CONVERTING A CONTINUOUS RANGE INTO A DISCRETE RANGE

The rates on newly issued Treasury bills over the 1984–1988 time period fluctuated between 5.18 and 10.49 percent, a range of values having a difference of 5.31 percent. Continuous ranges of values are difficult for GAs to handle. To solve this problem, we are going to divide this range into 32 discrete cutoff values. We can start by dividing the range by 32, which yields the following result:

$$\text{Range interval} = \frac{5.31}{32} = 0.166$$

Next, we obtain the cutoff values by starting with the range minimum and successively adding the range interval to it. This results in the following series of cutoff values:

  1. 5.180
  2. 5.180 + 0.166 = 5.346
  3. 5.346 + 0.166 = 5.512
       etc.
 32. 10.158 + 0.166 = 10.324

The last value is also equal to the range maximum minus the range interval (10.490 − 0.166 = 10.324). The numbers 1 through 32 can now serve as a type of shorthand for each specific numerical cutoff value.

Similar procedures could be followed to develop shorthand measures for the Y and Z parameters in our general rule. As an example, we could now discuss a rule like this:

IF the Treasury bill rate is LESS THAN cutoff value 5, AND the yield spread between long-term Treasury bonds and Treasury bills is LESS THAN cutoff value 18, AND the yield spread between corporate bonds and Treasury bonds is LESS THAN cutoff value 23, THEN invest in common stocks.

IF NOT, THEN invest in Treasury bills.

The cutoff values are being coded in increments of $\frac{1}{32}$, of the historical range of values. A value close to 1 is near the lower end of the historical range; a value near 32 is close to the upper end. The 5, 18, and 23 could easily be decoded into specific numerical cutoff values for the X, Y, and Z parameters.

CODING LOGIC COMBINATIONS

Next we will expand the LESS THAN condition by allowing it to be either a "less than" relationship or a "greater than or equal to" relationship. Both of these possibilities will be permitted for all three parts of the trading rule. Therefore, there are eight (2^3) possible combinations of "less than" and "greater than or equal to" relationships.

Finally, we will allow for the possibility of more complicated logical relationships between the three parts of the rule. For concision of expression, we need to introduce some additional shorthand. Let us define three conditions as follows:

Cond1 :   If the Treasury bill rate is greater than or equal to cutoff value X.
Cond2 :   If the yield spread between Treasury bonds and Treasury bills is greater than or equal to cutoff value Y.
Cond3 :   If the yield spread between corporate bonds and Treasury bonds is greater than or equal to cutoff value Z.

Each of the three conditions can independently be either true or false.

There are 8 different logical groupings of the three conditions. They are:

1.   If Cond1 OR (Cond2 AND Cond3)
2.   If Cond1 AND (Cond2 OR Cond3)
3.   If (Cond1 OR Cond2) AND Cond3
4.   If (Cond1 AND Cond2) OR Cond3
5.   If (Cond1 OR Cond3) AND Cond2
6.   If (Cond1 AND Cond3) OR Cond2
7.   If Cond1 OR Cond2 OR Cond3
8.   If Cond1 AND Cond2 AND Cond3

To clarify, let's consider logical grouping 3. Translating this back in its full form would yield the following statement:

IF either the Treasury bill rate is LESS THAN X OR the yield spread between long-term Treasury bonds and Treasury bills is LESS THAN Y AND the yield spread between corporate bonds and Treasury bonds is LESS THAN Z, THEN invest in common stocks.

IF NOT, THEN invest in Treasury bills.

In other words, the third condition must be true AND at least one of the first two conditions must also be true for the rule to signal "invest in stocks."

As if things aren't getting complicated enough, let's reconsider the eight possible different combinations of "less than" or "greater than or equal to" relationships. When eight possibilities along that dimension are combined with eight possible different logical groupings of the three conditions, we have 64 different possibilities. We can express the "less than" relationship form of condition 1 as "not(cond1)," meaning that if condition 1 is false (T-bill rates $\geq X$), then the opposite of this condition, not(cond1), is true—or if condition 1 is true, then not(cond1) is false. With this additional notational convenience, we could express one of the 64 possible rules as

If [not(Cond1) OR Cond2] AND Cond3

This rule is just a slight twist on logical grouping variation 3, discussed above. The only difference is the negation of condition 1. Expressed in full form, this would be

IF either the Treasury bill rate is LESS THAN or EQUAL TO X OR the yield spread between long-term Treasury bonds and Treasury bills is GREATER THAN Y AND the yield spread between corporate bonds and Treasury bonds is GREATER THAN Z, THEN invest in common stocks.

IF NOT, THEN invest in Treasury bills.

If you are slightly lost, don't panic! The basic point of all this is to add some additional complexity to our rule search. We want to make our problem somewhat challenging for our genetic algorithm. We are also trying to illustrate how you might formulate rules with a general structure based on some intuition, such as "interest rates are important," while allowing the computer to guide you toward attractive specific variations of the general structure.

OUR PROBLEM

We have now set up a problem of decent size. The number of possible combinations of our general rule can be calculated as follows:

	32	possible X values
$\times$	32	possible Y values
$\times$	32	possible Z values
$\times$	8	less than/greater than or equal to combinations
$\times$	8	logical grouping combinations
= 2,097,152		total possible combinations

This number of combinations has two advantages: a) it is small enough to use enumerative search, and b) it is large enough to let the GA flex its muscles and let us explore the impact of different GA methodological variations.

By *enumerative search* we mean cranking through all possible combinations one by one. From a computer programming standpoint, we create a series of nested loops that iterate through all of the roughly 2.1 million combinations, searching for the best-performing variations of our general rule.

That leads us to the next question: How do we tell a good rule from a bad one? Before trying to answer this question, we want to go back to the original purpose of our investigation of trading rules: making money, not in the past but in the immediate future. There is no trading system that can ever predict with certainty what the future holds. All we can really do is to try to tip the odds in our favor and go with a system that we think has a reasonable chance of working. The future is never exactly like the past. However, a common investment approach is to employ systems that would probably have worked well in the past and that seem to have a reasonable chance of doing well in the future. Investors either implicitly or explicitly have standards of "proof" when judging whether a system worked well in the past.

We will calculate the past performance of the rules over the 1984–1988 period. In a pure sense, back-testing (using historical data to simulate the past performance of an investment strategy) of trading systems is always flawed. The actions of each investor affect the market; had we employed a particular system in the past, it would have affected prices and returns. However, like other investors who use back-testing, we will assume that the impact of our actions on the observed performance would have been negligible, that our past actions were not done with billion dollar bills but with much smaller amounts that would not have moved the market in any significant fashion. Advocates of chaos theory might point out that small changes in initial conditions can have major consequences. We acknowledge these arguments but still feel that back-testing has logical merit.

We will also ignore transaction costs. This has become a trickier issue with the continued development and use of futures and options contracts. For example, some investors might choose to implement a market-timing strategy with index futures or index options. This complicates the analysis of transaction costs.

Our enumerative search yielded some interesting results. The top 50 of the roughly 2.1 million possible rules are summarized in Table 7.1; the best combination earned an average annual return of 16.273 percent. This rule was essentially as follows: If T-bill rates are roughly in the bottom half of their recent range OR the yield spread between Treasury bonds and Treasury bills is in the upper third of its range AND the yield spread between corporate bonds and Treasury bonds is in the upper eighth of its range, then invest in stocks; if not, invest in Treasury bills.

After completing the enumerative search, we turned a GA loose on the problem. The procedure was the same as that described in Chapter 6. The bit string representation of the problem was as follows:

Table 7.1 Enumerative Search—50 Best Rules

	Logic Code	)/(Code	Cutoff Values			Average Return
			Series 1	Series 2	Series 3	
1	3	4	14	21	27	**16.273**
2	3	4	14	21	26	**16.141**
3	6	6	14	21	21	**16.140**
4	6	6	13	21	18	**16.023**
5	7	4	14	21	27	**15.995**
6	7	4	14	21	28	**15.995**
7	6	6	13	21	21	**15.985**
8	6	6	14	21	20	**15.938**
9	6	6	14	21	19	**15.938**
10	6	6	14	21	18	**15.938**
11	6	6	14	21	23	**15.853**
12	6	6	15	21	21	**15.846**
13	6	6	14	21	22	**15.833**
14	6	6	14	21	24	**15.817**
15	7	4	15	21	27	**15.802**
16	7	4	15	21	28	**15.802**
17	6	8	13	21	31	**15.791**
18	6	6	13	21	20	**15.784**
19	6	6	13	21	19	**15.784**
20	6	6	14	18	21	**15.720**
21	3	4	14	21	23	**15.707**
22	3	4	14	21	24	**15.707**
23	7	4	18	21	27	**15.694**
24	7	4	18	21	28	**15.694**
25	3	4	14	20	27	**15.682**
26	3	4	14	20	26	**15.682**
27	6	6	14	21	26	**15.680**
28	6	6	13	21	22	**15.679**
29	6	6	15	21	19	**15.644**
30	6	6	15	21	18	**15.644**
31	6	6	15	21	20	**15.644**
32	6	6	13	21	7	**15.632**
33	3	4	14	18	27	**15.616**
34	3	4	14	18	26	**15.616**
35	6	6	13	18	18	**15.604**
36	7	4	16	21	28	**15.594**
37	7	4	16	21	27	**15.594**
38	6	8	13	18	31	**15.591**
39	7	4	19	21	27	**15.587**
40	7	4	19	21	28	**15.587**
41	3	4	14	21	22	**15.578**
42	3	4	14	23	26	**15.578**
43	6	4	14	21	27	**15.577**
44	7	4	14	18	27	**15.576**
45	4	3	14	21	7	**15.575**
46	6	2	16	15	14	**15.574**
47	6	6	13	21	23	**15.570**
48	6	6	13	18	21	**15.566**
49	7	4	14	18	28	**15.561**
50	6	6	15	21	23	**15.560**

Bit Position	Field
1–5	X Value
6–10	Y Value
11–15	Z Value
16–18	Logic code
19–21	Greater than/less than code

The fitness, or performance, measure was the compound annual rate of return earned through the use of the rule under consideration over the 1984–1988 time period. The rule generated monthly signals advising whether to be in or out of the equity market. It was assumed that one dollar was initially invested at the beginning of 1984. For each subsequent month the investment earned either the S&P 500 return or the T-bill rate, depending on the rule's signal. Full reinvestment was assumed each month so that the total wealth was either committed 100 percent to equities or 100 percent to T-bills. The final wealth figure at the end of the five-year period was then converted to a compound annual rate of return.

BASE-SETTING RESULTS

The GA was implemented as described in Chapter 6, but with an initial population size of 100 strings, or individuals. Crossover and mutation were also performed as described in Chapter 6, with respective probabilities of 0.6 and 0.001. Selection was accomplished with a ranking procedure, again as described in Chapter 6, with the three best-performing strings replacing the three worst-performing strings in each generation. Therefore, the best three performers had two copies each in the population prior to crossover and mutation. Strings with a performance rank between 4 and 97, inclusive, yielded one copy each prior to crossover and mutation. Fifty trials of the GA were performed, with a different random starting population for each trial. We will show graphs of the average population fitness and average population bias versus generation number. This will establish a base performance of the algorithm, showing the quality of solution and degree of convergence versus generation number. Later, we will see how these performance graphs change with changes in the crossover rate, mutation rate, and population size.

The results from these base settings of the GA are shown in Figures 7.1 and 7.2. Figure 7.1 shows how performance improved over time by plotting the average maximum fitness as a percent of the optimal value versus the generation number. To compute the average maximum fitness as a percent of the optimal value, we first capture the maximum fitness value in the population for each of the 50 trials; this is done for every generation and for every trial. We then average the maximum fitness values and divide that number by the optimal fitness value of 16.273 percent, which was obtained by enumerative search; this gives us the average maximum fitness as a percent of the optimal value by generation.

In Figure 7.1, the average maximum fitness of the first generation is about 88 percent of the optimal value. However, by the fiftieth generation, the algorithm has usually found at least one solution that is within about 96 percent of the optimal value. After the fiftieth generation, improvements come more slowly. There are diminishing returns to the search process.

Figure 7.2 shows how quickly the population converged by plotting the average bias versus the generation number (again, "average" bias means the average for the 50 trials). Convergence proceeds in a steadily increasing fashion. After 50 generations, the populations in the 50 trials average slightly over 80 percent convergence; after 75 generations, the convergence rate flattens out. We arbitrarily decided to define convergence at a bias level of just over 93 percent. With a mutation rate of 0.001 and a crossover rate of 0.6, there will be some continual change in the population; the bias will never reach 100 percent. Users must decide for themselves when to curtail the search. In both figures, the curves get more erratic at the upper right. This is due to the fact that 40 of the 50 trials reach convergence by generation 104. Because the sample size by generation number gradually gets smaller, the averages become more erratic on the extreme right-hand side of the graphs.

EXPERIMENTING WITH THE GA PARAMETERS

With performance measures from our base settings as a reference point, we will now examine possible variations in the basic procedure. We will study the effect of changes in crossover rate, mutation rate, and population size. For each different parameter setting, we will perform 50 trials of the algorithm and then compare the graphs of average maximum fitness and average bias with those obtained for the base setting. First, we will try crossover rates of 0.8 and 0.4. The results are shown in Figures 7.3 through 7.6, which are similar to Figures 7.1 and 7.2. It is somewhat difficult to see from Figures 7.3 and 7.5, but the maximum fitness values never get as high for these crossover settings as they do with the base setting of 0.6. In Figure 7.3, the maximum value is 97.27 percent of the optimal at generation 89. In Figure 7.5, the maximum value of 97.73 is reached at generation 88. For the base setting, a maximum of 99.45 was reached at generation 122. In Figure 7.4, the convergence rate is similar to that of the base setting. However, in Figure 7.6, convergence is slower due to the more disruptive influence of a higher crossover rate.

Second, we try mutation rates of 0.100 and 0.0001. The results are shown in Figures 7.7 through 7.10. As might be expected, the low mutation rate leads to poorer solutions but faster convergence. This can be seen in Figures 7.7 and 7.8. The higher mutation rate allows better solutions to be found, but the average bias stabilizes at slightly over 80 percent. The disruptive influence of a high mutation rate prohibits convergence to a high bias level.

Third, the population size is altered. Figures 7.11 through 7.14 show the results for population sizes of 50 and 125. With a small population we would expect poorer results and rapid convergence. That is exactly what happens, as shown in Figures 7.11 and 7.12. The reverse is true for the larger population of 125, which can be seen in Figures 7.13 and 7.14.

The results of these modifications are fairly intuitive. In most cases, the user can reasonably predict the general impact of various tweakings of the GA parameter settings. The results also show that the GA procedure is not highly sensitive to parameter changes; the GA still marches towards attractive solutions at a rapid rate. After experimenting with these changes, we chose to stick with the base parameter settings as a reasonable compromise between solution quality and speed of convergence.

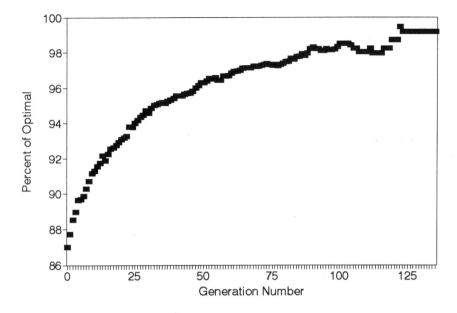

FIGURE 7.1 Base Parameter Settings: Percent of Optimal

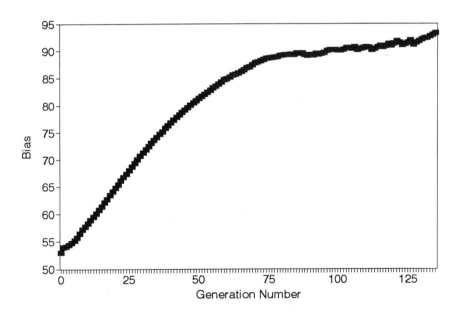

FIGURE 7.2 Base Parameter Settings: Bias

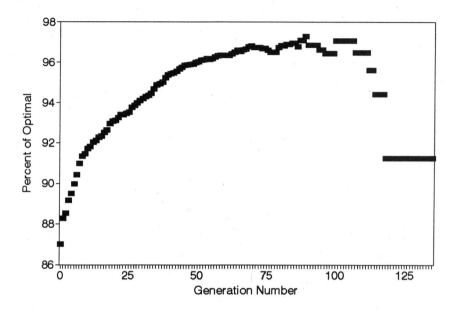

FIGURE 7.3   Crossover = 0.4: Percent of Optimal

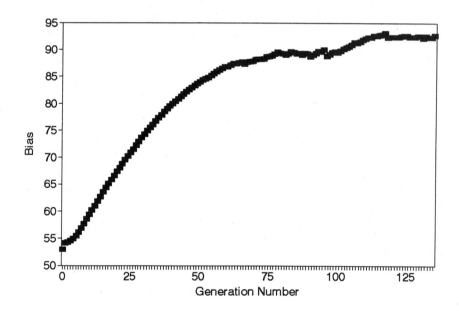

FIGURE 7.4   Crossover = 0.4: Bias

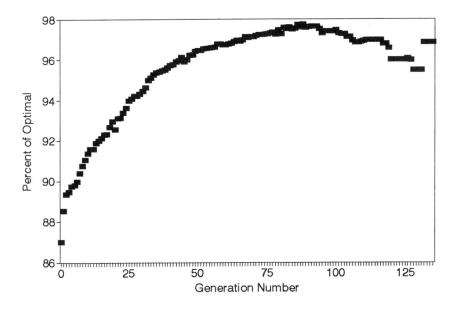

FIGURE 7.5   Crossover = 0.8: Percent of Optimal

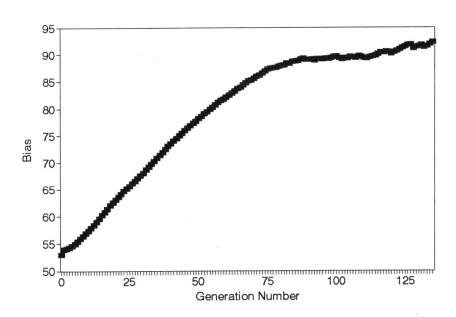

FIGURE 7.6   Crossover = 0.8: Bias

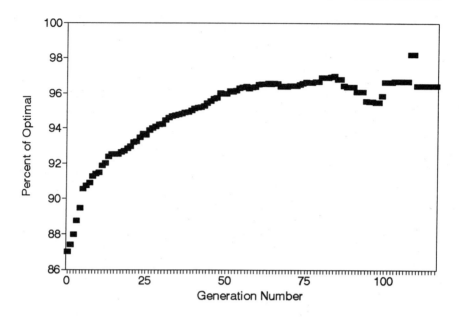

FIGURE 7.7   Mutation = 0.0001: Percent of Optimal

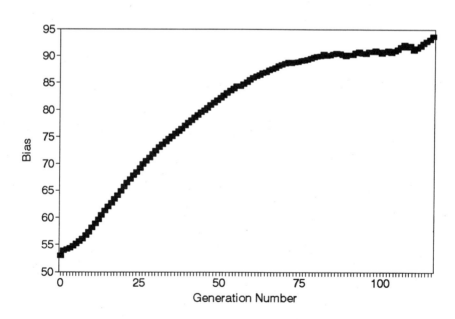

FIGURE 7.8   Mutation = 0.0001: Bias

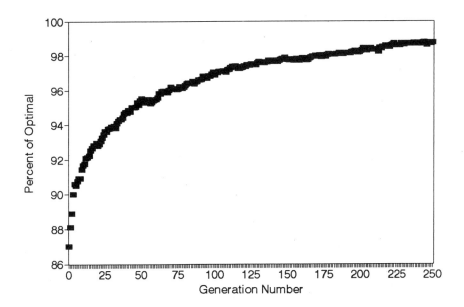

FIGURE 7.9 Mutation = 0.0010: Percent of Optimal

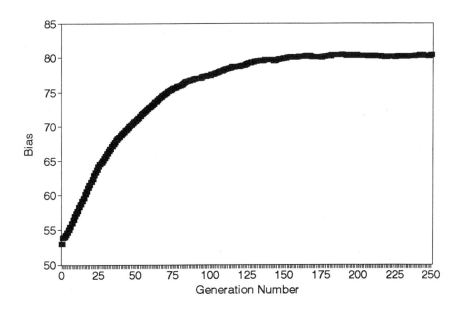

FIGURE 7.10 Mutation = 0.0010: Bias

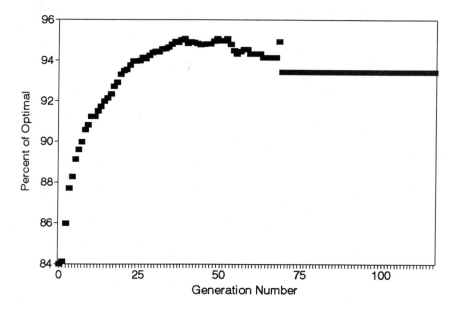

FIGURE 7.11   Population = 50: Percent of Optimal

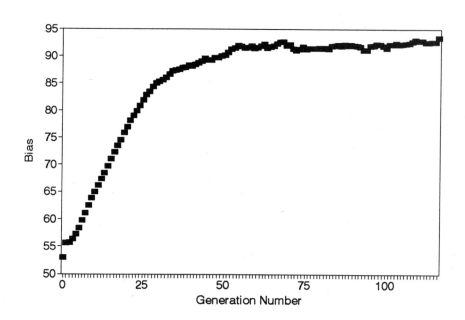

FIGURE 7.12   Population = 50: Bias

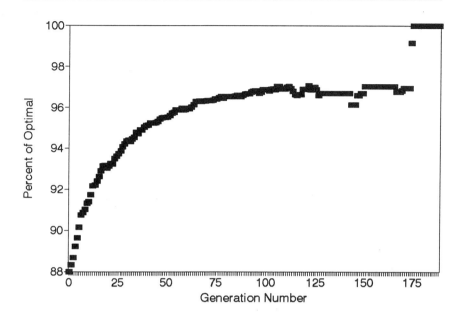

FIGURE 7.13   Population = 125: Percent of Optimal

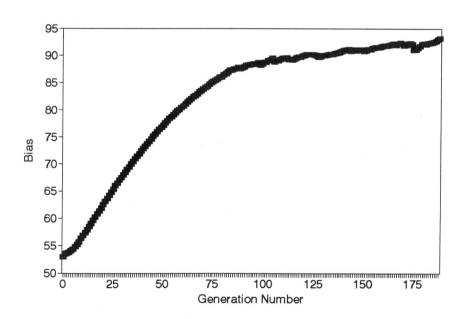

FIGURE 7.14   Population = 125: Bias

8

GA Applications

In a hot new field, those who develop interesting applications face a difficult choice: a) share your discoveries and win great praise or b) keep silent and expand your lead on the competition. Much of the current work in genetic algorithms is probably being kept secret for the latter reason. In addition, it is likely that some of the published work does not reveal all that the authors know about the subject. However, more GA applications are being reported than ever before.

There is much to learn from published application studies. In this chapter, we will describe some of the more important and interesting nonbusiness and business applications. The distinction between business and nonbusiness is tricky; applications that today seem more like "pure" research may have significant commercial potential. Because GAs were born out of computer science, many of the applications are most closely linked to that field.

It was difficult to decide how to organize this chapter. We have tried to group related applications together by topic area. In addition, some articles describe applications, but the real focus of the article may be an interesting twist on GA methodology. We chose to place this chapter before the chapter on advanced GA techniques, even though some knowledge of them would be helpful in understanding certain applications, because we felt that most readers were probably eager to learn more about possible applications before pressing into the technical details.

CRIMINAL SUSPECT RECOGNITION

In "Tracking a Criminal Suspect Through 'Face Space' with a Genetic Algorithm," (1991), C. Caldwell and V. S. Johnston describe a highly creative application: using GAs to aid witnesses in the identification of criminal suspects. From television and movies, we have probably all seen police artists working with crime witnesses to produce a sketch of the criminal suspect. That was the old-fashioned way, and it was a labor-intensive, time consuming process. Computers helped streamline this process, using image libraries of various facial features; however, they were limited because they relied on recall. Humans are extremely proficient at facial recognition but are far less proficient at recalling and describing what they saw. Many witnesses would be able to positively identify a suspect from a photograph, but describing a suspect from memory is far more difficult. The application developed by Caldwell and Johnston capitalizes on this ability of humans to recognize.

Their system works with a large library of basic facial features. The five building blocks are images of foreheads, eyes and their separations, noses, mouths, and chins, which allows for the generation of over 34 billion facial composites. These five categories were coded as a 35-bit binary string consisting of five 7-bit parameters. A given binary string could then be translated into a particular face with a unique combination of forehead, eyes, nose, mouth, and chin.

The system begins with a randomly generated population of 20 faces that are displayed on one computer screen. The witness studies the images and assigns each image a rating from one to nine that serves as the fitness value. A second generation is formed using selection of the fittest, crossover, and mutation. The witness evaluates the second generation, and the process is repeated.

One modification to a more traditional GA approach is that the witness can lock in a particular feature, thus limiting the search to other facial features. For example, the witness might decide that a particular nose image "looks right." The system can then "freeze" this feature and concentrate the search on the other four basic facial components.

This GA approach, with its freezing feature and other refinements, has proved highly effective. Convergence often occurs in only 20 generations—an incredible feat, considering the huge size of the "face-space."

MUSIC COMPOSITION

Music and electronic technology have become intertwined across many dimensions. Increasingly, computers aid both musicians and composers. It was only a matter of time before GAs entered the picture.

A. Horner and D. E. Goldberg, in "Genetic Algorithms and Computer-Assisted Music Composition" (1989), pursue an application called thematic bridging, in which a particular input pattern is gradually transformed into a desired output pattern over a specified duration of time. For example, a starting sequence of four notes might be gradually altered to become a sequence of three notes. The transformation is accomplished through various operations. For example, one operation might be "delete the last note," which would immediately transform a four-note pattern into a three-note pattern. Next, the order of the remaining three notes might be reversed. Finally, the first note might be mutated into a different note.

Horner and Goldberg developed a clever GA approach to the problem. First, a starting pattern was selected. Second, a population of binary strings was generated, with the length being related to the desired duration of the thematic bridging. Third, each binary string was decoded from left to right and interpreted as a sequence of various transforming operations. Certain bit patterns were assumed to represent the various transforming operations. Fourth, fitness was calculated. The fitness measure took into account the degree of match with the desired final pattern and the resulting duration of the transforming steps. Finally, traditional GA procedures involving selection, crossover, and mutation were used as the population evolved towards attractive solutions.

The authors report success. They have used the technique to build larger pieces of music from a collection of bridge passages. They even report that "tapes are available"—from the first author; to our knowledge they haven't hit the music stores yet.

SCHEDULING

The article "A System for Learning Routes and Schedules with Genetic Algorithms" (1989), by P. S. Gabbert, D. E. Brown, C. L. Huntley, B. P. Markowicz, and D. E. Sappington, describes how a GA can be used to explore routing and scheduling problems on a rail freight transportation network for CSX Transportation. (As an aside, CSX's 1991 Annual Report was voted one of the six best by a group of all-star financial analysts.) The GA approach proved to be especially useful for performing sensitivity analysis using various complex cost models.

Moving freight cars around the country is far more complex than it may seem. Cars are grouped into blocks that share a common originating yard and a common destination yard. A train is made up of locomotives and blocks. A routing is a sequence of yards across the country assigned to a particular block, and the schedule specifies the originating yard, the destination yard, and the departure time for each train.

The interactions between the various cost components are complex and often nonlinear. The total cost depends on the costs of freight car rental, fuel, crews, and locomotives. Some schedules might lead to delays at certain points in the network. However, a delay at one point might actually lower total cost if it permitted blocks, locomotives, or crews to be joined more efficiently.

We want to focus on the GA string coding for this problem. Each position in a string corresponded to a route taken by a given block. A master index of all routes was maintained in the system. A given string could be decoded by seeing which routes were being assigned to which blocks. Each route defined a train with a fixed origin, destination, and departure time. The path of each block and the schedule of the trains were implicit in each string. The fitness of a given string was the cost associated with that particular solution as the objective in this case was to minimize cost.

A major advantage of the system was its use in simulation exercises. The complexity of the cost interactions makes them difficult to analyze using traditional techniques. However, the GA approach easily accommodates changes to the cost function. The only portion of the GA system that must be altered is the fitness calculation, which allows the user to easily explore various cost scenarios, such as lower car-rental costs.

In "The Application of Genetic Algorithms to Resource Scheduling" (1991), G. Syswerda and J. Palmucci approach the problem of scheduling in a more general sense. They note that scheduling problems are usually computationally complex. Search techniques designed to exhaustively examine all possible combinations may fail due to time requirements. The use of heuristics may help, but optimal solutions may still be missed and problem-specific details make the development of a generic scheduling algorithm nearly impossible.

Syswerda and Palmucci try to develop a general approach to scheduling using GAs, but they refer to a specific application. The scheduling problem they describe was one faced by a Navy F-14 jet fighter–testing lab; the lab facilities had to be scheduled so as to balance task priorities; constraints on resources, time, and sequencing; and setup time requirements.

Problem representation is always an important decision in the use of GAs. Syswerda and Palmucci decided to let each string represent an ordered list of a given group of tasks to be scheduled. To evaluate the fitness, or performance, of a given string, a schedule optimizer was used to take the ordered list of tasks and produce a schedule. Each schedule was then assigned a score based on its overall desirability.

The purpose of using a GA in this case was to uncover the ordering of tasks that resulted in the best schedule. The GA efficiently searched through vast numbers of possible orderings. To aid in this search, Syswerda and Palmucci used several nonstandard variations of the mutation and crossover operations. One of these they called *order-based mutation*; in this operation, two tasks are randomly selected, and their positions are interchanged. It is not uncommon for GA researchers to tinker with some of the genetic operations to better fit the problem under investigation. In some respects, GA research is half art and half science.

The results of Syswerda and Palmucci's study would be of interest to anyone interested in using GAs to develop a scheduling application. However, the dream of a generic scheduling program seems remote. For the present, users will probably need to creatively modify approaches that have proved successful for other specific applications.

HORSE-RACE BETTING

Moving to a more whimsical application, M. de la Maza examined the use of GAs to develop rules that pick the winners of horse races in "A Seagull Visits the Race Track.'' The rules used variables such as the age of the horse, days elapsed since the last race, the odds of the last race, and the previous type of race. The GA was used to explore large numbers of rules that combined the basic variables. The system was built using a data base of race results for 500 races. The GA produced 37 rules utilizing 19 variables. When tested on a holdout sample of 1,500 races, the GA-derived rules correctly chose the winner 35.3 percent of the time. The system's pick to win the race finished in the money 78.3 percent of the time. These results are sufficient to qualify the system as an expert handicapper.

CHEMOMETRIC ANALYSIS

Chemometrics is a branch of analytical chemistry. For example, suppose a chemical monitoring device captures data over a given time period. Time series analysis of the data might provide useful insights into trends or periods present in the underlying chemical process. Chemometrics could also involve signal filtering, the design of sampling strategies, calibration of equipment, instrument optimization, and pattern recognition. Some of the problems encountered can be computationally complex and time consuming, so GAs are of potential use in this field.

In ''Application of Genetic Algorithms in Chemometrics'' (1989), Lucasius and Kateman investigate such possibilities. Specifically, they examined applications concerning adaptive filters, curve resolution, and DNA conformation analysis. For the adaptive filter problem, they used GAs to curve-fit noisy time series data associated with chromatograms. The GA minimized the differences between various attempted calculated curves and the experimental curve. The DNA conformation problem involves the various possible conformations of DNA molecules in motion due to temperature effects. In the GA representation, torsion angles of the molecules were represented as a binary string. One useful aspect of the GA approach was its lack of underlying assumptions about the problem space; it generated a rich mixture of conformational states, mimicking the extreme diversity found in nature. The authors conclude that GAs appear to show great promise with chemometric problems but that many details need additional refinement.

DATA BASE QUERY OPTIMIZATION

Modern data base management systems (DBMS) have become increasingly complex. Many systems permit users to formulate complex queries to the DBMS; these can involve multiple algebraic and logical relationships between items in the data Base. For example, a managerial user might request a profit center cost report linked to a list of all employees having a wage rate less than some value and having worked for the company more than five years.

The combinatorial possibilities of queries grows rapidly with the addition of more data items when complex algebraic and logical relationships are permitted. The search space can be extremely large. The DBMS takes queries and develops strategies for responding to them. Usually there are multiple potential strategies for answering a query. Various optimization procedures have been used to handle queries. However, as the size of systems has grown, many query optimizers have experienced difficulty.

K. Bennett, M. C. Ferris, and Y. E. Ioannidis developed a GA approach to database query optimization that they describe in an article published in 1989. Their method uses a novel encoding of chromosomes to represent binary tree query graphs. In addition, their system employs new variations of the crossover operator. They found that their GA approach was able to optimize large problems at which the traditional algorithm failed.

AIRCRAFT DESIGN

Designing modern aircraft is a complex process with many different steps, the first of which is the formulation of a general design concept—for example, the aircraft should have aluminum wings and an engine buried in the fuselage. Once this general concept has been formulated, the designer begins to concentrate on the various parameters associated with the design concept.

Design parameters include such items as wing loading, fuselage height and width, thrust-to-weight ratio, length of the aft and fore bodies, and so on. Each of these parameters may have a wide range of possible values, meaning that the parametric design problem is a combinatorial optimization problem; the task is to find the best parameter combination out of the set of possibilities.

In "Genetic Algorithms in Parametric Design of Aircraft," Mark F. Bramlette and Eugene E. Bouchard set up a search suite consisting of 16 different competing optimization methods. They examine two different GA-based approaches; the first was a fairly standard GA approach, although they use integer coding of parameters rather than binary coding. The second a GA coupled with a stochastic hill-climbing approach. They concluded that the latter GA-based approach and a simulated annealing approach produced the best answers of all 16 methods that were tested.

9
Advanced GA Techniques

The field of genetic algorithms is still relatively young, but the GA literature is already quite extensive. This book is designed to provide a broad overview of GAs, with special focus on investment applications, so we will not attempt to cover all or even most of the GA procedural variations and spin-off topics. However, we do want to cover some of them in this chapter.

Holland and others have laid down some theoretical foundations in the GA field, but the unknown still far surpasses the known. GAs are difficult to analyze mathematically. They do not neatly fit into traditional mathematical or statistical analysis, which has made theoretical work difficult. By contrast, experimental variations are easily conceived and implemented. Much of the GA literature reports the results of tests concerning ad hoc procedural modifications. Researchers often find some new twist that seems to work well but can't prove why it works or draw strong conclusions about its general applicability. Most of the topics in this chapter grew out of this body of empirical work.

CROSSOVER VARIATIONS

Crossover is critical to the search for better solutions, but there can be too much of a good thing. Crossover is disruptive; good chromosomes (strings) can be severely distorted. If crossover is too frequent, the search is chaotic and does not adequately capitalize on previous successes. Infrequent crossing keeps the search confined to narrow regions of the search space.

The crossover operation that we have been using is called *one-point crossover*, because only one cut is made in each chromosome. *Two-point crossover* involves two cuts and can be pictured this way:

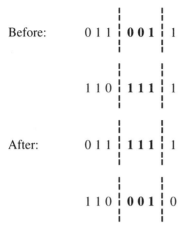

Before: 0 1 1 │ 0 0 1 │ 1

           1 1 0 │ 1 1 1 │ 1

After: 0 1 1 │ 1 1 1 │ 1

           1 1 0 │ 0 0 1 │ 0

Like most GA variations, two-point crossover has pros and cons. Consider the following two schemata:

Schemata 1: 1 * * * 0 1
Schemata 2: * * 0 0 * *

With one-point crossover, there is no way for schemata 1 to be combined with schemata 2 without losing at least one of the 1s at the endpoints of the string. However, with two-point crossover, the following could happen:

	Before			After
1 │ * * * │ 0 1			1 0 * 0 0 1	
* │ * 0 0 │ * *			* * * * * *	

However, there are other schemata that even two-point crossover cannot combine. Multiple-point crossovers have been developed and tested, as has another variation called *uniform crossover*.

Uniform crossover, developed by G. Syswerda in 1989, potentially allows any pattern to be swapped. It allows two parent strings to produce two children. First, we decide on a bit-by-bit basis how the child strings will relate to the parent strings. Let's consider two 5-bit strings as an example. As a first step, we flip five coins, one for each bit position, and record how they land. Instead of heads and tails, call the results "same" or "swap." Let's say we flip and get same-swap-same-swap-same. Now consider the following two parent strings:

Bit position:	1	2	3	4	5
Parent 1:	0	0	0	1	1
Parent 2:	1	1	1	0	0
Crossover pattern:	same	swap	same	swap	same

Next, we use the same-swap-same-swap-same pattern to form the two children. The pattern for the first bit position is "same." Parent 1 has a 0, so child 1 gets a 0. Parent 2 has a 1, so child 2 gets a 1. The pattern for bit position 2 is "swap," so child 1 gets the 1 from parent 2, and child 2 gets the 0 from parent 1. The final results are:

Bit position:	1	2	3	4	5
Child 1:	0	1	0	0	1
Child 2:	1	0	1	1	0

Uniform crossover permits great flexibility in the way strings are combined, which is an attractive feature. However, it can also wreak great havoc on strings through some drastic reconfigurations. There is yet no definitive answer concerning which form of crossover is best. It may well depend on the particular problem and how the string is translated into a fitness measure.

SELECTION

A major component of a GA is the scheme used to move from one generation to the next; this is a life-or-death decision! There are many possible variations concerning how potential parents are chosen and how they come together to produce new offspring. Selection can range from being very heavy-handed, placing strong emphasis on fitness, to very subtle schemes that weight fitness more lightly. David E. Goldberg and Kalyanmoy Deb, in "A Comparative Analysis of Selection Schemes Used in Genetic Algorithms," analyzed various alternative selection procedures, identifying some of the strengths and weaknesses of each. We will explain some of these procedures and summarize their findings.

1. Roulette wheel proportionate. This procedure utilizes a weighted selection based on fitness. As a highly simplified example (which will also be used to explain the second and third methods), consider a population of ten individuals. It contains six identical individuals that we label as type A and four identical individuals that we label as type B. Assume that type A individuals have a fitness value of 12, whereas type B individuals have a fitness of only 7. The total fitness of all ten is 6 × 12 plus 4 × 7, or 100. Type A captures 72 percent of the total fitness, and type B captures 28 percent. One method of proportionate reproduction is the *weighted roulette wheel technique*. With this approach, we construct a wheel, 72 percent of which is labeled A, with 28 percent labeled B. To choose the next generation, we merely give the wheel ten spins and create a new mixture of A and B types. When the new generation is created, it will, on average, contain about seven (based on 72 percent) type A members and three (based on 28 percent) type B members. Because the spins of the wheels are controlled by chance (using a random number generator in the computer implementation), the actual A/B split could end up anywhere from 0/10 to 10/0. However, on average this method rewards higher fitness values.

2. Stochastic remainder selection. Consider the ten-member A-B population described above. The expected number of copies of type A individuals is 7.2, while the expected number of type B individuals is 2.8. With stochastic remainder selection, we first concentrate on the integer components of the expected values, 7 and 2. Seven copies of A are allocated to the next generation, as are two copies of B. To determine the identity of the tenth member, the fractional remainders are used to weight a roulette wheel. Here, B gets a 0.8 (80 percent) weighting, and A gets only a 0.2 (20 percent) weighting. This method will give rise to a new generation with either a 7/3 or 8/2 split between A and B members. Note that this method is more heavy handed in that it forces the next generation to closely parallel the relative fitness proportions.

3. Stochastic universal selection. This method is another variation of the previous two, but will take slightly more imagination to visualize it. Picture the same roulette wheel with 72 percent of the wheel marked A and 28 percent marked B. Now imagine an outer ring of ten equally spaced markers. The roulette wheel is given one spin. To determine the composition of the next generation, the ten markers are examined; those opposite the A section are allocated to A types, and those opposite the B section are allocated to B types. This method will yield results similar to that of stochastic remainder selection; the split in this case will also be either 7/3 or 8/2.

4. Genitor selection. This is a GA variation developed by Whitley in 1989; it is a ranking-based procedure. This is basically the procedure that we have employed in our research. The population is ranked according to fitness, and then the best individuals replace the worst individuals.

5. Ranking selection with roulette wheel. This procedure begins by rank-ordering the population by fitness. Next, an assignment function gives each individual a probability of inclusion in the next generation. Higher-ranking individuals have a greater probability of inclusion. The assignment function can be linear or nonlinear, but normally it is the latter. A roulette wheel is then built with the slots determined by the assignment function. The next generation of an n-sized population is built by giving the wheel n spins. This procedure tips selection towards the better-performing members of the population but does not force any particular individuals into the next generation.

6. Tournament selection. Tournaments are like small jousting matches between members of the population to see who gets to participate in the next generation. They can involve two or more individuals at a time. In our example tournament, two members are chosen at random from the population, and then their fitness values are compared. The better performing of the two members could either be automatically chosen to be part of the next generation, or a simulated, weighted coin could be flipped to choose between them. For example, we might decide to choose the better performer 75 percent of the time; to do so, we would flip a "coin" with a 0.75 probability of heads coming up. If the coin does come up heads, then we select the better performer; if not, we choose the other. Tournaments are repeatedly performed in this fashion until the next generation of the population is completely filled.

GAs face an inherent conflict between exploitation and exploration. *"Exploitation"* here refers to taking advantage of information already obtained in the search. For example, suppose that a GA finds that strings in the population with a 1010 pattern in bits 5 through 8 seem to have much better fitness values. If the algorithm leads to a rapid "fixing" of these bit positions with the 1010 pattern, then that knowledge is being exploited in an effort to improve average fitness in the population. The risk of fixing bits too quickly is that the search could be curtailed; further exploration might show that a 0110 pattern in those four bits coupled with another pattern elsewhere in the string is more effective. This tension between exploitation and exploration is always present.

The selection method has a major impact on the balance between exploitation and exploration. A more heavy-handed approach seeks to exploit the available information. For example, well-performing strings may be almost forced into the next generation. Alternatively, the selection may involve only a subtle tipping of the odds towards the survival of the fittest. Roulette wheel proportionate selection slightly tips the odds in favor of better performers. However, a ranking procedure with an assignment function that strongly weights higher-ranking performers is far more heavy handed.

For investment applications, the choice of selection method and the desired balance between exploitation and exploration may depend on the problem being investigated. If decisions must be made quickly, especially those in real-time trading environments, then quicker convergence through exploitation may be more desirable. For longer-term decisions that are not as time-sensitive, then a slower, higher-quality search may be preferable.

CLASSIFIER SYSTEMS

Classifier systems are a fascinating extension of genetic algorithms. The power of this technique is extraordinary. In Chapter 16, we will discuss how classifier systems are being used to build stock market trading systems.

Classifier systems are sets of rules that perform certain actions when the rule conditions are met. As an example, let's consider a system to manage a stock portfolio. The portfolio manager examines the stocks of many different companies, deciding which to purchase and which to sell. These decisions might revolve around various criteria such as earnings growth, shares outstanding, institutional ownership, dividend growth, leverage, and price-to-book ratio. The rules in the classifier system could be encoded as shown in Table 9.1. The left-hand portion

Table 9.1   Classifier System Example

Example Number	Input						Output	
	High Earnings Growth	High Shares Outstanding	High Institutional Ownership	High Dividend Growth	Acceptable Leverage	High Price-to-Book	Buy	Sell
1	1	#	#	#	1	#	1	0
2	1	#	#	#	1	0	1	0
3	#	1	#	#	#	#	0	1

of the rule represents the environmental input, and the right-hand side represents the output.

The input side is coded with 0s, 1s, and #s, which make up a *ternary* (three-part) alphabet. The 0 and 1 are used to indicate whether or not the stock possesses the given qualifying attribute, such as high earnings growth. If earnings growth is encoded in position 1 of the string, then a 1 in that position indicates the stock has high earnings growth. A # in the first position indicates that earnings growth is not an important factor in the rule.

The output side has two positions. A 1 in the first output position signals that the portfolio manager should buy the stock; a 1 in the second position indicates a sale. The following patterns would indicate that no action is needed: 00, 11, #0, 0#, and ##.

With the rule coding as shown in Table 9.1, a buy is indicated for the first example. This is a rule for a stock with high earnings growth and an acceptable debt level. The input coding of 1###1# means that high earnings growth and an acceptable debt level trigger a buy but that all other attributes are irrelevant to the buy decision. The output is coded as a 10, which indicates a purchase.

The second rule is a slight variation of the first. The coding of 1###10 indicates that earnings growth and debt are important but that the stock must also be a good value as reflected in the acceptable P/E ratio. If the P/E is too high, then the stock is perhaps overpriced and should not be purchased.

The third rule is simple. It merely states that when the institutional ownership gets too high, then it is time to sell regardless of the other factors. The input side is represented as #1####.

There are many ways that a classifier system might be constructed to handle this problem. We will briefly outline one possible approach that is simple but contains many of the major features of classifier systems.

The initial rule population could be created randomly or seeded with a given set of trial rules. The randomization procedure would work with the ternary alphabet to create perhaps 100 initial random rules. With classifier systems, rules maintain an associated level of *strength*. As a starting point, all rules are assigned the same arbitrary level of strength.

Each cycle of the classifier system routine is called a *timestep*. Rules bid in a simulated auction to see which ones get activated in a given timestep. Again, there are many ways we might construct the classifier system in this example. Let's assume that we present each of the rules a dataset of stocks with fields describing the attributes discussed earlier, such as high earnings growth. After reading through the dataset, some rules might be applicable and some might not. For example, one rule might "see" several stocks that it wants to buy because they meet the rule's purchase criteria. We might say that the dataset has caused certain rules to "fire"; these could then bid in an auction to see which ones get to act.

Bids could be calculated in many ways, but they are often just a set percentage, such as 10 percent, of the strength level. At this point, we could merely examine the bids of all the rules and go with the highest bidder. However, classifier systems normally rely on a noisy bidding process in which randomly generated noise is added to each bid value—in other words, the bids are all randomly perturbed by a slight amount. Rule A might have a strength level of 100 and a bid of 10. Rule B might have a strength level of 95 and a bid of 9.5. However, rule B might win the auction because it receives 1 unit of positive noise, while rule A gets 0.7 units of negative noise, resulting in effective bids of 9.3 and 10.5, respectively.

The strength of rules in the classifier system is adjusted in several ways. The winning rule's strength would be reduced by the amount of its bid. Some classifier systems impose a simulated tax on the rule strength economy; for example, each rule might pay a tax proportional to its strength. In more complicated classifier systems, rules might fire each other in chains, and bid payments might proceed backward in the chain. One such payment mechanism is called the *bucket brigade*. Rules can also receive rewards, which add to their strength.

In our example, the reward calculation could be complex. The winning rule might get to buy or sell short the applicable stocks in the data set. We might assume some arbitrary holding period such as one year. The rule's reward might then be linked to the return earned on the portfolio held over that year and could be either positive or negative. Note the basic risk-and-return principle that is occurring; rules must risk a bid to gain an uncertain reward.

In the second timestep, the rules might be confronted with a new data set and go through another bid-auction-reward cycle. As this process is repeated over many timesteps, the better rules gain strength, and the poorer rules lose strength.

New rules are introduced into the classifier system via genetic algorithms. As before, we have a population of strings that can be manipulated via selection, crossover, and mutation. However, the philosophy is a bit different in this case. With GAs we are trying to cast a broad search net, hoping to find the optimal solution, whereas with classifier systems we are trying to find a set of coadapted rules that work well in combination, not just one best rule. This requires some modifications to the GA procedures.

The GA procedure might get activated only at certain intervals, such as every 50 timesteps. Only a fraction of the population is replaced. The replacement procedure would tend to replace poor rules with good rules. Crossover might occur more delicately, depending on the rule structure; it might be undesirable to risk disruption of certain portions of the rule strings. Mutation would occur as before, but it would be modified slightly to accommodate the ternary alphabet.

Eventually the system should gravitate towards a set of rules that work well in combination. Clearly, this is a powerful technique, but classifier systems, like neural networks, require much tinkering with the system parameters. We will stick to a simpler, pure GA approach, but we'll touch on classifier system possibilities again in Chapters 15 and 16.

PART THREE
GENETIC ALGORITHMS AND INVESTMENT STRATEGIES

10
The Lure of Market Timing

The phrase *market timing* can mean different things to different investors. In recent years, similar concepts such as *tactical asset allocation* have created additional potential ambiguity. Before proceeding, we need to clarify what we mean by market timing.

D. Phillips and J. Lee, in a controversial article titled "Differentiating Tactical Asset Allocation from Market Timing" wrestle with definitions of tactical asset allocation, market timing, and strategic asset allocation, which they describe as "the proportion of assets allocated to each asset class to achieve the organization's long-term financial goals of the organization" (p. 14).

This description is reasonably clear, except that we could argue about what constitutes an asset class. For example, investor A might consider stocks and bonds to be two asset classes. However, investor B might want to make further refinements by considering the following to be separate asset classes: small- and large-firm stocks, long- and intermediate-term Treasury bonds, Treasury bills, long-term corporate bonds, and so on. We will follow an approach along the lines of investor B, which also coincides with the SBBI time series data.

An example of a strategic asset allocation would be to devote 60 percent of the portfolio to long-term Treasury bonds, 30 percent to common stocks, and 10 percent to Treasury bills. This allocation would be based on the risk tolerance and return objectives of the investor; it would be fairly conservative for an investor with a reasonably long investment horizon. With strategic asset allocation, the portfolio would be periodically reviewed and occasionally rebalanced, but the asset class allocations would be altered only infrequently.

Phillips and Lee view tactical asset allocation as a tilting of the asset mix based on current market conditions, but the tilting would only be done within limits. For example, the strategic allocation described above might include a stipulation that the equity component be permitted to range from 15 to 45 percent of the portfolio, with 30 percent being the average desired figure; the portfolio would never be totally concentrated in only one asset class. It should be noted that many practitioners disagree with this definition.

We part company with Phillips and Lee slightly when it comes to market timing. The following are several key quotes from their article:

> The singular objective [of market timing] is to outperform the equity market. The critical decision is whether to be in the equity market, or out of the equity market. (p. 15)

> The objective of the market timer is to maximize return. To a timer, risk is primarily opportunity cost—in particular, the gains foregone if he is out of the market when it takes off. Tactical asset allocation is concerned with both risk and return. (p. 15)

> The market timer's decision ultimately comes down to whether to be in or out of equities. (p. 15)

There is debate within the investment community about whether tactical asset allocation actually differs from market timing. In our tests, we will try to take a strong stand on a view of the market at any point in time, which leads naturally to more drastic allocation decisions such as 100 percent in or out. However, even staunch market timers may occasionally feel unsure of the market's direction and wish to hedge their position with a mixed allocation such as 50/50.

We will use market timing in a sense that is not limited to equities. For example, the investor might try to time the bond market, switching back and forth between Treasury bonds and Treasury bills. Or timing decisions could involve switches between Treasury bonds and corporate bonds. To us, market timing refers to major asset allocation shifts between asset classes. The classes do not have to be confined to equities, although they will be the principal focus. Equities receive primary attention because they are more volatile and therefore lead to greater potential rewards from successful timing.

Finally, market timers should not ignore risk. Let's say we develop a stock market timing strategy that yields roughly the same returns as a *buy-and-hold strategy*, one in which the asset is purchased at the beginning of the period and held continuously throughout the entire time span, and yet only requires equity exposure on average eight months out of the year. For the other four months of the year, again on average, the investor has a 100 percent Treasury bill portfolio. In this situation the two strategies offer the same return, but one has eight-twelfths (which equals 75 percent) as much risk. In our view, the market timing strategy would be clearly superior. We agree that it is far easier to get excited when a timing strategy offers returns superior to that of a buy-and-hold strategy, but we cannot as rational investors ignore risk considerations.

THE POTENTIAL REWARD

The potential reward to be earned from successful market timing is enormous. A brief examination of historical return data will prove the point. We will first examine returns over the past 30 years and then focus on just the past 3 years.

The numbers we will report are derived from the data in *Stocks, Bonds, Bills, and Inflation (SBBI): 1992 Yearbook*, published by Ibbotson Associates of Chicago. The data in *SBBI* is widely used for historical return comparisons.

As a comparative benchmark, let us examine the potential rewards that might have been earned from various asset class buy-and-hold strategies over the January 1962 through December 1991 period. This 30-year period spans several complete bull/bear markets, several full business cycles, different political climates, and disparate inflation environments. Table 10.1 shows the results of various investment strategies over the 1962–1991 period. It is organized to display the results of five buy-and-hold strategies and ten two-asset switching strategies. (We are ignoring transactions costs and the possibility of short sales for now.) In buy-and-hold strategies, all monetary distributions such as dividends and interest payments are assumed to be reinvested in the given asset.

The buy-and-hold results are shown in the blocks down the lower left diagonal. For example, if an investor had purchased $1,000 worth of Treasury bills at the beginning of January 1962 and continued to reinvest the original amount and all additional proceeds in Treasury bills, then the investor would have had $6,865 at the end of December 1991. This ending amount is called *terminal wealth*. The average annual compound return of 6.63 percent is shown just above the terminal wealth figure. A buy-and-hold strategy with equities would have been far more lucrative. Continuous investment in a Standard & Poor's 500 portfolio would have resulted in a terminal wealth of $18,711 (a compound return of 10.26 percent). Continuous investment in small-firm stocks would have resulted in a terminal wealth of $47,424 (a 13.73 percent annual return). *Small-firm stocks* are defined in SBBI as stocks in the smallest quintile (one-fifth) of market capitalization on the New York Stock Exchange. Market capitalization is calculated by multiplying the current stock price times the total number of outstanding shares of the stock. Buy-and-hold investments in either corporate or Treasury Bonds would have earned slightly more than T-bills.

Things get more interesting as we turn to optimal two-asset switching strategies. Consider the possibility of starting with $1,000 and clairvoyantly investing each month in the better performing of either T-bills or common stocks. Clearly, for months like October 1987 when stocks dropped 21.52 percent, it would have been far better to just earn the 0.6 percent that T-bills would have offered. However, in January 1987 stocks had climbed 13.43 percent. Catching all the peaks of stocks and avoiding the valleys would indeed be highly lucrative.

The large-firm stock results are enticing, but successful timing of small-firm stocks would have been even more lucrative. Perfect switching between Treasury bills and small-firm stocks would have led to a terminal wealth of $85,031,514, a 45.99 percent compound annual return. Perfect switching between small-firm stocks and Treasury bonds would have been the best of the ten two-asset switching combinations shown in Table 10.1, leading to a terminal wealth of $95,161,285, a compound annual return of 46.54 percent.

There are some important lessons to be learned from Table 10.1. First, the potential rewards to successful market timing are great. The range of terminal wealth from the same $1,000 initial investment goes from $6,865 for holding T-Bills to over $95 million from perfect timing between small-firm stocks and Treasury bonds; in percentage terms, the range is from 6.63 percent to 46.54 percent.

Second, the perfect switching strategies clobber the buy-and-hold strategies, as can be seen by comparing the diagonal results to the off-diagonal results. Nine of the ten switching strategies had compound annual returns over 19 percent and beat all five of the buy-and-hold strategies. The one switching strategy, Treasury bonds versus corporate bonds, that doesn't beat all five of the buy-and-hold op-

Table 10.1 Terminal Wealth of a $1,000 Initial Investment with Optimal Monthly Switching: January 1962–December 1991

	Treasury Bills	Common Stock	Small-Firm Stocks	Corporate Bonds	Treasury Bonds
Treasury Bills	(6.63) 6,865	(32.63) 4,774,992	(45.99) 85,031,514	(19.60) 214,484	(21.02) 306,332
Common Stock		(10.26) 18,711	(32.09) 4,227,932	(31.21) 3,462,767	(32.44) 4,579,619
Small-Firm Stocks			(13.73) 47,424	(45.16) 71,662,473	(46.54) 95,161,285
Corporate Bonds				(7.28) 8,236	(12.60) 35,184
Treasury Bonds					(6.77) 7,140

(Compound annual return shown in parentheses; table excludes short sales.)
Data derived from *Stocks, Bonds, Bills, and Inflation 1992 Yearbook*. Ibbotson Associates, Inc.: Chicago, Ill., 1983–1992.

tions beats four of them. Seven of the ten switching strategies had compound annual returns over 30 percent.

Third, over this time period small-firm stocks and switching strategies involving them significantly outperformed common stocks. The fact that small-firm stocks tend to outperform large-firm stocks, even on a risk-adjusted basis, is known as the *small-firm effect*.

Fourth, Treasury bonds are more intriguing than corporate bonds, at least where switching strategies are concerned. Because Treasury bonds are long-term default-free instruments, they are highly responsive to movements in the level of long-term interest rates. Corporate bonds respond both to interest rate movements and to changes in credit quality. Treasury bonds are less correlated with equities than are corporate bonds and therefore present a better option when "it's time to get out of stocks." The potential reward from optimal timing of Treasury bond–bill movements is attractive at 21.02 percent. Far less attractive is the return from optimal timing between corporate and Treasury bonds at 12.60 percent.

Before going on to examine results over a recent three-year period, we need to address several significant potential concerns. First, you may be wondering how hard it is to be successful at market timing. It is very hard. In the latter part of this chapter, we will recap both the academic research on market timing and the actual investment experience of market timers. Some of this research will put a damper on your expectations. Second, you may also have wondered about the transaction costs required in these switching strategies. It's true that they are concerns, but perhaps less than you might think. For the equity/T-bill switches, the potential rewards from accurately calling whether to be in or out of the market dwarf the transaction costs. In addition, market timing strategies would probably be implemented today using options and/or futures with fairly low transaction costs. We will say more about this later. For now, we will sweep transaction costs under the rug without forgetting they exist. Finally, we have not yet addressed the potential downside. We have presented potential results for perfect success but not for perfect failure. Being in the market at the wrong time, such as October 1987, can be costly. Results from the 1962–1991 period are interesting and contain several important lessons to be learned, but we might ask: Have the same general patterns continued to manifest themselves during recent years? Table 10.2 provides the answers with a format identical to that of Table 10.1.

Three out of the four lessons from Table 10.1 continue to be valid during the 1989–1991 time period. The potential rewards of successful market timing are great. Optimal monthly switches between common stocks and Treasury bills would have resulted in a terminal wealth of $2,748 from a $1,000 initial investment, a compound annual return of 40.06 percent. A buy-and-hold Treasury bill approach would have led to a terminal wealth of $1,234, an annual return of 7.26 percent. Also, the off-diagonal switching strategies beat all of the diagonal buy-and-hold strategies, except in one case. And finally, Treasury bond switching strategies look more attractive than corporate bond switching strategies.

Table 10.2   Terminal Wealth of a $1,000 Initial Investment with Optimal Monthly Switching: January 1989–December 1991

	Treasury Bills	Common Stock	Small-Firm Stocks	Corporate Bonds	Treasury Bonds
Treasury Bills	(7.26) 1,234	(40.06) 2,748	(35.66) 2,497	(20.40) 1,746	(23.17) 1,869
Common Stock		(18.46) 1,662	(29.03) 2,148	(40.36) 2,765	(40.50) 2,773
Small-Firm Stocks			(7.72) 1,250	(36.16) 2,524	(36.61) 2,549
Corporate Bonds				(14.17) 1,488	(17.75) 1,632
Treasury Bonds					(14.35) 1,495

(Compound annual return shown in parentheses; table excludes short sales.)
Data derived from *Stocks, Bonds, Bills, and Inflation 1992 Yearbook.* Ibbotson Associates, Inc.: Chicago, Ill., 1983–1992.

However, a significant difference exists between the small-firm/common stock results in Table 10.1 and those in Table 10.2. During the 1989–1991 period, the common stock buy-and-hold strategy soundly outperformed the small-firm buy-and-hold strategy (18.46 percent compound annual return versus 7.72 percent). Also, the switching strategies involving common stocks outperformed those using small-firm stocks.

Optimal two-asset switching strategies are intriguing, but the inclusion of additional assets makes the potential outcome extremely alluring. In Table 10.3, we report the results of calculations for optimal multi-asset switching strategies over the 1962–1991 time period. The numbers are mind-boggling. If the ''T-bill or common stock?'' decision is extended to include Treasury bonds, the optimal switching strategy would have resulted in a terminal wealth of nearly $26 million, or a 40.33 percent compound rate of return—all from an initial investment of only $1,000! However, the optimal T-bill/small-firm/Treasury bond scheme would have yielded over $509 million, for a rate of return of nearly 55 percent. Comparing back to Table 10.1, the best two-asset combination would have earned about $95 million, or about 46.5 percent compound annual return. Clearly, the addition of a third asset markedly improves the potential reward.

When we extend the selection possibilities to a fourth and fifth asset class, the numbers become stratospheric. The best four-asset combination results in a terminal wealth of over $1.3 billion, or an annual return of nearly 60 percent. The optimal scheme with all five asset classes leads to an ending wealth over $1.5 billion, or nearly 61 percent annual return.

Table 10.3   Multi-Asset Optimal Switching: January 1962–December 1991

	Assets	Terminal Wealth	Compound Return
1	Treasury Bills Common Stocks Treasury Bonds	25,960,554	40.33%
2	Treasury Bills Common Stocks Small Stocks	312,858,834	52.47%
3	Treasury Bills Small Stocks Treasury Bonds	509,070,346	54.96%
4	Treasury Bills Treasury Bonds Corporate Bonds	544,754	23.37%
5	Treasury Bills Common Stocks Small Stocks Treasury Bonds	1,321,523,558	59.97%
6	Treasury Bills Common Stocks Small Stocks Corporate Bonds	914,557,611	58.02%
7	Treasury Bills Common Stocks Small Stocks Treasury Bonds Corporate Bonds	1,560,377,604	60.86%

Table excludes short sales.
Data derived from *Stocks, Bonds, Bills, and Inflation 1992 Yearbook.* Ibbotson Associates, Inc.: Chicago, Ill., 1983–1992.

Before pushing completely into outer space, we need to return to earth for a few minutes. First, the inclusion of taxes would severely dampen the final results. If we were earning such phenomenal profits, the IRS, charities, and all of our "close" friends might soon be camped on our doorstep. Second, there is a subtle issue of "guts" underlying these calculations due to the assumption regarding complete reinvestment each month. Assume that you had earned $20 million in trading profits over some period of years. Would you really be willing to place that entire amount at risk every month that you moved your investment out of Treasury bills and into stocks? Would it bother you to see a one-month drop of $2 million in the value of your $20-million stake? Or what if you had just earned your first $200,000? Would a $20,000 downturn be distressing? That's exactly the kind of gutsiness implied in these calculations, which assume 100 percent reinvestment.

We said we were going to return to earth for just a few minutes; get ready to take off again. So far we have only assumed an ability to forecast the upside of asset value fluctuations—in short, we have ignored the possibility of short sales. In today's world, it has become much easier to "bet" on downward movements in securities. By selling stock index futures contracts or buying stock index put option contracts, we can win when the market turns down. So we'll try a few more calculations illustrating the potential rewards from correctly predicting both upside and downside movements.

Assume that we foresee returns of +5 percent, +2 percent, and −8 percent for assets X, Y, and Z, respectively. Without short sales, we would pick asset X. However, if we short asset Z, then the −8 percent return becomes +8 percent. As before, we are abstracting from the specific transaction cost concerns that would alter our numbers somewhat, but our general conclusions will still hold.

Table 10.4 shows the optimal two-asset results over the 1962–1991 time period with short sales being allowed. Note that just being able to go long or short, as appropriate, only in common stocks results in a terminal wealth of over $157 million, or about 49 percent annually. For the optimal small-firm/Treasury bond–switching scheme, the ending wealth is nearly $88 trillion, or a return of 84 percent annually. Remember, we said we were about to launch into outer space! Just as a matter of curiosity, the optimal switching pattern using all five asset classes, allowing short sales and ignoring transaction costs and taxes, is over $412 trillion, for a compound annual return over 93 percent.

Table 10.4   Terminal Wealth of a $1,000 Initial Investment with Optimal Monthly Switching (Short Sales Allowed): January 1962–December 1991

	Treasury Bills	Common Stock	Small-Firm Stocks	Corporate Bonds	Treasury Bonds
Treasury Bills	(6.63) 6,865	(49.67) 179,611,955	(74.16) 16,929,898,332	(26.31) 1,103,764	(29.41) 2,284,298
Common Stock		(49.01) 157,160,707	(85.42) 110,895,548,440	(57.31) 799,327,543	(59.67) 1,250,367,371
Small-Firm Stocks			(73.70) 15,640,041,362	(81.60) 59,360,458,467	(84.00) 87,966,728,639
Corporate				(25.55) 921,810	(33.04) 5,243,422
Treasury					(28.77) 1,967,705

(Compound annual return shown in parentheses.)
Data derived from *Stocks, Bonds, Bills, and Inflation 1992 Yearbook.* Ibbotson Associates, Inc.: Chicago, Ill., 1983–1992.

It's time to go back to earth. We do not want to suggest that these astronomical numbers are achievable or even remotely approachable. The basic conclusions are more important than the specific numerical results.

The main points to take away are these:

1. The consideration of additional asset classes in the market timing decision complicates the analysis but greatly increases the potential reward. We have discussed five different asset class choices; others that we have not included are gold, commodities, foreign equities, foreign bonds, and real estate.
2. The possibility of short sales complicates the decision but also greatly increases the potential reward. With the availability of futures and options contracts, it has become far easier to implement bearish strategies. These contracts also facilitate additional leveraging of returns, which we have ignored. Leveraging of the returns would increase both the risk and potential earnings.

We wanted you to experience some of the lure of market timing before reviewing the relevant literature. We will first examine the studies that have reached negative conclusions about the effectiveness of market-timing strategies and then finish the chapter on a more positive note.

MARKET TIMING LITERATURE: THE BAD NEWS

Based on our own informal conversations, it is rare to find someone really bullish about the concept of market timing. Of course, many investors speak against market timing and then describe how they have just moved funds into or out of the market based on what they foresee concerning general market conditions; they are "closet" market timers.

In our opinion, the generally negative opinion about market timing probably stems back to two important articles. Their influence is probably directly related to their high credibility; one was written by a Nobel laureate, and the other appeared in the *Harvard Business Review*.

In 1975, *Financial Analysts Journal* published an article by William Sharpe titled "Likely Gains from Market Timing." Sharpe, as one of the developers of the Capital Asset Pricing Model (CAPM), was one of three financial economists awarded the Nobel prize in 1990. These were the first Nobel prize awards granted to anyone who claimed "finance" as their domain, rather than "economics." Sharpe painted a very pessimistic view of market timing, summarizing his views as follows:

> The conclusion is fairly clear. Attempts to time the market are not likely to produce incremental returns of more than four percent per year over the long run. Moreover, unless a manager can predict whether the market will be good or bad each year with

considerable accuracy (e.g., be right at least seven times out of ten), he should probably avoid attempts to time the market altogether. (p. 69)

Sharpe examined annual switches, simply labeling a year as good or bad, depending on the performance of equities versus T-Bills.

The title of Robert Jeffrey's 1984 *HBR* article sums up his opinion: "The Folly of Market Timing." Jeffrey looked at the risk-reward characteristics of both annual and quarterly market timing strategies, examining the range of outcomes from worst to best for various levels of forecasting accuracy. He concluded: "Because the natural long-term odds vis-a-vis market timing are clearly stacked in favor of the house, extensive use of timing strategies should be confined to managing one's own money and not that of others." (p. 702) He described market timing as being basically contrarian in nature and therefore better suited to individuals than investment committees.

W. G. Droms, in "Market Timing as an Investment Policy" (1989), performed two significant extensions of Sharpe's study. First, he extended the time period under investigation from 1933–1972 to 1926–1986. Second, he examined annual, quarterly, and monthly timing strategies. He, too, was pessimistic about the advisability of market timing, concluding that successful timing required forecasting accuracy beyond the reach of most managers. He also pointed out that the superior potential rewards from more frequent switching can easily be negated due to higher transaction costs.

Many people argue against market timing in comparison to the buy-and-hold alternative based on the lumpiness of stock returns. Strong bull runs tend to be fairly short; if you miss them, it's hard to catch back up. The differential advantage is high in a few periods and much more narrow over many periods. Similarly, one can gain a significant advantage by merely avoiding the market's severe downturns, but these tend to be short and chaotic, making prediction difficult. Based on these considerations, buy-and-hold looks pretty attractive.

Some studies also document the difficulty of market timing in actual practice. R. T. Kleiman and A. P. Sahu, in their article, "An Empirical Investigation of the Timing Abilities of Insurance Company Investment Managers" (1989), studied the performance of 40 equity-oriented investment funds managed by life insurance companies and concluded that these funds failed to exhibit superior market timing ability. However, they also concluded that these funds showed poor security selections skills. Sinclair (1990) found significantly negative equity timing ability in the funds he examined.

Bond market timing can also be very difficult. G. H. Pink's article, "Market Timing by Canadian Bond Funds" (1988), found evidence of significantly negative timing ability among 34 Canadian bond funds over the 1976–1985 period. Robert C. Brown and Company, noted for its aggressive approach to interest rate timing, saw its assets decline nearly 50 percent in 1988 due to poor results. The firm was sold in 1989.

MARKET TIMING: THE GOOD NEWS

W. Sy in "Market Timing: Is It a Folly?" (1990), argues against the basic conclusions of Sharpe and Jeffrey. His study shows that market timers needed only about 60 percent predictive accuracy over the 1970–1989 time period to be successful. He also emphasizes the large potential rewards from successful monthly market timing. Finally, he argues that market timing can reduce the volatility, or risk, of returns.

Other studies cite the attractiveness of small-firm stock–switching strategies and the importance of short positions. G. W. Kester compares the returns from large-firm to small-firm stock switching in his article, "Market Timing with Small Versus Large-Firm Stocks: Potential Gains and Required Predictive Ability," showing that the latter is potentially far more lucrative. He finds that if transactions costs are less than 1 percent, market timing may outperform fixed-asset mix portfolios. G. A. Shilling, in "Market Timing: Better than a Buy-and-Hold Strategy" (1992), analyzes the impact of short selling in market-timing strategies. Successful shorting can offset some of the mistakes made in missing bull markets. Historically, there has been a negative bias against short positions.

Foreign markets offer attractive timing possibilities. Kester (1992) explores the potential rewards from market timing in the Japanese market. Hardy (1990) examines the risk premiums for six different countries. He argues that even with limited information, internationally diversified market timing may be appealing. As we noted earlier, the inclusion of additional assets can greatly increase the benefits of market timing.

It may be possible to construct good market-timing trading rules based on some relatively simple relationships. In "Market Timing with Imperfect Information" (1989), an article by R. G. Clarke, M. T. FitzGerald, P. Berent, and M. Statman, shows that some simple rules built around GNP may offer higher returns and lower risk than a buy-and-hold strategy. R. J. Fuller and J. L. Kling, in "Is the Stock Market Predictable?" (1990), examine the possibility that dividend yields may provide useful clues for market timing. (Interestingly, Sharpe himself is now selling market timing advice based on a relative-risk premium model.)

In the world of actual practice, Richard Fontaine, manager of the T. Rowe Price Capital Appreciation Fund, uses price-to-book value relationships to guide market-timing and sector rotation decisions. The fund has performed well compared to the S&P 500 since its 1986 inception.

Some market-timing newsletters have also experienced good performance. Mark Hulbert, editor of the *Hulbert Financial Digest*, which tracks newsletter recommendations, has identified five market-timing newsletters that beat the Wilshire 5000 index over a five-year period: *Investors' Intelligence*, *Fidelity Monitor*, *Systems and Forecasts*, *Telephone Switch*, and *Big Picture*. Dick Fabian's *Telephone Switch* has given some of the mutual funds fits with his abrupt buy-sell signals. In March 1990, roughly $40 million moved out and then back into Fidelity's Contra Fund over a four-day period based on Fabian's signals.

Some managers may be good at either market timing or stock selection, but not both. Peter Lynch, the highly successful manager of Fidelity's Magellan Fund for years, always concentrated on stock selection and avoided market timing. E. J. Weigel, in "The Performance of Tactical Asset Allocation" (1991), studied 17 investment managers and found an inverse relationship between market timing ability and other investment skills.

If the conclusions reached by G. L. Beebower and A. P. Varikooty in their 1991 article, "Measuring Market Timing Strategies," are correct, we may never know whether there are or are not any successful market timers. They show that most common statistical tests require extreme results to demonstrate statistically significant market timing ability. Managers beating the market by 2 percent per year over a lifetime or 1 percent per month for four years would qualify as certifiably good market timers.

CONCLUSION

After examining all the evidence, we are more encouraged than discouraged about market timing. The potential rewards are clearly quite attractive. The examination of optimal historical simulations points us strongly towards equity/T-Bill switches and a consideration of short positions.

Our review of market timing literature also leaves us in a bullish frame of mind. Although significant criticisms of market timing can be found, there are also many studies that demonstrate the theoretical possibility of succeeding at it. There also appear to be successful market timers out there in the market—and the ones who are *really* successful may not be talking.

11

Using GAs to Develop Investment Strategies

This chapter sets the stage for Chapters 12, 13, and 14, in which we explain why and how we have used GAs to develop specific investment strategies and present the actual results of our investigations. In this chapter we discuss the advantages of using GAs, our investment philosophy, back-testing, diversification and knowledge, trading rule portfolios, knowledge-based hedge portfolios, and the trading rule development process employed in the next three chapters.

WHY USE GAs?

Before answering the above question, we want to digress slightly and ask this one: Why use computers to develop investment trading systems? The answer is simple: Humans have limited cognitive ability. It's true that we do many things far better than machines, but we do have limits.

For example, humans can only process a limited number of relationships at any one time. Close your eyes and try to visualize a stack of bricks. How many separate bricks can you distinguish? Psychologists say that most people have a limit in the range of five to nine bricks. In a similar fashion, even grand master chess players can see only seven or so moves ahead during a game.

Computers, on the other hand, are good at keeping track of many relationships simultaneously. As an example, consider ten different variables. How many three-variable combinations are possible? The answer is 120. As humans, we might be able to get a firm mental grip on the ten variables and some of the possible pairings. But it would take us quite a long time to figure out all 120 combinations.

Therefore, it seems quite reasonable that computers should be highly useful in developing trading systems.

Another human weakness documented by psychologists is inconsistency in decision making. There has been increased interest in applying the results of research on this shortcoming to the process of investment management; we refer the interested reader to the works by P. Slovic et al. (1969, 1972) and R. Barach (1988) listed in the Bibliography. One way to avoid the pitfalls posed by this human failing is to use trading systems guided by carefully devised rules. Again, computers are potentially of great help.

There is certainly no shortage of quantitative approaches to investing. However, GAs offer several distinct advantages over other approaches: flexibility, speed, and ease of use. We will elaborate on all three of these points.

GAs are flexible because the user's imagination is probably the most limiting factor. We will present our method of using them to develop investment trading rules, but remember that it is just one out of many possible approaches. GAs can be used to develop either fundamentally based or technically based strategies. Because they are simply mathematical procedures, there is no particular investment philosophy tied to their use; GAs can be tailored to the user's preferences. And once the user has formulated the basic structure of an idea, endless variations are possible. From a computer implementation point of view, the only point where two separate problems differ is in the string interpretation and fitness calculation. GAs work on strings, and most of the GA procedure does not care what the strings represent.

Let's assume that we are using a GA to develop market timing trading rules and that our performance, or fitness, measure is the compound annual return earned in back-testing the rule over five years of historical data. What if we decide that returns during the past year are probably more important than returns from five years ago? We might decide to change our performance measure by making it a time-weighted return. With monthly data, five years represents 60 observations. The return from 60 months back might be given a weighting of 1, while the return from the past month might be given a weight of 60. Other months would be weighted using a linearly increasing scale from 1 to 60. With GAs, this type of change is easy to implement. The only part of the GA procedure that has to be changed is the performance calculation; everything else remains the same.

Potential variations surrounding the performance, or fitness, calculation are a key source of flexibility. In simple linear regression, for example, we try to minimize the sum of squared deviations around a line of best fit. What if we don't want squared deviations? What if we want to minimize the sum of the absolute value of cubed deviations? What if we want to time-weight the deviations? Or what if we want to minimize the sum of squared deviations, except that we are really worried about large deviations and want to take the absolute value of the cube of deviations beyond some value? That last change would introduce a complicated nonlinearity into the calculation. With GAs, it is easy to tailor the fitness calculation to the user's ideas, however complicated.

As we saw in Chapters 6 and 7, GAs are very swift. They are able to comb their way through large search spaces very quickly. With GAs we can attempt to develop trading rules that would be difficult to refine using traditional techniques. The speed of GAs makes them usable in a real-time trading environment. Our applications use monthly historical data, with monthly updating of trading rules possible. Although the size of the search space is very large, updated rules could be developed in hours or mere days. Other real-time trading applications might capitalize even more heavily on the speed of GAs.

One reason that GAs are easy to use is that they require minimal knowledge of the problem and problem solution techniques. For example, let's say the user has a portfolio optimization problem that could be solved using the XYZ method, but the user doesn't know that method. The problem might be solvable using GAs, provided the user can formulate a meaningful performance calculation. GAs try to find strings that yield optimal performance, so all that our XYZ-ignorant user has to do is correctly set up the problem in a general way; the GA will figure out how to actually do the optimization.

GAs are most easily used by someone with computer programming skills. Then when a change in the performance calculation is needed, it can be recoded by the user. However, good programmers could probably design and build a simple user interface that would allow the user to modify the GA without having to know anything about programming. GAs really are comparatively easy to use.

INVESTMENT PHILOSOPHY

Two basic alternative approaches to investing are market timing and security picking. Market timers, as described in Chapter 10, try to profit from well-timed movements into and out of various asset classes. Security pickers try to carefully choose individual stocks or bonds that are expected to perform better than average. It would be possible to use genetic algorithms for security selection. We have not done so (although we but have some ideas about how this might be accomplished), having instead chosen to concentrate on market timing applications. This decision was based on our own interests and also on convenience; our ideas about GAs and market timing have developed more quickly than our ideas about GAs and security selection.

The evidence concerning the effectiveness of market timing is mixed, as described in Chapter 10, but we lean towards the positive view. Investors pay attention to macroeconomic news to a lesser or greater degree, but presumably all investors are equally affected by economic developments. Even if they focus purely on security selection, the economic backdrop will probably color their thinking about the prospects of individual securities. U.S. companies all operate within the same legal, economic, and social environment, so we think it is reasonable to assume that careful analysis of macroeconomic conditions might lead to profitable market timing opportunities.

Basic finance and investments theory relates the value of stock to the prospects for associated dividend payments. If you buy stock, there are two possible monetary benefits: dividends and the resale value of your stock. The person who subsequently buys your stock has the same view; he or she is anticipating possible dividends and a future resale. From this chain of logic, we see that the value of any stock is strongly linked to the anticipated future dividend stream. The traditional methods of stock valuation differ primarily in their assumptions about the exact nature of this dividend stream. For example, will dividends grow at a constant rate, or will growth be "abnormally" high for a few years before settling down to a more normal growth rate?

Dividends ultimately depend on earnings. Higher earnings create the potential for greater dividends. Earnings are normally related to sales, and sales are primarily related to the health of the economy. Therefore, there is good reason to believe that macroeconomic news will affect the attractiveness of stocks as an investment.

However, this is not all of the story. Interest rates can be conceptually subdivided into three basic components: the real rate of interest, expected inflation, and a risk premium. Inflationary expectations are formed on the basis of various factors such as monetary growth, labor supply and demand, exchange rates, and governmental policies. For corporate and municipal bonds the default risk portion of the risk premium partially depends on the state of the economy. In tough times, the default risk becomes greater.

As interest rates react to economic news, the relative attractiveness of stocks and bonds changes. If interest rates go up, investors' required rates of return on stocks also rise, which affects the discounting of the future dividend stream. Dividends expected further into the future are perceived as less valuable. Bond values, which may depend in part on future coupon interest payments, are also adversely affected by rising interest rates. The changes in the relative valuation of stocks and bonds are subtle and not easy to predict, but it is clear that economic news is likely to have a significant impact.

Every trading system is based on assumptions. We approach the market primarily from a fundamental perspective; we believe that there are logical relationships between the economy, management decisions, and security prices. We place particular importance on macroeconomic variables. It seems reasonable to us that the monetary policy actions of the Federal Reserve and the fiscal policy actions of the federal government affect security prices.

In the United States, the bulk of our macroeconomic data is gathered, maintained, and distributed by the U.S. Department of Commerce (DOC); it publishes the monthly "Bible" of macroeconomic data, the *Survey of Current Business*, which is also accessible through the DOC's electronic economic bulletin board. The DOC provides monthly macroeconomic time series data on new housing starts, the consumer price index, manufacturers' new orders for durable goods, manufacturing and trade inventories, the capacity utilization rate, etc. These data, coupled with the historical return data from the 1992 *SBBI*, will provide the raw material for our construction of GA-based trading rules.

Our investigation of market timing trading rules uses what some might call technical analysis, but it is applied to fundamental variables. We examine relationships between the DOC macroeconomic time series data and security returns from both stocks and bonds. Our approach is technical in the sense that we do not prespecify the form of the relationships between the macroeconomic variables and security returns. We let the computer identify relationships that seem to be consistent.

We do not, however, recommend the mindless application of computer searches. When the computer finds what seems to be a consistent and tradable relationship between a macroeconomic variable or variables and security returns, it should be analyzed for reasonableness. For example, in some of our research we found a link between changes in the consumer price index in France and U.S. equity returns. Now it is possible that this is not a coincidence. Maybe French inflation has been a proxy for European business risk, and maybe events in Europe have presaged U.S. economic activity, but this seems like a stretch to us and not a relationship that we would want to bet on.

When examining many possible numerical relationships, there is always the risk of finding spurious correlations. Sure there may have been a strong statistical link between U.S. equity returns and some macroeconomic variable, but when you expand the number of variables under consideration, the combinatorial possibilities begin to explode. If you look at enough time series, you are almost bound to find at least one that will show a past numerical connection to security returns.

We don't feel comfortable betting on what may be spurious numerical connections between variables. So how is this prevented? One way is to attempt to build some robustness into the computations. We do this through a more complex fitness calculation and by diversifying across a portfolio of trading rules, limiting the impact of any one particular rule.

BACK-TESTING

Back-testing is using historical data to simulate how an investment strategy might have performed if it had been used in the past. There is a problem with this. If the strategy had actually been used, the trading activity that occurred in the past would have been different. Back-testers rely on the assumption that this interference would have been minimal and nonmaterial, essentially assuming that you are not playing this game with billion dollar bills. Chaos theory advocates might argue that even small changes in initial conditions can have large effects. Therefore, a different investment by even one small investor in the past might have led to significantly different results. We recognize these arguments but still feel that most reasonable investors would be more comfortable going forward with a strategy that looks good going backwards in time.

As a slight aside related to the above, George Soros, in his book, *The Alchemy of Finance* (New York: Simon and Schuster, 1987), describes what he calls the law of reflexivity:

> Instead of a determinate result, we have an interplay in which both the situation and the participants' views are dependent variables so that an initial change precipitates further changes both in the situation and in the participants' views. I call this interaction 'reflexivity', using the word as the French do when they describe a verb whose subject and object are the same.

Other complications when back-testing with strategies using macroeconomic data are data revisions and data availability issues. The DOC periodically revises historical data, correcting various problems. The data we are using now may not have been available in its present form during the actual dates of the back-testing period. Also, this data is released with lags; we have used the current lag timing. For example, February housing start data is typically available in April so that monthly trades based on this information could be implemented in May. We have not done an extensive check to verify that all current data availability lags are as they were during the back-testing period.

Another back-testing issue concerns trading costs and the accuracy of historical return data. We have used the *SBBI* historical return data, which is widely used in the industry. The common stock returns that are supposed to represent the S&P 500 index returns were probably achievable by large institutional investors but not by everyone. In addition, we have generally ignored the potential impact of trading costs.

Some researchers like to retain part of their data set to use as a "holdout sample test." For example, they might build trading rules by examining economic relationships over the 1984–1988 time period but then use data from the 1989–1991 time period as a holdout sample. The train of logic then would proceed along the following lines: "We built our rules using 1984–1988 data. What would have happened if we had then starting using these rules to guide investment decisions during the 1989–1991 time period? If the rules that were built using the earlier data continued to perform well in the holdout period, then the rules must be reasonably robust."

We disagree somewhat with the entire holdout sample concept, but we do it anyway; our problem with it concerns the notion of proof. If you believe in holdout testing, then essentially you are saying that you want a rule that performs well in the base period and in the holdout period. If this is true, why not just use the whole time period in your rule-building anyway? Regardless, we are going to forego our objection on this point and include holdout sample tests.

The notions of proof and truth are critical to the development of trading systems. The developer really needs to ask and answer several questions: What are my criteria for choosing a system? What do I consider to be adequate proof that a system seems to be working? Is past performance in any way related to future performance?

DIVERSIFICATION AND KNOWLEDGE

Practicing diversification is an admission of ignorance. Before we raise your eyebrows too high, we had best explain. Consider all the stocks that are included in the Standard and Poor's 500 stock index. In the next year, one of those stocks, and only one (ignoring a possible tie), will have the highest return of all 500 stocks. If you are clairvoyant or have a good forecasting system, then investing all your money in this one high-performing stock would lead to a higher ending wealth than investing in any other stock or portfolio of stocks. This one-stock portfolio would beat all the well-diversified portfolios.

If we can achieve higher wealth through a one-stock investment, then why has portfolio theory been so widely accepted? The answer goes back to our assumption about our own clairvoyance or knowledge; if we feel truly ignorant, then broad diversification makes sense. If we are confident about our ability to forecast, then we might select a more daring, less-diversified portfolio.

Indirectly, our portfolio decision relates to our notions of knowledge, truth, and proof. What does it take for us to be convinced that we have a fool-proof trading system? Some investors are easily convinced, and others have elaborate standards of proof. Do you need to see elaborate back-testing over long time periods before you are willing to invest based upon a certain rule or system? Or are you willing to accept only limited evidence? These are questions that every investor answers either explicitly or implicitly.

We can summarize by saying: If you think you're smart, go for it! If not, diversify.

PORTFOLIOS OF TRADING RULES

We think that genetic algorithms can be used to develop trading rules with a reasonable likelihood of doing well in the future. We repeat—*reasonable likelihood*. There is no sure thing. When we develop trading rules, we are developing a piece of logic that we think is true at least most of the time. We are developing an educated guess.

This leads to an interesting question: Should we aim to develop one really great trading rule, or should we diversify across a portfolio of rules? With normal diversification, the investor diversifies across assets, or stocks, but another way is to diversify across trading rules. If you have $50 to invest, then you invest $1 in each of 50 trading rules rather than betting all $50 on the performance of one rule.

We favor the portfolio of rules approach. Our results indicate that GAs can be used to tip the odds in your favor. But there is always risk; there is no sure thing. Rules that have worked well in the past sometimes cease to work well in subsequent time periods. Therefore, we have designed our searches to look for groups of attractive rules rather than one single, highly attractive rule. Few investors are confident (or foolish) enough to really put all their eggs into one basket.

KNOWLEDGE-BASED HEDGE PORTFOLIOS

In a hedge portfolio, partially or fully offsetting long and short positions are maintained simultaneously. For example, a hedge portfolio could be constructed around low and high price/earnings (P/E) stocks. The investor might go long, or buy, low P/E stocks while shorting, or selling, high P/E stocks in hopes that the low P/E stocks would outperform the high P/E stocks. If the dollar amounts of the long and short positions were equal, then the hedge portfolio would have a net investment of zero.

With a hedge portfolio, the investor tries to set up a zero dollar investment that yields a positive return. Let's say $10,000 is invested both long and short. Let's also assume that the low P/E portfolio earns 15 percent, while the high P/E portfolio earns 5 percent. The investor would then earn $1,500 on the long portfolio and lose $500 on the short portfolio. The net gain would be the difference in the two amounts, or $1,000.

Normally, hedge portfolios are constructed around groups of securities. Some securities are bought, others are sold. The net investment is zero; the long and short positions offset each other. However, another way of looking at hedge portfolios is to consider going long on good knowledge and going short on poor knowledge.

Assume that we have a trading rule, which we will call rule G, that tells us when to switch out of common stocks and into Treasury bills. Assume that rule G is correct 60 percent of the time. When rule G is wrong, we have invested in stocks when it is better to be in T-bills or vice versa. Assume that we have another trading rule, rule B, that is right only 40 percent of the time. Rule G is basically a good rule; rule B is basically a bad rule. We can create a knowledge-based hedge portfolio by going long with rule G and going short with rule B.

This may sound a bit strange. Table 11.1 should help clarify what we have in mind. It shows the hedge portfolio results for four investment scenarios in which common stocks outperform T-bills and four scenarios in which T-bills outperform common stocks. "In" indicates a signal to be "in" common stocks, while "Out" means the opposite (invest in Treasury bills). Consider scenario 7. The return on T-bills is +6 percent, but common stocks lose 3 percent. Rule G correctly says to be out of common stocks and be earning the T-bill return of 6 percent on $10,000, or $600. Rule B incorrectly advises to be in common stocks, but because this is a bad rule that we have shorted, we actually earn 3 percent, or $300, by shorting stocks. The return on the hedge portfolio is therefore 9 percent, or $900.

The logical question that quickly comes to mind is this: How much of a difference between good and bad rules do we need to make this concept of hedge portfolios interesting? To answer this question, we conducted a series of simulation experiments. The desired degrees of accuracy for the good rule and the bad rule were specified, and then a random number generator was used to create a series of trading decisions. We tested accuracy combinations going from 51/49 (51 percent accuracy for rule G, 49 percent for rule B) to 70/30, conducting a

Table 11.1 Hedge Portfolio Example: Terminal Wealth for
$10,000 Long and $10,000 Short

	Common Stock Return: +15% T-bill Return: +5%				Common Stock Return: −3% T-bill Return: +6%			
Rule G Signal	In		Out		In		Out	
Rule B Signal	In	Out	In	Out	In	Out	In	Out
Rule G Return	$1,500		$500		($300)		$600	
Rule B Return	$1,500	$500	$1,500	$500	($300)	$600	($300)	$600

Scenario	1	2	3	4	5	6	7	8
Hedge Portfolio Return	$0	$1,000	($1,000)	$0	$0	($900)	$900	$0

large number (250) of simulation trials for each accuracy combination. We also assumed a five-year test period for each simulation trial; as well, a five-year holding period for each trial was randomly selected over the 1967–1991 time period. Table 11.2 shows the results of these simulations. For each month, the maximum exposure was $10,000 invested long and $10,000 invested short. If the two rules both advocated the same investment action (either agreeing to be in the market or agreeing to be out of the market), then no investment action was taken. The third column shows the cumulative average return, or payoff (with no reinvestment), for each accuracy combination. These figures ignore transactions costs and assume that we can sell short at no cost. Because the net investment is zero in each period, rate of return calculations have no real meaning. A positive return is being generated with no net investment. A 60/40 predictive accuracy combination causes the results to become quite intriguing. With the hedge portfolio generating $4,333 on average, considerable costs could be incurred before the hedge portfolio would look unattractive.

RULE DEVELOPMENT PROCESS USED
IN CHAPTERS 12, 13, AND 14

In the next three chapters we present the results of our experiments using GAs to develop market timing trading rules. The format and structure of each chapter is similar; the only difference is the asset group being investigated. In Chapter

Table 11.2 Hedge Portfolio Simulation

Good Rule Accuracy	Bad Rule Accuracy	Average Cumulative Return
51%	49%	709
52%	48%	841
53%	47%	1,100
54%	46%	1,826
55%	45%	2,256
56%	44%	2,706
57%	43%	2,867
58%	42%	3,476
59%	41%	3,755
60%	40%	4,333
61%	39%	4,702
62%	38%	4,937
63%	37%	5,770
64%	36%	5,990
65%	35%	6,782
66%	34%	6,678
67%	33%	7,517
68%	32%	7,585
69%	31%	8,137
70%	30%	8,687
71%	29%	9,296
72%	28%	9,553
73%	27%	9,708
74%	26%	10,590
75%	25%	10,827

12, we develop market timing trading rules for the common stock/T-bill and small-firm stock/T-Bill switching decisions. In Chapter 13, we look at the Treasury bond/T-Bill and Treasury bond/corporate bond switching decisions. In Chapter 14, we explore switching between individual stocks and Treasury bills. We used the 1984–1988 time period to develop our trading rules, keeping the 1989–1991 period as a holdout testing period. The basic steps we followed are described below.

1. Examine correlations over the 1984–1988 period.

Our macroeconomic data base contains 167 different time series, which is a large set of variables to choose from. The situation gets even more complex when you consider the possibility of examining changes in the basic series. We felt that the monthly housing starts time series might have a less important linkage to monthly stock returns than changes in that series. Therefore, we also wanted to investigate 1- , 3- , and 12-month changes in each of the 167 different time series. The problem is this: How do you narrow this set down to a small, manageable number of variables?

To narrow the variable list in our search for attractive common stock timing rules, we ran regressions of all 167 different times series and the changes in these series against the monthly stock return series. The appropriate data availability lags were always considered. For example, February housing starts were linked with May stock returns due to the data availability lag. Next, we examined the regression runs and narrowed the list of variables down to the ten data series having the highest correlation with the asset series being considered, such as common stock returns.

It seems logical as a starting point to work with series that are basically correlated with the asset returns you are interested in. However, this procedure does implicitly assume that these correlations are likely to persist into the future. The relationship could change, but we are trying to gently play the odds, hoping that past patterns will persist, at least for the near future.

This procedure also opens us up to criticism about using counterintuitive or nonsensical relationships. An alternative approach would be to use economic theory, judgment, or the results from other studies to guide variable selection. One could, for example, try to use a set of variables patterned after the relationships described in John J. Murphy's book, *Intermarket Technical Analysis* (New York: John Wiley & Sons, 1991). We have performed some experiments along these lines and have not been satisfied with the results. In addition, we are trying to let the computer and numbers guide our decisions as much as possible, even if these decisions seem to go against our own logic at times. There is no reason why you could not select your own set of ten variables in this step and then proceed as we will now describe.

2. Create a string representation similar to that used in Chapter 7.

If we select three out of the ten possible variables, then we have created a situation similar to the one we studied in Chapter 7. We can then create a string identical in length and format to the one described there. Again, we investigate 64 different logical relationships between the variables in an attempt to find attractive rules of the following form:

> IF the one-month change in housing starts is LESS THAN X, AND the 12-month change in M1 is LESS THAN Y, AND the Treasury bill rate is GREATER THAN Z, THEN invest in common stocks.

> IF NOT, THEN invest in Treasury bills.

3. Use a performance calculation that projects future return performance.

In Chapter 7, we used a relatively simple fitness calculation that used the average annual return over a five-year period as the fitness value. The underlying assumption was that rules that performed well during the test period would perform well in the future. Now we wish to complicate things a bit more. Instead of just looking at the return over the five-year period, we are going to look at the pattern of the five-year moving average of five-year returns. Say what? Consider the five-year annual return for a particular rule as of January 1984. To calculate this, we compute the average annual return (for the trading rule being examined) over the February 1979–January 1984 time period. For February 1984, we use the return over March 1979–February 1984. In this fashion, we create a list of 60 five-year average annual return figures stretching over the 1984–1988 period.

The ideal situation would be to have a rule with consistently good, continually improving performance over the five-year period. If we visualize a plot of this pattern, we would see a group of points that seem to form a good fit about an upward-sloping line. The performance measure that we will report in Chapters 12–14 is based on such an approach. However, the specific details of its calculation are proprietary.

4. Conduct 240 GA runs, two for each of the 120 three-variable combinations.

With ten variables to choose from, we can create 120 different three-variable rules. We can also search for either good or bad rules and try to maximize or minimize performance. We do both by running two GA optimizations for all 120 combinations. In the first run, we try to maximize projected future returns for the trading rule under examination. In the second run, we try to minimize future performance. In short, we try to find 120 good trading rules and 120 bad trading rules.

5. Create a hedge portfolio from the rules identified in step 4.

Finally, we take the rules uncovered in step 4 and create a hedge portfolio as described earlier in this chapter. Essentially we go long with the good rules and go short with the bad rules. Ignoring transactions costs, this portfolio uses no net wealth. If there is no difference in performance between the two sets of rules, then the return on the hedge portfolio should on average be zero. If the good rules generally outperform the bad rules, then the hedge portfolio will generate a positive return.

12
Stock Market Results

In this chapter we really begin to apply our GA methods in earnest, starting with the search for attractive equity index timing rules. We also examine equity timing rules in Chapter 14, but for individual stocks. We examine bond market timing rules in Chapter 13. All three chapters have similar formats.

As we explained in Chapter 11, we had to find a way to limit the scope of our macroeconomic data base, which contained 167 different monthly time series for the period under consideration, so that we would be able to work with a small, manageable number of variables. To make matters more complex, we also considered changes in the various constituent series: 1- , 3- , and 12-month changes were investigated.

We chose to narrow the set of variables sharply by only considering series that showed high correlations with stock returns of the recent past, regressing the various macroeconomic time series and changes in them, which were adjusted for data availability lags, against the excess return of S&P stocks over Treasury bills over the 1984–1988 time period. For example, the January housing start numbers may not be available until March; therefore, a monthly trading decision based on these data might not be implemented until April. In cases like this, we would use the January housing start data against the April stock return data in our regression.

VARIABLE SELECTION FOR THE S&P/T-BILL TIMING DECISION

The results of our regression runs for the excess S&P returns, which are summarized in Table 12.1, have been sorted based on the absolute value of the correlation coefficient. (Note: the series description is shown exactly as it appears in the Department of Commerce data, but it has been truncated.) Only the 50 highest

127

correlations are reported. The series most highly correlated with the S&P returns over the 1984–1988 time period was three-month changes in the industrial production index for nondurable manufacturing; the correlation coefficient was − 0.3862, which, if squared, gives us an r-squared value that tells us how much of the variation in stock returns is "explained" by the changes in industrial production—in this case, 14.9 percent. This may sound low, but it is actually pretty good. Stock returns are extremely noisy. Market forecasters would surely agree that variations in returns are difficult to explain; forecasting the behavior of the stock market is an exceptionally challenging task.

The correlations in Table 12.1 are interesting and somewhat counterintuitive. For example, positive changes in industrial production are linked to negative stock returns and vice versa. As the economy improves, stocks tend to do worse. An examination of the other variables leads to the following conclusion: stocks tend to do better when labor cost goes up, capacity utilization goes down, unemployment goes up, or inflation is accelerating. The linkages here seem to have a contrarian bent. Contrarians go against the flow, betting on reversals of previous patterns.

Insights into many stock strategies can be gained by considering the pendulum on a grandfather clock. When the pendulum has passed the center point and is swinging out, it will continue until it reaches a point of reversal. Many stock strategies can be simply classified as "go with the flow" or "it's time for a reversal." For example, if you choose to invest in companies with sustained earnings increases, you are going with the flow. You think the pendulum will keep swinging out; success tends to breed success. If you buy only low P/E stocks, then you are betting on a reversal. The stock is cheap, which suggests that the pendulum has swung as far as it can go and is about to move back toward higher prices. Many of the linkages in Table 12.1 seem to point towards a reversal effect: Bad economic news is good for stocks; good news is bad news.

We chose ten of the top eleven series for further investigation; these are shown in boldface. The series ranked eighth was not chosen because it was quite similar to the series ranked first (both involved three-month changes in industrial production). A major potential weakness of this selection method is that we did not consider possible high correlations among the group of ten series. For example, changes in industrial production are probably highly correlated with changes in capacity utilization. If this is true, then the extra predictive value of combining changes in capacity utilization with changes in industrial production in some type of stock forecasting system may be minimal. This point is discussed further in Chapter 15.

We felt reasonably comfortable with our top ten list. We chose not to cast too much judgment on the underlying economic rationale of the relationships, but we did feel that the list contained mostly common sense variables. It seemed reasonable to us that stock returns would be influenced by inflation, unemployment, and production levels.

Table 12.1 Correlations with S&P Returns

	Series Number	Differencing Interval	Series Description	Correlation Coefficient
1	71	3	74. Industrial production, nondurable manufactures (1	− 0.3862
2	61	3	62a. Index of labor cost per unit of output, mfg. (1987 =	0.3659
3	251	3	(23) Spot price, lead scrap ($ per lb.) COPYRIGHTED (C	− 0.3565
4	234	3	952. Diffusion index of lagging indicators, 1-mo. span (pc	0.3422
5	77	3	82. Capacity utilization rate, manufacturing (pct.)	− 0.3342
6	42	3	45. Average weekly insured unemployment rate (pct.)	0.3169
7	225	12	920c. Coincident index, change over 3-mo. span (AR, pc	− 0.3150
8	72	3	75. Industrial production, consumer goods (1987 = 100)	− 0.3121
9	228	1	930c. Lagging index, change over 3-mo. span (AR, pct.)	0.3054
10	61	0	62a. Index of labor cost per unit of output, mfg.(1987 =	0.3047
11	141	3	323c. Change in CPI-U, less food & energy, 1-mo. span (pct	0.2986
12	229	3	940. Ratio, coincident index to lagging index (1982 = 100)	− 0.2871
13	197	3	733. Canada, consumer price index, NSA (1982-84 = 100)	− 0.2862
14	239	1	(98) Producer Price Index, lumber and wood products (19	− 0.2806
15	92	3	93. Free reserves, NSA (mil. $)	− 0.2699
16	63	0	62. Smoothed change in labor cost per unit output, mfg. (pc	0.2677
17	145	1	331c. Change in PPI, crude materials, 6-mo. span (AR, pct.	0.2651
18	246	3	(98) Producer Price Index, nonferrous scrap, NSA (1982 =	− 0.2626
19	89	1	92a. Mfrs' unfilled orders, durable goods indus. (bil. 1982	− 0.2624
20	88	0	92b. Change in mfrs.' unfilled orders, durables (bil. 1982	− 0.2623
21	223	3	920. Composite index of four coincident indicators (1982 =	− 0.2620
22	252	1	(23) Spot price, steel scrap ($ per ton) COPYRIGHTED (CRB	0.2610
23	225	0	920c. Coincident index, change over 3-mo. span (AR, pct.)	− 0.2561
24	210	1	746. France, stock prices, NSA (1967 = 100)	− 0.2523
25	229	0	940. Ratio, coincident index to lagging index (1982 = 100)	− 0.2511
26	110	1	108. Ratio, personal income to money supply M2 (ratio)	− 0.2501
27	125	12	120b. Change in CPI for services (AR, pct.)	− 0.2495
28	193	12	727. Italy, industrial production (1987 = 100)	− 0.2474
29	250	1	(23) Spot price, copper scrap ($ per lb.) COPYRIGHTED (CR	− 0.2437
30	63	3	62. Smoothed change in labor cost per unit output, mfg. (p	0.2432
31	179	3	602. Exports, excluding military aid shipments (mil. $)	− 0.2420
32	265	3	992. Experimental coincident index—modified methodo	− 0.2418
33	229	12	940. Ratio, coincident index to lagging index (1982 = 100)	− 0.2417
34	174	1	525. Defense Department prime contract awards in U.S. (m	− 0.2406
35	225	1	920c. Coincident index, change over 3-mo. span (AR, pct.)	− 0.2405
36	254	3	(23) Spot price, zinc, NSA ($ per lb.) COPYRIGHTED (CRB	− 0.2400
37	192	1	726. France, industrial production (1987 = 100)	− 0.2396
38	208	12	743. Canada, stock prices, NSA (1967 = 100)	− 0.2377
39	245	1	(98) Producer Price Index, aluminum base scrap (1982 = 1	− 0.2367
40	23	12	23. Spot prices, raw materials, NSA (1967 = 100) COPYR	− 0.2400
41	103	1	101. Commercial and industrial loans outstanding (mil. 198	0.2336
42	188	1	721. OECD, European countries, industrial production (198	− 0.2322
43	88	12	92b. Change in mfrs' unfilled orders, durables (bil. 1982 $)	− 0.2313
44	44	3	47. Index of industrial production (1987 = 100)	− 0.2294
45	90	1	92. Smoothed change in mfrs.' unfilled orders (bil. 1982 $)	− 0.2289
46	90	0	92. Smoothed change in mfrs.' unfilled orders (bil. 1982 $)	− 0.2284
47	18	1	19. United States, index of stock prices, NSA (1967 = 100)	− 0.2273
48	16	1	19. Index of stock prices, 500 common stocks, NSA (1941-	− 0.2273
49	150	12	333c. Change in PPI, capital equipment, 1-mo. span (pct.)	− 0.2269
50	106	3	105. Money supply M1 (bil. 1982 $)	0.2263

"GOOD" FORECASTING RULES FOR S&P STOCKS

With our list of ten variables, we next explored the 120 possible three-way combination rules that could be developed from this list, allowing for the possibility of eight different logical relationships and eight different greater than/less than relationships as outlined in Chapter 11. The range of cutoff values for each series was partitioned into 32 possible subintervals, as was also explained in that chapter.

We ran only one trial of the genetic algorithm for each of the possible three-way variable combinations, which means that we probably did not find the optimal (based on historical performance) rule parameters for each set of variables. This point will be addressed further in Chapter 15.

The list of 120 "good" rules is shown in Table 12.2. The rules are labeled as good because the GA's fitness calculation was structured to look for rules that had the best five-year moving average performance over the past five years, a procedure that is also explained in Chapter 11.

Reading Table 12.2 takes some effort; the rule structure is reasonably complicated and not easily summarized. We have tried our best to keep things as simple as possible. Really. Consider the first line in the table. This rule is based on the three-month changes in series numbers 71, 61, and 251, which can be seen from the six far right columns; these are the first three series chosen from Table 12.1. The underlying series relate to industrial production, labor costs, and the price of lead scrap. The fitness value of 1.7349 means that the GA calculated the projected five-year monthly moving average return of this rule to be 1.7349 percent. The cutoff values for the three series are 20, 13, and 13, respectively. Consider the value of 20 for series 1 and picture the 1984–1988 range of values for three-month changes in series 71 (which is based on industrial production). These numbers would have some range of values. Now consider breaking up this range into 32 equally spaced intervals. The value of 20 means that the critical point for trading decisions is at 20/32 of the range, so for any given month, to decide whether or not to invest in stocks, we must ask: "Are we above or below that 20/32 point?" Obviously, we need to know if we are more concerned about being above or below that point, which is where the greater than/less than (labeled $>/<$ in Table 12.2) comes into play.

Tables 12.3 and 12.4 allow us to decipher the greater than/less than codes and the logic codes. We will tackle both for rule 1, which we have been discussing. The logic code is 4, and the greater than/less than code is 3, which can be found in the first two columns of Table 12.3. From Table 12.4, we see that these codes correspond to:

> If (the change in series 71 is less than its cutoff value AND the change in series 61 is greater than its cutoff value) OR (the change in series 251 is less than its cutoff value), THEN invest in stocks.

The cutoff values of 20, 13, and 13 correspond very roughly to breakpoints at the two-thirds and one-third points of the range of historical values, respectively,

Table 12.2 Good Rules—S&P 500 Stocks

Rule #	Logic Code	)/(Code	Series 1	Series 2	Series 3	Fitness	1 #	Diff.	2 #	Diff.	3 #	Diff.
				Cutoff Values					Series Number and Differencing Interval			
1	4	3	20	13	13	1.7349	71	3	61	3	251	3
2	1	2	22	29	9	1.8468	71	3	61	3	234	3
3	1	3	17	16	16	1.8760	71	3	61	3	77	3
4	1	4	20	13	10	1.8463	71	3	61	3	42	3
5	7	2	4	12	14	1.9541	71	3	61	3	225	12
6	3	4	16	24	15	1.8827	71	3	61	3	228	1
7	7	4	14	13	22	1.9618	71	3	61	3	61	0
8	7	4	14	16	10	1.7987	71	3	61	3	141	3
9	2	4	16	10	22	1.8466	71	3	251	3	234	3
10	5	3	16	20	16	1.8892	71	3	251	3	77	3
11	6	3	20	16	6	1.7938	71	3	251	3	42	3
12	3	1	20	16	17	1.9009	71	3	251	3	225	12
13	2	4	15	19	21	1.7703	71	3	251	3	228	1
14	8	2	14	13	22	1.7803	71	3	251	3	61	0
15	3	4	20	13	3	1.7299	71	3	251	3	141	3
16	5	3	5	8	16	1.9571	71	3	234	3	77	3
17	2	4	16	15	11	1.8376	71	3	234	3	42	3
18	7	2	4	10	16	1.9551	71	3	234	3	225	12
19	6	4	16	22	13	2.0387	71	3	234	3	228	1
20	2	4	14	9	22	1.8773	71	3	234	3	61	0
21	2	4	16	23	7	1.8466	71	3	234	3	141	3
22	3	2	20	16	25	1.8517	71	3	77	3	42	3
23	7	5	11	16	20	1.8654	71	3	77	3	225	12
24	1	2	21	16	13	2.0670	71	3	77	3	228	1
25	5	6	18	16	7	1.8682	71	3	77	3	61	0
26	4	2	20	16	28	1.8566	71	3	77	3	141	3
27	1	3	20	10	25	1.8348	71	3	42	3	225	12
28	5	4	16	12	13	1.9267	71	3	42	3	228	1
29	4	4	21	9	22	1.7840	71	3	42	3	61	0
30	8	4	16	23	27	1.7737	71	3	42	3	141	3
31	2	2	5	14	13	2.0065	71	3	225	12	228	1
32	3	2	20	17	24	1.8794	71	3	225	12	61	0
33	7	7	3	17	3	1.7976	71	3	225	12	141	3
34	2	4	16	16	22	1.8193	71	3	228	1	61	0
35	7	2	16	13	1	1.8504	71	3	228	1	141	3
36	6	4	19	26	9	1.8214	71	3	61	0	141	3
37	4	6	14	18	22	1.8920	61	3	251	3	234	3
38	5	7	14	19	16	1.9957	61	3	251	3	77	3
39	3	6	16	18	18	1.8070	61	3	251	3	42	3
40	6	5	12	16	17	1.9304	61	3	251	3	225	12
41	7	3	10	21	13	1.8739	61	3	251	3	228	1
42	3	6	13	17	6	1.7817	61	3	251	3	61	0
43	7	7	13	21	22	1.7662	61	3	251	3	141	3
44	2	7	22	9	19	2.0114	61	3	234	3	77	3
45	6	8	16	23	6	1.8719	61	3	234	3	42	3
46	1	7	12	10	14	1.9132	61	3	234	3	225	12

Continued on next page

Table 12.2 *(continued)*

Rule #	Logic Code	)/(Code	Cutoff Value			Fitness	Series Number & Differencing Interval					
			Series 1	Series 2	Series 3		1		2		3	
							#	Diff	#	Diff	#	Diff
47	2	8	20	11	21	1.7818	61	3	234	3	228	1
48	5	8	22	11	7	1.8679	61	3	234	3	61	0
49	8	8	22	23	19	1.8839	61	3	234	3	141	3
50	7	5	13	16	14	1.9778	61	3	77	3	42	3
51	7	7	13	16	19	1.9413	61	3	77	3	225	12
52	2	6	26	16	13	2.0829	61	3	77	3	228	1
53	7	5	16	16	20	1.9148	61	3	77	3	61	0
54	4	6	12	16	27	1.9239	61	3	77	3	141	3
55	3	7	12	26	14	1.8662	61	3	42	3	225	12
56	4	8	20	8	21	1.8809	61	3	42	3	228	1
57	4	8	16	9	27	1.8516	61	3	42	3	61	0
58	2	6	19	14	13	1.7753	61	3	42	3	141	3
59	1	6	5	17	13	2.0386	61	3	225	12	228	1
60	7	5	14	17	20	1.9399	61	3	225	12	61	0
61	7	7	16	23	22	1.8799	61	3	225	12	141	3
62	7	8	19	13	22	1.8577	61	3	228	1	61	0
63	7	8	13	13	28	1.7530	61	3	228	1	141	3
64	2	8	19	12	16	1.7515	61	3	61	0	141	3
65	4	3	14	22	16	1.8367	251	3	234	3	77	3
66	7	4	16	8	10	1.8316	251	3	234	3	42	3
67	2	3	16	7	17	1.9273	251	3	234	3	225	12
68	4	4	18	8	21	1.8656	251	3	234	3	228	1
69	7	4	18	8	6	1.8384	251	3	234	3	61	0
70	1	4	21	9	6	1.8288	251	3	234	3	141	3
71	7	5	5	16	30	1.8718	251	3	77	3	42	3
72	7	1	16	16	25	1.8610	251	3	77	3	225	12
73	5	2	13	16	13	2.0876	251	3	77	3	228	1
74	6	7	19	16	24	1.8327	251	3	77	3	61	0
75	2	1	14	16	25	1.8726	251	3	77	3	141	3
76	2	3	16	8	17	1.8403	251	3	42	3	225	12
77	5	4	16	7	13	1.9042	251	3	42	3	228	1
78	2	4	17	9	7	1.7684	251	3	42	3	61	0
79	6	4	21	15	12	1.7968	251	3	42	3	141	3
80	2	2	1	14	13	1.9726	251	3	225	12	228	1
81	4	6	12	17	20	1.8847	251	3	225	12	61	0
82	6	3	21	14	10	1.8377	251	3	225	12	141	3
83	7	4	17	12	18	1.9282	251	3	228	1	61	0
84	2	4	18	20	10	1.8319	251	3	228	1	141	3
85	6	4	21	17	6	1.8035	251	3	61	0	141	3
86	4	6	6	16	28	1.9154	234	3	77	3	42	3
87	4	5	9	16	5	1.9480	234	3	77	3	225	12
88	2	6	31	16	13	2.0934	234	3	77	3	228	1
89	7	5	8	16	13	2.0038	234	3	77	3	61	0
90	1	5	8	16	25	1.9447	234	3	77	3	141	3
91	3	7	9	27	17	1.8894	234	3	42	3	225	12
92	2	8	22	8	13	1.8747	234	3	42	3	228	1

Continued on next page

Table 12.2 *(continued)*

Rule #	Logic Code	)/(Code	Cutoff Value Series 1	Cutoff Value Series 2	Cutoff Value Series 3	Fitness	1 #	1 Diff	2 #	2 Diff	3 #	3 Diff
93	1	8	9	6	5	1.8852	234	3	42	3	61	0
94	3	8	8	12	11	1.8201	234	3	42	3	141	3
95	7	7	17	17	13	2.0049	234	3	225	12	228	1
96	3	6	9	17	24	2.0094	234	3	225	12	61	0
97	3	5	8	17	1	1.8894	234	3	225	12	141	3
98	5	8	22	12	6	1.8690	234	3	228	1	61	0
99	3	6	10	17	9	1.7847	234	3	228	1	141	3
100	3	8	8	22	9	1.8505	234	3	61	0	141	3
101	2	1	16	17	13	1.8209	77	3	42	3	225	12
102	5	4	16	24	13	2.0635	77	3	42	3	228	1
103	4	2	19	27	24	1.8880	77	3	42	3	61	0
104	3	4	16	6	8	1.8312	77	3	42	3	141	3
105	3	4	16	15	13	2.1165	77	3	225	12	228	1
106	6	3	16	13	2	1.8588	77	3	225	12	61	0
107	6	1	16	6	24	1.8940	77	3	225	12	141	3
108	3	4	16	13	30	2.1430	77	3	228	1	61	0
109	2	2	16	13	8	1.8606	77	3	228	1	141	3
110	6	4	19	24	3	1.9334	77	3	61	0	141	3
111	1	6	6	17	13	2.0390	42	3	225	12	228	1
112	6	3	25	17	24	1.8173	42	3	225	12	61	0
113	3	5	6	17	13	1.7900	42	3	225	12	141	3
114	7	8	8	13	20	1.9362	42	3	228	1	61	0
115	7	8	11	13	12	1.8977	42	3	228	1	141	3
116	6	8	9	20	8	1.7874	42	3	61	0	141	3
117	4	4	15	13	27	2.0906	225	12	228	1	61	0
118	1	4	14	13	0	1.9726	225	12	228	1	141	3
119	6	2	14	24	24	1.7853	225	12	61	0	141	3
120	3	8	12	18	12	1.8834	228	1	61	0	141	3

Table 12.3   Logic Codes

Logic Code	Invest in the S&P IF
1	Condition1 OR (Condition2 AND Condition3)
2	Condition1 AND (Condition2 OR Condition3)
3	(Condition1 OR Condition2) AND Condition3
4	(Condition1 AND Condition2) OR Condition3
5	(Condition1 OR Condition3) AND Condition2
6	(Condition1 AND Condition3) OR Condition2
7	Condition1 OR Condition2 OR Condition3
8	Condition1 AND Condition2 AND Condition3

Table 12.4   Greater Than/Less Than Codes

>/< Code	Series 1 Relationship	Series 2 Relationship	Series 3 Relationship
1	<	<	<
2	<	<	>
3	<	>	<
4	<	>	>
5	>	<	<
6	>	<	>
7	>	>	<
8	>	>	>

because 20 is roughly two-thirds of 32 and 13 is roughly one-third of 32. We realize we are doing some crude "ballparking" of numbers here; the purpose is to put the rule into a form that's easier to grasp.

Therefore, a rough translation of the rule might be as follows:

IF (the three-month change in industrial production is in the lower two-thirds of its historical range AND the three-month change in labor costs is in the upper two-thirds of its range) OR (the three-month change in the price of lead scrap is in the bottom third of its range) THEN invest in stocks. IF NOT, THEN invest in Treasury bills.

Whew! We know that is cumbersome. Fortunately, we are not as concerned with the specifics of given rules as we are with the performance of the entire group of 120 rules.

However, before we move on, there are some interesting observations from the details in Table 12.2. If you scan down the list of logic codes for the 120 rules, you will see that all eight possible values show up. The distribution is not heavily skewed, except that logic code 8 only shows up a few times. Similarly, all eight possible greater than/less than codes appear in the Table 12.3. However, there are few 1s and quite a few 4s. The fact that all eight codes do appear in both cases lends support to their use. A more restrictive approach might not uncover some of these relationships. The 64 different possible combinations associated with the two codes form a rich set of rules to explore.

The distribution of cutoff values also appears to be reasonable. In most cases, the values represent numbers in the middle two quartiles of the range. Often the cutoff is near the midpoint of the range, which says that what is most important is merely whether or not the series is in the upper or lower half of its historical range.

The range of fitness values is fairly great. Some rules have fitness values over 2.1, while the lowest have values under 1.8. Because these represent projected five-year monthly moving average returns, this is a substantial range. One reason for this large spread may be the fact that only one trial of the GA was performed for each variable combination. If the best of, say, five trials was used, the spread of fitness values might narrow.

PERFORMANCE OF THE GOOD RULES

The trends in performance of the good rule portfolio are summarized in Figures 12.1 and 12.2. The percentage of correct calls, shown in Figure 12.1, generally trends upward over the rule-building period and into the holdout period, but there are several up and down periods. By 1988, the percentage of correct calls was nearing 60 percent. The average return graph in Figure 12.2 shows a similar pattern. Figures 12.3 and 12.4 display the same information but over a shorter time period, focusing on the holdout period results. The percentage of correct calls remained high into 1990, before starting a downward drift. Average return peaked in the middle of 1989 and then began to decline.

The individual performance of all 120 good rules is shown in Table 12.5. The columns show the average annual return and the percentage of correct calls for each rule for four different time periods. The rules were built using data from the 1984–1988 time period; the performance over the 1971–1983 period is shown only for comparison. The holdout period was 1989–1991, and results for that entire period are shown in the last two columns. The results for 1989 are shown separately, because this represents the first year of the three-year holdout period.

The average percentage accuracy of the good rule portfolio dropped sharply during the holdout period. During the rule-building period, the rules were making correct calls 61.6 percent of the time, and the average annual return was 21.96

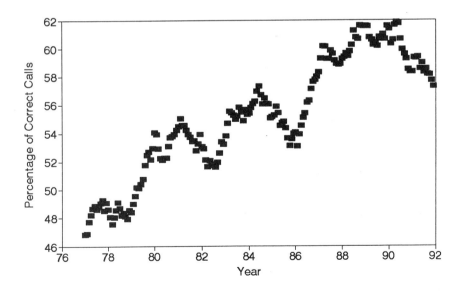

FIGURE 12.1   Percentage Correct Calls (S&P—Good Rules) 1977–1991

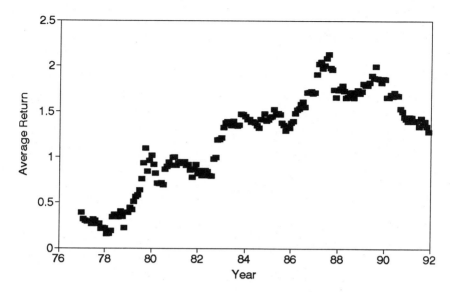

FIGURE 12.2   Average Return (S&P—Good Rules) 1977–1991

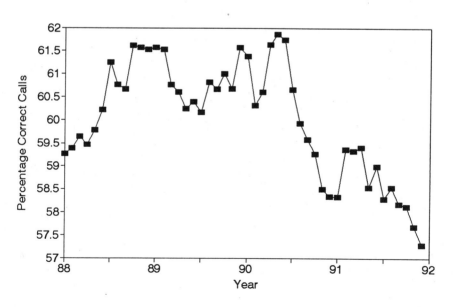

FIGURE 12.3   Percentage Correct Calls (S&P—Good Rules) 1988–1991

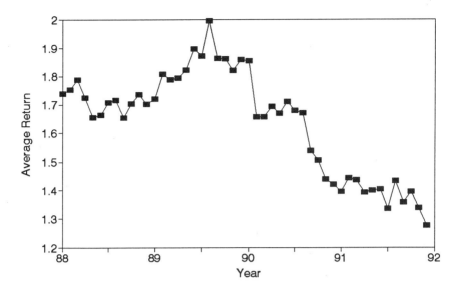

FIGURE 12.4 Average Return (S&P—Good Rules) 1988–1991

percent. During the 1989 holdout year, the accuracy of calls declined to 21.96 percent, but the average return was 22.74 percent. For the entire 1989–1991 holdout period, the accuracy was 53.06 percent, and the average annual return was 14.96 percent—less than that of a buy-and-hold strategy, which would have earned a 18.46 percent average annual return over the same period.

These results seem somewhat disappointing. However, there are two additional factors to consider. First, we are ultimately going to look at a hedge portfolio that mixes two rule portfolios with contrasting performance. We are primarily interested in the difference in performance between the two rule portfolios, not how each portfolio does individually. Second, we must consider risk. A buy-and-hold strategy exposes the investor to equity market risk 12 months of the year. Our rule portfolio signals when to be in and when to be out of the market. The 14.96 percent average annual return involved an average annual equity market exposure of about 8 months, so this portfolio earned 81 percent (14.96/18.46) as much as the buy-and-hold strategy but had only 75 percent (8/12) as much risk.

"BAD" FORECASTING RULES FOR S&P STOCKS

The "bad" forecasting rules for S&P stocks are detailed in Table 12.6. Let's decode the rule with the highest fitness (the worst rule of the 120): rule 65. The fitness value is 12.2547, which means that the projected monthly moving average return is −2.2547 percent. The logic code and greater than code are 4 and 5, respectively. The rule relates to three-month changes in series 251, 234, and 77;

Table 12.5 Performance Summary—Good Rules—S&P 500 Stocks

Rule #	Fitness	1971–1983 Period		1984–1988 Period		1989		1989–1991 Period	
		% Correct	Average Return	% Correct	Average Return	% Correct	Average Return	% Correct	Average Return
1	1.7349	50.00	8.61	58.33	17.59	66.67	31.50	61.11	16.96
2	1.8468	50.69	8.02	61.67	20.83	58.33	19.30	58.33	14.06
3	1.8760	51.39	8.10	43.33	7.10	33.33	8.40	41.67	7.26
4	1.8463	50.00	8.81	65.00	25.99	66.67	27.20	61.11	15.73
5	1.9541	54.17	10.42	51.67	10.64	41.67	9.70	44.44	5.22
6	1.8827	50.69	7.51	63.33	23.54	50.00	23.60	55.56	14.62
7	1.9618	53.47	9.95	58.33	21.79	50.00	21.20	52.78	10.66
8	1.7987	47.92	8.52	63.33	24.62	58.33	25.70	61.11	16.50
9	1.8466	50.69	8.23	58.33	14.95	66.67	31.50	58.33	16.59
10	1.8892	59.03	12.48	56.67	14.66	25.00	12.50	41.67	8.12
11	1.7938	50.00	8.73	63.33	25.91	58.33	25.90	55.56	16.74
12	1.9009	54.17	10.16	60.00	19.95	25.00	12.50	41.67	8.44
13	1.7703	50.00	7.38	51.67	13.75	66.67	31.50	55.56	16.32
14	1.7803	52.08	7.59	51.67	11.38	58.33	27.40	52.78	16.50
15	1.7299	48.61	8.59	61.67	24.21	58.33	25.90	50.00	11.76
16	1.9571	54.17	8.38	48.33	8.62	66.67	26.50	52.78	10.41
17	1.8376	49.31	8.78	60.00	25.17	50.00	23.80	55.56	16.91
18	1.9551	53.47	9.23	51.67	9.70	66.67	26.50	55.56	12.79
19	2.0387	46.53	8.04	70.00	26.40	33.33	12.30	44.44	8.97
20	1.8773	52.08	7.82	58.33	23.87	41.67	20.00	50.00	12.74
21	1.8466	51.39	8.58	65.00	27.14	50.00	23.80	55.56	14.62
22	1.8517	53.47	9.15	63.33	25.59	58.33	25.90	55.56	14.93
23	1.8654	52.78	8.75	65.00	26.25	58.33	25.90	58.33	19.00
24	2.0670	50.00	7.80	50.00	15.02	41.67	10.20	38.89	7.12
25	1.8682	46.53	6.29	56.67	13.01	58.33	31.40	47.22	15.85
26	1.8566	51.39	8.97	66.67	28.22	58.33	25.90	55.56	14.93
27	1.8348	49.31	5.56	66.67	28.27	66.67	27.50	52.78	10.90
28	1.9267	54.86	8.71	60.00	18.99	66.67	31.50	55.56	18.09
29	1.7840	51.39	7.26	66.67	26.85	66.67	31.50	58.33	16.59
30	1.7737	50.00	7.32	63.33	26.30	58.33	29.30	55.56	15.95
31	2.0065	54.17	11.64	53.33	12.88	25.00	5.10	38.89	4.40
32	1.8794	48.61	7.92	65.00	25.94	58.33	25.90	58.33	15.33
33	1.7976	44.44	6.31	63.33	25.79	66.67	31.50	61.11	17.49
34	1.8193	52.08	9.10	61.67	26.34	58.33	29.30	58.33	18.64
35	1.8504	51.39	8.63	73.33	28.06	33.33	12.80	47.22	12.35
36	1.8214	47.22	8.11	58.33	22.71	58.33	25.90	55.56	16.74
37	1.8920	50.69	9.01	58.33	15.12	41.67	19.40	55.56	16.03
38	1.9957	61.81	14.42	56.67	14.66	25.00	12.40	41.67	10.22
39	1.8070	47.92	8.52	63.33	24.62	58.33	25.70	61.11	16.50
40	1.9304	54.86	10.03	60.00	19.95	25.00	12.50	41.67	10.17
41	1.8739	48.61	10.02	58.33	20.48	33.33	8.90	38.89	8.04
42	1.7817	48.61	9.11	63.33	23.63	66.67	27.20	58.33	17.20
43	1.7662	51.39	11.43	66.67	24.57	50.00	19.00	50.00	14.52
44	2.0114	49.31	8.55	60.00	15.44	50.00	25.30	47.22	13.24
45	1.8719	45.83	7.48	66.67	27.75	58.33	25.70	61.11	15.28
46	1.9132	54.86	9.09	43.33	8.46	58.33	20.70	50.00	12.11

Continued on next page

Table 12.5 *(continued)*

Rule #	Fitness	1971–1983 Period		1984–1988 Period		1989		1989–1991 Period	
		% Correct	Average Return	% Correct	Average Return	% Correct	Average Return	% Correct	Average Return
47	1.7818	51.39	9.93	58.33	20.91	41.67	14.20	52.78	13.91
48	1.8679	49.31	9.98	63.33	20.62	50.00	27.80	52.78	17.08
49	1.8839	52.08	11.15	63.33	22.42	41.67	14.20	47.22	9.31
50	1.9778	52.78	8.75	63.33	25.42	58.33	25.90	61.11	19.40
51	1.9413	53.47	9.04	68.33	28.92	66.67	27.20	63.89	19.81
52	2.0829	50.00	8.71	51.67	18.60	33.33	12.50	41.67	13.29
53	1.9148	52.78	8.75	65.00	26.25	58.33	25.90	58.33	19.00
54	1.9239	52.08	9.22	66.67	27.88	66.67	27.20	63.89	19.81
55	1.8662	47.22	10.31	41.67	8.39	25.00	7.00	47.22	11.49
56	1.8809	53.47	7.78	58.33	20.05	50.00	19.30	58.33	16.27
57	1.8516	50.69	7.30	66.67	27.00	58.33	25.70	61.11	16.50
58	1.7753	47.92	8.62	65.00	25.35	41.67	14.20	52.78	12.06
59	2.0386	45.83	8.20	51.67	11.20	41.67	13.20	38.89	6.15
60	1.9399	47.22	8.06	63.33	25.79	66.67	31.50	61.11	18.88
61	1.8799	49.31	8.45	66.67	27.00	58.33	25.70	61.11	16.50
62	1.8577	50.69	9.48	66.67	27.14	41.67	17.70	52.78	14.80
63	1.7530	50.69	9.67	71.67	27.91	50.00	15.90	55.56	16.05
64	1.7515	49.31	8.98	61.67	24.57	58.33	21.30	55.56	15.33
65	1.8367	54.17	7.64	45.00	5.61	66.67	27.10	58.33	12.21
66	1.8316	48.61	9.26	63.33	20.07	58.33	29.30	52.78	17.47
67	1.9273	57.64	11.59	55.00	12.08	58.33	23.30	58.33	15.25
68	1.8656	47.92	6.88	66.67	28.30	41.67	23.80	47.22	13.29
69	1.8384	48.61	9.26	63.33	20.07	58.33	29.30	52.78	17.47
70	1.8288	50.69	10.59	68.33	26.78	41.67	17.70	44.44	13.75
71	1.8718	52.78	8.75	65.00	26.25	58.33	25.90	58.33	19.00
72	1.8610	52.78	8.75	65.00	26.25	58.33	25.90	58.33	19.00
73	2.0876	50.00	7.62	48.33	14.56	41.67	10.20	38.89	8.83
74	1.8327	52.78	9.15	58.33	18.80	58.33	25.90	58.33	19.00
75	1.8726	52.78	8.97	65.00	26.25	58.33	25.90	55.56	16.74
76	1.8403	57.64	11.58	61.67	19.49	25.00	16.30	41.67	11.06
77	1.9042	54.86	8.71	60.00	18.99	66.67	31.50	55.56	18.09
78	1.7684	52.78	8.63	63.33	24.23	66.67	31.50	58.33	18.45
79	1.7968	54.86	9.54	60.00	19.89	66.67	27.20	55.56	16.81
80	1.9726	49.31	8.63	50.00	10.49	33.33	8.40	36.11	1.74
81	1.8847	47.92	9.84	56.67	22.17	58.33	21.60	58.33	14.78
82	1.8377	50.00	9.57	63.33	24.58	58.33	25.90	55.56	16.74
83	1.9282	49.31	9.20	68.33	19.89	25.00	12.30	41.67	12.35
84	1.8319	48.61	8.31	66.67	27.74	41.67	25.40	47.22	14.37
85	1.8035	49.31	8.66	61.67	21.68	58.33	25.90	55.56	16.74
86	1.9154	50.00	8.13	68.33	30.23	58.33	25.90	55.56	17.37
87	1.9480	54.86	9.91	70.00	29.01	50.00	23.80	52.78	17.59
88	2.0934	50.69	7.25	50.00	15.42	41.67	10.20	41.67	10.93
89	2.0038	52.08	8.09	68.33	26.70	50.00	23.80	55.56	18.33
90	1.9447	54.17	9.50	70.00	30.46	50.00	23.80	52.78	18.00
91	1.8894	49.31	10.68	45.00	5.03	33.33	19.90	47.22	17.66
92	1.8747	51.39	8.36	63.33	20.52	66.67	31.50	58.33	18.45

Continued on next page

Table 12.5 *(continued)*

Rule #	Fitness	1971–1983 Period		1984–1988 Period		1989		1989–1991 Period	
		% Correct	Average Return	% Correct	Average Return	% Correct	Average Return	% Correct	Average Return
93	1.8852	53.47	8.51	70.00	29.28	58.33	29.30	52.78	17.47
94	1.8201	58.33	10.56	65.00	23.59	58.33	29.30	50.00	17.11
95	2.0049	45.83	8.61	56.67	16.15	33.33	15.70	38.89	9.78
96	2.0094	50.00	10.51	66.67	28.11	58.33	29.30	55.56	17.88
97	1.8894	50.69	9.75	70.00	30.90	58.33	29.30	55.56	17.88
98	1.8690	48.61	8.80	66.67	20.82	50.00	19.80	55.56	17.28
99	1.7847	48.61	9.26	63.33	20.07	58.33	29.30	52.78	17.47
100	1.8505	50.00	9.25	63.33	26.25	58.33	29.30	52.78	17.47
101	1.8209	47.92	8.64	56.67	17.53	58.33	25.90	61.11	19.35
102	2.0635	54.17	8.38	60.00	21.20	58.33	25.90	58.33	19.00
103	1.8880	51.39	8.72	68.33	26.93	66.67	31.50	58.33	18.93
104	1.8312	53.47	7.97	63.33	26.00	58.33	25.90	58.33	19.00
105	2.1165	49.31	8.64	51.67	11.10	33.33	8.40	33.33	4.65
106	1.8588	50.69	8.51	65.00	26.36	58.33	25.90	55.56	17.20
107	1.8940	52.08	9.03	63.33	26.00	58.33	25.90	58.33	19.00
108	2.1430	54.17	9.44	76.67	32.61	41.67	14.70	52.78	16.99
109	1.8606	52.08	8.50	66.67	27.36	58.33	25.90	58.33	19.00
110	1.9334	48.61	8.46	68.33	26.93	66.67	31.50	58.33	18.45
111	2.0390	48.61	8.40	51.67	11.20	41.67	13.20	38.89	6.15
112	1.8173	48.61	9.29	60.00	23.11	66.67	31.50	61.11	18.88
113	1.7900	52.78	8.49	65.00	26.46	66.67	31.50	61.11	18.88
114	1.9362	51.39	9.77	73.33	29.06	50.00	19.80	55.56	17.28
115	1.8977	49.31	9.36	66.67	20.82	50.00	19.80	55.56	17.28
116	1.7874	50.00	8.82	61.67	24.66	66.67	31.50	58.33	18.45
117	2.0906	51.39	9.28	73.33	30.96	50.00	19.80	58.33	17.69
118	1.9726	54.17	10.22	73.33	31.18	41.67	14.70	52.78	12.03
119	1.7853	52.78	10.95	63.33	25.67	58.33	25.90	55.56	16.74
120	1.8834	50.69	8.32	63.33	25.19	50.00	19.80	55.56	17.28

these series represent the spot price of lead scrap, the diffusion index of lagging indicators, and the manufacturing capacity utilization rate. The cutoff values are 18, 13, and 2, respectively. The complete translation of the rule would be roughly like this:

> If (the change in the price of lead scrap is in the upper half of its range AND the change in the diffusion index of lagging indicators is in the lower third of its range) OR (the change in capacity utilization is near the bottom of its range, then invest in the S&P 500).

Because 18 is close to 16 and the greater than code signals a greater than relationship, we translated the value of 18 as roughly "in the upper half of its range." Similar reasoning was used for the other two portions of the rule. Remembering

Table 12.6 Bad Rules—S&P 500 Stocks

Rule #	Logic Code	)/(Code	Cutoff Values				Series Number and Differencing Interval					
			Series 1	Series 2	Series 3	Fitness	1 #	Diff.	2 #	Diff.	3 #	Diff.
1	6	3	8	16	15	11.4712	71	3	61	3	251	3
2	8	1	2	4	6	11.6770	71	3	61	3	234	3
3	4	5	20	21	2	12.1414	71	3	61	3	77	3
4	8	6	30	16	26	11.2996	71	3	61	3	42	3
5	2	2	3	21	16	11.3706	71	3	61	3	225	12
6	8	1	3	6	13	11.7622	71	3	61	3	228	1
7	6	1	12	13	4	11.4352	71	3	61	3	61	0
8	4	1	25	16	10	11.5903	71	3	61	3	141	3
9	5	3	2	18	14	11.8252	71	3	251	3	234	3
10	7	6	20	6	2	12.0456	71	3	251	3	77	3
11	2	6	20	24	28	11.3317	71	3	251	3	42	3
12	3	6	10	10	16	11.1094	71	3	251	3	225	12
13	5	7	21	18	24	11.6410	71	3	251	3	228	1
14	5	5	30	23	7	11.3121	71	3	251	3	61	0
15	2	3	2	14	7	11.3761	71	3	251	3	141	3
16	6	7	15	6	19	11.6042	71	3	234	3	77	3
17	5	5	21	12	20	11.4901	71	3	234	3	42	3
18	8	6	21	6	30	11.4803	71	3	234	3	225	12
19	4	5	22	16	9	11.5144	71	3	234	3	228	1
20	8	6	20	4	27	11.8056	71	3	234	3	61	0
21	2	5	21	7	30	11.6381	71	3	234	3	141	3
22	4	8	0	19	24	11.2352	71	3	77	3	42	3
23	2	4	3	19	16	11.1856	71	3	77	3	225	12
24	3	7	2	19	13	11.8169	71	3	77	3	228	1
25	6	5	20	2	31	11.9132	71	3	77	3	61	0
26	8	5	19	2	7	11.8733	71	3	77	3	141	3
27	2	8	20	26	8	11.3411	71	3	42	3	225	12
28	2	7	21	13	13	11.5740	71	3	42	3	228	1
29	2	8	20	22	27	11.4717	71	3	42	3	61	0
30	4	7	19	14	10	11.5394	71	3	42	3	141	3
31	4	7	11	17	9	11.6965	71	3	225	12	228	1
32	8	7	20	16	7	11.4006	71	3	225	12	61	0
33	8	7	19	31	6	11.3900	71	3	225	12	141	3
34	8	5	21	9	3	11.7584	71	3	228	1	61	0
35	5	5	21	13	23	11.8223	71	3	228	1	141	3
36	2	1	3	5	16	11.2364	71	3	61	0	141	3
37	2	3	8	18	13	11.7932	61	3	251	3	234	3
38	4	4	12	15	16	11.2521	61	3	251	3	77	3
39	4	4	19	18	28	11.3411	61	3	251	3	42	3
40	3	2	16	24	17	11.1416	61	3	251	3	225	12
41	2	3	10	14	15	11.6958	61	3	251	3	228	1
42	2	1	16	25	4	11.7075	61	3	251	3	61	0
43	7	2	16	14	7	11.7127	61	3	251	3	141	3
44	4	1	16	16	2	12.2340	61	3	234	3	77	3
45	8	2	8	6	27	11.7534	61	3	234	3	42	3
46	8	2	8	6	31	11.5639	61	3	234	3	225	12

Continued on next page

141

Table 12.6 (continued)

Rule #	Logic Code	⟩/⟨ Code	Cutoff Values			Fitness	Series Number and Differencing Interval					
			Series 1	Series 2	Series 3		1 #	Diff.	2 #	Diff.	3 #	Diff.
47	5	1	16	5	31	11.6001	61	3	234	3	228	1
48	7	1	16	16	11	11.5700	61	3	234	3	61	0
49	5	1	8	6	23	11.6910	61	3	234	3	141	3
50	6	1	13	2	25	11.9343	61	3	77	3	42	3
51	2	4	13	16	14	11.2189	61	3	77	3	225	12
52	4	3	21	19	13	11.8810	61	3	77	3	228	1
53	6	1	16	2	26	11.9952	61	3	77	3	61	0
54	4	5	26	5	6	11.5645	61	3	77	3	141	3
55	2	4	16	26	8	11.4491	61	3	42	3	225	12
56	2	3	8	12	13	11.6258	61	3	42	3	228	1
57	2	3	16	15	9	11.6077	61	3	42	3	61	0
58	6	2	19	27	23	11.4849	61	3	42	3	141	3
59	7	2	10	8	15	11.5825	61	3	225	12	228	1
60	8	3	13	14	7	11.4233	61	3	225	12	61	0
61	2	1	16	25	7	11.5247	61	3	225	12	141	3
62	3	1	29	12	7	11.6534	61	3	228	1	61	0
63	5	1	9	13	21	11.7876	61	3	228	1	141	3
64	5	1	13	18	19	11.5904	61	3	61	0	141	3
65	4	5	18	13	2	12.2547	251	3	234	3	77	3
66	3	5	18	16	10	11.7952	251	3	234	3	42	3
67	1	6	18	13	5	11.8323	251	3	234	3	225	12
68	4	5	18	15	9	11.8043	251	3	234	3	228	1
69	7	7	18	23	27	12.0153	251	3	234	3	61	0
70	1	5	4	14	17	11.8263	251	3	234	3	141	3
71	6	4	21	19	26	11.3831	251	3	77	3	42	3
72	6	4	23	20	17	11.0059	251	3	77	3	225	12
73	6	6	15	19	15	12.0114	251	3	77	3	228	1
74	6	2	26	19	3	11.5924	251	3	77	3	61	0
75	3	5	5	2	10	11.6453	251	3	77	3	141	3
76	4	8	5	27	17	11.0914	251	3	42	3	225	12
77	6	1	29	7	9	11.6231	251	3	42	3	228	1
78	5	7	31	18	9	11.1798	251	3	42	3	61	0
79	4	3	13	26	7	11.2747	251	3	42	3	141	3
80	6	6	15	15	15	11.5623	251	3	225	12	228	1
81	4	7	0	16	7	11.1815	251	3	225	12	61	0
82	5	7	13	18	8	11.1333	251	3	225	12	141	3
83	4	5	14	15	4	11.8494	251	3	228	1	61	0
84	4	1	25	13	7	11.7731	251	3	228	1	141	3
85	7	1	15	15	15	11.4313	251	3	61	0	141	3
86	8	4	9	19	25	11.9018	234	3	77	3	42	3
87	6	4	11	19	11	12.0022	234	3	77	3	225	12
88	8	3	4	19	3	11.7102	234	3	77	3	228	1
89	2	1	6	30	3	11.5763	234	3	77	3	61	0
90	5	3	6	19	26	11.9444	234	3	77	3	141	3
91	5	2	13	10	11	11.6985	234	3	42	3	225	12
92	5	1	7	10	24	11.5001	234	3	42	3	228	1

Continued on next page

Table 12.6 *(continued)*

Rule #	Logic Code	)/(Code	Cutoff Values			Fitness	Series Number and Differencing Interval					
			Series 1	Series 2	Series 3		1 #	Diff.	2 #	Diff.	3 #	Diff.
93	3	3	14	13	4	11.5075	234	3	42	3	61	0
94	5	3	13	27	19	11.6470	234	3	42	3	141	3
95	4	3	23	15	13	11.6446	234	3	225	12	228	1
96	3	3	14	8	11	11.7015	234	3	225	12	61	0
97	5	3	6	17	22	11.7828	234	3	225	12	141	3
98	6	1	21	7	12	11.9787	234	3	228	1	61	0
99	5	1	13	13	16	11.7149	234	3	228	1	141	3
100	5	3	13	29	18	11.8429	234	3	61	0	141	3
101	2	2	2	6	19	11.7607	77	3	42	3	225	12
102	8	1	2	10	3	12.0004	77	3	42	3	228	1
103	2	8	19	20	27	11.5158	77	3	42	3	61	0
104	5	1	2	9	28	11.7349	77	3	42	3	141	3
105	7	6	19	6	13	12.0064	77	3	225	12	228	1
106	2	5	19	16	7	11.3926	77	3	225	12	61	0
107	2	3	2	14	8	11.7645	77	3	225	12	141	3
108	8	6	19	13	27	11.9363	77	3	228	1	61	0
109	5	5	19	13	30	12.0705	77	3	228	1	141	3
110	2	1	2	7	17	11.7991	77	3	61	0	141	3
111	8	7	29	17	13	11.7676	42	3	225	12	228	1
112	2	1	9	25	7	11.2757	42	3	225	12	61	0
113	4	3	9	24	8	11.0938	42	3	225	12	141	3
114	4	1	25	12	4	11.6604	42	3	228	1	61	0
115	2	1	7	13	21	11.6778	42	3	228	1	141	3
116	2	3	7	25	19	11.2350	42	3	61	0	141	3
117	3	1	23	9	7	11.8317	225	12	228	1	61	0
118	4	5	9	16	7	11.6332	225	12	228	1	141	3
119	5	5	16	7	27	11.5616	225	12	61	0	141	3
120	5	1	12	6	22	11.9311	228	1	61	0	141	3

that this is a bad rule, we would *not* want to invest in stocks when it tells us to do so.

If we scan down the list of rules, we see that change in capacity utilization near the low end of the range shows up in several of the higher fitness rules. This is true for the following rules: 3, 10, 25, 44, 50, 53, and 102. This type of microanalysis of the rule structure could point the analyst to some interesting macroeconomic/equity market relationships; it could also point the analyst towards other tests. For example, you could "lock in" the rule settings for capacity utilization and then examine all other possible variable combinations with it. There are many different ways to use the GA results.

PERFORMANCE OF THE BAD RULES

The aggregate performance of the bad rule portfolio is summarized in Figures 12.5 through 12.8. Figure 12.5 shows the percentage of correct calls declining slowly until 1986 and then starting a steep descent. This drop continued until 1990, when a reversal began to occur. Figure 12.6, which graphs the average return, shows a slightly different pattern. The moving average return was actually rising over the 1978–1984 period but then began to drop sharply. The fitness measure tried to project the average return based on the pattern from 1984–1988. Figure 12.7 more clearly highlights the reversal in accuracy. The bad rules got worse until about May of 1990, when they started improving sharply. The average return stayed fairly flat until 1991, when it began climbing abruptly, as shown in Figure 12.8.

The detailed performance of each rule is shown in Table 12.7. For 1989, the first year of the holdout period, most of the rules continued to make poor calls. The percentage correct column shows that most of the rules were correct only about 42 percent of the time, which means that if we had done the opposite of what the rule was suggesting, we would have been right 58 percent of the time. The rule portfolio did not do very well over the entire 1989–1991 period, but performance improved in 1990.

There are some rules that we might not actually want to include in a bad rule portfolio. For example, consider rule 76. First, it had a fitness value of only 11.9014, which was second lowest of the entire 120. Second, the percentage of correct calls during the rule-building period was 56.67 percent. Third, the average

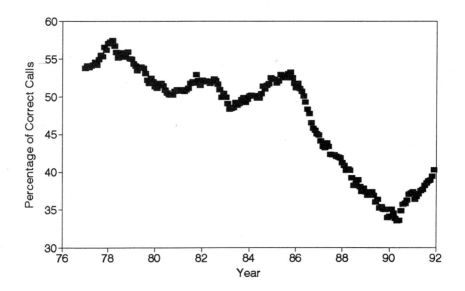

FIGURE 12.5 Percentage Correct (S&P—Bad Rules) 1977–1991

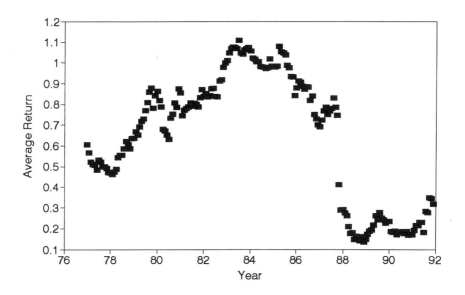

FIGURE 12.6 Average Return (S&P—Bad Rules) 1977–1991

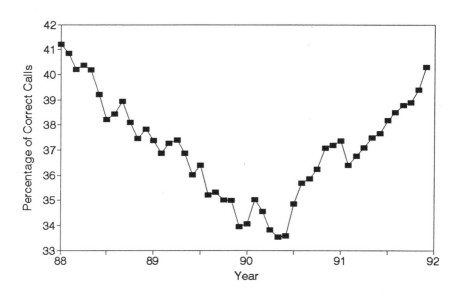

FIGURE 12.7 Percentage Correct (S&P—Bad Rules) 1988–1991

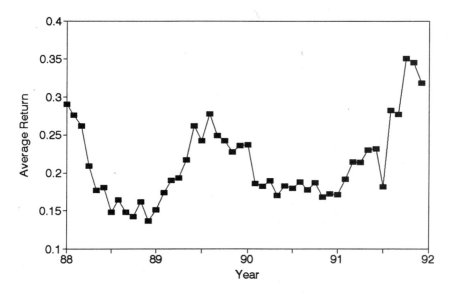

FIGURE 12.8 Average Return (S&P—Bad Rules) 1988–1991

annual return over the rule-building period was 15.83 percent. Subsequent performance supports the notion that this is not really a bad rule; it was right 50 percent of the time in 1989 and 58.33 percent of the time over the entire 1989–1991 holdout period, which suggests that there might be merit to a second cut of screening criteria with the rule portfolio before using it to make trading decisions. However, we have chosen to keeps things simple and use all 120 rules in constructing our hedge portfolio, which we will discuss later in this chapter.

VARIABLE SELECTION FOR THE SMALL-FIRM/T-BILL TIMING DECISION

As Chapter 10 demonstrated that the historical returns from optimal small-firm stock timing rules are extremely enticing. Small-firm stocks historically have been more volatile than large-firm stocks, thus making potential gains from successful timing very great. Table 12.8 shows the correlation results for the small-firm stock returns. There is a small overlap with the series that were selected for the S&P stocks; three of the ten variables are the same.

There are some interesting series that show up in this new list of ten. Changes in leading indicators are used twice, once involving one-month changes and again involving three-month changes. Market variables come into play with the one-month change in corporate bond yields and the three-month change in the index of stock prices. A series representing changes in Canadian price levels was also chosen for inclusion.

Table 12.7 Performance Summary—Bad Rules—S&P 500 Stocks

Rule #	Fitness	1971–1983 Period		1984–1988 Period		1989		1989–1991 Period	
		% Correct	Average Return	% Correct	Average Return	% Correct	Average Return	% Correct	Average Return
1	11.4712	56.94	11.31	41.67	3.05	41.67	9.90	38.89	7.84
2	11.6770	58.33	11.85	40.00	1.38	33.33	8.40	38.89	4.56
3	12.1414	51.39	8.37	36.67	−1.85	41.67	13.20	44.44	10.58
4	11.2996	52.08	10.02	41.67	2.85	33.33	15.70	36.11	11.04
5	11.3706	52.78	10.68	50.00	14.60	58.33	23.10	55.56	11.98
6	11.7622	56.94	11.10	38.33	0.32	33.33	12.00	38.89	5.67
7	11.4352	51.39	7.89	36.67	−0.04	33.33	12.00	41.67	8.41
8	11.5903	52.08	8.48	35.00	−1.27	41.67	13.40	38.89	10.38
9	11.8252	56.94	10.52	45.00	7.49	33.33	8.40	36.11	3.63
10	12.0456	51.39	8.83	36.67	−1.85	41.67	13.20	44.44	11.90
11	11.3317	51.39	8.83	36.67	−1.85	41.67	13.20	44.44	10.58
12	11.1094	43.06	6.65	45.00	8.35	66.67	20.20	55.56	12.29
13	11.6410	49.31	10.05	38.33	6.11	58.33	17.50	47.22	11.87
14	11.3121	51.39	7.72	45.00	8.55	41.67	17.30	47.22	11.79
15	11.3761	57.64	11.57	45.00	7.49	33.33	8.40	38.89	4.56
16	11.6042	54.86	11.25	38.33	3.89	33.33	8.40	47.22	11.25
17	11.4901	48.61	6.45	30.00	−3.61	50.00	11.50	44.44	6.68
18	11.4803	52.08	9.00	33.33	−3.70	33.33	8.40	44.44	10.47
19	11.5144	50.69	7.27	31.67	−4.36	41.67	10.20	44.44	7.40
20	11.8056	51.39	8.35	40.00	−0.12	41.67	13.20	47.22	12.08
21	11.6381	52.78	9.50	31.67	−4.44	33.33	8.40	44.44	10.47
22	11.2352	47.92	8.05	31.67	−2.64	33.33	8.40	41.67	6.82
23	11.1856	53.47	11.26	33.33	−2.28	33.33	8.40	38.89	4.13
24	11.8169	45.14	6.08	46.67	6.90	50.00	23.80	61.11	17.57
25	11.9132	57.64	12.83	33.33	−3.11	33.33	9.80	47.22	13.70
26	11.8733	56.25	12.53	43.33	3.95	50.00	13.30	55.56	13.03
27	11.3411	54.86	11.21	36.67	−1.83	33.33	11.80	47.22	14.57
28	11.5740	50.69	8.56	36.67	−0.73	33.33	8.40	41.67	8.97
29	11.4717	54.86	11.21	36.67	−1.83	33.33	11.80	47.22	14.57
30	11.5394	47.22	9.10	33.33	−3.40	41.67	13.20	41.67	10.22
31	11.6965	56.94	10.78	40.00	3.83	33.33	12.30	52.78	14.57
32	11.4006	55.56	11.65	40.00	1.11	33.33	9.80	47.22	14.52
33	11.3900	53.47	12.02	43.33	1.91	33.33	9.80	47.22	13.37
34	11.7584	54.17	10.20	33.33	−4.22	41.67	17.30	47.22	13.42
35	11.8223	47.22	6.74	28.33	−4.82	50.00	18.90	44.44	8.35
36	11.2364	52.78	10.31	41.67	0.73	33.33	8.40	38.89	4.56
37	11.7932	51.39	8.25	38.33	1.00	33.33	8.40	41.67	7.26
38	11.2521	38.89	3.20	43.33	7.77	75.00	26.60	58.33	15.68
39	11.3411	49.31	6.70	35.00	−1.98	50.00	15.10	50.00	11.92
40	11.1416	52.08	8.48	36.67	−0.83	41.67	13.40	38.89	9.06
41	11.6958	53.47	9.59	43.33	2.80	33.33	12.00	41.67	7.78
42	11.7075	52.08	8.05	38.33	0.51	41.67	13.40	44.44	12.13
43	11.7127	52.78	8.82	36.67	−0.83	41.67	13.20	38.89	7.32
44	12.2340	53.47	9.11	33.33	−3.02	41.67	13.40	41.67	8.44
45	11.7534	52.08	7.86	40.00	0.96	33.33	8.40	44.44	8.75
46	11.5639	55.56	9.36	35.00	−2.04	33.33	8.40	44.44	8.75

Continued on next page

Table 12.7 (continued)

Rule #	Fitness	1971–1983 Period		1984–1988 Period		1989		1989–1991 Period	
		% Correct	Average Return	% Correct	Average Return	% Correct	Average Return	% Correct	Average Return
47	11.6001	54.17	9.86	35.00	−2.64	41.67	13.40	41.67	10.55
48	11.5700	47.92	5.58	31.67	−3.04	50.00	15.30	44.44	7.87
49	11.6910	54.17	9.44	33.33	−2.77	33.33	8.40	44.44	8.75
50	11.9343	56.25	11.21	35.00	3.70	25.00	8.70	44.44	11.49
51	11.2189	46.53	7.96	31.67	−4.15	33.33	12.00	36.11	6.03
52	11.8810	52.78	9.00	48.33	7.30	50.00	23.80	58.33	14.60
53	11.9952	57.64	11.92	33.33	2.58	33.33	10.00	44.44	13.37
54	11.5645	58.33	11.66	48.33	12.10	41.67	8.40	52.78	9.67
55	11.4491	56.25	11.15	36.67	−0.81	33.33	12.00	41.67	13.00
56	11.6258	51.39	8.25	38.33	1.00	33.33	8.40	41.67	7.26
57	11.6077	52.08	8.48	36.67	−0.83	41.67	13.40	38.89	9.06
58	11.4849	56.25	11.25	36.67	−0.69	41.67	17.90	44.44	13.24
59	11.5825	47.22	6.25	56.67	12.93	75.00	35.50	50.00	10.14
60	11.4233	53.47	11.34	40.00	1.34	25.00	8.70	47.22	15.85
61	11.5247	56.25	11.32	45.00	4.83	33.33	10.00	44.44	13.37
62	11.6534	52.08	8.50	35.00	2.37	50.00	18.90	44.44	8.35
63	11.7876	50.00	7.53	28.33	−3.54	41.67	17.70	41.67	7.95
64	11.5904	49.31	7.93	41.67	3.58	58.33	24.70	50.00	12.43
65	12.2547	56.25	8.97	30.00	−4.87	50.00	12.10	52.78	10.96
66	11.7952	53.47	8.15	33.33	−4.08	66.67	18.70	58.33	13.52
67	11.8323	53.47	7.65	35.00	−2.79	50.00	12.10	50.00	9.45
68	11.8043	52.08	7.53	31.67	−4.77	66.67	18.70	61.11	14.22
69	12.0153	53.47	10.92	31.67	−4.22	66.67	22.70	52.78	13.86
70	11.8263	54.17	8.74	33.33	−1.80	58.33	21.50	52.78	12.66
71	11.3831	47.92	8.05	31.67	−2.64	33.33	8.40	41.67	6.82
72	11.0059	47.92	8.57	33.33	−2.52	33.33	8.40	41.67	6.82
73	12.0114	43.06	5.42	30.00	2.83	66.67	21.20	52.78	12.35
74	11.5924	54.86	11.99	30.00	−2.22	33.33	7.00	52.78	11.49
75	11.6453	56.25	11.14	56.67	15.83	50.00	26.20	58.33	15.28
76	11.0914	52.78	8.68	58.33	18.12	58.33	17.40	55.56	12.27
77	11.6231	48.61	9.67	36.67	−0.53	33.33	8.40	41.67	7.26
78	11.1798	50.69	8.04	41.67	1.91	33.33	8.40	41.67	7.26
79	11.2747	51.39	11.12	36.67	−0.53	25.00	7.00	41.67	9.75
80	11.5623	43.75	5.81	40.00	7.91	75.00	26.60	58.33	18.50
81	11.1815	56.94	11.68	43.33	3.14	25.00	5.10	47.22	15.03
82	11.1333	51.39	9.79	41.67	11.09	25.00	5.10	41.67	6.77
83	11.8494	53.47	9.25	33.33	1.79	50.00	11.80	44.44	5.04
84	11.7731	50.69	7.64	33.33	2.27	50.00	18.90	44.44	8.35
85	11.4313	50.69	8.34	43.33	3.30	33.33	8.40	41.67	7.26
86	11.9018	46.53	7.31	26.67	−5.79	41.67	10.20	47.22	7.72
87	12.0022	47.22	7.01	26.67	−3.61	41.67	10.20	44.44	7.43
88	11.7102	54.17	11.88	30.00	−2.24	33.33	7.00	52.78	11.49
89	11.5763	58.33	11.51	38.33	4.88	33.33	7.00	52.78	11.92
90	11.9444	49.31	7.99	31.67	0.00	33.33	8.40	44.44	8.29
91	11.6985	54.17	8.21	36.67	2.37	58.33	21.50	52.78	12.66
92	11.5001	50.69	10.73	31.67	−4.25	33.33	8.40	41.67	7.26

Continued on next page

Table 12.7 (*continued*)

Rule #	Fitness	1971–1983 Period		1984–1988 Period		1989		1989–1991 Period	
		% Correct	Average Return	% Correct	Average Return	% Correct	Average Return	% Correct	Average Return
93	11.5075	52.78	8.30	35.00	− 2.59	58.33	21.50	52.78	12.66
94	11.6470	52.78	9.12	38.33	2.11	41.67	17.40	41.67	9.39
95	11.6446	54.17	9.74	48.33	11.71	58.33	25.90	63.89	23.94
96	11.7015	54.86	8.74	35.00	− 0.48	58.33	21.50	52.78	12.66
97	11.7828	50.00	7.73	36.67	− 3.34	33.33	8.40	41.67	8.35
98	11.9787	51.39	8.20	33.33	2.27	50.00	18.90	44.44	8.35
99	11.7149	52.78	8.34	35.00	2.71	66.67	23.00	50.00	9.56
100	11.8429	55.56	9.90	40.00	1.85	50.00	19.40	47.22	10.79
101	11.7607	57.64	11.87	38.33	5.44	25.00	5.10	44.44	10.30
102	12.0004	55.56	13.56	31.67	− 2.09	25.00	5.10	44.44	10.30
103	11.5158	52.08	10.64	31.67	− 2.61	25.00	7.00	44.44	10.71
104	11.7349	50.69	10.10	33.33	− 2.00	25.00	5.10	38.89	6.41
105	12.0064	49.31	6.34	40.00	7.19	66.67	29.80	61.11	16.69
106	11.3926	52.08	10.66	38.33	2.13	25.00	5.10	47.22	11.04
107	11.7645	57.64	11.87	38.33	5.44	25.00	5.10	44.44	10.30
108	11.9363	46.53	7.10	35.00	− 2.52	50.00	18.90	47.22	12.43
109	12.0705	45.14	7.33	21.67	− 7.21	50.00	18.90	47.22	8.66
110	11.7991	52.08	9.93	35.00	− 1.21	25.00	5.10	44.44	10.30
111	11.7676	54.86	9.54	50.00	11.73	58.33	25.90	61.11	19.70
112	11.2757	53.47	11.99	43.33	4.35	25.00	5.10	47.22	11.49
113	11.0938	55.56	12.24	45.00	11.01	25.00	5.10	50.00	11.82
114	11.6604	52.78	9.31	35.00	2.37	50.00	18.90	47.22	10.19
115	11.6778	47.92	8.61	26.67	− 5.02	50.00	18.90	44.44	8.35
116	11.2350	48.61	9.67	36.67	− 0.53	33.33	8.40	41.67	7.26
117	11.8317	52.78	8.78	40.00	3.33	41.67	17.30	44.44	10.85
118	11.6332	56.94	10.56	38.33	2.69	66.67	23.00	52.78	11.23
119	11.5616	52.08	8.53	35.00	− 2.22	33.33	8.40	38.89	6.88
120	11.9311	50.00	7.72	36.67	0.16	50.00	18.90	47.22	10.63

"GOOD" FORECASTING RULES FOR SMALL-FIRM STOCKS

The list of good rules for small-firm stocks is shown in Table 12.9; notice that the fitness values are much lower than the corresponding list for S&P stocks (Table 12.2). This reflects the fact that small-firm stocks underperformed large-firm stocks over the 1984–1988 rule-building period. None of the rules in this list have a logic code of 8, which is the most stringent of the logical relationships (all AND conditions).

Rule 120 had the highest fitness of all the rules. It maintains that a good time to invest in small-firm stocks is when (the level of labor cost is not in the upper portion of its range *or* the three-month change in leading indicators is in the lower half of its range) *and* (the one-month change in corporate bond yields is in the lower half of its range). The latter portion of this rule seems logical. If corporate

Table 12.8 Correlations with Small-Firm Stock Returns

Series Number	Differencing Interval	Series Description	Correlation Coefficient
1	251	3	(23) Spot price, lead scrap ($ per lb.) COPYRIGHTED (C	− 0.4285
2	71	3	74. Industrial production, nondurable manufactures (198	− 0.3650
3	197	3	733. Canada, consumer price index, NSA (1982-84 = 100)	− 0.3441
4	18	3	19. United States, index of stock prices, NSA (1967 = 100)	− 0.3362
5	16	3	19. Index of stock prices, 500 common stocks, NSA (1941-	− 0.3360
6	61	3	62a. Index of labor cost per unit of output, mfg. (1987 = 100)	0.3167
7	42	3	45. Average weekly insured unemployment rate (pct.)	0.3112
8	63	3	62. Smoothed change in labor cost per unit output, mfg.	0.3061
9	220	1	910. Composite index of 11 leading indicators (1982 = 100)	− 0.2972
10	63	0	62. Smoothed change in labor cost per unit output, mfg.	0.2865
11	220	3	910. Composite index of 11 leading indicators (1982 = 100)	− 0.2821
12	119	1	116. Yield on new high-grade corporate bonds, NSA (pct	− 0.2767
13	141	3	323c. Change in CPI-U, less food & energy, 1-mo. span (pct.)	0.2747
14	222	0	910c. Leading index, change over 3-mo. span (AR, pct.)	− 0.2746
15	3	1	5. Average weekly initial claims, unemploy. insurance (tho	0.2738
16	246	3	(98) Producer Price Index, nonferrous scrap, NSA (1982 =	− 0.2732
17	90	1	92. Smoothed change in mfrs' unfilled orders (bil. 1982 $)	− 0.2711
18	208	3	743. Canada, stock prices, NSA (1967 = 100)	-0.2694
19	225	12	920c. Coincident index, change over 3-mo. span (AR, pct.)	− 0.2673
20	254	3	(23) Spot price, zinc, NSA ($ per lb.) COPYRIGHTED (CRB	− 0.2660
21	117	1	114. Discount rate on new 91-day Treasury bills, NSA (pct.	− 0.2607
22	77	3	82. Capacity utilization rate, mfg. (pct.)	-0.2585
23	18	1	19. United States, index of stock prices, NSA (1967 = 100)	− 0.2514
24	245	1	(98) Producer Price Index, aluminum base scrap (1982 = 1	− 0.2514
25	16	1	19. Index of stock prices, 500 common stocks, NSA (1941-	− 0.2511
26	208	12	743. Canada, stock prices, NSA (1967 = 100)	− 0.2503
27	229	3	940. Ratio, coincident index to lagging index (1982 = 100)	− 0.2480
28	90	3	92. Smoothed change in mfrs.' unfilled orders (bil. 1982 $)	− 0.2468
29	199	3	735. Germany, consumer price index, NSA (1982-84 = 10	− 0.2465
30	30	1	31. Change in manufacturing and trade inventories (AR, bil.	0.2442
31	89	1	92a. Mfrs.' unfilled orders, durable goods indus. (bil. 1982	− 0.2442
32	88	0	92b. Change in mfrs.' unfilled orders, durables (bil. 1982	− 0.2441
33	72	3	75. Industrial production, consumer goods (1987 = 100)	− 0.2435
34	264	1	991. CIBCR short-leading composite index (1967 = 100)	− 0.2410
35	3	3	5. Average weekly initial claims, unemploy. insurance (tho	0.2373
36	150	1	333c. Change in PPI, capital equipment, 1-mo. span (pct.)	− 0.2366
37	118	1	115. Yield on long-term Treasury bonds, NSA (pct.)	− 0.2363
38	150	12	333c. Change in PPI, capital equipment, 1-mo. span (pct.)	− 0.2352
39	89	3	92a. Mfrs' unfilled orders, durable goods indus. (bil. 1982	− 0.2280
40	174	1	525. Defense Department prime contract awards in U.S. (m	− 0.2264
41	264	3	991. CIBCR short-leading composite index (1967 = 100)	− 0.2248
42	92	3	93. Free reserves, NSA (mil. $)	− 0.2244
43	193	3	727. Italy, industrial production (1987 = 100)	− 0.2216
44	61	0	62a. Index of labor cost per unit of output, mfg. (1987 = 100	0.2214
45	206	3	738c. Japan, 6-mo. change in consumer prices (AR, pct.)	− 0.2187
46	204	3	737c. Italy, 6-mo. change in consumer prices (AR, pct.)	− 0.2141
47	98	3	99b. Change in sensitive materials prices (pct.)	0.2111
48	140	3	323. CPI-U, all items less food & energy (1982–1984 =	0.2098
49	172	12	452. Labor force participation rate, females 20 and over	0.2087
50	30	3	31. Change in manufacturing and trade inventories (AR, bi	0.2070

Table 12.9 Good Rules—Small-Firm Stocks

Rule #	Logic Code	⟩/⟨ Code	Cutoff Values			Fitness	Series Number and Differencing Interval					
			Series 1	Series 2	Series 3		1 #	Diff.	2 #	Diff.	3 #	Diff.
1	1	1	17	17	29	1.4210	251	3	71	3	197	3
2	7	5	25	14	23	1.1825	251	3	71	3	18	3
3	5	8	10	2	6	1.2351	251	3	71	3	42	3
4	5	8	30	3	6	1.2271	251	3	71	3	63	3
5	7	1	17	16	26	1.2586	251	3	71	3	220	1
6	7	5	31	20	27	1.2501	251	3	71	3	63	0
7	5	7	12	3	26	1.2114	251	3	71	3	220	3
8	5	5	24	20	25	1.3580	251	3	71	3	119	1
9	7	1	17	29	20	1.4327	251	3	197	3	18	3
10	5	6	12	22	8	1.2912	251	3	197	3	42	3
11	7	7	19	30	6	1.2790	251	3	197	3	63	3
12	7	3	17	28	28	1.5709	251	3	197	3	220	1
13	1	2	17	29	13	1.4210	251	3	197	3	63	0
14	3	2	17	16	20	1.4311	251	3	197	3	220	3
15	5	5	12	23	25	1.4492	251	3	197	3	119	1
16	5	2	17	25	10	1.4474	251	3	18	3	42	3
17	5	8	10	22	5	1.2203	251	3	18	3	63	3
18	7	3	2	25	8	0.9583	251	3	18	3	220	1
19	5	1	17	25	27	1.4030	251	3	18	3	63	0
20	3	2	17	20	20	1.1571	251	3	18	3	220	3
21	4	5	13	21	16	1.4676	251	3	18	3	119	1
22	1	2	17	27	12	1.4445	251	3	42	3	63	3
23	7	6	20	10	27	1.2901	251	3	42	3	220	1
24	7	6	17	9	30	1.2944	251	3	42	3	63	0
25	5	5	12	27	26	1.2682	251	3	42	3	220	3
26	7	1	2	25	25	1.4334	251	3	42	3	119	1
27	6	6	25	12	29	1.0938	251	3	63	3	220	1
28	7	2	17	13	17	1.2416	251	3	63	3	63	0
29	5	7	12	20	26	1.2453	251	3	63	3	220	3
30	5	7	31	6	25	1.5635	251	3	63	3	119	1
31	7	5	12	24	27	1.1518	251	3	220	1	63	0
32	5	7	12	7	26	1.2290	251	3	220	1	220	3
33	5	7	12	5	25	1.4144	251	3	220	1	119	1
34	2	1	1	27	26	1.3674	251	3	63	0	220	3
35	7	6	23	13	24	1.3790	251	3	63	0	119	1
36	2	3	1	4	25	1.3338	251	3	220	3	119	1
37	1	1	16	29	30	1.2672	71	3	197	3	18	3
38	7	3	16	29	20	1.3357	71	3	197	3	42	3
39	7	1	16	30	21	1.3286	71	3	197	3	63	3
40	3	2	20	14	19	1.3333	71	3	197	3	220	1
41	5	6	8	11	12	1.2911	71	3	197	3	63	0
42	3	2	16	14	20	1.4806	71	3	197	3	220	3
43	5	3	16	14	25	1.5667	71	3	197	3	119	1
44	1	1	16	25	25	1.2949	71	3	18	3	42	3
45	1	6	2	31	6	1.2933	71	3	18	3	63	3
46	3	1	15	25	23	1.2525	71	3	18	3	220	1

Continued on next page

Table 12.9 *(continued)*

Rule #	Logic Code	⟩/⟨ Code	Cutoff Values			Fitness	Series Number and Differencing Interval					
			Series 1	Series 2	Series 3		1		2		3	
							#	Diff.	#	Diff.	#	Diff.
47	1	1	20	29	27	1.3672	71	3	18	3	63	0
48	5	5	11	23	30	1.3036	71	3	18	3	220	3
49	4	1	16	21	16	1.5495	71	3	18	3	119	1
50	7	6	2	6	15	1.2455	71	3	42	3	63	3
51	7	8	2	6	15	1.2552	71	3	42	3	220	1
52	1	3	20	9	27	1.4771	71	3	42	3	63	0
53	5	5	9	28	26	1.2847	71	3	42	3	220	3
54	5	5	13	27	25	1.4732	71	3	42	3	119	1
55	3	1	16	0	27	1.2202	71	3	63	3	220	1
56	1	3	20	6	27	1.4104	71	3	63	3	63	0
57	1	7	3	7	26	1.3372	71	3	63	3	220	3
58	5	3	10	6	25	1.5652	71	3	63	3	119	1
59	1	1	16	27	27	1.3404	71	3	220	1	63	0
60	3	5	2	20	26	1.2777	71	3	220	1	220	3
61	6	5	5	11	25	1.4474	71	3	220	1	119	1
62	1	1	19	29	27	1.4080	71	3	63	0	220	3
63	5	5	7	25	25	1.4953	71	3	63	0	119	1
64	3	5	3	26	14	1.4309	71	3	220	3	119	1
65	2	2	4	25	6	1.2542	197	3	18	3	42	3
66	1	2	31	30	6	1.3134	197	3	18	3	63	3
67	2	1	31	20	20	1.0911	197	3	18	3	220	1
68	5	1	13	25	27	1.2624	197	3	18	3	63	0
69	2	2	10	25	25	1.2033	197	3	18	3	220	3
70	5	3	18	22	25	1.4861	197	3	18	3	119	1
71	1	4	31	8	6	1.3464	197	3	42	3	63	3
72	7	4	13	10	15	1.3919	197	3	42	3	220	1
73	3	4	31	10	19	1.3241	197	3	42	3	63	0
74	7	4	14	7	20	1.4561	197	3	42	3	220	3
75	5	1	14	27	25	1.4593	197	3	42	3	119	1
76	7	4	15	5	19	1.3883	197	3	63	3	220	1
77	1	3	30	6	30	1.3241	197	3	63	3	63	0
78	2	3	4	6	26	1.3146	197	3	63	3	220	3
79	5	3	1	6	25	1.5635	197	3	63	3	119	1
80	3	2	31	23	13	1.3236	197	3	220	1	63	0
81	3	3	30	31	26	1.3635	197	3	220	1	220	3
82	5	3	15	19	25	1.5733	197	3	220	1	119	1
83	7	4	16	12	23	1.5671	197	3	63	0	220	3
84	5	1	21	24	25	1.4614	197	3	63	0	119	1
85	2	3	13	20	25	1.5661	197	3	220	3	119	1
86	1	4	30	9	6	1.3155	18	3	42	3	63	3
87	7	2	25	9	23	1.3318	18	3	42	3	220	1
88	1	3	29	6	27	1.4303	18	3	42	3	63	0
89	7	4	15	9	8	1.2591	18	3	42	3	220	3
90	2	1	19	28	25	1.4376	18	3	42	3	119	1
91	2	4	20	6	5	1.1976	18	3	63	3	220	1
92	5	3	16	12	27	1.2887	18	3	63	3	63	0

Continued on next page

Table 12.9 *(continued)*

Rule #	Logic Code	⟩/⟨ Code	Cutoff Values			Fitness	Series Number and Differencing Interval					
			Series 1	Series 2	Series 3		1 #	Diff.	2 #	Diff.	3 #	Diff.
93	1	3	30	7	26	1.2616	18	3	63	3	220	3
94	5	3	14	6	25	1.5635	18	3	63	3	119	1
95	5	4	21	29	10	1.1233	18	3	220	1	63	0
96	5	3	5	5	26	1.1958	18	3	220	1	220	3
97	2	3	21	7	16	1.5185	18	3	220	1	119	1
98	1	1	30	29	26	1.4370	18	3	63	0	220	3
99	2	1	21	25	16	1.6192	18	3	63	0	119	1
100	5	3	24	20	25	1.5057	18	3	220	3	119	1
101	1	8	6	6	5	1.3331	42	3	63	3	220	1
102	1	7	7	6	27	1.5049	42	3	63	3	63	0
103	1	3	27	6	26	1.2934	42	3	63	3	220	3
104	1	7	7	6	23	1.5090	42	3	63	3	119	1
105	3	7	8	29	27	1.2939	42	3	220	1	63	0
106	1	5	10	27	29	1.2345	42	3	220	1	220	3
107	5	5	10	20	25	1.4872	42	3	220	1	119	1
108	3	3	25	13	24	1.2784	42	3	63	0	220	3
109	1	5	7	27	25	1.5492	42	3	63	0	119	1
110	3	1	25	16	16	1.4988	42	3	220	3	119	1
111	3	7	12	30	30	1.2933	63	3	220	1	63	0
112	6	1	23	19	26	1.2668	63	3	220	1	220	3
113	3	5	6	0	25	1.5635	63	3	220	1	119	1
114	1	5	6	30	26	1.5020	63	3	63	0	220	3
115	1	7	6	13	25	1.6133	63	3	63	0	119	1
116	6	5	6	2	25	1.5635	63	3	220	3	119	1
117	7	1	21	27	26	1.4458	220	1	63	0	220	3
118	7	2	17	5	16	1.4275	220	1	63	0	119	1
119	5	7	5	3	25	1.4083	220	1	220	3	119	1
120	3	1	27	15	16	1.6385	63	0	220	3	119	1

bond yields are declining, then stocks become relatively more attractive. However, the portion of the rule that relates to leading indicators is counterintuitive because it emphasizes decreases in the index of leading indicators. Again, this represents more of a contrarian philosophy.

PERFORMANCE OF THE SMALL-FIRM GOOD RULES

Once again, the GA seems to have done well in finding a group of rules that are behaving as desired. Figure 12.9 shows that the percentage of correct calls for this group of rules was rising rapidly over the 1984–1988 rule-building period; this trend continued until the end of 1989, when it seems to have reversed (see Figure 12.10). The moving average return for this group of rules was actually

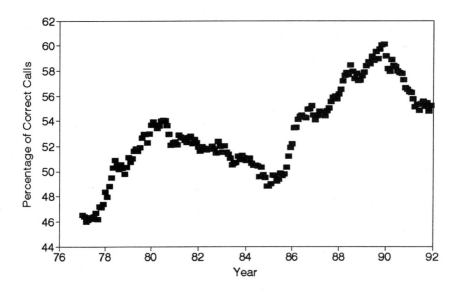

FIGURE 12.9   Percentage Correct (Small-Firm—Good Rules) 1977–1991

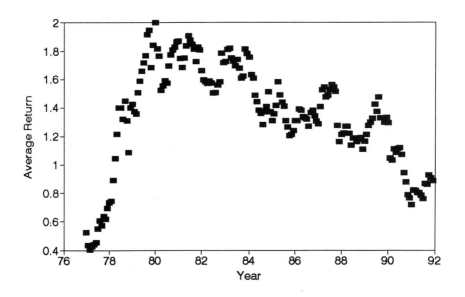

FIGURE 12.10   Percentage Correct (Small-Firm—Good Rules) 1988–1991

falling over the rule-building period (see Figure 12.11), but this was due to the general decline in returns for small-firm stocks. As can be seen in Figure 12.12, the average return was fairly stable in 1988 and increased in 1989 before declining further.

The detailed results are shown in Table 12.10. Performance in 1989 was not great, but this was a difficult year for small-firm stocks, which showed a return of 10.18 percent. In fact, they underperformed T-bills in six months of that year, which included zero or negative returns in the last four months. The return in 1990 was especially bad at −21.56 percent. Things improved greatly in 1991 when the annual return was 44.63 percent. All in all, the holdout period was an extremely volatile period for small-firm stocks; their average annual return during that time was only 7.72 percent.

The average annual return of the good rule portfolio for the 1989–1991 period was 6.71 percent. On average, the rules were correct 52.2 percent of the time. The average return for 1989 was 9.63 percent, with 52.5 percent correct calls. Apparently, the further one goes into the holdout period, the poorer the performance of the rule portfolio, which is not greatly surprising. This problem might be solved by annual, or even monthly, updating of the rule portfolio.

The individual rule results show the need for a portfolio approach. Rule 58, for example, had a relatively high fitness value at 1.5652 and made correct calls over 58 percent of the time in the rule-building period. However, this rule earned 7.9 percent in 1989 and had an average annual return of only 2.44 percent over the holdout period. The percentage of correct calls also slipped to 50 percent. Rule 18, on the other hand, had the lowest fitness of the entire set but performed well during the holdout period, averaging 13.7 percent overall. It is hard to predict the subsequent performance of any particular rule; it's a better idea to rely on the behavior of the portfolio.

"BAD" FORECASTING RULES FOR SMALL-FIRM STOCKS

The list of bad rules for small-firm stocks is shown in Table 12.11. Logic code 8 shows up in about one-fourth of the list. Apparently, very stringent rule conditions lead to bad rules, which would seem to make sense. Many of the rules also have extreme cutoff values.

Rule 29 has the highest fitness value, which makes it the number-one candidate to be a poor performing rule. Translated, the rule dictates that if (the three-month change in the price of lead scrap is in the bottom three-fourths of its range *and* the three-month change in labor cost is in the bottom half of its range) *or* (the three-month change in the index of leading indicators is in the top fifth of its range), then invest in small-firm stocks. Again we are pointed towards a possibly contrarian approach. If leading indicators are strongly rising, the rule says to invest in stocks. But remember—this is a bad rule. We want to do the opposite.

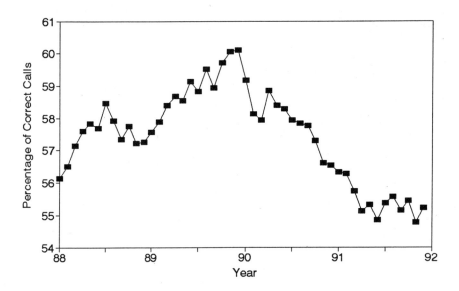

FIGURE 12.11 Average Return (Small-Firm—Good Rules) 1977–1991

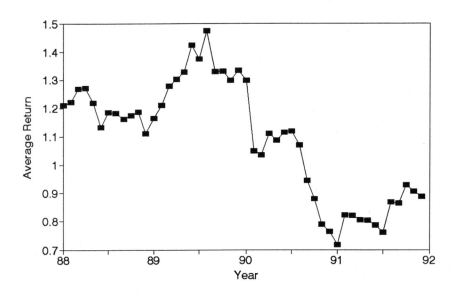

FIGURE 12.12 Average Return (Small-Firm—Good Rules) 1988–1991

Table 12.10 Performance Summary—Good Rules—Small-Firm Stocks

Rule #	Fitness	1971–1983 Period		1984–1988 Period		1989		1989–1991 Period	
		% Correct	Average Return	% Correct	Average Return	% Correct	Average Return	% Correct	Average Return
1	1.4210	52.08	14.03	63.33	18.66	33.33	1.50	41.67	4.86
2	1.1825	54.17	12.59	51.67	14.46	33.33	2.00	47.22	4.16
3	1.2351	47.22	14.34	50.00	4.71	66.67	18.10	58.33	9.33
4	1.2271	47.22	14.34	50.00	4.71	66.67	18.10	58.33	9.33
5	1.2586	51.39	11.51	58.33	16.75	41.67	4.90	52.78	4.28
6	1.2501	54.86	16.24	56.67	16.57	50.00	7.90	55.56	5.25
7	1.2114	51.39	18.16	53.33	13.57	58.33	10.20	61.11	12.13
8	1.3580	54.17	15.78	56.67	16.82	58.33	10.20	58.33	6.00
9	1.4327	47.92	16.84	56.67	16.57	66.67	15.80	55.56	5.07
10	1.2912	52.08	16.95	53.33	5.37	50.00	9.10	47.22	−2.08
11	1.2790	49.31	17.44	53.33	11.39	66.67	17.60	52.78	3.70
12	1.5709	47.22	12.04	66.67	19.83	41.67	8.40	38.89	2.28
13	1.4210	50.69	13.99	58.33	12.27	41.67	8.40	36.11	0.50
14	1.4311	49.31	11.86	61.67	18.22	33.33	1.50	50.00	17.13
15	1.4492	46.53	17.48	56.67	13.64	66.67	15.80	52.78	2.69
16	1.4474	48.61	18.02	56.67	15.75	58.33	8.30	55.56	7.32
17	1.2203	49.31	16.71	50.00	3.73	58.33	10.20	58.33	7.72
18	0.9583	45.14	15.14	50.00	12.17	66.67	15.60	63.89	13.70
19	1.4030	47.92	17.49	58.33	16.63	58.33	12.50	63.89	17.13
20	1.1571	51.39	15.71	63.33	18.66	33.33	1.50	41.67	6.56
21	1.4676	49.31	12.99	53.33	14.04	41.67	8.40	41.67	4.25
22	1.4445	46.53	7.39	63.33	16.65	41.67	4.30	36.11	0.10
23	1.2901	47.92	7.47	60.00	17.50	66.67	13.20	55.56	2.73
24	1.2944	47.22	7.00	58.33	16.86	58.33	10.20	52.78	1.15
25	1.2682	47.22	14.72	53.33	6.50	66.67	13.20	55.56	4.03
26	1.4334	47.22	14.72	53.33	6.50	66.67	13.20	55.56	4.03
27	1.0938	53.47	19.27	56.67	9.15	41.67	5.10	44.44	3.04
28	1.2416	55.56	20.05	58.33	19.21	41.67	4.60	47.22	7.26
29	1.2453	49.31	15.38	48.33	3.44	50.00	9.10	52.78	4.13
30	1.5635	52.08	17.29	56.67	5.09	58.33	8.60	52.78	2.66
31	1.1518	52.78	14.81	63.33	16.63	33.33	1.50	47.22	8.94
32	1.2290	47.92	12.26	58.33	13.59	25.00	1.00	38.89	5.13
33	1.4144	52.08	13.92	61.67	13.79	33.33	1.50	44.44	5.34
34	1.3674	48.61	11.14	53.33	6.17	50.00	6.50	50.00	6.44
35	1.3790	47.92	9.31	51.67	12.45	41.67	6.30	47.22	8.89
36	1.3338	53.47	12.75	53.33	13.41	50.00	7.90	41.67	−3.24
37	1.2672	47.22	9.05	61.67	17.91	50.00	11.90	50.00	2.22
38	1.3357	44.44	9.22	63.33	16.38	50.00	11.90	50.00	3.10
39	1.3286	50.00	16.25	51.67	14.48	66.67	17.60	55.56	4.71
40	1.3333	54.86	15.99	58.33	15.10	41.67	6.10	47.22	4.03
41	1.2911	47.92	12.20	50.00	4.73	75.00	21.60	61.11	12.16
42	1.4806	50.00	9.81	56.67	14.65	33.33	3.10	50.00	11.55
43	1.5667	44.44	13.73	61.67	17.07	50.00	10.20	47.22	0.23
44	1.2949	45.14	7.49	56.67	17.36	58.33	12.40	61.11	10.85
45	1.2933	45.83	13.14	53.33	12.07	58.33	10.20	61.11	12.79
46	1.2525	44.44	7.10	56.67	17.03	58.33	12.40	61.11	13.55

Continued on next page

Table 12.10 *(continued)*

Rule #	Fitness	1971–1983 Period % Correct	1971–1983 Period Average Return	1984–1988 Period % Correct	1984–1988 Period Average Return	1989 % Correct	1989 Average Return	1989–1991 Period % Correct	1989–1991 Period Average Return
47	1.3672	53.47	15.66	56.67	14.55	58.33	13.40	66.67	16.94
48	1.3036	46.53	15.94	60.00	18.45	66.67	14.40	63.89	13.32
49	1.5495	46.53	10.53	53.33	14.94	41.67	8.40	47.22	7.98
50	1.2455	47.92	8.31	58.33	17.03	58.33	10.20	61.11	12.79
51	1.2552	52.78	13.88	60.00	17.23	58.33	10.20	58.33	7.72
52	1.4771	48.61	8.41	60.00	20.20	58.33	10.90	52.78	1.64
53	1.2847	47.22	14.72	53.33	6.50	66.67	13.20	55.56	4.03
54	1.4732	47.22	14.72	53.33	6.50	66.67	13.20	55.56	4.03
55	1.2202	50.00	10.11	53.33	13.07	41.67	4.90	50.00	1.28
56	1.4104	54.86	17.13	58.33	15.10	58.33	8.60	52.78	2.66
57	1.3372	50.69	12.85	56.67	13.08	58.33	8.60	55.56	8.44
58	1.5652	50.69	16.40	58.33	12.74	50.00	7.90	50.00	2.44
59	1.3404	49.31	10.19	61.67	19.86	41.67	4.90	47.22	4.16
60	1.2777	45.83	9.16	56.67	13.40	33.33	1.50	44.44	7.69
61	1.4474	51.39	13.80	60.00	14.32	41.67	8.70	47.22	8.04
62	1.4080	51.39	10.62	58.33	16.64	50.00	7.90	55.56	6.71
63	1.4953	48.61	13.18	53.33	6.17	41.67	6.30	50.00	12.61
64	1.4309	48.61	9.48	58.33	17.51	50.00	7.90	55.56	11.41
65	1.2542	45.83	15.88	50.00	12.17	66.67	15.60	63.89	13.70
66	1.3134	47.92	17.25	56.67	12.96	66.67	17.60	58.33	7.32
67	1.0911	47.92	17.02	56.67	14.69	66.67	17.60	55.56	4.98
68	1.2624	45.83	15.59	55.00	15.10	66.67	15.60	66.67	15.05
69	1.2033	45.14	8.97	55.00	11.74	41.67	8.40	47.22	10.52
70	1.4861	43.75	8.41	61.67	19.27	66.67	15.60	55.56	10.60
71	1.3464	50.69	13.48	61.67	17.95	66.67	17.60	58.33	7.32
72	1.3919	52.78	16.57	61.67	16.90	33.33	3.00	50.00	4.43
73	1.3241	50.69	13.48	61.67	17.95	66.67	17.60	58.33	7.32
74	1.4561	50.69	14.70	56.67	14.97	41.67	5.00	61.11	16.35
75	1.4593	47.22	14.72	53.33	6.50	66.67	13.20	55.56	4.03
76	1.3883	47.92	12.56	53.33	11.91	58.33	11.90	55.56	13.11
77	1.3241	50.00	14.88	63.33	15.60	58.33	15.20	47.22	1.19
78	1.3146	53.47	17.97	60.00	13.97	58.33	8.60	55.56	4.56
79	1.5635	52.08	17.29	58.33	12.74	58.33	8.60	52.78	2.66
80	1.3236	47.92	17.25	56.67	14.69	66.67	17.60	58.33	7.32
81	1.3635	46.53	12.91	60.00	14.27	50.00	11.90	50.00	8.26
82	1.5733	52.08	17.42	70.00	16.60	41.67	8.90	47.22	7.98
83	1.5671	48.61	14.93	56.67	16.01	75.00	18.10	55.56	6.74
84	1.4614	47.22	11.66	53.33	6.17	41.67	6.30	50.00	10.87
85	1.5661	45.14	11.25	58.33	15.11	58.33	14.80	41.67	1.25
86	1.3155	53.47	14.31	63.33	18.26	66.67	18.10	63.89	11.25
87	1.3318	47.22	10.18	58.33	17.09	66.67	17.00	55.56	3.85
88	1.4303	48.61	9.41	65.00	18.60	75.00	21.50	58.33	6.50
89	1.2591	53.47	14.31	60.00	17.23	58.33	10.20	58.33	7.72
90	1.4376	45.14	13.41	53.33	6.50	66.67	13.20	55.56	4.03
91	1.1976	53.47	18.46	65.00	17.68	58.33	8.60	55.56	4.74
92	1.2887	53.47	20.53	51.67	11.50	41.67	5.10	47.22	1.80

Continued on next page

Table 12.10 *(continued)*

Rule #	Fitness	1971–1983 Period		1984–1988 Period		1989		1989–1991 Period	
		% Correct	Average Return	% Correct	Average Return	% Correct	Average Return	% Correct	Average Return
93	1.2616	52.78	17.02	61.67	14.28	66.67	16.40	58.33	6.97
94	1.5635	52.08	17.29	58.33	12.74	58.33	8.60	55.56	3.97
95	1.1233	50.69	12.39	53.33	7.46	41.67	8.40	41.67	3.76
96	1.1958	49.31	12.47	58.33	13.59	33.33	1.50	36.11	1.38
97	1.5185	49.31	12.91	48.33	13.38	41.67	8.40	47.22	10.17
98	1.4370	48.61	11.14	58.33	14.90	58.33	14.10	52.78	8.91
99	1.6192	48.61	13.26	48.33	5.71	41.67	8.20	47.22	8.75
100	1.5057	51.39	13.31	55.00	15.12	58.33	16.30	55.56	6.09
101	1.3331	56.25	18.20	68.33	20.73	58.33	8.60	55.56	5.70
102	1.5049	54.17	16.38	63.33	16.77	58.33	8.60	52.78	2.66
103	1.2934	50.69	14.94	60.00	14.23	66.67	11.60	52.78	2.09
104	1.5090	52.08	14.23	61.67	15.52	58.33	8.60	52.78	5.16
105	1.2939	52.08	12.96	65.00	21.17	41.67	4.90	50.00	6.85
106	1.2345	52.78	13.45	60.00	17.88	41.67	4.90	44.44	4.89
107	1.4872	56.94	16.47	65.00	16.91	33.33	1.50	47.22	8.94
108	1.2784	47.22	14.72	53.33	6.50	66.67	13.20	55.56	4.03
109	1.5492	50.00	11.06	60.00	17.14	41.67	6.30	50.00	12.61
110	1.4988	48.61	8.61	55.00	14.16	41.67	4.30	50.00	9.11
111	1.2933	54.86	22.07	56.67	15.12	41.67	5.10	44.44	3.04
112	1.2668	52.08	15.47	58.33	14.15	33.33	1.50	41.67	8.44
113	1.5635	54.17	17.35	66.67	15.45	41.67	2.10	50.00	9.36
114	1.5020	47.92	9.99	65.00	17.60	50.00	5.00	50.00	5.19
115	1.6133	45.83	8.70	65.00	18.52	41.67	4.70	50.00	11.31
116	1.5635	55.56	17.69	63.33	17.62	58.33	8.60	52.78	4.49
117	1.4458	47.92	11.09	53.33	6.17	58.33	10.20	52.78	7.66
118	1.4275	50.00	9.07	50.00	13.89	33.33	1.00	47.22	12.27
119	1.4083	54.86	14.35	55.00	14.22	50.00	7.90	47.22	−0.81
120	1.6385	47.92	8.64	56.67	14.52	33.33	1.50	55.56	15.35

PERFORMANCE OF THE SMALL-FIRM BAD RULES

Figure 12.13 illustrates the steep decline in forecasting accuracy for this bad rule portfolio that began in about 1985. Figure 12.14 shows how the decline continued until about 1990, at which time the accuracy began a slight improvement that accelerated in 1991. Figure 12.15 shows a similar pattern for the average return; note the sharp discontinuity that occurred around the crash of 1987. From Figure 12.16, we can see that average returns seemed to bounce around within a band until late 1990, when they dropped substantially.

The detailed results of the small-firm bad rule portfolio can be seen in Table 12.12. The average return for 1989 was 7.84 percent, with 45.35 percent correct calls, and the average annual return for the entire holdout period was 7.88 percent, with 47.22 percent correct calls. These rules appear to be making calls that are

Table 12.11   Bad Rules—Small-Firm Stocks

Rule #	Logic Code	>/< Code	Cutoff Values			Fitness	Series Number and Differencing Interval					
			Series 1	Series 2	Series 3		1 #	Diff.	2 #	Diff.	3 #	Diff.
1	6	4	22	17	18	12.5806	251	3	71	3	197	3
2	6	4	25	16	21	12.2145	251	3	71	3	18	3
3	4	1	27	8	7	12.4652	251	3	71	3	42	3
4	8	5	24	2	13	12.1064	251	3	71	3	63	3
5	4	4	26	16	27	11.9183	251	3	71	3	220	1
6	6	4	21	20	27	12.4389	251	3	71	3	63	0
7	2	4	13	5	26	11.9920	251	3	71	3	220	3
8	4	4	19	16	25	12.0872	251	3	71	3	119	1
9	4	4	21	18	25	12.7289	251	3	197	3	18	3
10	4	3	24	17	6	12.6222	251	3	197	3	42	3
11	7	2	16	21	6	12.4638	251	3	197	3	63	3
12	7	4	23	21	21	12.4198	251	3	197	3	220	1
13	4	3	21	18	13	12.5970	251	3	197	3	63	0
14	4	4	20	13	26	12.5601	251	3	197	3	220	3
15	4	4	27	26	25	12.7397	251	3	197	3	119	1
16	4	7	16	25	7	12.1998	251	3	18	3	42	3
17	4	3	25	21	9	12.1792	251	3	18	3	63	3
18	6	2	14	25	22	12.2459	251	3	18	3	220	1
19	6	4	21	25	27	12.6262	251	3	18	3	63	0
20	8	4	13	30	26	12.1255	251	3	18	3	220	3
21	5	4	14	25	7	12.2451	251	3	18	3	119	1
22	4	3	26	25	6	12.2420	251	3	42	3	63	3
23	8	2	13	9	27	12.1123	251	3	42	3	220	1
24	2	1	13	8	30	11.9634	251	3	42	3	63	0
25	8	2	13	7	26	12.3094	251	3	42	3	220	3
26	4	4	25	26	25	12.3573	251	3	42	3	119	1
27	4	2	25	14	27	12.7184	251	3	63	3	220	1
28	6	3	21	5	29	12.5994	251	3	63	3	63	0
29	4	2	24	14	26	12.9190	251	3	63	3	220	3
30	8	2	10	6	25	12.6556	251	3	63	3	119	1
31	4	8	17	12	27	11.9447	251	3	220	1	63	0
32	6	2	29	27	20	12.1517	251	3	220	1	220	3
33	4	2	14	7	25	12.6131	251	3	220	1	119	1
34	6	1	30	7	20	11.9447	251	3	63	0	220	3
35	4	4	27	27	25	12.8998	251	3	63	0	119	1
36	6	4	13	26	24	12.0258	251	3	220	3	119	1
37	8	8	20	28	29	12.2150	71	3	197	3	18	3
38	8	7	20	29	7	12.2710	71	3	197	3	42	3
39	4	3	8	12	13	12.6585	71	3	197	3	63	3
40	8	8	16	29	27	12.4078	71	3	197	3	220	1
41	2	8	20	13	20	12.0902	71	3	197	3	63	0
42	8	8	19	28	27	12.3920	71	3	197	3	220	3
43	8	8	20	29	25	12.6499	71	3	197	3	119	1
44	6	6	15	24	23	12.1187	71	3	18	3	42	3
45	5	7	17	25	18	12.1562	71	3	18	3	63	3
46	6	4	8	29	12	12.1372	71	3	18	3	220	1

Continued on next page

Table 12.11 *(continued)*

Rule #	Logic Code	⟩/⟨ Code	Cutoff Values				Series Number and Differencing Interval					
			Series 1	Series 2	Series 3	Fitness	1 #	Diff.	2 #	Diff.	3 #	Diff.
47	8	8	20	25	27	12.0018	71	3	18	3	63	0
48	8	8	17	29	27	12.0416	71	3	18	3	220	3
49	2	8	17	21	17	12.1234	71	3	18	3	119	1
50	8	1	3	9	13	12.4199	71	3	42	3	63	3
51	2	2	8	8	6	12.3049	71	3	42	3	220	1
52	8	6	20	6	27	12.0493	71	3	42	3	63	0
53	2	2	8	10	3	12.3049	71	3	42	3	220	3
54	5	2	8	8	1	12.3049	71	3	42	3	119	1
55	2	2	2	14	6	12.1390	71	3	63	3	220	1
56	6	3	8	13	18	12.5541	71	3	63	3	63	0
57	2	2	3	13	9	12.4960	71	3	63	3	220	3
58	8	2	2	6	25	12.8781	71	3	63	3	119	1
59	2	8	17	20	19	12.0720	71	3	220	1	63	0
60	2	4	3	21	26	12.0668	71	3	220	1	220	3
61	7	4	8	11	25	12.4232	71	3	220	1	119	1
62	4	4	8	19	30	12.1102	71	3	63	0	220	3
63	4	4	2	24	25	12.3333	71	3	63	0	119	1
64	8	4	3	30	25	12.4398	71	3	220	3	119	1
65	4	7	31	19	9	12.0504	197	3	18	3	42	3
66	2	7	30	25	18	12.4513	197	3	18	3	63	3
67	2	8	31	24	27	12.3306	197	3	18	3	220	1
68	2	7	31	25	23	12.4512	197	3	18	3	63	0
69	8	8	30	29	26	12.4479	197	3	18	3	220	3
70	7	8	31	19	25	12.5277	197	3	18	3	119	1
71	4	7	15	25	13	12.2545	197	3	42	3	63	3
72	8	6	16	0	24	11.9349	197	3	42	3	220	1
73	6	7	13	10	19	12.4417	197	3	42	3	63	0
74	6	5	15	7	20	12.5378	197	3	42	3	220	3
75	8	6	30	7	25	12.6481	197	3	42	3	119	1
76	4	6	12	20	24	12.2865	197	3	63	3	220	1
77	2	6	31	20	19	12.2613	197	3	63	3	63	0
78	6	5	15	13	18	12.5463	197	3	63	3	220	3
79	2	8	30	12	23	12.6322	197	3	63	3	119	1
80	2	8	30	20	19	12.4056	197	3	220	1	63	0
81	2	8	31	21	26	12.2583	197	3	220	1	220	3
82	3	6	13	16	25	12.7551	197	3	220	1	119	1
83	4	8	29	9	26	12.2517	197	3	63	0	220	3
84	8	8	26	30	25	12.3427	197	3	63	0	119	1
85	2	8	30	8	24	12.5685	197	3	220	3	119	1
86	4	7	19	28	13	12.2856	18	3	42	3	63	3
87	8	5	25	8	5	12.2271	18	3	42	3	220	1
88	6	7	24	9	16	12.2610	18	3	42	3	63	0
89	8	8	29	24	26	12.0305	18	3	42	3	220	3
90	3	6	21	10	16	12.3026	18	3	42	3	119	1
91	6	7	24	13	22	12.2689	18	3	63	3	220	1
92	7	7	25	20	19	12.7377	18	3	63	3	63	0

Continued on next page

Table 12.11 *(continued)*

Rule #	Logic Code	⟩/⟨ Code	Cutoff Values			Fitness	Series Number and Differencing Interval					
			Series 1	Series 2	Series 3		1		2		3	
							#	Diff.	#	Diff.	#	Diff.
93	4	6	20	13	27	12.3591	18	3	63	3	220	3
94	2	5	25	19	10	12.1297	18	3	63	3	119	1
95	3	7	25	26	23	11.8871	18	3	220	1	63	0
96	8	6	29	7	26	11.9979	18	3	220	1	220	3
97	1	8	20	17	16	12.1812	18	3	220	1	119	1
98	8	8	29	27	26	12.2229	18	3	63	0	220	3
99	3	8	20	25	16	12.2456	18	3	63	0	119	1
100	4	6	24	14	25	12.1967	18	3	220	3	119	1
101	2	1	7	20	28	12.2783	42	3	63	3	220	1
102	2	2	9	20	19	12.8194	42	3	63	3	63	0
103	6	7	28	13	1	12.2205	42	3	63	3	220	3
104	8	6	25	12	24	12.7041	42	3	63	3	119	1
105	4	4	20	27	27	11.9667	42	3	220	1	63	0
106	8	2	10	5	26	12.1382	42	3	220	1	220	3
107	8	2	7	5	25	12.4605	42	3	220	1	119	1
108	2	6	24	26	26	11.9630	42	3	63	0	220	3
109	8	4	8	27	25	12.2019	42	3	63	0	119	1
110	2	4	9	8	21	12.2362	42	3	220	3	119	1
111	6	4	20	31	19	12.5190	63	3	220	1	63	0
112	4	4	13	6	27	12.4602	63	3	220	1	220	3
113	2	4	6	17	24	12.3720	63	3	220	1	119	1
114	4	4	20	19	30	12.7001	63	3	63	0	220	3
115	8	4	12	29	24	12.5760	63	3	63	0	119	1
116	8	4	6	29	25	12.4690	63	3	220	3	119	1
117	4	4	29	27	26	12.0845	220	1	63	0	220	3
118	4	4	11	29	25	12.4162	220	1	63	0	119	1
119	8	4	7	29	25	12.3591	220	1	220	3	119	1
120	2	8	27	26	14	12.2611	63	0	220	3	119	1

less reliable than a coin flip over the entire holdout period. Once again, the expected performance is worse the further you stretch past the rule-building period. Regular updating of the rule base is probably necessary.

HEDGE PORTFOLIO RESULTS

As described in Chapter 11, a hedge portfolio might be constructed by going long on the good rules and going short on the bad rules. Let's say that 90 of the 120 good rules indicate ''Invest in the S&P 500!'' and the remaining 30 rules signal Treasury bills as being the better investment. An investor might use these signals to maintain a 75 percent S&P stocks/25 percent Treasury bill allocation in the given month. However, let's also suppose that the bad rules suggest a 20 percent

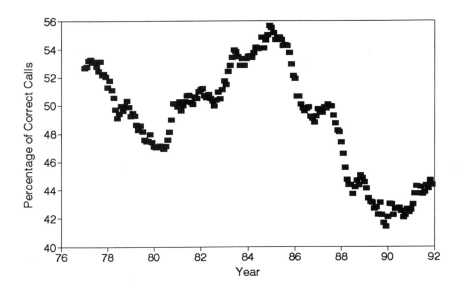

FIGURE 12.13 Percentage Correct (Small-Firm—Bad Rules) 1977–1991

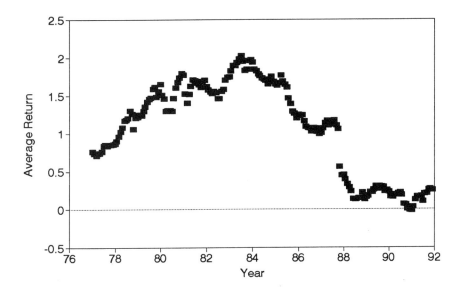

FIGURE 12.14 Percentage Correct (Small-Firm—Bad Rules) 1988–1991

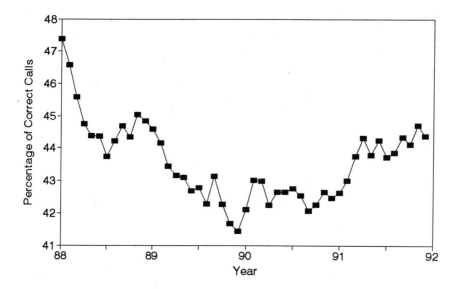

FIGURE 12.15   Average Return (Small-Firm—Bad Rules) 1977–1991

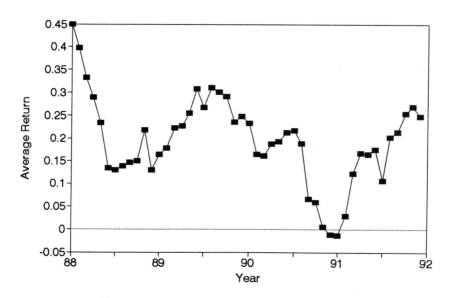

FIGURE 12.16   Average Return (Small-Firm—Bad Rules) 1988–1991

Table 12.12 Performance Summary—Bad Rules—Small-Firm Stocks

Rule #	Fitness	1971–1983 Period % Correct	1971–1983 Period Average Return	1984–1988 Period % Correct	1984–1988 Period Average Return	1989 % Correct	1989 Average Return	1989–1991 Period % Correct	1989–1991 Period Average Return
1	12.5806	47.22	14.62	46.67	−1.17	50.00	10.70	44.44	9.75
2	12.2145	48.61	16.18	41.67	−2.55	58.33	13.90	47.22	10.82
3	12.4652	52.78	13.18	50.00	8.26	25.00	−1.80	36.11	3.07
4	12.1064	55.56	14.60	50.00	5.76	41.67	6.50	50.00	5.67
5	11.9183	49.31	16.64	41.67	−2.75	58.33	13.90	47.22	10.82
6	12.4389	45.14	11.45	43.33	−2.39	50.00	10.70	44.44	9.75
7	11.9920	52.08	12.68	50.00	2.04	41.67	8.80	47.22	13.60
8	12.0872	50.69	16.04	46.67	−1.80	41.67	8.40	41.67	9.00
9	12.7289	58.33	15.89	46.67	−0.46	33.33	3.10	38.89	3.07
10	12.6222	56.25	23.15	48.33	9.02	41.67	6.70	50.00	7.09
11	12.4638	56.25	16.59	45.00	6.62	33.33	1.50	44.44	14.29
12	12.4198	54.17	12.91	46.67	−0.42	33.33	3.10	47.22	13.29
13	12.5970	55.56	21.12	53.33	11.66	41.67	5.30	44.44	3.85
14	12.5601	57.64	15.72	48.33	−0.77	33.33	3.10	41.67	3.51
15	12.7397	54.17	10.98	45.00	0.28	33.33	3.10	47.22	12.53
16	12.1998	51.39	10.09	43.33	−1.38	41.67	10.20	38.89	5.58
17	12.1792	52.78	17.90	50.00	7.80	58.33	10.20	55.56	7.49
18	12.2459	56.94	14.91	48.33	0.38	33.33	3.30	41.67	5.25
19	12.6262	54.86	12.51	46.67	−0.96	33.33	3.30	36.11	1.61
20	12.1255	53.47	13.74	46.67	1.08	41.67	5.30	41.67	6.41
21	12.2451	56.94	16.40	51.67	2.09	33.33	3.30	41.67	6.94
22	12.2420	52.08	20.31	40.00	−3.15	33.33	5.40	44.44	11.06
23	12.1123	52.08	19.05	43.33	−1.40	41.67	8.80	50.00	12.56
24	11.9634	50.00	17.16	43.33	−1.17	41.67	8.80	47.22	13.60
25	12.3094	52.08	19.05	43.33	−1.40	41.67	8.80	50.00	12.56
26	12.3573	52.78	12.93	46.67	6.85	33.33	5.40	44.44	11.06
27	12.7184	55.56	18.31	46.67	8.26	58.33	13.60	58.33	15.51
28	12.5994	48.61	9.85	40.00	−0.59	41.67	8.40	47.22	12.00
29	12.9190	55.56	18.31	45.00	7.86	50.00	11.20	52.78	13.24
30	12.6556	50.69	13.83	43.33	2.85	58.33	14.20	55.56	17.86
31	11.9447	51.39	17.40	36.67	−3.94	66.67	17.60	61.11	10.68
32	12.1517	52.08	13.43	46.67	4.91	66.67	10.00	58.33	10.19
33	12.6131	50.69	15.94	38.33	0.00	75.00	18.20	61.11	12.66
34	11.9447	47.92	11.62	48.33	1.29	41.67	6.10	50.00	10.55
35	12.8998	51.39	14.47	46.67	7.17	58.33	12.40	50.00	2.60
36	12.0258	45.83	11.97	38.33	−3.47	50.00	10.70	44.44	4.62
37	12.2150	51.39	16.07	40.00	−3.34	41.67	3.70	47.22	11.95
38	12.2710	50.00	15.76	41.67	−1.93	41.67	3.70	47.22	11.95
39	12.6585	52.78	16.61	50.00	10.02	33.33	0.30	38.89	2.66
40	12.4078	52.08	15.81	38.33	−3.50	41.67	5.40	47.22	12.58
41	12.0902	53.47	17.04	45.00	−1.63	41.67	5.30	50.00	14.93
42	12.3920	49.31	12.64	41.67	−2.75	33.33	2.40	44.44	11.52
43	12.6499	52.08	14.27	43.33	−2.15	41.67	5.30	47.22	14.11
44	12.1187	58.33	18.47	48.33	−1.38	50.00	6.50	38.89	0.00
45	12.1562	47.92	8.10	46.67	7.10	41.67	8.40	41.67	7.26
46	12.1372	53.47	13.69	41.67	−1.04	25.00	−2.00	36.11	3.01

Continued on next page

Table 12.12 *(continued)*

Rule #	Fitness	1971–1983 Period		1984–1988 Period		1989		1989–1991 Period	
		% Correct	Average Return	% Correct	Average Return	% Correct	Average Return	% Correct	Average Return
47	12.0018	51.39	16.20	45.00	− 2.44	33.33	3.30	36.11	3.26
48	12.0416	48.61	15.19	45.00	− 0.04	41.67	5.30	33.33	− 1.18
49	12.1234	52.78	16.18	48.33	0.22	58.33	10.20	52.78	7.00
50	12.4199	47.92	17.33	45.00	− 0.08	41.67	8.40	41.67	3.35
51	12.3049	52.78	13.18	50.00	8.26	25.00	− 1.80	36.11	3.07
52	12.0493	51.39	19.50	40.00	− 5.34	41.67	7.70	47.22	13.68
53	12.3049	50.00	13.46	45.00	5.21	25.00	− 1.80	36.11	3.07
54	12.3049	52.08	19.10	41.67	− 2.09	25.00	− 1.80	36.11	3.07
55	12.1390	59.72	16.65	55.00	10.28	58.33	11.90	47.22	3.91
56	12.5541	52.08	11.51	46.67	0.71	50.00	10.30	52.78	14.42
57	12.4960	54.86	12.25	48.33	7.14	50.00	8.90	41.67	2.50
58	12.8781	49.31	14.30	43.33	1.11	41.67	9.90	44.44	6.56
59	12.0720	54.86	22.86	50.00	0.57	50.00	14.00	55.56	8.52
60	12.0668	53.47	18.55	43.33	0.34	66.67	17.70	55.56	7.29
61	12.4232	50.00	14.99	40.00	− 0.85	50.00	6.60	47.22	4.31
62	12.1102	51.39	16.69	45.00	7.04	33.33	5.20	41.67	6.21
63	12.3333	52.08	14.90	46.67	7.17	58.33	12.40	50.00	2.60
64	12.4398	49.31	17.03	46.67	− 0.20	50.00	10.70	41.67	3.66
65	12.0504	52.08	10.67	46.67	1.63	33.33	1.50	47.22	10.55
66	12.4513	52.08	10.49	43.33	− 0.77	33.33	1.50	44.44	9.42
67	12.3306	53.47	11.05	45.00	1.10	33.33	2.40	36.11	− 0.23
68	12.4512	52.08	10.49	43.33	− 0.77	33.33	1.50	41.67	7.69
69	12.4479	53.47	11.45	41.67	− 1.36	41.67	5.30	38.89	0.76
70	12.5277	54.86	12.70	45.00	− 1.57	33.33	3.30	38.89	1.90
71	12.2545	50.00	16.81	41.67	− 0.79	33.33	5.40	47.22	13.96
72	11.9349	54.17	17.66	46.67	0.53	33.33	4.60	47.22	4.07
73	12.4417	53.47	20.07	46.67	− 0.73	25.00	0.90	44.44	3.63
74	12.5378	49.31	12.95	43.33	− 1.02	58.33	13.70	38.89	− 0.67
75	12.6481	52.08	15.87	38.33	− 3.75	33.33	1.50	44.44	7.61
76	12.2865	55.56	19.21	46.67	2.20	58.33	12.10	50.00	5.55
77	12.2613	51.39	11.05	43.33	− 1.46	33.33	1.50	41.67	7.69
78	12.5463	51.39	15.29	43.33	0.28	50.00	6.60	52.78	4.89
79	12.6322	51.39	11.53	48.33	2.29	33.33	1.50	44.44	6.79
80	12.4056	53.47	19.30	48.33	0.12	33.33	3.30	52.78	9.28
81	12.2583	53.47	15.05	40.00	− 0.44	50.00	6.70	50.00	5.97
82	12.7551	50.69	13.38	35.00	− 1.13	66.67	15.80	66.67	17.98
83	12.2517	53.47	16.48	45.00	6.78	41.67	5.10	52.78	9.47
85	12.5685	47.92	12.93	41.67	− 1.74	50.00	6.60	50.00	7.72
86	12.2856	50.00	17.62	43.33	− 0.46	33.33	5.40	47.22	12.08
87	12.2271	52.08	17.42	43.33	− 3.47	33.33	3.30	36.11	1.61
88	12.2610	53.47	18.17	46.67	− 2.77	33.33	3.00	36.11	1.51
89	12.0305	52.78	12.93	40.00	− 1.31	25.00	− 1.80	41.67	8.49
90	12.3026	53.47	18.18	48.33	− 0.51	33.33	3.00	44.44	2.95
91	12.2689	53.47	11.72	46.67	0.22	58.33	13.60	55.56	13.44
92	12.7377	52.08	11.74	41.67	− 4.44	41.67	5.30	38.89	1.12

Continued on next page

Table 12.12 *(continued)*

Rule #	Fitness	1971–1983 Period		1984–1988 Period		1989		1989–1991 Period	
		% Correct	Average Return	% Correct	Average Return	% Correct	Average Return	% Correct	Average Return
93	12.3591	52.08	11.73	48.33	1.70	58.33	13.60	52.78	12.64
94	12.1297	54.17	11.29	43.33	−1.68	33.33	3.30	41.67	3.51
95	11.8871	54.17	11.88	48.33	0.04	41.67	5.30	38.89	2.28
96	11.9979	50.69	15.27	40.00	0.67	58.33	9.60	61.11	13.03
97	12.1812	50.69	18.63	48.33	−0.12	66.67	18.20	52.78	3.01
98	12.2229	52.08	17.10	40.00	−1.02	41.67	4.50	47.22	6.03
99	12.2456	54.86	20.48	50.00	9.59	58.33	10.40	52.78	4.31
100	12.1967	47.22	13.17	45.00	−1.34	41.67	3.10	47.22	13.16
101	12.2783	51.39	18.55	41.67	−2.22	58.33	12.10	55.56	8.66
102	12.8194	46.53	14.30	40.00	−3.59	41.67	8.40	44.44	10.93
103	12.2205	53.47	14.56	43.33	−1.74	50.00	10.50	52.78	13.00
104	12.7041	49.31	12.34	50.00	2.92	50.00	10.50	55.56	14.27
105	11.9667	47.92	9.16	41.67	−1.13	58.33	13.90	55.56	10.17
106	12.1382	49.31	17.44	43.33	−0.51	66.67	17.70	63.89	13.96
107	12.4605	45.83	15.44	40.00	−0.69	66.67	17.70	61.11	13.91
108	11.9630	52.78	12.93	46.67	6.85	33.33	5.40	44.44	11.06
109	12.2019	50.00	16.66	40.00	−2.86	58.33	12.40	50.00	2.60
110	12.2362	45.83	13.83	53.33	1.63	66.67	17.10	50.00	6.62
111	12.5190	51.39	20.04	50.00	1.34	66.67	20.30	58.33	10.06
112	12.4602	54.17	13.97	40.00	−1.68	66.67	16.90	55.56	8.38
113	12.3720	47.22	11.34	33.33	−2.86	58.33	16.90	50.00	5.67
114	12.7001	54.17	18.02	38.33	3.44	50.00	14.00	41.67	4.19
115	12.5760	52.08	19.22	46.67	0.90	75.00	17.80	61.11	6.50
116	12.4690	43.75	9.39	36.67	−3.27	41.67	9.90	47.22	10.58
117	12.0845	51.39	16.57	46.67	7.17	50.00	12.10	50.00	8.55
118	12.4162	51.39	14.47	46.67	7.17	58.33	12.40	50.00	2.60
119	12.3591	45.14	13.25	46.67	1.00	58.33	11.20	61.11	20.05
120	12.2611	52.78	20.16	36.67	−3.99	50.00	10.70	44.44	6.38

S&P 500/80 percent Treasury bill split. For simplicity, we'll use $10,000 as a base investment figure. The good rules say to put $7,500 in stocks and $2,500 in T-Bills, whereas the bad rules say to short $2,000 of stocks and short $8,000 in T-bills; the net effect of the combination is to short $5,500 in T-bills and invest $5,500 in stocks.

We need to digress a moment to talk about transaction costs because we are simplifying life greatly here by ignoring them and other real-world constraints. However, in today's world of derivative securities, there are many implementation possibilities for our basic concept of the hedge portfolio. It is also possible to use leverage to magnify the benefits of small, but consistent, return differentials. We reiterate that our purpose in this book is not to show precisely how you could make money using strategies derived by using genetic algorithms but to suggest possibilities that seem to warrant further investigation.

The hedge portfolio results for S&P 500 stocks are shown in Table 12.13. As you can see, it performs reasonably well. The long portfolio does outperform the short portfolio for 1989 and for the entire 1989–1991 holdout period. Two return figures are reported: the monthly return and the cumulative return.

The "returns" on the hedge portfolio require some tricky interpretation because the net investment is zero. Let's assume that we are willing to go short a

Table 12.13   Hedge Portfolio Results—S&P 500 Stocks

		Cumulative Return			Hedge Portfolio	
Year	Month	Buy and Hold	Long Portfolio	Short Portfolio	Return	Cumulative Return
1989	1	7.23	5.78	1.33	4.45	4.45
	2	4.56	3.83	1.61	−2.12	2.34
	3	7.03	5.54	2.73	0.54	2.87
	4	12.55	8.18	4.96	0.34	3.21
	5	17.07	11.71	6.15	2.13	5.33
	6	16.44	11.29	6.74	−0.93	4.41
	7	26.90	18.83	9.77	3.93	8.34
	8	29.35	20.77	10.90	0.60	8.94
	9	28.84	20.69	11.28	−0.42	8.53
	10	25.84	18.39	11.20	−1.83	6.70
	11	28.46	20.37	12.37	0.63	7.32
	12	31.49	22.72	13.55	0.90	8.23
1990	1	22.67	16.57	12.47	−4.06	4.16
	2	24.25	17.90	13.24	0.46	4.62
	3	27.52	20.63	14.23	1.44	6.06
	4	24.37	18.83	13.39	−0.76	5.30
	5	36.49	28.08	16.05	5.44	10.74
	6	35.54	27.54	16.61	−0.91	9.83
	7	35.11	27.27	17.34	−0.83	9.00
	8	22.91	16.80	16.98	−7.91	1.08
	9	16.86	12.50	16.66	−3.40	−2.32
	10	16.43	12.56	17.13	−0.36	−2.68
	11	23.92	18.16	19.12	3.28	0.60
	12	27.32	20.83	20.39	1.19	1.79
1991	1	32.95	24.91	22.54	1.59	3.39
	2	42.47	32.60	25.58	3.67	7.06
	3	45.86	35.42	26.86	1.10	8.16
	4	46.26	35.84	27.42	−0.13	8.03
	5	52.52	41.01	29.68	2.03	10.06
	6	45.55	37.20	26.67	−0.37	9.69
	7	52.37	41.28	30.83	−0.31	9.38
	8	55.95	43.53	32.13	0.60	9.97
	9	53.39	43.01	31.16	0.37	10.34
	10	55.44	44.25	32.22	0.07	10.41
	11	49.16	41.78	31.12	−0.89	9.52
	12	66.21	52.63	35.60	4.24	13.76

maximum of $10,000 with an offsetting $10,000 long position. Calculating our net position as described above, this extreme position would occur only if 100 percent of the good rules and 100 percent of the bad rules gave the same signals. Our actual position might be $5,500 long in stocks and $5,500 short in T-Bills, as in our previous example.

After the first eight months of the holdout period, the hedge portfolio has a cumulative positive return of 8.94 percent. If the maximum base investment was always $10,000, then the cumulative dollar advantage would have been $894. The cumulative return becomes negative in 1990 but finishes in the black by 13.76 percent. Clearly, the long and short portfolio seem to be performing differently. The GA has successfully identified sets of rules with different return characteristics. Further refinements might accentuate this difference, making it even more attractive. Figure 12.17 graphically displays the hedge portfolio results.

The hedge portfolio results for small-firm stocks are not highly attractive, but they do show some promise. As can be seen in Table 12.14, the cumulative return starts positively and stays that way through the first year of the holdout period. After that time, the bad rule portfolio begins to actually outperform the good rule portfolio, leading to negative results for the hedged position. The reason why this still shows promise is that in actual application we would probably be updating our rule portfolios at least annually. As long as we can develop a long portfolio that outperforms a short portfolio going into the future, even if the path into the future is short-lived, we create the possibility of a lucrative investment strategy.

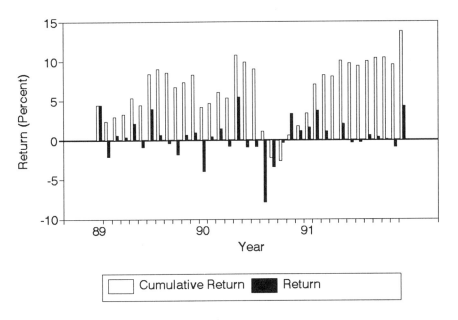

FIGURE 12.17 Hedge Portfolio—S&P 500 Stocks

Table 12.14   Hedge Portfolio Results—Small-Firm Stocks

		Cumulative Return			Hedge Portfolio	
Year	Month	Buy and Hold	Long Portfolio	Short Portfolio	Return	Cumulative Return
1989	1	4.04	3.14	1.22	1.92	1.92
	2	4.90	3.94	1.88	0.12	2.04
	3	8.66	6.70	3.33	1.24	3.28
	4	11.69	8.27	5.32	−0.46	2.82
	5	15.73	11.34	7.34	0.92	3.74
	6	13.41	10.32	6.57	−0.20	3.54
	7	18.02	13.26	9.23	0.17	3.70
	8	19.46	14.44	10.35	0.02	3.72
	9	19.46	14.80	10.65	0.04	3.77
	10	12.25	10.76	7.56	−0.73	3.04
	11	11.68	10.58	7.74	−0.33	2.71
	12	10.18	9.64	7.84	−0.94	1.77
1990	1	1.76	3.81	6.32	−3.90	−2.13
	2	3.66	5.38	7.20	0.68	−1.45
	3	7.48	8.83	8.51	2.05	0.60
	4	4.62	6.42	8.29	−2.01	−1.41
	5	10.49	10.69	11.20	1.31	−0.09
	6	12.08	11.92	12.33	0.10	0.01
	7	7.80	9.08	10.99	−1.35	−1.34
	8	−6.17	0.76	3.03	−0.45	−1.80
	9	−13.95	−5.35	0.29	−3.41	−5.20
	10	−18.87	−8.40	−1.60	−1.33	−6.54
	11	−15.22	−5.32	−0.23	1.97	−4.57
	12	−13.58	−3.70	0.62	0.87	−3.70
1991	1	−6.31	3.32	3.78	4.14	0.44
	2	4.12	9.51	11.56	−1.51	−1.07
	3	11.20	12.54	17.14	−2.23	−3.29
	4	11.58	13.07	17.58	0.09	−3.21
	5	15.30	14.39	20.95	−1.70	−4.90
	6	9.71	13.06	16.46	2.55	−2.36
	7	14.18	15.67	19.61	−0.39	−2.74
	8	17.16	17.49	21.51	−0.02	−2.76
	9	17.53	17.95	21.97	0.01	−2.75
	10	21.26	19.77	24.64	−0.64	−3.39
	11	17.91	18.13	23.36	−0.34	−3.74
	12	25.00	22.40	26.49	1.08	−2.66

For example, if we could develop a system for finding a long rule portfolio that outperforms a short rule portfolio for three months, we could merely update our rule portfolios every three months and have an ongoing, attractive hedge portfolio. It might even be better to only project one month forward and then update the rule base. This is certainly an avenue worthy of further investigation.

CONCLUSIONS

The results are intriguing. They do not point to some sure-fire method of beating the market, but they do show great promise. In Chapter 15 we will elaborate on possible additional refinements to our basic approach. There are many simple modifications that could prove to be more profitable. We have drawn several major conclusions from the results in this chapter, which are summarized below.

1. The GA is indeed finding rules with the characteristics that we specified. The graphs of average return shown in Figures 12.2, 12.6, 12.11, and 12.15 clearly demonstrate this. The good rules, as a group, show patterns of attractive returns that appear to be increasing; the bad rules have opposite patterns. Furthermore, the performance summary tables show patterns of average return and percentage of correct calls that are consistent with the fitness calculation.

2. The behavior of the rules does seem to persist into the holdout period. This can be most clearly seen by focusing on the 1989 results. In aggregate, the behavior of the rule portfolios continued the 1984–1988 trends into 1989. This is encouraging because it points to a link between past performance and future performance.

3. The performance of the rule portfolios seems to degrade over time. The good rules become less attractive, and the bad rules become more attractive. This is not surprising. If there are predictable links between macroeconomic variables and stock returns, the market will probably find them and predictability will diminish over time. We do not mean to suggest that the market is explicitly finding and acting on rules of the type that we have formulated, but it may implicitly be doing this in other ways.

4. The hedge portfolio approach seems promising. We clearly seem to be identifying rule portfolios with different performance characteristics. The good rules are definitely outperforming the bad rules into the holdout period. The question becomes: Is this differential performance enough to be meaningful? We have not examined leveraged strategies that would tend to accentuate and capitalize on this differential performance. In addition, refinements to the basic procedure might heighten the difference in returns between the good rule and bad rules, making hedge portfolios much more attractive.

5. It is probably better to focus on a portfolio of rules rather than on individual rules. When we examined the subsequent performance of individual rules, we saw inconsistencies. Some rules that looked highly promising over the rule-building period broke down in the holdout period. The opposite was also true. However, when viewed as a group, the behavior becomes more predictable. We are simply trying to gently tip the odds in our favor.

13

Bond Market Results

The format of this chapter follows that of Chapter 12. The basic pattern of tests that we ran is identical, with the only difference being the assets under consideration. Here we examine rules that involve switches between Treasury bonds, corporate bonds, and Treasury bills. Before describing the specific results, there are a few basic principles of bond investment worth reviewing.

The *yield curve,* or term structure of interest rates, is the relationship between bond yields and term to maturity. Because municipal and corporate bonds differ in default risk, you must remove default risk from consideration when examining the link between yield and maturity. For this reason, yield curves are constructed using only Treasury securities, which presumably have zero default risk. The so-called normal yield curve is upward sloping; yields on longer-term bonds exceed those for shorter-term bonds. Occasionally the reverse occurs, and the yield curve is said to be *inverted.*

The major rationale offered for upward-sloping yield curves is that investors demand extra yield for tying up their money in longer-term securities. The yield curve also reflects expectations about future movements in interest rates. If investors think that rates will rise in the future, they will demand higher yields on longer-term securities, which also leads to an upward-sloping yield curve. Therefore, a strongly upward-sloping yield curve combines the effects of interest rate expectations and a premium for investing in longer-term instruments.

Some people think that bonds are boring because they are simple. They pay contractually agreed amounts of interest and principal at stated time periods over a fixed period of time. For Treasury bonds, this payment pattern has been perfectly predictable. However, changes in interest rates can have a significant impact on bond prices, making them far less boring.

The yields in shorter-term bonds are more volatile than changes in the yields of longer-term bonds, but the price volatility of long-term bonds is greater. Bond prices and yields move inversely; a drop in interest rates causes bond prices to rise. Consider two Treasury bonds that are identical in all respects except for the term to maturity, which is 2 years and 15 years, respectively. If yields drop by 1 percent on both bonds, the percentage price change will be far greater for the 15-year bond. Therefore, returns are more volatile for long-term bonds than for short-term bonds.

Owing to the difference in response to interest rate changes, switching back and forth at the most appropriate time between Treasury bonds, which are longer-term securities, and Treasury bills, which are shorter-term securities, can be lucrative, as shown in Chapter 10. Treasury bond traders focus primarily on the yield curve and expected changes in it. If they think yields are headed down, then they will want to switch into longer maturities, but if they think yields are headed up, then they worry about bond price decreases and so switch into shorter maturities. Alternatively, if traders were confident of yield increases, then long term bonds could be sold short.

With corporate bonds, the risk of default enters into the picture. Bonds with higher bond ratings presumably have lower default risk, which means that investors will pay more for the bond, resulting in a lower yield. With lower risk, investors are willing to accept a lower yield. Many bond traders focus on changes in credit quality and how these affect bond yields and prices. The spread between the yield on Treasury bonds and corporate bonds is closely monitored; investors demand larger yields on the latter because they are riskier. The corporate/Treasury yield spread will change as economic conditions change. When the economy becomes shaky, the risk of default increases and the yield spread will widen.

All of the above means that there are many investors concerned about the relative attractiveness of Treasury bonds, Treasury bills, and corporate bonds. We will apply our GA methodology to the problem of developing profitable bond market-timing trading rules. We focus first on the Treasury market.

VARIABLE SELECTION FOR TREASURY BONDS

The correlations of the various series with the difference between Treasury bond returns and Treasury bill returns are shown in Table 13.1. Interestingly, the highest of these is a negative correlation with 1-month changes in stock prices in the United Kingdom. The third-highest correlation is with the 3-month change in the diffusion index of coincident indicators. *Diffusion indexes* represent the number of components of the base series, which in this case is the index of coincident indicators that are rising. If the index of coincident indicators is rising, then the economy is picking up. This increases the demand for loans and tends to increase interest rates, which hurts bond prices, leading to negative bond returns. Therefore, this relationship seems logical. Among the ten series that we chose for further investigation was 3-month changes in consumer installment debt. Here

Table 13.1   Correlations with Treasury Bond Returns

	Series Number	Differencing Interval	Series Description	Correlation Coefficient
1	207	1	742. United Kingdom, stock prices, NSA (1967 = 100)	−0.3984
2	229	3	940. Ratio, coincident index to lagging index (1982 = 1	−0.3914
3	233	3	951. Diffusion index of coincident indicators, 6-mo. span	−0.3311
4	255	3	(23) Spot price, burlap, NSA ($ per yd.) COPYRIGHTED	−0.3309
5	5	3	7. Mfrs.' new orders, durable goods industries (bil. 1982 $)	−0.3122
6	86	12	91. Average duration of unemployment in weeks (weeks)	−0.3084
7	193	3	727. Italy, industrial production (1987 = 100)	−0.2962
8	66	3	66. Consumer installment credit outstanding (mil. $)	0.2959
9	234	3	952. Diffusion index of lagging indicators, 1-mo. span (pct.	0.2938
10	178	12	570. Employment, defense products industries (thous.)	−0.2902
11	100	0	99. Smoothed change in sensitive materials (prices (pct.)	−0.2836
12	205	12	738. Japan, consumer price index, NSA (1982–1984 =	0.2815
13	228	1	930c. Lagging index, change over three-mo. span (AR, pc	0.2813
14	66	12	66. Consumer installment credit outstanding (mil. $)	0.2801
15	202	12	736c. France, 6-mo. change in consumer prices (AR, pct.)	−0.2786
16	13	3	14. Current liabilities of business failures, NSA (mil. $)	0.2777
17	226	3	930. Composite index of seven lagging indicators (1982 =	0.2774
18	247	12	(98) Producer Price Index, sand, gravel, and stone (1982	0.2708
19	61	3	62a. Index of labor cost per unit of output, mfg. (1987 =	0.2693
20	94	3	95. Ratio, consumer installment credit to personal income	0.2638
21	67	1	69. Mfrs.' mach. & equip. sales + bus. constr. exp. (AR, bi	0.2633
22	71	3	74. Industrial production, nondurable manufactures (1987	−0.2615
23	178	1	570. Employment, defense products industries (thous.)	−0.2605
24	8	0	9. Construction contracts (mil. sq. ft.) COPYRIGHTED (Mc	0.2588
25	92	0	93. Free reserves, NSA (mil. $)	−0.2579
26	34	3	37. Number of persons unemployed (thous.)	0.2544
27	94	12	95. Ratio, consumer installment credit to personal income	0.2533
28	141	0	323c. Change in CPI-U, less food & energy, 1-mo. span (p	0.2523
29	228	0	930c. Lagging index, change over 3-mo. span (AR, pct.)	0.2521
30	40	3	43. Civilian unemployment rate (pct.)	0.2513
31	196	3	732c. United Kingdom, 6-mo. change in consumer prices	−0.2496
32	21	1	21. Average weekly overtime hours, mfg. (hours)	0.2491
33	202	3	736c. France, 6-mo. change in consumer prices (AR, pct.)	−0.2482
34	13	0	14. Current liabilities of business failures, NSA (mil. $)	0.2442
35	98	0	99b. Change in sensitive materials prices (pct.)	−0.2423
36	172	3	452. Labor force participation rate, females 20 and over	0.2417
37	99	1	99a. Index of sensitive materials prices (1982 = 100)	−0.2412
38	3	1	5. Average weekly initial claims, unemploy. insurance (th	0.2384
39	223	3	920. Composite index of four coincident indicators (1982	−0.2378
40	71	12	74. Industrial production, nondurable manufactures (1987	−0.2376
41	233	12	951. Diffusion index of coincident indicators, 6-mo. span	−0.2371
42	225	0	920c. Coincident index, change over 3-mo. span (AR, pct	−0.2367
43	77	3	82. Capacity utilization rate, manufacturing)pct.)	−0.2351
44	172	12	452. Labor force participation rate, females 20 and over	0.2338
45	99	3	99a. Index of sensitive materials prices (1982 = 100)	−0.2336
46	229	12	940. Ratio, coincident index to lagging index (1982 =	−0.2322
47	265	3	992. Experimental coincident index—modified methodol	−0.2306
48	138	1	320c. Change in CPI-U, all items, 1-mo. span (pct.)	0.2290
49	239	12	(98) Producer Price Index, lumber and wood products (19	−0.2279
50	99	12	99a. Index of sensitive materials prices (1982 = 100)	−0.2266

the correlation with bond returns was positive. The logic in this case might be as clear-cut as this: If consumer debt has increased, interest rates may need to come down to entice consumers to take on more debt. Lower interest rates would lead to positive bond returns. The last variable that was chosen was 12-month changes in Japanese consumer prices. Increases in Japanese inflation seem to be good for the Treasury bond market.

GOOD RULES FOR TREASURY BONDS

The list of 120 good rules for the Treasury bond/Treasury bill timing decision is shown as Table 13.2. Rule 23, which involved U.K. stock prices, changes in the duration of unemployment, and changes in the diffusion index of lagging indicators had the highest level of fitness. All eight logic codes appear in the list. All of the greater than codes also appear, but most of the codes have a value of 4 or less. Greater than codes of 3 or less involve at least two less than relationships. There are many extreme values in the three columns of cutoff values.

Figures 13.1–13.4 show the percentage of correct calls and the moving average returns of the good rule portfolio. The pattern differs somewhat from that of the stock market. Figure 13.1 shows that the percentage of correct calls for this rule portfolio increased rapidly and steadily over the 1980s. In Figure 13.2 we see that this trend peaked in 1988 and then declined during the holdout period. This is an example of a reversal in a strong trend of past performance. In Figure 13.3 we see that average returns also increased sharply, as the 1980s were good years for the bond market overall. From Figure 13.4, we see that the moving average monthly return peaked in 1989 before entering a steady downtrend for the remainder of the holdout period. This rule portfolio exhibits stronger sustained trends than the stock market rule portfolios that we examined in Chapter 12.

The detailed rule results can be seen in Table 13.3. The average return for these rules was 15.45 percent in 1989, with 53.96 percent correct calls—a substantial drop from the 66 percent accuracy obtained during the rule-building period. A buy-and-hold strategy earned 18.10 percent in 1989. It seems that the market entered into a new phase sometime during the 1988–1989 period. The average annual return for the good rule portfolio over the entire 1989–1991 period was 10.51 percent, with about 46 percent accuracy. This would have underperformed a buy-and-hold strategy, which earned an average annual return of 14.35 percent. Clearly there was a major degradation in the performance of these rules during the holdout period.

The best-performing rule of the group was number 103, which was generating large returns during the rule-building period and was making accurate calls 70 percent of the time. The fitness measure was above average, but not in the upper range. This raises the question: How could this happen? The fitness was probably penalized by high volatility in the stream of returns. Our fitness calculation method rewards high and increasing returns but penalizes volatile returns. In 1989 this rule gave correct signals 75 percent of the time and earned a 22.8 percent

Table 13.2 Good Rules—Treasury Bonds

Rule #	Logic Code	>/< Code	Series 1	Series 2	Series 3	Fitness	1 #	Diff.	2 #	Diff.	3 #	Diff.
1	2	1	23	22	29	1.6211	207	1	229	3	233	3
2	5	2	20	17	4	1.4815	207	1	229	3	5	3
3	5	1	27	14	18	1.6327	207	1	229	3	86	12
4	6	3	27	14	13	1.5763	207	1	229	3	66	3
5	2	2	20	17	4	1.5371	207	1	229	3	234	3
6	7	1	28	22	1	1.5652	207	1	229	3	178	12
7	8	1	20	17	2	1.6456	207	1	229	3	100	0
8	6	1	29	17	17	1.5537	207	1	229	3	205	12
9	3	2	29	30	29	1.4469	207	1	233	3	5	3
10	2	1	23	30	18	1.6198	207	1	233	3	86	12
11	6	3	28	0	16	1.3758	207	1	233	3	66	3
12	1	2	29	29	4	1.4582	207	1	233	3	234	3
13	7	1	27	31	4	1.3809	207	1	233	3	178	12
14	7	1	24	26	16	1.4961	207	1	233	3	100	0
15	3	1	29	30	16	1.4060	207	1	233	3	205	12
16	2	1	21	24	18	1.5480	207	1	5	3	86	12
17	5	2	26	17	16	1.4641	207	1	5	3	66	3
18	4	4	27	6	29	1.3825	207	1	5	3	234	3
19	3	1	28	19	26	1.4057	207	1	5	3	178	12
20	8	1	24	0	12	1.4422	207	1	5	3	100	0
21	3	1	29	19	13	1.4169	207	1	5	3	205	12
22	1	2	28	18	0	1.5905	207	1	86	12	66	3
23	1	2	28	19	8	1.7350	207	1	86	12	234	3
24	3	1	28	18	23	1.6350	207	1	86	12	178	12
25	3	1	28	18	10	1.6711	207	1	86	12	100	0
26	6	1	27	18	18	1.5817	207	1	86	12	205	12
27	5	4	4	16	10	1.4632	207	1	66	3	234	3
28	3	3	28	17	23	1.4515	207	1	66	3	178	12
29	7	2	23	16	25	1.4958	207	1	66	3	100	0
30	3	3	28	24	18	1.5385	207	1	66	3	205	12
31	7	4	26	6	30	1.4372	207	1	234	3	178	12
32	1	3	28	8	28	1.5592	207	1	234	3	100	0
33	3	4	28	10	28	1.5109	207	1	234	3	205	12
34	6	1	28	0	28	1.4353	207	1	178	12	100	0
35	6	1	29	23	17	1.4029	207	1	178	12	205	12
36	2	2	24	12	6	1.4422	207	1	100	0	205	12
37	4	2	22	25	31	1.5283	229	3	233	3	5	3
38	7	1	18	27	16	1.6694	229	3	233	3	86	12
39	5	2	17	8	19	1.5225	229	3	233	3	66	3
40	1	2	22	27	5	1.5865	229	3	233	3	234	3
41	3	1	22	18	22	1.4941	229	3	233	3	178	12
42	7	1	18	28	2	1.5511	229	3	233	3	100	0
43	1	2	22	28	10	1.5539	229	3	233	3	205	12
44	8	3	17	30	16	1.6072	229	3	5	3	86	12
45	3	2	22	1	18	1.4888	229	3	5	3	66	3
46	2	2	13	18	13	1.5582	229	3	5	3	234	3

Continued on next page

Table 13.2 *(continued)*

Rule #	Logic Code	⟩/⟨ Code	Cutoff Values			Fitness	Series Number and Differencing Interval					
			Series 1	Series 2	Series 3		1		2		3	
							#	Diff.	#	Diff.	#	Diff.
47	4	1	18	19	4	1.4584	229	3	5	3	178	12
48	7	1	18	26	2	1.4771	229	3	5	3	100	0
49	4	2	18	19	28	1.5474	229	3	5	3	205	12
50	2	1	17	16	28	1.5867	229	3	86	12	66	3
51	5	2	19	18	4	1.6783	229	3	86	12	234	3
52	6	1	19	16	30	1.6112	229	3	86	12	178	12
53	3	1	27	18	3	1.5645	229	3	86	12	100	0
54	2	2	17	16	6	1.5571	229	3	86	12	205	12
55	1	4	22	18	8	1.5895	229	3	66	3	234	3
56	3	3	22	18	24	1.5591	229	3	66	3	178	12
57	4	3	17	17	2	1.5706	229	3	66	3	100	0
58	7	4	17	16	24	1.5273	229	3	66	3	205	12
59	7	2	17	7	20	1.4591	229	3	234	3	178	12
60	7	2	17	6	6	1.5479	229	3	234	3	100	0
61	8	4	17	26	28	1.5562	229	3	234	3	205	12
62	5	1	17	4	27	1.4317	229	3	178	12	100	0
63	8	1	12	6	18	1.3861	229	3	178	12	205	12
64	8	2	17	2	29	1.4817	229	3	100	0	205	12
65	5	1	29	3	18	1.5712	233	3	5	3	86	12
66	6	4	27	31	16	1.4029	233	3	5	3	66	3
67	1	2	31	19	6	1.4734	233	3	5	3	234	3
68	3	1	30	19	8	1.4761	233	3	5	3	178	12
69	3	1	30	19	12	1.5176	233	3	5	3	100	0
70	5	4	29	28	10	1.3738	233	3	5	3	205	12
71	7	3	27	18	30	1.5982	233	3	86	12	66	3
72	1	2	22	18	10	1.6941	233	3	86	12	234	3
73	3	1	30	18	23	1.6038	233	3	86	12	178	12
74	4	1	23	18	2	1.6071	233	3	86	12	100	0
75	7	1	20	18	16	1.6022	233	3	86	12	205	12
76	7	4	9	15	8	1.4465	233	3	66	3	234	3
77	3	3	30	24	23	1.3862	233	3	66	3	178	12
78	6	6	2	16	11	1.3808	233	3	66	3	100	0
79	3	4	30	15	27	1.3953	233	3	66	3	205	12
80	3	3	30	10	23	1.3573	233	3	234	3	178	12
81	3	3	31	26	13	1.5067	233	3	234	3	100	0
82	1	4	26	4	10	1.4262	233	3	234	3	205	12
83	5	1	29	0	25	1.3110	233	3	178	12	100	0
84	3	2	28	8	10	1.3129	233	3	178	12	205	12
85	3	2	31	13	24	1.4053	233	3	100	0	205	12
86	7	1	24	18	24	1.5523	5	3	86	12	66	3
87	2	6	29	18	8	1.6933	5	3	86	12	234	3
88	6	5	27	18	23	1.5600	5	3	86	12	178	12
89	4	1	24	18	4	1.6096	5	3	86	12	100	0
90	8	2	10	16	27	1.5584	5	3	86	12	205	12
91	5	8	30	17	9	1.5348	5	3	66	3	234	3
92	7	2	19	16	26	1.4587	5	3	66	3	178	12

Continued on next page

Table 13.2 (continued)

Rule #	Logic Code	>/< Code	Cutoff Values			Fitness	Series Number and Differencing Interval					
			Series 1	Series 2	Series 3		1 #	Diff.	2 #	Diff.	3 #	Diff.
93	5	7	31	17	25	1.5664	5	3	66	3	100	0
94	7	4	19	19	27	1.5000	5	3	66	3	205	12
95	4	3	19	13	23	1.4544	5	3	234	3	178	12
96	4	3	20	19	12	1.4712	5	3	234	3	100	0
97	4	4	19	13	26	1.5271	5	3	234	3	205	12
98	6	1	19	23	24	1.3082	5	3	178	12	100	0
99	8	2	19	1	28	1.3609	5	3	178	12	205	12
100	4	4	19	0	28	1.3609	5	3	100	0	205	12
101	3	2	18	10	10	1.6396	86	12	66	3	234	3
102	3	4	18	18	25	1.4999	86	12	66	3	178	12
103	4	3	18	16	10	1.5917	86	12	66	3	100	0
104	2	4	16	4	27	1.5592	86	12	66	3	205	12
105	3	3	18	10	0	1.6346	86	12	234	3	178	12
106	1	3	18	8	27	1.6823	86	12	234	3	100	0
107	3	3	18	10	5	1.6346	86	12	234	3	205	12
108	2	1	18	30	12	1.5452	86	12	178	12	100	0
109	3	2	18	30	21	1.5507	86	12	178	12	205	12
110	2	2	18	12	5	1.5273	86	12	100	0	205	12
111	7	6	16	8	23	1.4916	66	3	234	3	178	12
112	1	7	15	10	25	1.6873	66	3	234	3	100	0
113	3	7	16	10	3	1.4632	66	3	234	3	205	12
114	6	5	17	23	25	1.5589	66	3	178	12	100	0
115	2	6	17	24	27	1.4060	66	3	178	12	205	12
116	4	5	15	25	1	1.4963	66	3	100	0	205	12
117	4	7	25	22	13	1.4222	234	3	178	12	100	0
118	5	6	10	23	10	1.3191	234	3	178	12	205	12
119	4	6	10	20	28	1.4247	234	3	100	0	205	12
120	5	2	10	28	10	1.2456	178	12	100	0	205	12

return. The average annual return over the 1989–1991 period was 15.58 percent, with 58.33 percent accuracy. The fact that this rule looked extremely good on several levels during the rule-building phase and performed well in the holdout period but did not have extremely high fitness raises questions about the effectiveness of the fitness calculation. This issue will be addressed in Chapter 15.

BAD RULES FOR TREASURY BONDS

The list of bad rules for Treasury bonds is shown in Table 13.4. These rules use all eight logic codes, but they, unlike the good rules, are tilted towards higher greater than codes, meaning that many of them involve greater than relationships. Again, many of the cutoff values are fairly extreme. The rule with the highest

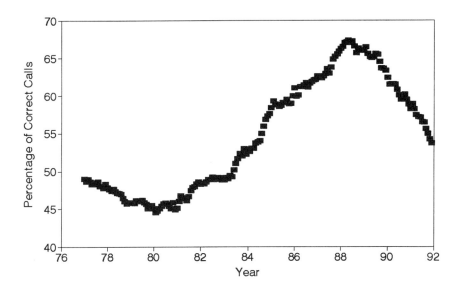

FIGURE 13.1 Percentage Correct (Treasury Bonds—Good Rules) 1977–1991

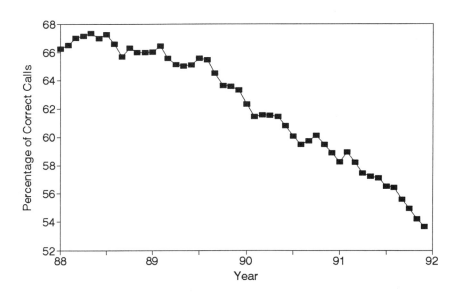

FIGURE 13.2 Percentage Correct (Treasury Bonds—Good Rules) 1988–1991

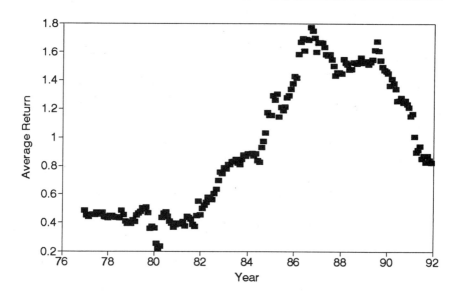

FIGURE 13.3   Average Return (Treasury Bonds—Good Rules) 1977–1991

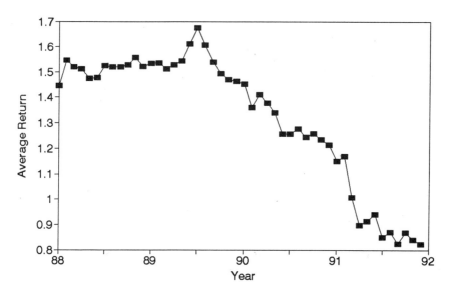

FIGURE 13.4   Average Return (Treasury Bonds—Good Rules) 1988–1991

Table 13.3 Performance Summary: Good Rules—Treasury Bonds

Rule #	Fitness	1971–1983 Period % Correct	1971–1983 Period Average Return	1984–1988 Period % Correct	1984–1988 Period Average Return	1989 % Correct	1989 Average Return	1989–1991 Period % Correct	1989–1991 Period Average Return
1	1.6211	46.53	6.69	66.67	20.79	66.67	18.10	47.22	9.75
2	1.4815	50.00	8.15	70.00	21.78	50.00	15.80	41.67	9.92
3	1.6327	45.83	5.47	75.00	22.14	41.67	13.90	33.33	7.98
4	1.5763	45.14	5.33	76.67	23.81	50.00	15.50	61.11	15.68
5	1.5371	50.00	8.15	70.00	21.78	50.00	15.80	41.67	9.92
6	1.5652	46.53	6.69	70.00	23.34	50.00	13.40	44.44	9.00
7	1.6456	46.53	5.59	73.33	22.85	50.00	15.80	38.89	10.03
8	1.5537	46.53	5.59	68.33	19.74	50.00	15.80	33.33	8.29
9	1.4469	45.14	5.33	71.67	21.41	50.00	16.40	63.89	15.85
10	1.6198	44.44	5.89	63.33	18.02	66.67	18.10	55.56	13.32
11	1.3758	54.86	9.87	63.33	14.72	50.00	13.40	66.67	15.73
12	1.4582	56.94	11.28	63.33	14.43	50.00	13.40	58.33	13.86
13	1.3809	47.22	6.88	68.33	20.43	41.67	14.50	55.56	13.75
14	1.4961	48.61	5.32	53.33	16.07	33.33	14.60	50.00	12.71
15	1.4060	47.92	7.03	71.67	21.31	50.00	16.40	55.56	13.96
16	1.5480	53.47	6.08	66.67	19.90	25.00	11.10	47.22	11.49
17	1.4641	49.31	7.75	55.00	11.55	50.00	10.10	50.00	11.15
18	1.3825	45.14	6.29	71.67	20.55	41.67	7.10	66.67	13.13
19	1.4057	44.44	5.23	68.33	21.23	50.00	13.40	61.11	15.05
20	1.4422	51.39	6.38	55.00	16.80	33.33	12.70	47.22	12.48
21	1.4169	52.78	7.24	70.00	20.97	33.33	11.20	44.44	10.68
22	1.5905	46.53	6.18	73.33	24.53	50.00	13.40	33.33	6.09
23	1.7350	46.53	5.69	61.67	18.71	50.00	13.40	41.67	8.01
24	1.6350	47.22	4.96	75.00	22.86	50.00	13.40	47.22	8.83
25	1.6711	46.53	6.18	73.33	24.53	50.00	13.40	33.33	6.09
26	1.5817	46.53	6.18	70.00	22.04	66.67	18.10	36.11	7.23
27	1.4632	52.78	7.51	66.67	19.75	75.00	22.80	44.44	10.52
28	1.4515	45.14	5.33	71.67	21.62	50.00	13.40	63.89	14.85
29	1.4958	52.78	7.51	63.33	15.61	50.00	11.80	36.11	7.09
30	1.5385	45.83	5.57	61.67	18.96	50.00	13.40	63.89	14.85
31	1.4372	45.83	4.59	70.00	22.62	33.33	8.10	52.78	12.74
32	1.5592	48.61	5.57	73.33	23.31	50.00	13.40	61.11	13.75
33	1.5109	45.14	4.33	80.00	25.95	50.00	13.40	61.11	13.75
34	1.4353	49.31	8.23	56.67	17.72	50.00	13.40	63.89	14.85
35	1.4029	59.03	10.37	48.33	14.44	33.33	8.40	52.78	13.44
36	1.4422	54.86	7.89	55.00	15.62	41.67	14.70	52.78	11.55
37	1.5283	44.44	5.43	61.67	18.57	66.67	18.10	55.56	11.80
38	1.6694	47.22	6.33	71.67	21.20	50.00	15.80	33.33	8.29
39	1.5225	52.78	6.83	43.33	7.54	33.33	8.40	36.11	7.26
40	1.5865	54.86	10.76	60.00	15.60	66.67	15.10	52.78	11.47
41	1.4941	47.22	7.13	65.00	21.10	66.67	18.10	50.00	11.60
42	1.5511	46.53	6.12	71.67	21.20	50.00	15.80	33.33	8.29
43	1.5539	55.56	11.12	60.00	15.60	66.67	15.10	52.78	11.47
44	1.6072	50.69	6.96	70.00	20.03	58.33	16.40	52.78	12.21
45	1.4888	49.31	8.40	38.33	5.42	75.00	15.20	44.44	7.52
46	1.5582	51.39	5.65	75.00	21.63	41.67	14.50	38.89	10.08

Continued on next page

Table 13.3 (continued)

Rule #	Fitness	1971–1983 Period		1984–1988 Period		1989		1989–1991 Period	
		% Correct	Average Return	% Correct	Average Return	% Correct	Average Return	% Correct	Average Return
47	1.4584	51.39	7.03	70.00	20.03	33.33	11.20	33.33	7.29
48	1.4771	47.22	5.67	71.67	20.49	41.67	14.70	30.56	7.95
49	1.5474	52.78	7.14	71.67	19.87	41.67	11.80	36.11	7.14
50	1.5867	44.44	5.27	73.33	24.63	58.33	16.40	33.33	8.09
51	1.6783	44.44	5.51	73.33	22.96	66.67	18.10	33.33	6.03
52	1.6112	46.53	6.35	75.00	23.89	66.67	18.10	36.11	6.97
53	1.5645	45.83	6.38	71.67	22.91	66.67	18.10	36.11	7.23
54	1.5571	44.44	5.27	71.67	24.21	58.33	16.40	33.33	8.09
55	1.5895	54.86	7.96	70.00	22.23	66.67	20.20	47.22	11.04
56	1.5591	46.53	6.69	63.33	18.94	66.67	18.10	44.44	8.52
57	1.5706	52.78	6.81	70.00	20.33	58.33	17.30	52.78	13.08
58	1.5273	54.17	7.77	66.67	20.18	58.33	20.40	41.67	10.79
59	1.4591	42.36	4.02	68.33	20.79	58.33	16.40	47.22	11.06
60	1.5479	47.22	4.95	70.00	21.09	50.00	15.80	33.33	8.29
61	1.5562	47.22	5.40	75.00	21.93	50.00	15.80	36.11	8.32
62	1.4317	56.25	9.74	51.67	15.26	50.00	15.80	33.33	8.29
63	1.3861	49.31	6.15	61.67	20.00	50.00	17.00	52.78	14.67
64	1.4817	46.53	6.19	71.67	21.87	50.00	15.80	33.33	8.52
65	1.5712	54.86	7.88	66.67	20.27	25.00	11.10	47.22	11.98
66	1.4029	52.78	8.58	43.33	6.47	75.00	15.20	55.56	10.93
67	1.4734	54.86	9.85	68.33	20.53	16.67	2.90	47.22	9.31
68	1.4761	54.17	8.70	68.33	20.77	33.33	11.20	50.00	12.00
69	1.5176	54.17	8.70	68.33	20.77	33.33	11.20	50.00	12.00
70	1.3738	49.31	7.87	56.67	13.12	50.00	11.20	50.00	10.41
71	1.5982	48.61	7.48	70.00	23.17	66.67	18.10	41.67	8.60
72	1.6941	48.61	7.95	56.67	18.41	66.67	18.10	41.67	8.60
73	1.6038	49.31	6.55	65.00	18.60	66.67	18.10	55.56	11.58
74	1.6071	47.92	7.45	70.00	23.17	66.67	18.10	41.67	8.60
75	1.6022	46.53	6.18	70.00	23.05	66.67	18.10	38.89	8.21
76	1.4465	52.08	6.55	66.67	19.75	75.00	22.80	41.67	10.14
77	1.3862	47.92	7.03	63.33	19.92	66.67	18.10	58.33	14.37
78	1.3808	58.33	11.44	65.00	18.99	75.00	22.80	58.33	13.44
79	1.3953	52.78	7.41	68.33	21.02	75.00	22.80	47.22	11.52
80	1.3573	47.92	7.03	61.67	17.42	66.67	18.10	58.33	14.37
81	1.5067	52.78	7.96	53.33	9.16	25.00	5.90	44.44	9.47
82	1.4262	47.22	5.65	70.00	21.87	58.33	17.50	52.78	13.05
83	1.3110	56.94	9.45	51.67	15.55	50.00	15.90	55.56	15.20
84	1.3129	48.61	6.92	61.67	17.42	66.67	18.10	58.33	14.37
85	1.4053	55.56	10.03	56.67	16.29	33.33	10.60	38.89	9.64
86	1.5523	46.53	6.18	70.00	22.04	66.67	18.10	36.11	7.23
87	1.6933	46.53	6.51	58.33	16.71	66.67	18.10	38.89	7.26
88	1.5600	45.14	5.65	70.00	21.69	66.67	18.10	36.11	7.23
89	1.6096	46.53	6.32	75.00	23.96	50.00	16.40	33.33	7.09
90	1.5584	41.67	3.00	70.00	22.70	58.33	16.40	55.56	12.77
91	1.5348	54.86	8.07	66.67	19.75	66.67	18.00	47.22	10.33
92	1.4587	52.78	7.51	66.67	18.90	66.67	19.00	41.67	9.36

Continued on next page

Table 13.3 (continued)

Rule #	Fitness	1971–1983 Period		1984–1988 Period		1989		1989–1991 Period	
		% Correct	Average Return	% Correct	Average Return	% Correct	Average Return	% Correct	Average Return
93	1.5664	56.25	8.44	60.00	14.32	41.67	7.30	41.67	6.97
94	1.5000	54.86	8.10	70.00	21.72	58.33	19.10	44.44	10.68
95	1.4544	46.53	6.65	60.00	15.37	66.67	18.10	58.33	14.17
96	1.4712	51.39	8.10	55.00	11.35	41.67	11.10	38.89	9.78
97	1.5271	54.17	7.63	71.67	22.80	50.00	14.30	50.00	10.33
98	1.3082	59.03	10.67	48.33	14.65	33.33	8.40	55.56	13.65
99	1.3609	54.86	7.19	70.00	17.76	33.33	11.20	47.22	11.01
100	1.3609	49.31	6.46	65.00	18.49	33.33	11.20	47.22	11.01
101	1.6396	46.53	6.18	70.00	22.04	66.67	18.10	36.11	7.23
102	1.4999	54.86	7.96	71.67	22.07	66.67	20.20	47.22	11.04
103	1.5917	52.78	8.04	70.00	22.62	75.00	22.80	58.33	15.58
104	1.5592	43.06	3.90	68.33	21.83	58.33	16.40	38.89	7.98
105	1.6346	45.83	6.00	78.33	25.87	58.33	17.50	33.33	7.03
106	1.6823	47.92	6.41	73.33	23.36	58.33	17.50	33.33	7.03
107	1.6346	45.83	6.00	71.67	22.58	58.33	17.50	33.33	7.03
108	1.5452	45.83	6.26	70.00	22.04	66.67	18.10	36.11	7.23
109	1.5507	46.53	6.18	70.00	22.04	66.67	18.10	36.11	7.23
110	1.5273	47.22	5.91	70.00	22.04	66.67	18.10	44.44	7.95
111	1.4916	50.00	6.47	68.33	20.29	58.33	17.50	52.78	12.56
112	1.6873	51.39	6.53	63.33	19.22	66.67	22.20	38.89	9.92
113	1.4632	52.78	7.51	75.00	24.01	66.67	22.20	41.67	10.33
114	1.5589	58.33	10.25	53.33	16.74	50.00	15.00	58.33	15.70
115	1.4060	53.47	7.65	66.67	19.75	66.67	18.00	47.22	10.33
116	1.4963	53.47	7.61	71.67	23.12	75.00	22.80	41.67	10.14
117	1.4222	50.00	6.75	60.00	18.53	33.33	8.40	36.11	7.26
118	1.3191	44.44	4.49	60.00	11.66	58.33	17.50	61.11	14.14
119	1.4247	44.44	4.89	66.67	20.36	41.67	8.70	52.78	10.14
120	1.2456	48.61	5.56	50.00	8.58	58.33	15.20	55.56	10.38

fitness is rule 32, which makes it the best candidate for being a rotten rule. (Yes, that does sound odd, but we are in search of consistently bad rules.) This rule involves U.K. stock prices, the diffusion index of lagging indicators, and the smoothed change in sensitive materials prices. Coincidentally, two of these three variables also showed up in the rule having the highest fitness of the good rules.

The aggregate performance of the bad rule portfolio is summarized in Figures 13.5–13.8. Figure 13.5 is almost the mirror image of Figure 13.1. It shows a strong steady decline in the forecasting accuracy of the bad rule portfolio over the 1983–1988 period. Figure 13.6 shows the decline bottoming out in 1988, when the performance of these rules underwent a complete reversal. The average return pattern shown in Figure 13.7 is more erratic. Returns dropped precipitously in 1987 and then subsequently bounce around, as seen in Figure 13.8.

Table 13.4 Bad Rules—Treasury Bonds

Rule #	Logic Code	⟩/⟨ Code	Cutoff Values Series 1	Series 2	Series 3	Fitness	1 #	Diff.	2 #	Diff.	3 #	Diff.
1	7	8	27	9	18	11.1050	207	1	229	3	233	3
2	7	6	27	13	11	11.3428	207	1	229	3	5	3
3	1	8	11	9	16	11.3806	207	1	229	3	86	12
4	3	7	20	17	12	11.0112	207	1	229	3	66	3
5	4	7	27	10	11	11.7361	207	1	229	3	234	3
6	1	8	20	9	18	11.3077	207	1	229	3	178	12
7	4	8	28	6	25	11.2758	207	1	229	3	100	0
8	3	7	27	8	10	11.0581	207	1	229	3	205	12
9	7	6	27	10	14	10.9475	207	1	233	3	5	3
10	2	8	28	8	18	11.7393	207	1	233	3	86	12
11	2	7	28	5	13	11.7233	207	1	233	3	66	3
12	2	7	28	9	8	11.6932	207	1	233	3	234	3
13	1	8	20	3	14	11.0396	207	1	233	3	178	12
14	2	7	28	17	2	11.1752	207	1	233	3	100	0
15	2	8	28	8	30	11.1215	207	1	233	3	205	12
16	2	8	28	9	16	11.4141	207	1	5	3	86	12
17	2	5	28	20	12	11.3791	207	1	5	3	66	3
18	8	7	28	30	9	11.6629	207	1	5	3	234	3
19	1	8	25	12	11	11.0241	207	1	5	3	178	12
20	7	8	28	15	25	11.3916	207	1	5	3	100	0
21	2	7	29	24	29	10.9063	207	1	5	3	205	12
22	2	8	28	23	7	11.2746	207	1	86	12	66	3
23	7	6	28	8	12	11.6627	207	1	86	12	234	3
24	2	7	28	24	27	11.6131	207	1	86	12	178	12
25	2	8	28	16	25	11.4597	207	1	86	12	100	0
26	5	7	28	18	31	11.3806	207	1	86	12	205	12
27	2	7	28	5	8	11.7655	207	1	66	3	234	3
28	2	5	28	10	27	11.4625	207	1	66	3	178	12
29	2	8	28	3	25	11.2758	207	1	66	3	100	0
30	6	7	28	13	7	10.9816	207	1	66	3	205	12
31	6	7	28	10	1	11.6269	207	1	234	3	178	12
32	8	6	28	12	25	12.1561	207	1	234	3	100	0
33	2	6	28	8	11	11.6269	207	1	234	3	205	12
34	2	8	28	4	25	11.2758	207	1	178	12	100	0
35	2	7	28	29	22	10.8793	207	1	178	12	205	12
36	2	8	28	24	18	11.3362	207	1	100	0	205	12
37	1	8	17	4	4	10.8132	229	3	233	3	5	3
38	1	8	6	6	16	11.7315	229	3	233	3	86	12
39	7	6	17	7	13	11.7035	229	3	233	3	66	3
40	7	6	17	3	9	11.2513	229	3	233	3	234	3
41	1	8	9	7	3	11.3275	229	3	233	3	178	12
42	4	8	17	5	23	11.1064	229	3	233	3	100	0
43	7	8	17	4	31	11.1276	229	3	233	3	205	12
44	5	8	9	13	16	11.5995	229	3	5	3	86	12
45	2	7	17	9	12	11.1135	229	3	5	3	66	3
46	3	7	9	18	8	11.3668	229	3	5	3	234	3

Continued on next page

Table 13.4 (continued)

Rule #	Logic Code	$\rangle/\langle$ Code	Cutoff Values			Fitness	Series Number and Differencing Interval					
			Series 1	Series 2	Series 3		1		2		3	
							#	Diff.	#	Diff.	#	Diff.
47	5	8	18	18	4	10.8283	229	3	5	3	178	12
48	5	8	30	15	20	10.7854	229	3	5	3	100	0
49	5	7	18	24	26	11.0952	229	3	5	3	205	12
50	5	7	18	25	24	10.8396	229	3	86	12	66	3
51	3	7	9	16	9	11.7704	229	3	86	12	234	3
52	3	8	9	18	30	11.4249	229	3	86	12	178	12
53	4	4	22	25	25	11.0102	229	3	86	12	100	0
54	3	7	9	16	7	11.3806	229	3	86	12	205	12
55	3	5	9	15	8	11.6311	229	3	66	3	234	3
56	3	6	9	15	26	11.3105	229	3	66	3	178	12
57	4	6	9	16	25	11.2833	229	3	66	3	100	0
58	6	5	17	12	25	11.0948	229	3	66	3	205	12
59	1	6	9	24	6	11.4735	229	3	234	3	178	12
60	6	7	9	12	20	11.3776	229	3	234	3	100	0
61	4	5	13	6	10	11.2470	229	3	234	3	205	12
62	7	8	9	16	24	10.9968	229	3	178	12	100	0
63	3	5	17	2	26	10.9387	229	3	178	12	205	12
64	6	6	17	24	26	11.2290	229	3	100	0	205	12
65	1	8	8	9	16	11.7603	233	3	5	3	86	12
66	6	6	2	24	14	11.3296	233	3	5	3	66	3
67	1	7	8	9	22	11.0352	233	3	5	3	234	3
68	1	8	4	8	6	10.9418	233	3	5	3	178	12
69	2	8	25	16	20	10.8538	233	3	5	3	100	0
70	4	7	15	18	10	10.8075	233	3	5	3	205	12
71	3	7	5	18	13	11.5653	233	3	86	12	66	3
72	3	7	9	16	8	11.8863	233	3	86	12	234	3
73	7	8	5	16	31	11.5875	233	3	86	12	178	12
74	7	8	7	16	22	11.7263	233	3	86	12	100	0
75	4	7	6	16	10	11.6396	233	3	86	12	205	12
76	3	5	7	14	8	11.6372	233	3	66	3	234	3
77	7	5	14	14	26	11.2124	233	3	66	3	178	12
78	7	7	9	14	22	11.2554	233	3	66	3	100	0
79	4	5	4	13	10	11.3820	233	3	66	3	205	12
80	1	6	4	23	3	11.1755	233	3	234	3	178	12
81	4	6	5	12	25	11.4577	233	3	234	3	100	0
82	8	5	23	9	10	11.2791	233	3	234	3	205	12
83	7	8	8	13	23	10.8682	233	3	178	12	100	0
84	7	6	5	5	10	10.8069	233	3	178	12	205	12
85	6	6	22	25	31	11.0895	233	3	100	0	205	12
86	3	7	9	16	8	11.3601	5	3	86	12	66	3
87	4	7	13	16	8	11.9631	5	3	86	12	234	3
88	1	8	9	16	8	11.3601	5	3	86	12	178	12
89	7	6	9	16	5	11.4978	5	3	86	12	100	0
90	4	7	9	16	4	11.3601	5	3	86	12	205	12
91	4	5	13	15	9	11.6500	5	3	66	3	234	3
92	5	1	6	15	27	10.9419	5	3	66	3	178	12

Continued on next page

Table 13.4 *(continued)*

Rule #	Logic Code	>/< Code	Series 1	Series 2	Series 3	Fitness	1 #	1 Diff.	2 #	2 Diff.	3 #	3 Diff.
93	3	6	9	14	25	11.1297	5	3	66	3	100	0
94	7	5	9	14	28	10.9897	5	3	66	3	205	12
95	1	6	9	26	19	11.1982	5	3	234	3	178	12
96	4	2	27	8	25	11.3721	5	3	234	3	100	0
97	6	5	19	10	25	11.4546	5	3	234	3	205	12
98	7	6	18	12	2	10.6995	5	3	178	12	100	0
99	3	7	18	31	23	10.6910	5	3	178	12	205	12
100	3	7	18	25	28	10.9948	5	3	100	0	205	12
101	7	6	16	4	9	11.4585	86	12	66	3	234	3
102	3	7	16	11	27	11.4269	86	12	66	3	178	12
103	3	7	16	7	2	11.3110	86	12	66	3	100	0
104	5	7	18	31	31	11.0576	86	12	66	3	205	12
105	6	5	16	10	27	11.4324	86	12	234	3	178	12
106	3	6	6	12	25	11.4573	86	12	234	3	100	0
107	3	5	16	22	12	11.4381	86	12	234	3	205	12
108	3	6	16	27	23	11.6905	86	12	178	12	100	0
109	3	5	16	27	27	11.4233	86	12	178	12	205	12
110	3	5	16	2	28	11.1922	86	12	100	0	205	12
111	6	1	15	10	27	11.3028	66	3	234	3	178	12
112	2	1	14	9	29	11.0552	66	3	234	3	100	0
113	6	1	15	8	28	11.4470	66	3	234	3	205	12
114	2	3	14	23	2	10.5315	66	3	178	12	100	0
115	2	3	13	9	10	10.6624	66	3	178	12	205	12
116	3	3	15	24	31	11.0451	66	3	100	0	205	12
117	2	4	12	26	24	11.4839	234	3	178	12	100	0
118	2	3	8	25	11	11.1965	234	3	178	12	205	12
119	8	3	12	25	10	11.7208	234	3	100	0	205	12
120	4	7	1	25	10	10.7722	178	12	100	0	205	12

The detailed performance summary of the bad Treasury bond rule portfolio is shown in Table 13.5. The average return of these rules was 11.56 percent in 1989, with 49.58 percent accuracy. Over the entire 1989–1991 holdout period, the average annual return was 11.25 percent, with 55 percent accuracy. These rules experienced a dramatic turnaround in their effectiveness (or lack thereof).

Because we were actually trying to find bad rules, we can examine the worst performer of this group: rule 34, which earned a return of 11.00 percent in 1989, even though it was correct 58.33 percent of the time. Over the entire holdout period, its return was 4.4 percent, with only 33.33 percent accuracy. This rule says to invest in Treasury bonds when the one-month change in U.K. stock prices is not unusually low *and* (the annual change in defense employment is high *or* the smoothed change in sensitive materials prices is not in the low end of its range).

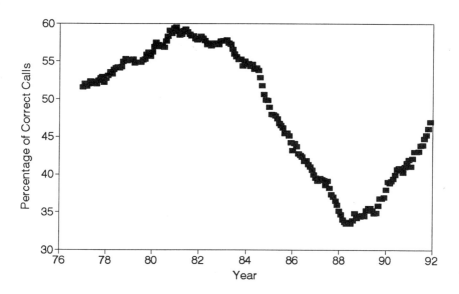

FIGURE 13.5 Percentage Correct (Treasury Bonds—Bad Rules) 1977–1991

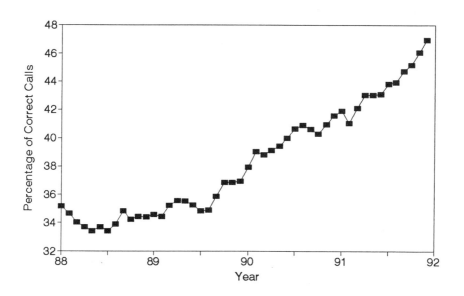

FIGURE 13.6 Percentage Correct (Treasury Bonds—Bad Rules) 1988–1991

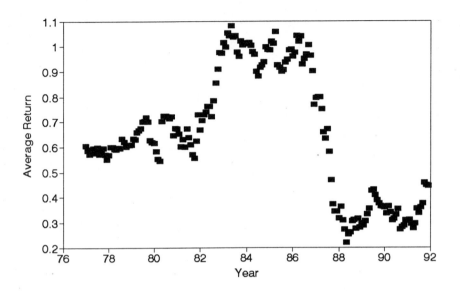

FIGURE 13.7   Average Return (Treasury Bonds—Bad Rules) 1977–1991

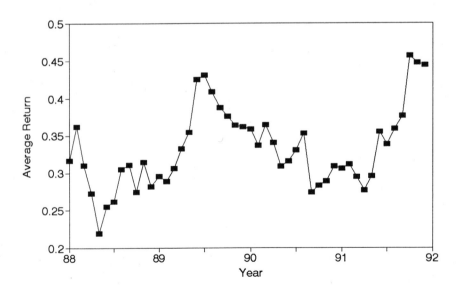

FIGURE 13.8   Average Return (Treasury Bonds—Bad Rules) 1988–1991

Table 13.5 Performance Summary: Bad Rules—Treasury Bonds

Rule #	Fitness	1971–1983 Period % Correct	1971–1983 Period Average Return	1984–1988 Period % Correct	1984–1988 Period Average Return	1989 % Correct	1989 Average Return	1989–1991 Period % Correct	1989–1991 Period Average Return
1	11.1050	54.86	8.10	25.00	0.81	58.33	12.90	66.67	13.75
2	11.3428	55.56	8.25	23.33	−0.55	41.67	10.30	36.11	5.88
3	11.3806	54.86	7.98	35.00	2.82	50.00	11.70	66.67	13.65
4	11.0112	48.61	5.75	43.33	6.36	66.67	19.40	63.89	14.80
5	11.7361	51.39	6.35	38.33	4.83	66.67	20.20	36.11	8.63
6	11.3077	54.17	7.95	25.00	0.83	50.00	10.60	61.11	11.47
7	11.2758	54.17	7.26	26.67	0.92	50.00	12.80	50.00	10.71
8	11.0581	54.86	8.05	28.33	1.96	58.33	14.70	36.11	7.00
9	10.9475	55.56	8.25	30.00	1.89	58.33	11.80	38.89	6.12
10	11.7393	54.86	7.44	30.00	1.59	50.00	12.80	44.44	8.55
11	11.7233	54.17	7.74	28.33	1.25	50.00	12.80	36.11	6.79
12	11.6932	54.86	8.10	28.33	1.25	50.00	12.80	36.11	6.79
13	11.0396	54.86	9.87	46.67	6.59	75.00	15.90	63.89	12.64
14	11.1752	54.86	8.10	28.33	1.25	50.00	12.80	36.11	6.79
15	11.1215	52.08	6.37	30.00	1.59	50.00	12.80	44.44	8.55
16	11.4141	50.00	7.91	41.67	4.60	75.00	18.30	61.11	12.16
17	11.3791	50.00	6.46	33.33	6.30	58.33	16.20	36.11	8.80
18	11.6629	56.25	7.11	30.00	3.78	58.33	16.20	41.67	8.86
19	11.0241	58.33	10.41	45.00	4.66	66.67	13.60	47.22	7.58
20	11.3916	55.56	8.27	28.33	1.00	50.00	10.00	36.11	5.37
21	10.9063	54.86	7.92	25.00	0.86	50.00	10.00	38.89	6.03
22	11.2746	52.78	8.48	25.00	0.22	50.00	12.80	52.78	12.71
23	11.6627	52.78	7.39	31.67	1.76	58.33	15.80	38.89	7.72
24	11.6131	53.47	8.02	25.00	0.40	50.00	12.80	38.89	9.08
25	11.4597	54.86	9.61	28.33	1.06	50.00	12.80	52.78	11.25
26	11.3806	56.94	8.77	26.67	−0.96	50.00	12.80	66.67	15.63
27	11.7655	56.94	9.82	28.33	1.25	50.00	12.80	30.56	6.71
28	11.4625	54.17	8.51	30.00	1.34	50.00	12.80	50.00	11.52
29	11.2758	54.86	8.10	38.33	7.55	75.00	24.00	44.44	10.22
30	10.9816	50.69	8.05	30.00	1.34	50.00	12.80	61.11	13.70
31	11.6269	54.86	9.12	20.00	−2.24	50.00	12.80	38.89	7.84
32	12.1561	53.47	7.71	35.00	2.75	41.67	9.10	38.89	6.59
33	11.6269	54.86	8.10	28.33	1.25	50.00	12.80	36.11	6.79
34	11.2758	42.36	3.13	46.67	5.73	58.33	11.00	33.33	4.40
35	10.8793	54.86	8.10	28.33	1.25	50.00	12.80	36.11	6.79
36	11.3362	53.47	8.23	30.00	0.65	50.00	12.80	36.11	6.79
37	10.8132	55.56	8.94	28.33	1.27	50.00	10.60	66.67	13.29
38	11.7315	55.56	11.27	43.33	6.48	66.67	15.10	69.44	14.40
39	11.7035	54.17	8.37	28.33	1.27	50.00	10.60	66.67	13.29
40	11.2513	55.56	8.94	28.33	1.27	50.00	10.60	66.67	13.29
41	11.3275	55.56	11.06	38.33	4.88	66.67	15.10	72.22	14.80
42	11.1064	53.47	7.66	30.00	1.68	50.00	10.60	66.67	13.29
43	11.1276	52.78	7.17	30.00	1.68	50.00	10.60	66.67	13.29
44	11.5995	50.00	7.91	41.67	5.60	75.00	15.20	58.33	10.87
45	11.1135	50.00	7.95	35.00	4.65	41.67	10.10	61.11	13.08
46	11.3668	50.00	9.04	30.00	4.04	75.00	16.70	63.89	12.66

Continued on next page

189

Table 13.5 (continued)

Rule #	Fitness	1971–1983 Period % Correct	1971–1983 Period Average Return	1984–1988 Period % Correct	1984–1988 Period Average Return	1989 % Correct	1989 Average Return	1989–1991 Period % Correct	1989–1991 Period Average Return
47	10.8283	48.61	7.62	30.00	2.91	75.00	15.20	69.44	14.37
48	10.7854	50.00	6.75	33.33	4.09	66.67	15.10	55.56	10.68
49	11.0952	51.39	7.46	26.67	3.31	41.67	10.00	61.11	13.26
50	10.8396	56.25	8.41	31.67	4.23	50.00	10.60	47.22	7.52
51	11.7704	60.42	12.35	35.00	1.27	50.00	11.80	72.22	14.57
52	11.4249	57.64	10.55	30.00	0.88	33.33	8.40	72.22	14.73
53	11.0102	54.86	9.61	41.67	6.92	33.33	8.40	52.78	11.76
54	11.3806	59.03	12.16	35.00	2.24	50.00	11.80	72.22	14.57
55	11.6311	53.47	11.08	33.33	2.82	25.00	4.20	66.67	11.71
56	11.3105	53.47	11.08	33.33	5.96	50.00	14.50	75.00	15.28
57	11.2833	53.47	10.27	40.00	7.70	50.00	14.50	72.22	14.88
58	11.0948	51.39	8.51	36.67	4.83	50.00	10.60	63.89	13.70
59	11.4735	50.00	8.38	43.33	10.68	58.33	14.60	63.89	13.08
60	11.3776	52.08	8.90	38.33	5.00	58.33	15.60	58.33	12.90
61	11.2470	54.86	9.12	31.67	2.69	41.67	9.00	41.67	8.49
62	10.9968	43.75	4.94	51.67	7.58	66.67	18.10	72.22	14.70
63	10.9387	55.56	9.22	40.00	8.30	50.00	10.60	66.67	13.29
64	11.2290	47.92	6.84	31.67	2.83	50.00	10.60	66.67	13.29
65	11.7603	54.17	9.55	41.67	5.81	75.00	15.20	58.33	10.90
66	11.3296	56.25	9.11	41.67	6.39	41.67	9.80	50.00	10.22
67	11.0352	55.56	10.06	56.67	10.39	41.67	10.10	52.78	12.58
68	10.9418	52.78	9.24	51.67	8.72	66.67	13.60	63.89	12.64
69	10.8538	49.31	5.90	33.33	3.17	66.67	15.10	52.78	9.67
70	10.8075	47.92	7.59	36.67	6.90	91.67	22.40	66.67	14.42
71	11.5653	57.64	9.37	45.00	6.48	33.33	7.50	61.11	13.08
72	11.8863	65.28	13.60	38.33	3.10	50.00	11.80	63.89	13.52
73	11.5875	63.19	12.70	30.00	0.98	50.00	11.80	63.89	13.52
74	11.7263	57.64	10.02	30.00	0.98	50.00	11.80	63.89	14.24
75	11.6396	63.89	13.03	43.33	4.95	50.00	11.80	63.89	13.52
76	11.6372	56.94	11.47	36.67	4.13	25.00	4.80	58.33	12.11
77	11.2124	48.61	7.36	35.00	3.24	25.00	4.80	58.33	11.60
78	11.2554	56.94	11.47	36.67	4.13	25.00	4.80	58.33	12.11
79	11.3820	52.08	8.56	36.67	5.21	33.33	8.40	52.78	11.74
80	11.1755	54.17	10.33	41.67	5.13	58.33	9.90	55.56	11.87
81	11.4577	56.25	8.71	46.67	7.92	33.33	5.40	44.44	7.58
82	11.2791	55.56	8.84	30.00	1.04	41.67	9.00	47.22	8.49
83	10.8682	47.92	5.72	51.67	7.58	66.67	18.10	61.11	13.34
84	10.8069	54.17	9.51	46.67	5.98	66.67	15.10	66.67	14.22
85	11.0895	55.56	8.82	33.33	2.00	33.33	8.40	41.67	7.26
86	11.3601	56.94	11.17	41.67	4.26	41.67	10.00	58.33	12.24
87	11.9631	57.64	10.57	41.67	4.21	41.67	10.00	58.33	11.87
88	11.3601	56.25	11.12	30.00	0.18	41.67	10.00	58.33	12.24
89	11.4978	56.25	11.12	30.00	0.18	41.67	10.00	58.33	12.24
90	11.3601	56.25	11.12	31.67	0.51	41.67	10.00	58.33	12.24
91	11.6500	52.78	9.15	33.33	2.82	33.33	7.70	58.33	11.36
92	10.9419	47.22	6.68	31.67	2.49	33.33	7.40	61.11	12.50

Continued on next page

Table 13.5 *(continued)*

Rule #	Fitness	1971–1983 Period		1984–1988 Period		1989		1989–1991 Period	
		% Correct	Average Return	% Correct	Average Return	% Correct	Average Return	% Correct	Average Return
93	11.1297	48.61	8.92	40.00	5.90	41.67	11.80	61.11	12.69
94	10.9897	48.61	7.36	35.00	3.24	25.00	4.80	53.33	11.60
95	11.1982	51.39	8.98	46.67	8.16	41.67	10.80	41.67	10.27
96	11.3721	52.08	8.47	45.00	6.92	33.33	8.40	44.44	8.66
97	11.4546	49.31	8.37	23.33	−0.08	66.67	15.10	52.78	11.55
98	10.6995	47.92	7.29	35.00	2.66	75.00	15.20	55.56	10.55
99	10.6910	55.56	10.30	43.33	8.37	33.33	8.40	44.44	10.11
100	10.9948	46.53	7.32	33.33	3.30	75.00	15.20	55.56	10.55
101	11.4585	56.94	10.52	31.67	1.25	50.00	11.80	50.00	9.89
102	11.4269	56.94	9.58	31.67	1.06	50.00	11.80	63.89	14.22
103	11.3110	57.64	9.66	35.00	1.81	50.00	11.80	63.89	12.90
104	11.0576	53.47	7.23	30.00	0.88	33.33	8.40	63.89	14.40
105	11.4324	59.03	10.54	23.33	−1.42	58.33	12.40	66.67	14.42
106	11.4573	53.47	7.71	45.00	7.30	33.33	5.40	44.44	7.58
107	11.4381	57.64	10.70	28.33	−0.04	50.00	11.80	58.33	13.73
108	11.6905	56.94	9.58	31.67	1.06	50.00	11.80	63.89	14.22
109	11.4233	59.72	11.61	30.00	2.60	50.00	11.80	63.89	14.22
110	11.1922	56.94	9.38	35.00	2.09	50.00	11.80	63.89	14.22
111	11.3028	52.08	8.13	23.33	−0.81	33.33	4.80	61.11	11.58
112	11.0552	50.00	7.62	26.67	−0.30	33.33	5.40	61.11	11.79
113	11.4470	52.08	8.13	23.33	−0.81	33.33	4.80	61.11	11.58
114	10.5315	48.61	7.36	35.00	3.24	25.00	4.80	58.33	11.60
115	10.6624	50.69	8.05	36.67	5.21	33.33	8.40	58.33	12.48
116	11.0451	47.92	6.85	33.33	2.82	25.00	4.20	58.33	11.39
117	11.4839	39.58	2.70	45.00	5.29	33.33	5.40	38.89	7.23
118	11.1965	54.86	9.12	31.67	2.69	41.67	9.00	41.67	8.49
119	11.7208	57.64	11.66	41.67	8.78	41.67	8.00	44.44	10.08
120	10.7722	56.25	10.15	48.33	11.42	41.67	11.10	44.44	11.12

GOOD RULES FOR CORPORATE BONDS

Five of the ten series that were used to develop Treasury bond trading rules were also used to develop corporate bond rules. The correlations (shown in Table 13.6) were similar in magnitude and direction to those used with Treasury bonds. This is not surprising. Employment-related series appear four times in the list. Certainly a good argument could be made for dropping one or two of these series on the basis of high correlations between them, but we chose to let the GA use all four. Possible modifications to our variable selection procedure will be addressed in Chapter 15. One hundred readers could probably look at the list of variables in Table 13.6 and come up with nearly 100 different lists of ten most-promising variables.

The list of good rules for corporate bonds is shown in Table 13.7. Rule 26 has the most fitness. It suggests that a good time to invest in corporate bonds is when

Table 13.6 Correlations with Corporate Bond Returns

	Series Number	Differencing Interval	Series Description	Correlation Coefficient
1	207	1	742. United Kingdom, stock prices, NSA (1967 = 100)	−0.3931
2	229	3	940. Ratio, coincident index to lagging index (1982 =	−0.3658
3	86	12	91. Average duration of unemployment in weeks (weeks)	−0.3430
4	178	1	570. Employment, defense products industries (thous.)	−0.3262
5	255	3	(23) Spot price, burlap, NSA ($ per yd.) COPYRIGHTED	−0.3205
6	193	3	727. Italy, industrial production (1987 = 100)	−0.3099
7	34	3	37. Number of persons employed (thous.)	0.3087
8	202	12	736c. France, 6-mo. change in consumer prices (AR, pct.)	−0.3083
9	205	12	738. Japan, consumer price index, NSA (1982–1984 = 100)	0.2992
10	40	3	43. Civilian unemployment rate (pct.)	0.2974
11	100	0	99. Smoothed change in sensitive materials prices (pct.)	−0.2973
12	172	3	452. Labor force participation rate, females 20 and over	0.2924
13	66	3	66. Consumer installment credit outstanding (mil. $)	0.2909
14	206	12	738c. Japan, 6-mo. change in consumer prices (AR, pct.)	0.2898
15	141	0	323c. Change in CPI-U, less food & energy, 1-mo. span (pc	0.2878
16	5	3	7. Mfrs.' new orders, durable goods industries (bil. 1982 $)	−0.2840
17	66	12	66. Consumer installment credit outstanding (mil. $)	0.2820
18	8	0	9. Construction contracts (mil. sq. ft.) COPYRIGHTED (McG	0.2790
19	74	12	77. Ratio, mfg., and trade inventories in sales in 1982 $ (ra	0.2755
20	13	3	14. Current liabilities of business failures, NSA (mil. $)	0.2741
21	172	12	452. Labor force participation rate, females 20 and over	0.2712
22	94	3	95. Ratio, consumer installment credit to personal income	0.2700
23	233	12	951. Diffusion index of coincident indicators, 6-mo. span	−0.2663
24	141	1	323c. Change in CPI-U, less food & energy, 1-mo. span (pc	0.2584
25	247	12	(98) Producer Price Index, sand, gravel, and stone (1982	0.2582
26	79	1	83. Consumer expectations, NSA (1966:I = 100) COPYR	−0.2555
27	233	3	951. Diffusion index of coincident indicators, 6-mo. span	−0.2551
28	79	12	83. Consumer expectations, NSA (1966:I = 100) COPYRI	−0.2550
29	140	1	323. CPI-U, all items less food and energy (1982–1984 =	0.2540
30	225	12	920c. Coincident index, change over 3-mo. span (AR, pct.)	−0.2529
31	207	3	742. United Kingdom, stock prices, NSA (1967 = 100)	−0.2524
32	99	3	99a. Index of sensitive materials prices (1982 = 100)	−0.2515
33	234	3	952. Diffusion index of lagging indicators, 1-mo. span (pct.	0.2503
34	114	0	111. Change in business and consumer credit (AR, pct.)	0.2496
35	226	3	930. Composite index of seven lagging indicators (1982 =	0.2486
36	229	12	940. Ratio, coincident index to lagging index (1982 = (1	−0.2473
37	173	3	453. Labor force participation rate, 16–19 years of age (pct	0.2472
38	226	12	930. Composite index of seven lagging indicators (1982 =	0.2461
39	188	3	721. OECD, European countries, industrial production (19	−0.2458
40	86	3	91. Average duration of unemployment in weeks (weeks)	−0.2438
41	142	3	323c. Change in CPI-U, less food & energy, 6-mo. span (A	−0.2428
42	196	3	732c. United Kingdom, 6-mo. change in consumer prices	−0.2428
43	138	1	320c. Change in CPI-U, all items, 1-mo. span (pct.)	0.2427
44	110	3	108. Ratio, personal income to money supply M2 (ratio)	−0.2417
45	66	1	66. Consumer installment credit outstanding (mil. $)	0.2409
46	116	0	113. Net change in consumer installment credit (AR, bil. $)	0.2409
47	68	12	70. Manufacturing and trade inventories (bil. 1982 $)	0.2389
48	94	12	95. Ratio, consumer installment credit to personal income	0.2385
49	239	12	(98) Producer Price Index, lumber and wood products (198	−0.2381
50	99	1	99a. Index of sensitive materials prices (1982 = 100)	−0.2368

Table 13.7 Good Rules—Corporate Bonds

Rule #	Logic Code	)/(Code	Cutoff Values Series 1	Series 2	Series 3	Fitness	1 #	Diff.	2 #	Diff.	3 #	Diff.
1	8	1	23	18	13	1.4065	207	1	229	3	86	12
2	8	1	23	18	20	1.3658	207	1	229	3	178	1
3	3	2	28	20	16	1.4683	207	1	229	3	34	3
4	3	1	28	27	8	1.3651	207	1	229	3	202	12
5	1	2	28	22	3	1.3137	207	1	229	3	205	12
6	1	4	28	2	8	1.5387	207	1	229	3	40	3
7	8	1	23	19	12	1.4222	207	1	229	3	100	0
8	6	3	27	14	8	1.4589	207	1	229	3	172	3
9	7	1	28	18	27	1.4022	207	1	86	12	178	1
10	4	2	27	22	17	1.4158	207	1	86	12	34	3
11	6	5	22	18	13	1.4110	207	1	86	12	202	12
12	3	1	28	18	18	1.5340	207	1	86	12	205	12
13	3	2	28	13	10	1.4554	207	1	86	12	40	3
14	3	1	28	18	12	1.4596	207	1	86	12	100	0
15	6	3	27	16	14	1.5184	207	1	86	12	172	3
16	3	2	28	9	9	1.4554	207	1	178	1	34	3
17	8	1	23	7	18	1.4152	207	1	178	1	202	12
18	4	4	27	30	27	1.2100	207	1	178	1	205	12
19	3	2	28	25	8	1.4554	207	1	178	1	40	3
20	4	3	24	9	12	1.3609	207	1	178	1	100	0
21	5	2	28	7	14	1.3320	207	1	178	1	172	3
22	2	3	23	16	18	1.5752	207	1	34	3	202	12
23	3	4	28	9	30	1.4554	207	1	34	3	205	12
24	7	2	28	9	3	1.4554	207	1	34	3	40	3
25	3	3	28	9	7	1.4554	207	1	34	3	100	0
26	3	4	28	18	15	1.5447	207	1	34	3	172	3
27	3	1	28	18	17	1.5152	207	1	202	12	205	12
28	7	3	23	25	15	1.4247	207	1	202	12	40	3
29	2	1	24	18	23	1.4555	207	1	202	12	100	0
30	2	2	23	17	13	1.4555	207	1	202	12	172	3
32	3	1	28	18	12	1.4770	207	1	205	12	100	0
33	3	2	28	18	16	1.4463	207	1	205	12	172	3
34	4	3	28	8	4	1.4554	207	1	40	3	100	0
35	3	4	28	21	13	1.5327	207	1	40	3	172	3
36	3	2	28	13	12	1.4693	207	1	100	0	172	3
37	7	5	2	18	14	1.3712	229	3	86	12	178	1
38	6	7	22	18	18	1.4644	229	3	86	12	34	3
39	6	1	20	18	27	1.4463	229	3	86	12	202	12
40	6	1	19	18	27	1.4317	229	3	86	12	205	12
41	7	1	14	18	25	1.3908	229	3	86	12	40	3
42	3	1	27	18	21	1.4513	229	3	86	12	100	0
43	3	2	24	17	17	1.4370	229	3	86	12	172	3
44	8	2	20	21	16	1.3669	229	3	178	1	34	3
45	5	1	22	20	23	1.3776	229	3	178	1	202	12
46	8	2	18	31	24	1.2918	229	3	178	1	205	12

Continued on next page

Table 13.7 *(continued)*

Rule #	Logic Code	)/(Code	Cutoff Values				Series Number and Differencing Interval					
			Series 1	Series 2	Series 3	Fitness	1 #	Diff.	2 #	Diff.	3 #	Diff.
47	4	4	20	31	19	1.3834	229	3	178	1	40	3
48	6	1	18	20	27	1.2512	229	3	178	1	100	0
49	4	4	13	30	13	1.2736	229	3	178	1	172	3
50	4	3	27	16	7	1.4185	229	3	34	3	202	12
51	6	4	20	16	22	1.3723	229	3	34	3	205	12
52	6	4	20	16	5	1.3669	229	3	34	3	40	3
53	5	3	18	17	27	1.4110	229	3	34	3	100	0
54	3	8	2	18	17	1.4597	229	3	34	3	172	3
55	6	3	26	17	10	1.2862	229	3	202	12	205	12
56	6	3	27	5	15	1.4038	229	3	202	12	40	3
57	7	1	22	20	10	1.4077	229	3	202	12	100	0
58	7	3	21	25	15	1.4188	229	3	202	12	172	3
59	3	8	4	27	17	1.4480	229	3	205	12	40	3
60	4	1	18	29	12	1.2981	229	3	205	12	100	0
61	2	4	18	11	14	1.3558	229	3	205	12	172	3
62	3	3	26	15	20	1.3788	229	3	40	3	100	0
63	3	4	28	17	13	1.4047	229	3	40	3	172	3
64	3	2	26	20	11	1.3324	229	3	100	0	172	3
65	8	2	18	16	18	1.4028	86	12	178	1	34	3
66	2	3	18	29	13	1.4110	86	12	178	1	202	12
67	2	1	18	30	16	1.3676	86	12	178	1	205	12
68	2	4	18	22	22	1.3688	86	12	178	1	40	3
69	6	1	18	12	27	1.4077	86	12	178	1	100	0
70	8	2	16	9	16	1.4068	86	12	178	1	172	3
71	2	3	18	18	20	1.4597	86	12	34	3	202	12
72	3	2	18	27	30	1.4053	86	12	34	3	205	12
73	2	2	18	23	22	1.4157	86	12	34	3	40	3
74	2	3	18	18	21	1.4363	86	12	34	3	100	0
75	8	4	16	18	24	1.4380	86	12	34	3	172	3
76	2	1	18	17	16	1.4355	86	12	202	12	205	12
77	8	2	16	7	22	1.4335	86	12	202	12	40	3
78	2	1	18	17	25	1.4781	86	12	202	12	100	0
79	2	2	16	18	14	1.4866	86	12	202	12	172	3
80	2	2	18	27	20	1.4329	86	12	205	12	40	3
81	2	1	18	15	21	1.4289	86	12	205	12	100	0
82	2	4	16	19	17	1.4303	86	12	205	12	172	3
83	2	4	18	8	26	1.3946	86	12	40	3	100	0
84	2	4	18	19	11	1.4288	86	12	40	3	172	3
85	2	2	18	20	14	1.4457	86	12	100	0	172	3
86	6	6	31	17	11	1.3860	178	1	34	3	202	12
87	8	4	20	16	26	1.3421	178	1	34	3	205	12
88	7	8	13	16	5	1.3202	178	1	34	3	40	3
89	2	3	26	16	27	1.3594	178	1	34	3	100	0
90	6	8	30	18	18	1.4175	178	1	34	3	172	3
91	8	1	21	20	4	1.2237	178	1	202	12	205	12
92	8	2	6	13	19	1.3551	178	1	202	12	40	3

Continued on next page

Table 13.7 *(continued)*

Rule #	Logic Code	⟩/⟨ Code	Cutoff Values			Fitness	Series Number and Differencing Interval					
			Series 1	Series 2	Series 3		1 #	Diff.	2 #	Diff.	3 #	Diff.
93	2	1	8	25	25	1.3819	178	1	202	12	100	0
94	7	3	12	27	4	1.3181	178	1	202	12	172	3
95	2	4	24	6	15	1.3042	178	1	205	12	40	3
96	4	7	29	25	21	1.1317	178	1	205	12	100	0
97	7	4	31	10	13	1.2639	178	1	205	12	172	3
99	2	4	4	15	6	1.3061	178	1	40	3	172	3
100	8	2	12	12	12	1.2668	178	1	100	0	172	3
101	3	5	16	18	17	1.4944	34	3	202	12	205	12
102	7	5	15	25	3	1.3923	34	3	202	12	40	3
103	3	5	15	25	0	1.3923	34	3	202	12	100	0
104	7	7	18	24	17	1.5047	34	3	202	12	172	3
105	4	8	9	27	17	1.3546	34	3	205	12	40	3
106	2	8	16	24	15	1.3436	34	3	205	12	100	0
107	2	8	18	10	14	1.4595	34	3	205	12	172	3
108	3	5	16	6	27	1.3594	34	3	40	3	100	0
109	2	8	18	4	16	1.4175	34	3	40	3	172	3
110	6	7	16	8	5	1.3820	34	3	100	0	172	3
111	5	4	20	10	8	1.3547	202	12	205	12	40	3
112	3	1	25	21	22	1.3880	202	12	205	12	100	0
113	3	4	24	28	13	1.3709	202	12	205	12	172	3
114	7	4	24	8	25	1.4463	202	12	40	3	100	0
115	6	4	30	21	14	1.4545	202	12	40	3	172	3
116	3	2	25	14	12	1.4078	202	12	100	0	172	3
117	4	7	11	8	20	1.3782	205	12	40	3	100	0
118	6	8	10	18	14	1.4215	205	12	40	3	172	3
119	6	7	12	16	11	1.3456	205	12	100	0	172	3
120	2	6	17	29	16	1.4063	40	3	100	0	172	3

(the one-month change in French stock prices has not been near the top of its range *or* the three-month change in the number of persons unemployed is in the upper half of its range) *and* the three-month change in the labor force participation rate of females is in the upper half of its range.

The aggregate performance of the good rule portfolio can be seen in Figures 13.9–13.12. The percentage of correct calls climbed steeply and steadily from 1982 to 1988. It began dropping sharply in the last half of 1989 but then flattened out from mid-1990 through 1991. Average returns rose quickly through the mid-1980s, but they peaked in 1986 and then started a general decline that was interrupted briefly with a minor peak in 1989, after which the decline continued until 1991. During most of 1991 the moving average return, as shown in Figure 13.12, was fairly steady. Unfortunately for our results, some type of fundamental reversal

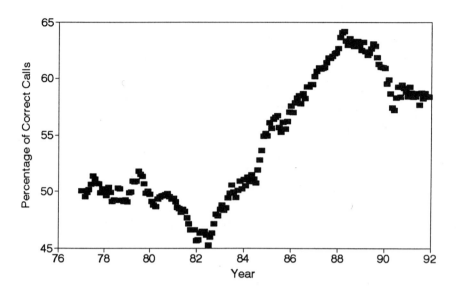

FIGURE 13.9   Percentage Correct (Corporate Bonds—Good Rules) 1977–1991

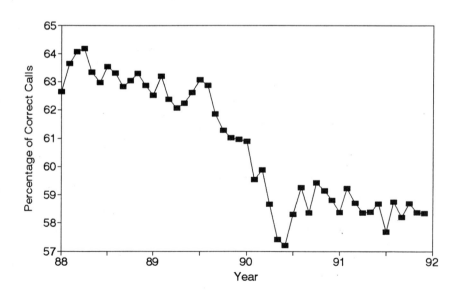

FIGURE 13.10   Percentage Correct (Corporate Bonds—Good Rules) 1988–1991

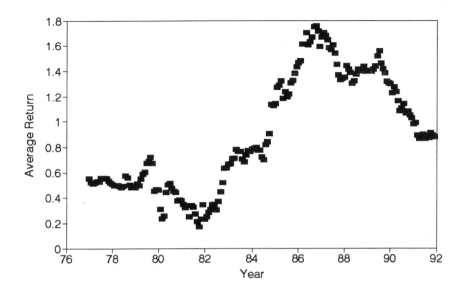

FIGURE 13.11 Average Return (Corporate Bonds—Good Rules) 1977–1991

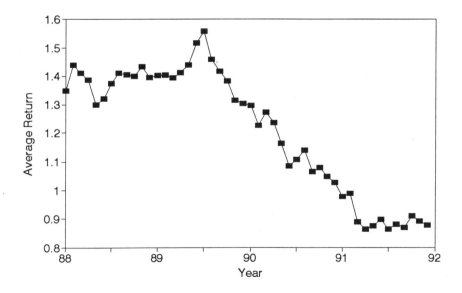

FIGURE 13.12 Average Return (Corporate Bonds—Good Rules) 1988–1991

in the effectiveness of this rule portfolio seems to have occurred in the 1986–1988 period.

The patterns that appear in the graphs of the aggregate performance of the various rule portfolios may be providing valuable clues to chaotic changes in the structure of the markets. Several chaos theory researchers have suggested that financial markets go through phases. At times they appear to exhibit somewhat consistent behavior—*somewhat* consistent because markets never fall into easily definable patterns—and at other times they are in transition. These changes could be due to fundamental political/legal changes or could be driven more by changes in general sentiment.

The detailed performance of the good rule portfolio is summarized in Table 13.8. Corporate bonds performed well over the 1989–1991 period, earning an annual compound rate of 14.17 percent. They did slightly better in 1989, with a buy-and-hold return of 16.23 percent. For the entire 1989–1991 test period, 45 of the 120 rules equaled or outperformed the buy-and-hold alternative. Rule 8 had the best average return, at 15.40 percent; it made correct calls about 69 percent of the time.

BAD RULES FOR CORPORATE BONDS

The list of bad rules is shown in Table 13.9; the overall performance of the bad rule portfolio can be seen in Figures 13.13–13.16. As demonstrated in Figure 13.13, the GA procedure has certainly identified a group of rules with a strong downward trend in forecasting accuracy. This poor performance seemed to bottom out in 1988 and then reversed course about 1989, as seen in Figure 13.14. The average return, shown in Figure 13.15, also experienced a precipitous drop over the 1987–1988 period. As shown in Figure 13.16, average return increased in 1989 and then declined a bit before starting to rise again.

The detailed performance of the bad rule portfolio can be seen in Table 13.10. Only one rule from this entire group matches the performance of the buy-and-hold alternative. If we compare this to the 45 good rules that equaled or exceeded the performance of the buy-and-hold alternative, we see that there is a sharp contrast in the performance of the good and bad rule portfolios. This difference in performance is what we try to exploit with hedge portfolios.

HEDGE PORTFOLIO RESULTS

Because the concept of hedge portfolios was described in Chapters 11 and 12, we will not repeat the discussion here but instead merely report the results for bond market-timing strategies. The hedge portfolio results for Treasury bonds are shown in Table 13.11 and are fairly encouraging. The cumulative return did become negative early into the holdout period but was positive for all but four months of the 1989–1991 period. At the end of the first year, the cumulative return was 3.63 percent. The long portfolio seemed to be generally outperforming

Table 13.8 Performance Summary: Good Rules—Corporate Bonds

Rule #	Fitness	1971–1983 Period % Correct	1971–1983 Period Average Return	1984–1988 Period % Correct	1984–1988 Period Average Return	1989 % Correct	1989 Average Return	1989–1991 Period % Correct	1989–1991 Period Average Return
1	1.4065	45.83	5.16	70.00	19.25	58.33	14.60	50.00	11.20
2	1.3658	45.83	5.26	66.67	18.88	58.33	16.20	47.22	10.25
3	1.4683	47.22	6.05	71.67	19.88	58.33	12.60	72.22	14.29
4	1.3651	47.92	5.56	73.33	20.68	58.33	12.60	61.11	12.35
5	1.3137	50.69	8.79	65.00	19.98	58.33	12.60	50.00	9.11
6	1.5387	53.47	11.07	61.67	14.73	58.33	12.60	69.44	14.01
7	1.4222	46.53	5.36	58.33	19.17	58.33	16.20	47.22	10.25
8	1.4589	47.22	6.05	76.67	21.32	58.33	15.00	69.44	15.40
9	1.4022	47.22	6.18	63.33	20.22	58.33	16.20	27.78	7.43
10	1.4158	46.53	5.92	55.00	13.29	50.00	11.40	66.67	12.82
11	1.4110	47.22	6.18	63.33	20.22	58.33	16.20	27.78	7.43
12	1.5340	47.22	6.18	70.00	21.45	58.33	12.60	30.56	6.53
13	1.4554	47.22	6.05	71.67	19.88	58.33	12.60	72.22	14.29
14	1.4596	47.22	6.18	70.00	21.45	58.33	12.60	30.56	6.53
15	1.5184	47.92	6.13	73.33	21.35	50.00	15.00	66.67	15.05
16	1.4554	47.22	6.05	71.67	19.88	58.33	12.60	72.22	14.29
17	1.4152	52.08	8.02	56.67	12.55	25.00	5.70	38.89	8.35
18	1.2100	47.22	6.05	53.33	13.26	58.33	16.20	66.67	14.17
19	1.4554	47.22	6.05	71.67	19.88	58.33	12.60	72.22	14.29
20	1.3609	55.56	8.95	60.00	15.96	41.67	10.70	52.78	11.47
21	1.3320	47.22	6.05	70.00	18.01	58.33	12.60	72.22	14.29
22	1.5752	52.08	7.76	58.33	13.34	33.33	9.10	41.67	9.50
23	1.4554	48.61	6.32	78.33	23.08	58.33	12.60	72.22	14.29
24	1.4554	48.61	6.32	78.33	23.08	58.33	12.60	72.22	14.29
25	1.4554	47.92	6.17	73.33	21.17	58.33	12.60	72.22	14.29
26	1.5447	48.61	6.93	73.33	21.90	58.33	12.60	72.22	14.29
27	1.5152	58.33	10.91	63.33	17.51	41.67	8.40	44.44	9.33
28	1.4247	59.03	8.37	53.33	10.89	50.00	10.00	52.78	10.27
29	1.4555	60.42	11.62	66.67	20.13	41.67	10.70	52.78	10.27
30	1.4555	56.25	8.36	58.33	13.01	25.00	5.70	38.89	7.49
31	1.4099	47.22	6.05	58.33	16.29	33.33	9.40	58.33	11.90
32	1.4770	52.78	8.10	63.33	12.60	50.00	11.40	36.11	8.24
33	1.4463	47.22	6.05	71.67	19.88	58.33	12.60	72.22	14.29
34	1.4554	47.22	6.16	75.00	21.63	58.33	12.60	72.22	14.29
35	1.5327	49.31	6.57	73.33	21.90	58.33	12.60	72.22	14.29
36	1.4693	47.22	6.05	71.67	19.88	58.33	12.60	72.22	14.29
37	1.3712	46.53	6.53	63.33	20.22	58.33	16.20	27.78	7.43
38	1.4644	45.14	6.00	56.67	17.18	58.33	16.20	47.22	12.29
39	1.4463	43.06	3.65	66.67	20.78	58.33	16.20	38.89	8.32
40	1.4317	43.06	3.65	68.33	21.08	58.33	16.20	36.11	7.52
41	1.3908	47.22	6.18	63.33	20.22	58.33	16.20	27.78	7.43
42	1.4513	47.92	4.95	61.67	17.05	58.33	16.20	36.11	8.12
43	1.4370	46.53	5.27	58.33	16.08	58.33	16.20	52.78	10.77
44	1.3669	47.22	6.05	55.00	15.05	58.33	16.20	66.67	14.17
45	1.3776	52.78	8.10	46.67	8.79	41.67	8.40	33.33	7.26
46	1.2918	47.22	6.05	55.00	15.05	58.33	16.20	66.67	14.17

Continued on next page

Table 13.8 (continued)

Rule #	Fitness	1971–1983 Period		1984–1988 Period		1989		1989–1991 Period	
		% Correct	Average Return	% Correct	Average Return	% Correct	Average Return	% Correct	Average Return
47	1.3834	47.22	6.05	53.33	13.26	58.33	16.20	66.67	14.17
48	1.2512	52.78	8.10	46.67	8.79	41.67	8.40	33.33	7.26
49	1.2736	47.22	6.05	53.33	13.26	58.33	16.20	66.67	14.17
50	1.4185	47.92	5.66	63.33	19.38	58.33	16.20	55.56	12.21
51	1.3723	51.39	7.11	65.00	20.48	58.33	16.20	66.67	14.17
52	1.3669	50.00	6.92	68.33	21.14	58.33	16.20	66.67	14.17
53	1.4110	44.44	3.68	73.33	21.47	66.67	16.50	52.78	10.79
54	1.4597	53.47	9.46	63.33	20.18	58.33	14.80	66.67	13.39
55	1.2862	47.22	6.41	61.67	16.96	58.33	16.20	55.56	11.04
56	1.4038	50.00	7.03	53.33	10.95	58.33	16.20	55.56	12.21
57	1.4077	54.17	9.41	63.33	19.71	33.33	7.80	33.33	6.03
58	1.4188	59.03	8.57	65.00	17.93	50.00	10.00	52.78	10.77
59	1.4480	50.69	9.50	46.67	12.80	50.00	14.60	61.11	13.08
60	1.2981	52.78	9.01	60.00	13.97	58.33	13.20	38.89	8.83
61	1.3558	47.22	6.05	55.00	16.04	50.00	14.60	63.89	13.63
62	1.3788	47.22	5.54	61.67	16.96	58.33	16.20	52.78	10.77
63	1.4047	47.92	5.71	61.67	18.15	58.33	16.20	55.56	12.21
64	1.3324	47.22	5.54	61.67	16.96	58.33	16.20	52.78	10.77
65	1.4028	47.22	6.05	55.00	15.05	58.33	16.20	66.67	14.17
66	1.4110	47.22	6.18	63.33	20.22	58.33	16.20	27.78	7.43
67	1.3676	47.22	6.18	63.33	20.22	58.33	16.20	27.78	7.43
68	1.3688	47.22	6.05	55.00	15.05	58.33	16.20	66.67	14.17
69	1.4077	52.78	8.10	46.67	8.79	41.67	8.40	33.33	7.26
70	1.4068	47.22	6.05	55.00	15.05	58.33	16.20	66.67	14.17
71	1.4597	50.00	7.25	63.33	20.12	58.33	16.20	33.33	9.08
72	1.4053	45.83	5.51	65.00	20.74	58.33	16.20	27.78	7.43
73	1.4157	51.39	7.76	63.33	20.22	58.33	16.20	30.56	6.47
74	1.4363	47.92	6.94	65.00	20.53	58.33	16.20	36.11	10.52
75	1.4380	49.31	7.03	66.67	19.50	58.33	16.20	66.67	14.17
76	1.4355	47.22	6.47	65.00	19.30	58.33	16.20	27.78	7.43
77	1.4335	44.44	5.61	56.67	17.21	58.33	16.20	47.22	10.96
78	1.4781	48.61	7.21	66.67	19.72	58.33	16.20	27.78	6.56
79	1.4866	50.69	6.65	66.67	19.70	41.67	13.30	36.11	8.49
80	1.4329	46.53	6.54	56.67	17.10	58.33	16.20	27.78	7.43
81	1.4289	47.22	6.18	61.67	18.15	58.33	16.20	27.78	7.43
82	1.4303	47.92	6.19	60.00	17.69	41.67	13.30	61.11	13.21
83	1.3946	45.83	6.21	63.33	20.22	58.33	16.20	52.78	11.74
84	1.4288	48.61	6.74	66.67	20.75	58.33	16.20	66.67	14.17
85	1.4457	50.00	6.24	68.33	21.18	58.33	16.20	33.33	8.60
86	1.3860	49.31	6.47	58.33	17.62	58.33	14.80	66.67	13.68
87	1.3421	51.39	7.11	65.00	20.48	58.33	16.20	66.67	14.17
88	1.3202	51.39	7.11	65.00	20.48	58.33	16.20	66.67	14.17
89	1.3594	46.53	4.30	68.33	21.04	66.67	16.50	52.78	10.79
90	1.4175	51.39	7.37	58.33	16.35	58.33	14.80	66.67	13.68
91	1.2237	55.56	8.81	65.00	18.68	33.33	7.80	47.22	8.89
92	1.3551	42.36	5.36	51.67	14.09	58.33	16.20	55.56	12.50

Continued on next page

Table 13.8 *(continued)*

Rule #	Fitness	1971–1983 Period		1984–1988 Period		1989		1989–1991 Period	
		% Correct	Average Return	% Correct	Average Return	% Correct	Average Return	% Correct	Average Return
93	1.3819	56.94	8.49	63.33	18.43	50.00	10.00	52.78	10.77
94	1.3181	53.47	6.96	60.00	16.62	75.00	19.30	72.22	15.18
95	1.3042	47.22	6.05	50.00	14.51	50.00	14.60	63.89	13.63
96	1.1317	45.14	5.52	60.00	12.50	58.33	16.20	66.67	14.17
97	1.2639	47.22	6.05	58.33	17.25	58.33	16.20	66.67	14.17
98	1.2765	50.00	6.48	53.33	14.77	58.33	16.20	66.67	14.17
99	1.3061	50.69	6.75	61.67	19.69	58.33	16.20	66.67	14.17
100	1.2668	47.22	6.05	55.00	15.05	58.33	16.20	66.67	14.17
101	1.4944	61.11	11.56	61.67	18.35	41.67	8.40	41.67	8.04
102	1.3923	58.33	9.21	68.33	20.61	50.00	10.00	52.78	10.77
103	1.3923	59.03	9.33	68.33	20.61	50.00	10.00	52.78	10.77
104	1.5047	56.94	8.00	61.67	17.29	50.00	10.00	52.78	10.77
105	1.3546	47.22	6.05	50.00	13.46	50.00	14.60	63.89	13.63
106	1.3436	50.00	6.40	68.33	20.68	58.33	16.20	66.67	14.17
107	1.4595	47.22	6.05	56.67	15.99	58.33	16.20	66.67	14.17
108	1.3594	47.92	4.89	68.33	20.80	66.67	16.50	50.00	10.25
109	1.4175	50.69	6.75	61.67	19.69	58.33	16.20	66.67	14.17
110	1.3820	51.39	7.11	65.00	20.48	58.33	16.20	66.67	14.17
111	1.3547	47.22	6.05	60.00	18.10	58.33	16.20	66.67	14.17
112	1.3880	52.78	8.10	50.00	10.51	41.67	8.40	33.33	7.26
113	1.3709	55.56	7.86	55.00	15.89	50.00	10.00	52.78	10.77
114	1.4463	55.56	7.01	68.33	20.78	41.67	9.70	61.11	12.00
115	1.4545	50.69	6.58	63.33	19.01	58.33	16.20	66.67	14.17
116	1.4078	56.94	8.49	63.33	18.43	50.00	10.00	52.78	10.77
117	1.3782	47.22	6.05	50.00	14.30	58.33	16.20	66.67	14.17
118	1.4215	49.31	6.57	65.00	20.38	58.33	16.20	66.67	14.17
119	1.3456	47.22	6.05	58.33	17.08	58.33	16.20	66.67	14.17
120	1.4063	52.78	7.58	60.00	15.89	58.33	16.20	66.67	14.17

Table 13.9 Good Rules—S&P 500 Stocks

Rule #	Logic Code	⟩/⟨ Code	Cutoff Values			Fitness	Series Number and Differencing Interval					
			Series 1	Series 2	Series 3		1 #	Diff.	2 #	Diff.	3 #	Diff.
1	1	8	18	6	16	11.2006	207	1	229	3	86	12
2	3	7	27	8	14	10.6652	207	1	229	3	178	1
3	7	8	27	8	29	11.3661	207	1	229	3	34	3
4	2	8	28	9	27	11.1345	207	1	229	3	202	12
5	2	7	28	22	27	10.6121	207	1	229	3	205	12
6	7	8	28	7	29	11.1733	207	1	229	3	40	3
7	7	8	27	9	25	11.0054	207	1	229	3	100	0
8	7	6	27	13	4	11.0847	207	1	229	3	172	3
9	2	7	28	21	31	11.1070	207	1	86	12	178	1
10	4	6	28	31	29	11.0180	207	1	86	12	34	3
11	5	8	25	28	20	11.1408	207	1	86	12	202	12
12	1	7	23	16	28	10.7931	207	1	86	12	205	12
13	4	8	27	14	30	11.0566	207	1	86	12	40	3
14	7	6	27	14	2	11.0809	207	1	86	12	100	0
15	1	7	17	16	22	10.7199	207	1	86	12	172	3
16	4	7	28	14	9	10.7843	207	1	178	1	34	3
17	1	8	25	9	20	10.7563	207	1	178	1	202	12
18	3	7	28	20	9	10.4740	207	1	178	1	205	12
19	4	7	28	8	10	10.7843	207	1	178	1	40	3
20	2	7	28	22	2	10.9103	207	1	178	1	100	0
21	2	5	28	31	4	10.8146	207	1	178	1	172	3
22	8	8	28	31	24	10.9468	207	1	34	3	202	12
23	8	7	28	29	0	11.0180	207	1	34	3	205	12
24	6	7	23	17	29	11.0451	207	1	34	3	40	3
25	3	6	23	17	24	10.9519	207	1	34	3	100	0
26	2	8	28	29	17	11.2687	207	1	34	3	172	3
27	7	8	28	20	17	10.6093	207	1	202	12	205	12
28	4	8	25	19	31	10.9787	207	1	202	12	40	3
29	2	8	28	10	25	10.9593	207	1	202	12	100	0
30	2	5	28	28	4	10.7447	207	1	202	12	172	3
31	2	5	28	26	10	10.7843	207	1	205	12	40	3
32	3	6	23	10	24	10.7843	207	1	205	12	100	0
33	2	5	28	24	12	10.6661	207	1	205	12	172	3
34	3	8	21	31	23	10.7688	207	1	40	3	100	0
35	8	7	28	29	4	11.0233	207	1	40	3	172	3
36	2	7	28	25	23	10.9729	207	1	100	0	172	3
37	7	6	9	16	6	11.1926	229	3	86	12	178	1
38	3	7	6	16	17	11.2587	229	3	86	12	34	3
39	1	8	6	16	16	11.2496	229	3	86	12	202	12
40	1	8	6	16	5	11.2059	229	3	86	12	205	12
41	3	7	6	16	15	11.2149	229	3	86	12	40	3
42	7	8	6	16	23	11.2825	229	3	86	12	100	0
43	3	8	6	16	30	11.2114	229	3	86	12	172	3
44	5	5	14	18	17	10.6148	229	3	178	1	34	3
45	3	6	9	1	27	10.9318	229	3	178	1	202	12
46	1	7	18	12	31	10.4769	229	3	178	1	205	12

Continued on next page

Table 13.9 *(continued)*

Rule #	Logic Code	)/(Code	Cutoff Values			Fitness	Series Number and Differencing Interval					
			Series 1	Series 2	Series 3		1		2		3	
							#	Diff.	#	Diff.	#	Diff.
47	4	8	18	31	29	10.5777	229	3	178	1	40	3
48	3	6	8	31	20	10.6418	229	3	178	1	100	0
49	5	5	12	6	15	10.5593	229	3	178	1	172	3
50	3	8	9	27	27	11.2681	229	3	34	3	202	12
51	6	6	18	28	25	10.9368	229	3	34	3	205	12
52	6	7	8	17	28	11.2719	229	3	34	3	40	3
53	4	6	6	17	25	10.8936	229	3	34	3	100	0
54	3	7	8	26	12	11.1490	229	3	34	3	172	3
55	4	7	9	27	10	10.9763	229	3	202	12	205	12
56	3	8	9	27	27	11.2925	229	3	202	12	40	3
57	1	8	9	27	11	10.9318	229	3	202	12	100	0
58	3	7	9	27	6	11.1151	229	3	202	12	172	3
59	4	6	18	25	30	10.8182	229	3	205	12	40	3
60	3	6	1	10	25	10.7268	229	3	205	12	100	0
61	7	5	18	26	5	10.4452	229	3	205	12	172	3
62	5	8	18	28	22	10.7176	229	3	40	3	100	0
63	3	5	9	15	4	10.8004	229	3	40	3	172	3
64	1	7	12	7	12	10.6915	229	3	100	0	172	3
65	4	5	25	31	17	11.0695	86	12	178	1	34	3
66	1	8	16	3	20	10.7499	86	12	178	1	202	12
67	3	5	16	31	28	11.1036	86	12	178	1	205	12
68	3	5	16	31	15	10.9994	86	12	178	1	40	3
69	3	6	16	31	24	11.4168	86	12	178	1	100	0
70	3	5	16	31	21	11.0398	86	12	178	1	172	3
71	6	7	28	17	20	10.9702	86	12	34	3	202	12
72	6	5	21	17	31	10.9091	86	12	34	3	205	12
73	3	7	13	29	16	10.9900	86	12	34	3	40	3
74	3	6	16	17	24	11.0207	86	12	34	3	100	0
75	3	7	16	28	20	11.2269	86	12	34	3	172	3
76	3	7	16	20	27	10.9372	86	12	202	12	205	12
77	3	8	16	20	28	11.1470	86	12	202	12	40	3
78	3	7	16	20	11	11.1658	86	12	202	12	100	0
79	1	5	16	31	19	10.9857	86	12	202	12	172	3
80	3	5	18	31	22	10.9371	86	12	205	12	40	3
81	3	6	16	28	23	11.1234	86	12	205	12	100	0
82	6	5	28	10	11	10.7862	86	12	205	12	172	3
83	3	5	13	15	2	10.9062	86	12	40	3	100	0
84	6	6	16	29	19	11.1282	86	12	40	3	172	3
85	3	7	15	23	4	10.7323	86	12	100	0	172	3
86	3	8	6	27	24	10.7798	178	1	34	3	202	12
87	4	7	4	29	10	10.7808	178	1	34	3	205	12
88	3	7	10	29	15	10.9156	178	1	34	3	40	3
89	6	7	31	17	23	10.7896	178	1	34	3	100	0
90	6	6	11	28	10	10.6633	178	1	34	3	172	3
91	1	8	5	20	5	10.3760	178	1	202	12	205	12
92	6	4	31	24	31	10.7541	178	1	202	12	40	3

Continued on next page

Table 13.9 *(continued)*

Rule #	Logic Code	)/(Code	Cutoff Values			Fitness	Series Number and Differencing Interval					
			Series 1	Series 2	Series 3		1 #	Diff.	2 #	Diff.	3 #	Diff.
93	7	4	31	27	24	10.9784	178	1	202	12	100	0
94	4	7	12	24	6	10.4175	178	1	202	12	172	3
95	6	7	7	10	30	10.6695	178	1	205	12	40	3
96	5	8	31	17	24	10.5436	178	1	205	12	100	0
97	5	1	31	24	10	10.5033	178	1	205	12	172	3
98	6	1	31	16	16	10.6741	178	1	40	3	100	0
99	7	1	31	17	16	10.6241	178	1	40	3	172	3
100	5	3	30	11	11	10.6723	178	1	100	0	172	3
101	2	7	28	27	27	10.8255	34	3	202	12	205	12
102	2	2	17	22	28	10.9739	34	3	202	12	40	3
103	7	4	20	27	24	11.0473	34	3	202	12	100	0
104	2	7	28	20	12	10.9494	34	3	202	12	172	3
105	8	5	28	10	8	11.0893	34	3	205	12	40	3
106	2	4	17	21	24	10.8308	34	3	205	12	100	0
107	6	7	29	10	16	11.0316	34	3	205	12	172	3
108	2	4	17	28	24	10.9977	34	3	40	3	100	0
109	6	7	28	16	16	11.1720	34	3	40	3	172	3
110	2	7	29	12	11	11.2207	34	3	100	0	172	3
111	2	6	24	31	28	10.8293	202	12	205	12	40	3
112	6	7	27	10	24	10.7356	202	12	205	12	100	0
113	3	5	20	12	11	10.5025	202	12	205	12	172	3
114	6	8	24	30	12	10.8984	202	12	40	3	100	0
115	8	7	24	30	6	10.8169	202	12	40	3	172	3
116	1	3	30	11	11	10.6849	202	12	100	0	172	3
117	5	4	24	29	22	10.6709	205	12	40	3	100	0
118	7	1	22	17	18	10.6241	205	12	40	3	172	3
119	5	3	18	11	12	10.6723	205	12	100	0	172	3
120	6	2	22	25	7	10.7668	40	3	100	0	172	3

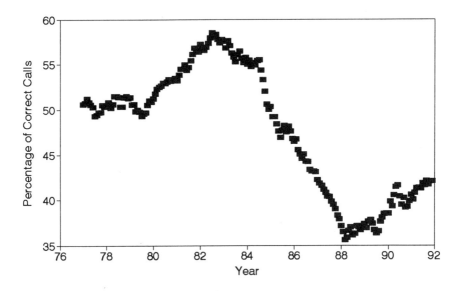

FIGURE 13.13 Percentage Correct (Corporate Bonds—Bad Rules) 1977–1991

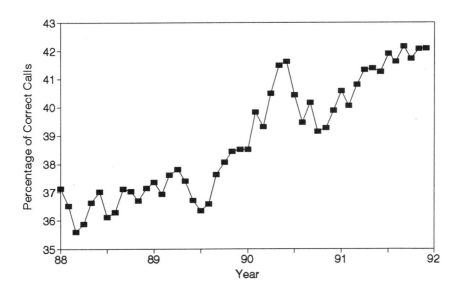

FIGURE 13.14 Percentage Correct (Corporate Bonds—Bad Rules) 1988–1991

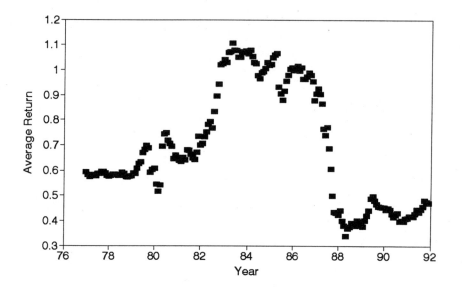

FIGURE 13.15   Average Return (Corporate Bonds—Bad Rules) 1977–1991

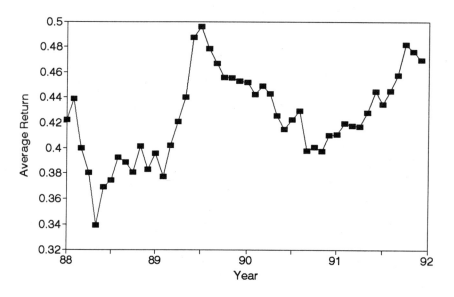

FIGURE 13.16   Average Return (Corporate Bonds—Bad Rules) 1988–1991

Table 13.10 Performance Summary: Bad Rules—Corporate Bonds

Rule #	Fitness	1971–1983 Period % Correct	1971–1983 Period Average Return	1984–1988 Period % Correct	1984–1988 Period Average Return	1989 % Correct	1989 Average Return	1989–1991 Period % Correct	1989–1991 Period Average Return
1	11.2006	55.56	9.24	33.33	4.86	50.00	11.10	58.33	12.08
2	10.6652	52.78	8.14	28.33	3.61	50.00	13.10	33.33	7.58
3	11.3661	54.17	9.36	21.67	0.88	41.67	10.80	38.89	8.38
4	11.1345	52.08	8.59	26.67	2.11	41.67	11.90	38.89	9.00
5	10.6121	52.08	7.52	35.00	3.24	41.67	11.90	36.11	10.08
6	11.1733	53.47	9.23	26.67	2.11	33.33	9.60	36.11	7.98
7	11.0054	52.78	8.59	25.00	1.49	41.67	10.80	41.67	9.78
8	11.0847	53.47	8.23	23.33	1.57	33.33	9.20	27.78	6.03
9	11.1070	54.17	10.23	28.33	2.47	41.67	11.90	58.33	12.85
10	11.0180	51.39	6.64	28.33	2.58	41.67	11.90	30.56	7.92
11	11.1408	52.08	8.82	40.00	4.95	41.67	8.40	41.67	8.63
12	10.7931	54.86	9.87	31.67	2.94	58.33	11.10	55.56	10.79
13	11.0566	50.00	6.39	21.67	1.23	41.67	9.50	30.56	6.41
14	11.0809	52.78	8.14	21.67	1.44	41.67	9.50	30.56	6.41
15	10.7199	55.56	9.00	38.33	4.18	58.33	11.10	41.67	7.81
16	10.7843	52.78	8.10	30.00	4.41	41.67	11.90	27.78	7.14
17	10.7563	53.47	8.85	43.33	6.65	58.33	13.70	41.67	8.66
18	10.4740	52.78	8.10	28.33	2.78	41.67	11.90	27.78	7.14
19	10.7843	52.78	8.10	30.00	4.41	41.67	11.90	27.78	7.14
20	10.9103	52.78	8.10	28.33	2.78	41.67	11.90	27.78	7.14
21	10.8146	52.78	8.10	30.00	4.41	41.67	11.90	27.78	7.14
22	10.9468	50.69	7.57	26.67	4.75	50.00	11.90	52.78	10.22
23	11.0180	57.64	11.77	26.67	2.75	41.67	11.90	44.44	10.19
24	11.0451	54.17	11.11	36.67	2.53	33.33	9.50	41.67	9.92
25	10.9519	48.61	8.25	31.67	3.26	58.33	13.20	52.78	10.93
26	11.2687	57.64	11.77	26.67	2.75	41.67	11.90	44.44	10.19
27	10.6093	44.44	5.35	35.00	3.83	66.67	16.90	52.78	12.48
28	10.9787	48.61	6.60	35.00	3.15	58.33	13.70	41.67	9.83
29	10.9593	43.06	5.66	30.00	2.76	58.33	16.90	41.67	9.70
30	10.7447	53.47	9.12	31.67	4.75	41.67	11.90	27.78	7.14
31	10.7843	52.78	8.10	31.67	3.03	41.67	11.90	27.78	7.14
32	10.7843	49.31	6.46	53.33	10.10	41.67	7.80	50.00	9.31
33	10.6661	52.78	8.10	38.33	4.71	41.67	11.90	27.78	7.14
34	10.7688	52.78	7.69	53.33	11.62	58.33	10.90	55.56	9.17
35	11.0233	58.33	11.06	23.33	1.53	41.67	11.90	44.44	10.19
36	10.9729	52.78	8.10	28.33	2.78	41.67	11.90	27.78	7.14
37	11.1926	59.72	13.77	33.33	1.59	58.33	11.10	69.44	13.13
38	11.2587	53.47	10.84	50.00	12.34	58.33	16.20	61.11	13.37
39	11.2496	58.33	12.93	33.33	1.59	58.33	11.10	66.67	12.90
40	11.2059	58.33	12.93	33.33	1.59	58.33	11.10	66.67	12.90
41	11.2149	54.17	11.04	43.33	8.92	58.33	16.20	61.11	13.37
42	11.2825	56.25	11.18	33.33	1.59	58.33	11.10	69.44	13.37
43	11.2114	58.33	12.93	33.33	1.59	58.33	11.10	66.67	12.90
44	10.6148	52.78	8.10	46.67	8.79	41.67	8.40	33.33	7.26
45	10.9318	54.86	11.63	41.67	8.23	50.00	13.90	61.11	12.82
46	10.4769	59.64	9.92	50.00	8.79	50.00	10.00	58.33	10.49

Continued on next page

Table 13.10 *(continued)*

Rule #	Fitness	1971–1983 Period		1984–1988 Period		1989		1989–1991 Period	
		% Correct	Average Return	% Correct	Average Return	% Correct	Average Return	% Correct	Average Return
47	10.5777	46.53	5.94	53.33	13.26	58.33	16.20	66.67	14.17
48	10.6418	53.47	11.07	45.00	10.12	50.00	13.90	61.11	12.82
49	10.5593	52.78	8.10	46.67	8.79	41.67	8.40	33.33	7.26
50	11.2681	56.94	12.43	41.67	6.59	33.33	8.10	44.44	9.94
51	10.9368	62.50	12.63	35.00	5.50	33.33	9.70	58.33	12.32
52	11.2719	55.56	12.11	35.00	2.49	33.33	9.50	44.44	10.41
53	10.8936	53.47	9.95	31.67	1.79	33.33	9.50	50.00	11.55
54	11.1490	55.56	12.04	38.33	4.36	33.33	8.10	50.00	10.77
55	10.9763	54.17	12.31	45.00	8.46	25.00	5.60	27.78	6.32
56	11.2925	52.78	10.85	38.33	4.13	25.00	5.60	27.78	6.32
57	10.9318	52.78	10.85	38.33	4.13	25.00	5.60	27.78	6.32
58	11.1151	54.86	12.05	36.67	4.07	25.00	5.60	27.78	6.32
59	10.8182	50.00	6.50	33.33	3.87	50.00	11.90	61.11	11.95
60	10.7268	46.53	5.77	58.33	11.05	33.33	7.20	58.33	11.12
61	10.4452	50.69	7.92	30.00	3.01	41.67	9.90	33.33	7.78
62	10.7176	58.33	11.14	46.67	8.72	41.67	9.70	55.56	9.75
63	10.8004	49.31	7.38	35.00	2.35	41.67	8.40	33.33	7.26
64	10.6915	52.08	8.29	41.67	7.01	33.33	8.10	30.56	6.00
65	11.0695	57.64	11.56	46.67	8.79	41.67	8.40	50.00	10.98
66	10.7499	56.25	10.07	35.00	3.05	58.33	11.10	72.22	13.70
67	11.1036	59.03	11.62	46.67	6.73	50.00	10.00	63.89	11.58
68	10.9994	59.03	11.62	46.67	6.73	50.00	10.00	63.89	11.58
69	11.4168	56.25	10.07	35.00	3.05	58.33	11.10	72.22	13.70
70	11.0398	59.03	11.62	46.67	6.73	50.00	10.00	63.89	11.58
71	10.9702	50.00	8.14	36.67	2.53	41.67	9.70	38.89	8.52
72	10.9091	51.39	8.02	38.33	2.75	41.67	9.70	58.33	12.58
73	10.9900	53.47	10.71	31.67	1.68	41.67	8.40	50.00	10.60
74	11.0207	52.08	9.57	30.00	1.29	41.67	8.40	55.56	11.31
75	11.2269	61.11	12.51	31.67	2.55	50.00	9.50	58.33	12.71
76	10.9372	56.25	10.07	35.00	3.05	58.33	11.10	72.22	13.70
77	11.1470	52.08	8.78	31.67	2.75	58.33	11.10	55.56	11.79
78	11.1658	53.47	10.21	36.67	4.65	58.33	11.10	55.56	11.79
79	10.9857	56.94	9.72	48.33	7.42	41.67	8.40	44.44	8.86
80	10.9371	54.86	10.24	36.67	2.49	41.67	8.40	38.89	7.12
81	11.1234	56.25	10.07	35.00	3.05	58.33	11.10	72.22	13.70
82	10.7862	52.78	8.10	40.00	4.35	41.67	8.40	33.33	7.26
83	10.9062	50.00	7.48	35.00	2.35	41.67	8.40	33.33	7.26
84	11.1282	56.94	10.47	31.67	3.07	33.33	8.10	47.22	10.52
85	10.7323	60.42	12.27	45.00	4.88	41.67	8.40	36.11	9.17
86	10.7798	50.69	7.57	40.00	6.99	50.00	9.70	55.56	10.82
87	10.7808	56.25	11.48	38.33	4.76	33.33	8.10	47.22	10.52
88	10.9156	56.25	10.85	36.67	3.92	33.33	8.10	47.22	10.52
89	10.7896	46.53	5.74	35.00	3.00	50.00	11.30	36.11	8.24
90	10.6633	57.64	11.57	38.33	4.76	33.33	8.10	47.22	10.52
91	10.3760	44.44	5.35	35.00	3.83	66.67	16.90	52.78	12.48
92	10.7541	44.44	6.28	36.67	4.04	50.00	14.50	47.22	10.58

Continued on next page

Table 13.10 *(continued)*

Rule #	Fitness	1971–1983 Period		1984–1988 Period		1989		1989–1991 Period	
		% Correct	Average Return	% Correct	Average Return	% Correct	Average Return	% Correct	Average Return
93	10.9784	45.83	6.16	38.33	4.13	25.00	5.60	27.78	6.32
94	10.4175	46.53	7.43	40.00	5.96	50.00	14.50	47.22	10.58
95	10.6695	50.69	6.29	43.33	5.21	50.00	10.40	61.11	11.41
96	10.5436	48.61	6.39	63.33	13.98	33.33	7.20	58.33	11.12
97	10.5033	52.78	8.10	40.00	4.35	41.67	8.40	33.33	7.26
98	10.6741	49.31	7.38	38.33	2.96	41.67	8.40	33.33	7.26
99	10.6241	49.31	7.46	38.33	3.12	41.67	8.40	33.33	7.26
100	10.6723	52.08	8.34	46.67	8.79	41.67	8.40	36.11	7.87
101	10.8255	59.03	11.85	43.33	7.05	33.33	8.10	47.22	10.52
102	10.9739	49.31	7.46	36.67	2.53	41.67	9.70	33.33	7.72
103	11.0473	45.83	6.16	38.33	4.13	25.00	5.60	27.78	6.32
104	10.9494	59.03	11.85	43.33	7.05	33.33	8.10	47.22	10.52
105	11.0893	59.03	11.85	38.33	4.29	33.33	8.10	47.22	10.52
106	10.8308	45.83	6.03	53.33	9.75	33.33	8.50	58.33	11.58
107	11.0316	57.64	11.77	38.33	4.29	33.33	8.10	47.22	10.52
108	10.9977	52.78	9.73	33.33	2.26	33.33	9.50	50.00	11.55
109	11.1720	55.56	11.12	36.67	2.91	33.33	8.10	47.22	10.52
110	11.2207	57.64	11.77	43.33	7.05	33.33	8.10	47.22	10.52
111	10.8293	46.53	7.65	48.33	9.13	41.67	13.90	38.89	7.29
112	10.7356	47.92	6.41	40.00	4.35	25.00	5.60	27.78	6.32
113	10.5025	52.78	8.10	40.00	4.68	41.67	8.40	33.33	7.26
114	10.8984	47.22	8.73	35.00	4.21	50.00	14.50	52.78	12.66
115	10.8169	47.22	8.53	31.67	3.07	50.00	14.50	52.78	12.66
116	10.6849	52.78	8.10	45.00	7.10	41.67	8.40	33.33	7.26
117	10.6709	59.03	11.13	43.33	7.73	50.00	11.30	52.78	11.58
118	10.6241	47.92	7.01	36.67	4.04	50.00	11.90	36.11	8.41
119	10.6723	52.78	8.09	48.33	8.82	33.33	8.10	30.56	7.17
120	10.7668	52.78	7.87	45.00	8.08	41.67	8.40	41.67	10.36

Table 13.11   Hedge Portfolio Results—Treasury Bonds

Year	Month	Cumulative Return Buy and Hold	Cumulative Return Long Portfolio	Short Portfolio	Hedge Portfolio Return	Hedge Portfolio Cumulative Return
1989	1	2.03	1.45	1.25	0.20	0.20
	2	0.20	−0.10	1.63	−1.90	−1.70
	3	1.43	0.81	2.67	−0.11	−1.81
	4	3.04	2.06	3.76	0.18	−1.63
	5	7.17	5.36	5.41	1.64	0.01
	6	13.07	10.52	6.92	3.47	3.48
	7	15.76	12.78	8.22	0.83	4.30
	8	12.76	10.93	8.00	−1.44	2.86
	9	12.97	11.29	8.57	−0.20	2.67
	10	17.25	14.45	10.24	1.30	3.96
	11	18.17	15.31	11.02	0.04	4.00
	12	18.10	15.43	11.56	−0.37	3.63
1990	1	14.05	12.82	11.49	−2.20	1.43
	2	13.76	12.96	11.67	−0.05	1.38
	3	13.26	13.18	11.93	−0.03	1.35
	4	10.97	12.48	11.18	0.05	1.40
	5	15.58	14.71	13.93	−0.49	0.91
	6	18.24	16.26	15.71	−0.21	0.70
	7	19.50	17.14	16.81	−0.20	0.50
	8	14.49	17.20	12.58	3.68	4.18
	9	15.83	18.19	13.61	−0.07	4.11
	10	18.32	19.69	15.42	−0.33	3.78
	11	23.08	22.23	18.27	−0.35	3.43
	12	25.38	23.79	19.48	0.25	3.69
1991	1	27.01	25.00	20.41	0.21	3.89
	2	27.39	25.48	20.92	−0.05	3.85
	3	27.88	25.99	21.43	−0.01	3.83
	4	29.67	27.15	22.53	0.01	3.85
	5	29.67	27.52	22.73	0.13	3.98
	6	28.85	27.35	22.62	−0.04	3.93
	7	30.87	28.45	24.10	−0.35	3.58
	8	35.32	30.36	27.29	−1.08	2.51
	9	39.42	31.74	30.38	−1.37	1.14
	10	40.18	32.33	31.05	−0.07	1.07
	11	41.33	32.96	31.99	−0.24	0.83
	12	49.54	35.09	37.81	−2.81	−1.98

Table 13.12 Hedge Portfolio Results—Corporate Bonds

Year	Month	Cumulative Return			Hedge Portfolio	
		Buy and Hold	Long Portfolio	Short Portfolio	Return	Cumulative Return
1989	1	2.02	1.66	1.00	0.66	0.66
	2	0.70	0.68	1.27	−1.24	−0.57
	3	1.35	1.33	1.94	−0.01	−0.58
	4	3.51	2.96	3.13	0.44	−0.14
	5	7.43	6.27	4.33	2.05	1.91
	6	11.67	9.81	5.74	1.97	3.88
	7	13.66	11.48	6.83	0.50	4.38
	8	11.81	10.20	7.05	−1.36	3.02
	9	12.26	10.74	7.58	0.00	3.02
	10	15.35	13.15	8.93	0.92	3.94
	11	16.16	13.94	9.68	0.01	3.94
	12	16.23	14.05	10.30	−0.47	3.47
1990	1	14.01	12.18	10.52	−1.84	1.63
	2	13.87	12.29	10.75	−0.10	1.53
	3	13.75	12.28	11.34	−0.54	0.99
	4	11.58	10.43	11.31	−1.63	−0.64
	5	15.87	13.78	12.95	1.56	0.92
	6	18.38	15.78	14.08	0.77	1.68
	7	19.58	16.86	14.98	0.15	1.83
	8	16.09	15.12	13.68	−0.36	1.47
	9	17.15	16.07	14.46	0.13	1.61
	10	18.69	17.41	15.39	0.35	1.95
	11	22.08	20.02	17.29	0.57	2.52
	12	24.12	21.54	18.67	0.10	2.62
1991	1	25.98	22.93	19.92	0.08	2.70
	2	27.50	24.05	20.94	0.07	2.78
	3	28.88	25.16	21.76	0.21	2.98
	4	30.66	26.31	23.01	−0.11	2.88
	5	31.17	26.85	23.53	0.00	2.88
	6	30.93	26.84	23.69	−0.14	2.74
	7	33.12	28.49	25.04	0.22	2.96
	8	36.78	30.75	27.19	0.04	2.99
	9	40.48	33.07	28.97	0.38	3.37
	10	41.09	33.63	29.51	0.00	3.37
	11	42.58	34.74	30.30	0.22	3.59
	12	48.80	38.82	32.31	1.49	5.08

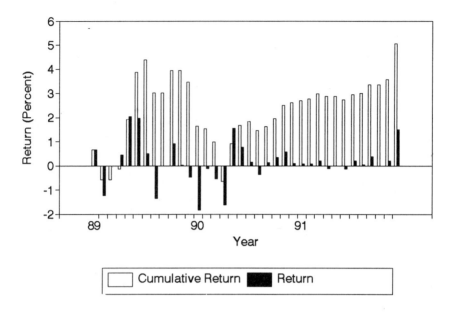

FIGURE 13.17   Hedge Portfolio—Corporate Bonds

the short portfolio over the first portion of the holdout period. As we mentioned in the preceding chapter, more frequent updating of the rule portfolios might improve the results substantially.

The hedge portfolio results for corporate bonds are shown in Table 13.12. The results are quite similar to those for Treasury bonds. The hedge portfolio has a cumulative positive return of 3.47 percent after one year. At the end of the holdout period, the cumulative return is a positive 5.08 percent. Figure 13.17 graphically illustrates the performance of the hedge portfolio.

In general, we conclude that the GA procedure is working. The performance of the long (good rule) portfolio is generally better than that of the short (bad rule) portfolio. The hedge portfolio concept shows promise. In Chapter 15, we will discuss further refinements and research possibilities in more detail.

14
Results for Individual Stocks

In this chapter we move away from asset class timing rules to the development of market timing rules for the following stocks: IBM, Mobil, McDonald's, and Consolidated Edison. The timing choice is whether to be fully invested in the particular company's stock or to be invested in Treasury bills.

These four stocks were chosen in accordance with some of the chaos theory research of E. E. Peters. In his article "A Chaotic Attractor for the S&P 500" (1991), Peters uses rescaled range (R/S) analysis to examine the level and average cycle length of persistence in stock returns. The results for these four stocks are as follows:

	Hurst Exponent	Cycle Length
IBM	0.72	18 months
Mobil	0.72	36 months
McDonald's	0.65	42 months
Consolidated Edison	0.68	90 months

As was explained in Chapter 4, the Hurst exponent measures the level of persistence in returns. An exponent of 0.5 indicates that the returns follow a random walk, i.e., there is no pattern of any kind. The greater the exponent, the greater the level of persistence. The cycle length is a measure of how frequently the pattern of persistence changes.

We felt that these stocks would make an interesting sample for our research because it might be easier to develop profitable trading rules for stocks with a high level of persistence in returns. It is also probably easier to develop rules for stocks with a longer cycle time. A shorter cycle means that the underlying relationships are getting scrambled more frequently. If the stock enters into a new cycle, then rules based on past relationships probably will not continue to work.

VARIABLE SELECTION FOR THE FOUR INDIVIDUAL STOCKS

The correlation results for all four stocks are shown in Tables 14.1 through 14.4. IBM's stock returns (Table 14.1) are positively correlated with business loan activity and negatively correlated with inflation and increases in personal income. Mobil's stock returns (Table 14.2) are positively linked to increases in the money supply and negatively correlated with inflation and worldwide stock returns. Stock returns for McDonald's (Table 14.3) seem to lag behind the general economy as evinced by the negative correlation with changes in the coincident index and positive correlation with lagging indicators. The returns for Consolidated Edison (Table 14.4) are higher when labor costs are rising and consumer sentiment is high. The only common factor among all four stock return series is that they demonstrate a high negative correlation with inflation.

TIMING RULES FOR IBM

The good and bad rule portfolios for IBM are shown in Tables 14.5 and 14.6, respectively. We are going to cheat a bit by looking ahead and discussing one of the trading rules that performed best over the holdout period. Rule 61 (in Table 14.5) says that an attractive time to invest in IBM seems to be when (the change in business loans is in the top half of its range *or* the 12-month change in Canadian stock prices is in the lower third of its range) *and* the 1-month change in lumber product prices is in the lower half of its range. This rule generated a 16.03 percent annual return over the test period.

IBM has the shortest cycle length of the four stocks under investigation. Figure 14.1 shows the moving average percentage of correct calls for the portfolio of 120 good trading rules over the 1984–1991 period. As before, the rules were constructed based on 1984–1988 data, and the 1988–1991 period was used as a holdout test period. The moving average return for this same period is shown in Figure 14.2. The pattern of average return is far more erratic than the percentage of correct calls, with several ups and downs occurring before the crash of 1987. Average return for the good rule portfolio continued to decline after the crash, with some leveling off in 1991. The average percentage of correct calls climbed steadily into 1988 before starting a fairly steady drop.

The detailed results for the good rule portfolio are shown in Table 14.7. The rules performed well during the 1984–1988 rule-building period, with a 58.7 percent rate of correct calls. However, subsequent performance was somewhat disappointing. The average return for 1989 was a loss of 6.8 percent. This sounds bad, but the return on a buy-and-hold strategy for IBM was −19.4 percent, so the rule portfolio actually outperformed the passive buy-and-hold alternative. The average annual buy-and-hold return over the 1989–1991 period was 5.7 percent,

Table 14.1 Correlations with IBM Stock Returns

	Series Number	Differencing Interval	Series Description	Correlation Coefficient
1	49	1	51. Personal income less transfer payments (AR, bil. 1987	−0.3775
2	51	1	52. Personal income (AR, bil. 1987 $)	−0.3715
3	239	1	(98) Producer Price Index, lumber and wood products (19	−0.3578
4	197	3	733. Canada, consumer price index, NSA (1982–1984 =	−0.3068
5	115	0	112. Net change in business loans (AR, bil. $)	0.3062
6	229	3	940. Ratio, coincident index to lagging index (1982 = 10	−0.3009
7	110	1	108. Ratio, personal income to money supply M2 (ratio)	−0.3000
8	103	1	101. Commercial and industrial loans outstanding (mil.	0.2958
9	189	1	722. United Kingdom, industrial production (1987 = 100)	−0.2956
10	69	1	72. Commercial and industrial loans outstanding (mil. $)	0.2914
11	208	12	743. Canada, stock prices, NSA, (1967 = 100)	−0.2859
12	89	1	92a. Mfrs.' unfilled orders, durable goods indus. (bil. 1982	−0.2828
13	88	0	92b. Change in mfrs.' unfilled orders, durables (bil. 1982	−0.2827
14	265	1	992. Experimental coincident index—modified methodol	−0.2765
15	225	12	920c. Coincident index, change over 3-mo. span (AR, pct.	−0.2764
16	225	1	920c. Coincident index, change over 3-mo. span (AR, pct.	−0.2677
17	79	1	83. Consumer expectations, NSA (1966:I = 100) COPYR	−0.2673
18	88	12	92b. Change in mfrs.' unfilled orders, durables (bil. 1982	−0.2663
19	220	1	910. Composite index of 11 leading indicators (1982 = 1	−0.2638
20	251	3	(23) Spot price, lead scrap ($ per lb.) COPYRIGHTED (CR	−0.2627
21	228	1	930c. Lagging index, change over 3-mo. span (AR, pct.)	0.2620
22	245	3	(98) Producer Price Index, aluminum base scrap (1982 =	−0.2611
23	229	1	940. Ratio, coincident index to lagging index (1982 = 10	−0.2605
24	71	3	74. Industrial production, nondurable manufactures (1987	−0.2595
25	61	3	62a. Index of labor cost per unit of output, mfg. (1987 =	0.2593
26	3	1	5. Average weekly initial claims, unemploy. insurance (th	0.2574
27	179	3	602. Exports, excluding military aid shipments (mil. $)	−0.2561
28	92	3	93. Free reserves, NSA (mil. $)	−0.2556
29	223	1	920. Composite index of four coincident indicators (1982	−0.2543
30	103	3	101. Commercial and industrial loans outstanding (mil. 19	0.2513
31	193	1	727. Italy, industrial production (1987 = 100)	0.2486
32	110	3	108. Ratio,personal income to money supply M2 (ratio)	−0.2439
33	232	1	951. Diffusion index of coincident indicators, 1-mo. span	−0.2392
34	18	12	19. United States, index of stock prices, NSA (1967 =	−0.2376
35	16	12	19. Index of stock prices, 500 common stocks, NSA (1941	−0.2373
36	145	12	331c. Change in PPI, crude materials, 6-mo. span (AR, pc	−0.2365
37	77	3	82. Capacity utilization rate, manufacturing (pct.)	−0.2348
38	200	3	735c. Germany, 6-mo. change in consumer prices (AR, pc	−0.2347
39	69	3	72. Commercial and industrial loans outstanding (mil. $)	0.2342
40	15	12	112. Net change in business loans (AR, bil. $)	0.2330.
41	253	1	(23) Spot price, tin, NSA ($ per lb.) COPYRIGHTED (CRB)	0.2315
42	234	3	952. Diffusion index of lagging indicators, 1-mo. span (pct.	0.2313
43	123	1	120. Smoothed change in CPI for services (AR, pct.)	−0.2309
44	63	0	62. Smoothed change in labor cost per unit output, mfg. (p	0.2282
45	98	1	99b. Change in sensitive materials prices (pct.)	−0.2275
46	253	3	(23) Spot price, tin, NSA ($ per lb.) COPYRIGHTED (CRB)	0.2274
47	254	3	(23) Spot price, zinc, NSA ($ per lb.) COPYRIGHTED (CR	−0.2263
48	245	1	(98) Producer Price Index, aluminum base scrap (1982 =	−0.2214
49	90	1	92. Smoothed change in mfrs.' unfilled orders (bil. 1982 $)	−0.2211
50	106	3	105. Money supply M1 (bil. 1982 $)	0.2180

Table 14.2 Correlations with Mobil Stock Returns

	Series Number	Differencing Interval	Series Description	Correlation Coefficient
1	92	3	93. Free reserves, NSA (mil. $)	−0.3491
2	210	1	746. France, stock prices, NSA (1967 = 100)	−0.3377
3	46	1	48. Employee hours in nonag. establishments (AR, bil. hou	−0.3221
4	208	3	743. Canada, stock prices, NSA (1967 = 100)	−0.3094
5	209	1	745. Federal Republic of Germany, stock prices, NSA (1	−0.2974
6	46	3	48. Employee hours in nonag. establishments (AR, bil. hou	−0.2931
7	197	3	733. Canada, consumer price index, NSA (1982–1984 =	−0.2892
8	150	12	333c. Change in PPI, capital equipment, 1-mo. span (pct.)	−0.2838
9	106	1	105. Money supply M1 (bil. 1982 $)	0.2836
10	18	1	19. United States, index of stock prices, NSA (1967 = 100	−0.2825
11	16	1	19. Index of stock prices, 500 common stocks, NSA (194	−0.2825
12	106	3	105. Money supply M1 (bil. 1982 $)	0.2803
13	232	12	951. Diffusion index of coincident indicators, 1-mo. span	−0.2753
14	232	0	951. Diffusion index of coincident indicators, 1-mo. span	−0.2738
15	205	1	738. Japan, consumer price index, NSA (1982–1984 = 10	0.2685
16	252	1	(23) Spot price, steel scrap ($ per ton) COPYRIGHTED (CR	0.2681
17	86	1	91. Average duration of unemployment in weeks (weeks)	0.2681
18	139	12	320c. Change in CPI-U, all items, 6-mo. span (AR, pct.)	−0.2669
19	110	1	108. Ratio, personal income to money supply M2 (ratio)	−0.2660
20	209	3	745. Federal Republic of Germany, stock prices, NSA (19	−0.2639
21	16	1	557. Industrial production, defense & space equipment (1	−0.2590
22	18	3	19. United States, index of stock prices, NSA (1967 = 10	−0.2563
23	16	3	19. Index of stock prices, 500 common stocks, NSA (1941	−0.2561
24	57	1	58. Consumer sentiment, NSA (1966:I = 100) COPYR	−0.2558
25	196	3	732c. United Kingdom, 6-mo. change in consumer prices	0.2525
26	26	3	28. New private housing units started (AR, thous.)	−0.2509
27	121	1	118. Secondary market yields on FHA mortgages, NSA (p	0.2473
28	207	3	742. United Kingdom, stock prices, NSA (1967 = 100)	−0.2458
29	9	1	10. Contracts and orders for plant and equipment (bil.$)	0.2383
30	115	1	112. Net change in business loans (AR, bil. $)	0.2345
31	1	1	1. Average weekly hours, mfg. (hours)	−0.2341
32	92	1	93. Free reserves, NSA (mil. $)	−0.2338
33	42	3	45. Average weekly insured unemployment rate (pct.)	0.2316
34	107	3	106. Money supply M2 (bil. 1982 $)	0.2300
35	89	3	92a. Mfrs.' unfilled orders, durable goods indus. (bil. 1982	−0.2296
36	141	3	323c. Change in CPI-U, less food & energy, 1-mo. span (pc	0.2294
37	90	1	92. Smoothed change in mfrs.' unfilled orders (bil. 1982 $)	−0.2272
38	154	12	334c. Change in PPI, finished cons. goods, 6-mo. span (A	−0.2252
39	5	1	7. Mfrs.' new orders, durable goods industries (bil. 1982 $)	0.2229
40	90	3	92. Smoothed change in mfrs.' unfilled orders (bil. 1982 $)	−0.2220
41	179	3	602. Exports, excluding military aid shipments (mil. $)	−0.2203
42	194	1	728. Japan, industrial production (1987 = 100)	−0.2192
43	19	1	20. Contracts and orders for plant and equipment (bil. 198	0.2189
44	9	12	10. Contracts and orders for plant and equipment (bil. $)	−0.2170
45	240	1	(98) Producer Price Index, wastepaper, news (1982 = 100	0.2164
46	240	3	(98) Producer Price Index, wastepaper, news (1982 = 100	0.2162
47	25	12	27. Mfrs.' new orders, nondefense capital goods (bil. 1982	−0.2154
48	110	3	108. Ratio, personal income to money supply M2 (ratio	−0.2139
49	155	12	336. Producer Price Index, finished goods (1982 = 100)	−0.2134
50	46	12	48. Employee hours in nonag. establishments (Ar, bil. hou	−0.2125

Table 14.3 Correlations with McDonald's Stock Returns

	Series Number	Differencing Interval	Series Description	Correlation Coefficient
1	234	3	952. Diffusion index of lagging indicators, 1-mo. span (pct.	0.3940
2	228	1	930c. Lagging index, change over 3-mo. span (AR, pct.)	0.3731
3	229	3	940. Ratio, coincident index to lagging index (1982 = 100	− 0.3485
4	193	3	727. Italy, industrial production (1987 = 100)	− 0.3462
5	61	0	62a. Index of labor cost per unit of output, mfg. (1987 =	0.3462
6	239	1	(98) Producer Price Index, lumber and wood products (19	− 0.3331
7	225	12	920c. Coincident index, change over 3-mo. span (AR, pct.	− 0.3320
8	225	1	920c. Coincident index, change over 3-mo. span (AR, pct.	− 0.3206
9	71	3	74. Industrial production, nondurable manufactures (1987	− 0.3165
10	190	1	723. Canada, industrial production (1987 = 100)	− 0.3133
11	61	3	62a. Index of labor cost per unit of output, mfg. (1987 =	0.3099
12	77	3	82. Capacity utilization rate, manufacturing (pct.)	− 0.3038
13	66	12	66. Consumer installment credit outstanding (mil. $)	0.2966
14	251	3	(23) Spot price, lead scrap ($ per lb.) COPYRIGHTED (CR	− 0.2961
15	265	3	992. Experimental coincident index—modified methodo	− 0.2954
16	103	1	101. Commercial and industrial loans outstanding (mil. 1	0.2933
17	223	3	920. Composite index of four coincident indicators (1982	− 0.2823
18	234	0	952. Diffusion index of lagging indicators, 1-mo. span (pct.	0.2820
19	246	3	(98) Producer Price Index, nonferrous scrap, NSA (1982 =	− 0.2811
20	72	3	75. Industrial production, consumer goods (1987 = 100)	− 0.2775
21	145	1	331c. Change in PPI, crude materials, 6-mo. span (AR, pc	0.2774
22	139	3	320c. Change in CPI-U, all items, 6-mo. span (AR, pct.)	0.2751
23	110	1	108. Ratio, personal income to money supply M2 (ratio)	− 0.2722
24	192	1	726. France, industrial production (1987 = 100)	− 0.2699
25	245	3	(98) Producer Price Index, aluminum base scrap (1982 =	− 0.2696
26	63	0	62. Smoothed change in labor cost per unit output, mfg.	0.2683
27	229	12	940. Ratio, coincident index to lagging index (1982 = 10	− 0.2661
28	225	0	920c. Coincident index, change over 3-mo. span (AR, pct.	− 0.2659
29	229	1	940. Ratio, coincident index to lagging index (1982 = 10	− 0.2634
30	110	3	108. Ratio, personal income to money supply M2 (ratio)	− 0.2618
31	174	0	525. Defense Department prime contract awards in U.S.	− 0.2584
32	208	0	743. Canada, stock prices, NSA (1967 = 100)	− 0.2566
33	226	1	930. Composite index of seven lagging indicators (1982 =	0.2558
34	229	0	940. Ratio, coincident index to lagging index (1982 = 100	− 0.2554
35	13	12	14. Current liabilities of business failures, NSA (mil. $)	0.2546
36	23	12	23. Spot prices, raw materials, NSA (1967 = 100) COPYR	− 0.2546
37	115	0	112. Net change in business loans (AR, bil. $)	0.2502
38	245	1	(98) Producer Price Index, aluminum base scrap (1982 =	− 0.2490
39	94	12	95. Ratio, consumer installment credit to personal income	0.2467
40	49	1	51. Personal income less transfer payments (Ar, bil. 1987	− 0.2446
41	251	0	(23) Spot price, lead scrap ($ per lb.) COPYRIGHTED (CR	− 0.2441
42	21	1	21. Average weekly overtime hours, mfg. (hours)	0.2409
43	145	3	331c. Change in PPI, crude materials, 6-mo. span (AR, pc	0.2407
44	103	12	101. Commercial and industrial loans outstanding (mil. 198	0.2396
45	98	3	99b. Change in sensitive materials prices (pct.)	0.2386
46	49	3	51. Personal income less transfer payments (AR, bil. 1987	− 0.2373
47	208	12	743. Canada, stock prices, NSA (1967 = 100)	− 0.2363
48	42	3	45. Average weekly insured unemployment rate (pct.)	0.2353
49	51	1	52. Personal income (AR, bil. 1987 $)	− 0.2343
50	251	12	(23) Spot price, lead scrap ($ per lb.) COPYRIGHTED (CR	− 0.2339

Table 14.4 Correlations with Consolidated Edison Stock Returns

	Series Number	Differencing Interval	Series Description	Correlation Coefficient
1	71	3	74. Industrial production, nondurable manufactures (1987	−0.3975
2	173	3	453. Labor force participation rate, 16–19 years of age (pct	0.3903
3	61	3	62a. Index of labor cost per unit of output, mfg. (1987 =	0.3858
4	193	12	727. Italy, industrial production (1987 = 100)	−0.3831
5	192	1	726. France, industrial production (1987 = 100)	−0.3645
6	252	1	(23) Spot price, steel scrap ($ per ton) COPYRIGHTED (C	0.3439
7	229	3	940. Ratio, coincident index to lagging index (1982 = 10	−0.3399
8	23	3	23. Spot prices, raw materials, NSA (1967 = 100) COPYR	−0.3293
9	234	3	952. Diffusion index of lagging indicators, 1-mo. span (pct.	0.3287
10	182	3	612. General imports (mil. $)	−0.3208
11	193	3	727. Italy, industrial production (1987 = 100)	−0.3201
12	77	3	82. Capacity utilization rate, manufacturing (pct.)	−0.3157
13	68	1	70. Manufacturing and trade inventories (bil. 1982 $)	0.3083
14	210	1	746. France, stock prices, NSA (1967 = 100)	−0.3078
15	5	1	7. Mfrs.' new orders, durable goods industries (Bil. 1982 $)	−0.3040
16	211	3	747. Italy, stock prices, NSA (1967 = 100)	0.3034
17	226	3	930. Composite index of seven lagging indicators (1982 =	0.2945
18	99	3	99a. Index of sensitive materials prices (1982 = 100)	−0.2872
19	228	1	930c. Lagging index, change over 3-mo. span (AR, pct.)	0.2865
20	57	0	58. Consumer sentiment, NSA (1966:I = 100) COPYRIG	0.2847
21	233	3	951. Diffusion index of coincident indicators, 6-mo. span	−0.2758
22	37	1	41. Employees on nonag. payrolls (thous.)	0.2721
23	228	0	930c. Lagging index, change over 3-mo. span (AR, pct.)	0.2716
24	174	0	525. Defense Department prime contract awards in U.S.	−0.2692
25	196	1	732c. United Kingdom, 6-mo. change in consumer prices	−0.2678
26	256	1	(23) Spot price, cotton ($ per lb.) COPYRIGHTED (CRB)	−0.2665
27	207	1	742. United Kingdom, stock prices, NSA (1967 = 100)	−0.2654
28	173	1	453. Labor force participation rate, 16–19 years of age (pct	0.2634
29	72	3	75. Industrial production, consumer goods (1987 = 100)	−0.2606
30	248	1	(98) Producer Price Index, raw cotton (1982 = 100)	−0.2597
31	205	12	738. Japan, consumer price index, NSA (1982–1984 = 10	0.2596
32	98	0	99b. Change in sensitive materials prices (pct.)	−0.2596
33	72	1	75. Industrial production, consumer goods (1987 = 100)	0.2587
34	148	3	332c. Change in PPI, intermed. materials, 6-mo. span (AR,	−0.2583
35	188	1	721. OECD, European countries, industrial production (19	−0.2578
36	44	3	47. Index of industrial production (1987 = 100)	−0.2572
37	6	1	8. Mfrs.' new orders, consumer goods and materials (bil.	−0.2537
38	107	1	106. Money supply M2 (bil. 1982 $)	0.2536
39	23	1	23. Spot prices, raw materials, NSA (1967 = 100) COPYR	−0.2536
40	99	1	99a. Index of sensitive materials prices (1982 = 100)	−0.2508
41	192	12	726. France, industrial production (1987 = 100)	−0.2499
42	123	0	120. Smoothed change in CPI for services (AR, pct.)	0.2406
43	98	12	99b. Change in sensitive materials prices (pct.)	−0.2395
44	152	3	334. Producer Price Index, finished consumer goods (1982	−0.2373
45	55	1	57. Manufacturing and trade sales (mil. 1982 $)	0.2363
46	174	12	525. Defense Department prime contract awards in U.S.	−0.2363
47	63	3	62. Smoothed change in labor cost per unit output, mfg.	0.2362
48	155	3	336. Producer Price Index, finished goods (1982 = 100)	−0.2358
49	253	3	(23) Spot price, tin, NSA ($ per lb.) COPYRIGHTED (CRB)	−0.2342
50	13	12	14. Current liabilities of business failures, NSA (mil. $)	0.2313

Table 14.5 Good Rules—IBM Stock

Rule #	Logic Code	)/(Code	Series 1	Series 2	Series 3	Fitness	1 #	Diff.	2 #	Diff.	3 #	Diff.
1	5	3	16	20	27	1.6309	88	0	115	0	49	1
2	1	4	23	16	5	1.4434	88	0	115	0	69	1
3	6	3	22	9	17	1.4420	88	0	115	0	103	1
4	1	7	3	20	20	1.6110	88	0	115	0	110	1
5	1	3	23	16	14	1.5993	88	0	115	0	239	1
6	1	3	23	16	12	1.7703	88	0	115	0	197	3
7	6	6	13	23	13	1.4034	88	0	115	0	229	3
8	6	6	13	20	22	1.4069	88	0	115	0	208	12
9	4	6	7	21	26	1.3450	88	0	49	1	69	1
10	7	3	6	26	17	1.6981	88	0	49	1	103	1
11	3	5	6	18	13	1.6736	88	0	49	1	110	1
12	7	1	16	27	8	1.6973	88	0	49	1	239	1
13	1	1	24	26	12	1.8669	88	0	49	1	197	3
14	7	5	7	21	4	1.3395	88	0	49	1	229	3
15	1	1	24	26	29	1.7799	88	0	49	1	208	12
16	5	2	23	16	17	1.4316	88	0	69	1	103	1
17	4	3	14	20	13	1.6922	88	0	69	1	110	1
18	1	1	24	31	14	1.5663	88	0	69	1	239	1
19	6	6	13	20	9	1.3994	88	0	69	1	197	3
20	3	3	23	17	13	1.5409	88	0	69	1	229	3
21	1	4	23	16	2	1.5217	88	0	69	1	208	12
22	4	3	14	17	13	1.6914	88	0	103	1	110	1
23	3	3	23	23	14	1.7330	88	0	103	1	239	1
24	7	2	4	17	12	1.5590	88	0	103	1	197	3
25	3	3	22	16	15	1.4772	88	0	103	1	229	3
26	7	2	22	17	12	1.5212	88	0	103	1	208	12
27	5	3	23	29	14	1.5599	88	0	110	1	239	1
28	7	1	10	13	10	1.8538	88	0	110	1	197	3
29	6	1	14	13	16	1.5685	88	0	110	1	229	3
30	6	3	14	13	22	1.6952	88	0	110	1	208	12
31	2	1	6	14	12	1.7113	88	0	239	1	197	3
32	1	1	24	14	22	1.6308	88	0	239	1	229	3
33	3	1	24	14	10	1.6460	88	0	239	1	208	12
34	3	2	21	11	18	1.4105	88	0	197	3	229	3
35	7	1	22	12	13	1.4878	88	0	197	3	208	12
36	6	3	16	14	10	1.4194	88	0	229	3	208	12
37	3	5	20	28	20	1.4254	115	0	49	1	69	1
38	1	6	16	28	17	1.7290	115	0	49	1	103	1
39	8	5	26	19	13	1.6408	115	0	49	1	110	1
40	4	5	20	27	10	1.6390	115	0	49	1	239	1
41	1	5	16	27	12	1.8498	115	0	49	1	197	3
42	7	5	20	26	13	1.6811	115	0	49	1	229	3
43	1	5	16	28	26	1.6551	115	0	49	1	208	12
44	6	8	16	20	17	1.3830	115	0	69	1	103	1
45	4	5	26	28	13	1.6170	115	0	69	1	110	1
46	1	5	16	30	14	1.5513	115	0	69	1	239	1

Continued on next page

219

Table 14.5 *(continued)*

Rule #	Logic Code	)/(Code	Cutoff Values				Series Number and Differencing Interval					
			Series 1	Series 2	Series 3	Fitness	1 #	Diff.	2 #	Diff.	3 #	Diff.
47	1	3	30	17	12	1.5412	115	0	69	1	197	3
48	7	6	20	16	13	1.4421	115	0	69	1	229	3
49	3	8	20	23	14	1.2387	115	0	69	1	208	12
50	4	3	29	27	13	1.6493	115	0	103	1	110	1
51	5	5	20	19	14	1.7267	115	0	103	1	239	1
52	1	7	16	17	11	1.5944	115	0	103	1	197	3
53	7	5	20	30	13	1.3662	115	0	103	1	229	3
54	7	6	16	17	11	1.3791	115	0	103	1	208	12
55	4	5	20	20	10	1.7932	115	0	110	1	239	1
56	1	5	4	13	12	1.7317	115	0	110	1	197	3
57	7	5	20	13	13	1.5681	115	0	110	1	229	3
58	2	1	2	13	29	1.5918	115	0	110	1	208	12
59	7	1	19	14	11	1.7213	115	0	239	1	197	3
60	5	5	27	14	22	1.5923	115	0	239	1	229	3
61	3	5	16	14	10	1.5921	115	0	239	1	208	12
62	7	5	20	11	16	1.5573	115	0	197	3	229	3
63	1	5	12	12	24	1.3863	115	0	197	3	208	12
64	6	7	20	14	14	1.4900	115	0	229	3	208	12
65	1	4	27	16	17	1.7290	49	1	69	1	103	1
66	5	3	1	20	20	1.5908	49	1	69	1	110	1
67	3	3	27	22	14	1.7110	49	1	69	1	239	1
68	1	3	23	14	12	1.8431	49	1	69	1	197	3
69	3	3	26	20	13	1.6657	49	1	69	1	229	3
70	1	3	27	16	29	1.6934	49	1	69	1	208	12
71	3	3	23	17	13	1.7247	49	1	103	1	110	1
72	3	3	26	22	14	1.7396	49	1	103	1	239	1
73	1	3	23	17	12	1.9270	49	1	103	1	197	3
74	1	4	23	17	2	1.7136	49	1	103	1	229	3
75	7	4	24	17	23	1.7913	49	1	103	1	208	12
76	8	1	19	13	12	1.6876	49	1	110	1	239	1
77	1	1	26	17	14	1.8555	49	1	110	1	197	3
78	5	1	19	13	27	1.6012	49	1	110	1	229	3
79	5	1	26	13	29	1.6748	49	1	110	1	208	12
80	5	1	23	10	12	1.8716	49	1	239	1	197	3
81	4	2	27	14	24	1.6436	49	1	239	1	229	3
82	5	1	23	12	29	1.8421	49	1	239	1	208	12
83	4	1	22	12	5	1.8442	49	1	197	3	229	3
84	3	1	23	10	9	1.8871	49	1	197	3	208	12
85	6	2	26	28	29	1.7280	49	1	229	3	208	12
86	4	3	27	27	13	1.6493	69	1	103	1	110	1
87	1	5	16	30	14	1.5117	69	1	103	1	239	1
88	6	6	17	25	12	1.5591	69	1	103	1	197	3
89	7	2	20	17	21	1.3567	69	1	103	1	229	3
90	2	8	20	17	17	1.3561	69	1	103	1	208	12
91	7	5	23	13	20	1.6152	69	1	110	1	239	1
92	1	5	16	18	12	1.7619	69	1	110	1	197	3

Continued on next page

Table 14.5 *(continued)*

Rule #	Logic Code	⟩/⟨ Code	Cutoff Values			Fitness	Series Number and Differencing Interval					
			Series 1	Series 2	Series 3		1 #	Diff.	2 #	Diff.	3 #	Diff.
93	4	6	20	20	26	1.6711	69	1	110	1	229	3
94	7	5	23	13	23	1.6890	69	1	110	1	208	12
95	5	5	23	14	11	1.6640	69	1	239	1	197	3
96	1	5	16	14	21	1.6272	69	1	239	1	229	3
97	3	1	30	14	10	1.5980	69	1	239	1	208	12
98	7	5	17	11	13	1.5910	69	1	197	3	229	3
99	3	5	17	12	4	1.5579	69	1	197	3	208	12
100	2	5	20	15	22	1.4415	69	1	229	3	208	12
101	3	1	29	13	12	1.5896	103	1	110	1	239	1
102	2	5	25	13	12	1.8283	103	1	110	1	197	3
103	6	7	23	13	13	1.6178	103	1	110	1	229	3
104	5	6	23	13	8	1.6491	103	1	110	1	208	12
105	2	5	23	14	12	1.7860	103	1	239	1	197	3
106	2	5	25	14	20	1.6626	103	1	239	1	229	3
107	2	5	25	15	28	1.6082	103	1	239	1	208	12
108	7	5	17	12	13	1.5928	103	1	197	3	229	3
109	3	5	17	12	7	1.6058	103	1	197	3	208	12
110	3	6	17	16	17	1.5017	103	1	229	3	208	12
111	6	1	13	12	10	1.8142	110	1	239	1	197	3
112	4	2	13	21	28	1.6606	110	1	239	1	229	3
113	2	2	13	14	23	1.6986	110	1	239	1	208	12
114	7	3	13	12	25	1.7905	110	1	197	3	229	3
115	4	1	13	12	9	1.8576	110	1	197	3	208	12
116	2	1	13	15	18	1.6399	110	1	229	3	208	12
117	7	3	14	11	25	1.7650	239	1	197	3	229	3
118	4	1	14	12	10	1.7047	239	1	197	3	208	12
119	2	1	14	16	22	1.6692	239	1	229	3	208	12
120	7	1	10	20	6	1.3524	197	3	229	3	208	12

while the average annual return for the good rule portfolio was 3.02 percent. Four of the rules did exceptionally well, averaging 16 percent annually or better and continuing to have correct calls at least 60 percent of the time.

The percentage of correct calls and the average return for the 120 bad rules (as before, a "bad" rule is one that seems to give poor timing signals) are shown in Figures 14.3 and 14.4. As in the corresponding figures for the good rule portfolios, the average return graph displays a more erratic pattern; however, after the crash of 1987, the average return seemed to oscillate within a certain band. The percentage of correct calls declined steadily until mid-1988, when it began to rise.

The detailed results for the bad rule portfolio are shown in Table 14.8. In aggregate, the average results are slightly confusing when compared to the good rule portfolio. The bad rule portfolio averaged a 4.0 percent loss in 1989, but this

Table 14.6 . Bad Rules—IBM Stock

Rule #	Logic Code	)/(Code	Cutoff Values			Fitness	Series Number and Differencing Interval					
			Series 1	Series 2	Series 3		1		2		3	
							#	Diff.	#	Diff.	#	Diff.
1	8	2	6	20	23	12.8915	88	0	115	0	49	1
2	8	1	6	20	11	12.4683	88	0	115	0	69	1
3	6	1	6	20	22	12.4723	88	0	115	0	103	1
4	8	2	7	20	29	12.6619	88	0	115	0	110	1
5	8	2	8	16	15	13.0814	88	0	115	0	239	1
6	2	1	7	20	19	12.5345	88	0	115	0	197	3
7	8	2	6	20	21	12.8358	88	0	115	0	229	3
8	8	2	7	16	29	12.6073	88	0	115	0	208	12
9	8	7	31	28	20	12.5230	88	0	49	1	69	1
10	8	7	24	26	17	12.6694	88	0	49	1	103	1
11	2	4	7	19	13	12.5562	88	0	49	1	110	1
12	2	4	8	10	14	13.1418	88	0	49	1	239	1
13	4	8	13	22	12	12.7391	88	0	49	1	197	3
14	8	4	8	23	19	12.9750	88	0	49	1	229	3
15	8	4	7	23	29	13.1108	88	0	49	1	208	12
16	8	1	8	20	2	12.4465	88	0	69	1	103	1
17	5	1	7	20	22	12.8269	88	0	69	1	110	1
18	2	2	7	25	15	13.1248	88	0	69	1	239	1
19	2	1	7	20	22	12.5127	88	0	69	1	197	3
20	6	7	5	20	22	12.4212	88	0	69	1	229	3
21	8	5	23	16	11	12.9227	88	0	69	1	208	12
22	6	3	6	17	1	12.3573	88	0	103	1	110	1
23	8	2	8	10	15	13.0558	88	0	103	1	239	1
24	6	3	13	17	12	12.7959	88	0	103	1	197	3
25	2	2	8	17	13	12.6731	88	0	103	1	229	3
26	6	3	6	17	0	12.3573	88	0	103	1	208	12
27	2	4	8	3	14	13.1939	88	0	110	1	239	1
28	8	4	6	13	10	12.6766	88	0	110	1	197	3
29	2	4	7	13	14	12.6634	88	0	110	1	229	3
30	7	3	13	22	22	12.5367	88	0	110	1	208	12
31	6	4	13	15	12	13.4191	88	0	239	1	197	3
32	6	2	8	15	26	13.0529	88	0	239	1	229	3
33	8	3	8	14	11	13.3422	88	0	239	1	208	12
34	6	8	16	12	13	12.5821	88	0	197	3	229	3
35	6	8	17	12	13	12.1416	88	0	197	3	208	12
36	8	5	21	2	11	12.4245	88	0	229	3	208	12
37	7	4	20	12	30	12.1450	115	0	49	1	69	1
38	5	3	20	23	27	12.6830	115	0	49	1	103	1
39	6	2	20	29	22	12.8495	115	0	49	1	110	1
40	6	4	20	23	7	12.7844	115	0	49	1	239	1
41	8	4	15	26	12	12.8972	115	0	49	1	197	3
42	8	4	20	28	22	12.6485	115	0	49	1	229	3
43	2	3	20	23	23	12.7935	115	0	49	1	208	12
44	3	1	20	16	17	12.2736	115	0	69	1	103	1
45	5	1	20	20	22	12.4475	115	0	69	1	110	1
46	6	4	23	30	9	12.4611	115	0	69	1	239	1

Continued on next page

Table 14.6 *(continued)*

Rule #	Logic Code	⟩/⟨ Code	Cutoff Values			Fitness	Series Number and Differencing Interval					
			Series 1	Series 2	Series 3		1		2		3	
							#	Diff.	#	Diff.	#	Diff.
47	2	4	20	2	21	12.2891	115	0	69	1	197	3
48	8	4	20	30	21	12.5165	115	0	69	1	229	3
49	6	5	21	20	11	12.7649	115	0	69	1	208	12
50	3	3	20	20	20	12.4986	115	0	103	1	110	1
51	1	2	23	23	8	12.4853	115	0	103	1	239	1
52	8	2	16	17	12	12.5906	115	0	103	1	197	3
53	3	1	20	15	27	12.2462	115	0	103	1	229	3
54	7	2	20	2	11	12.6057	115	0	103	1	208	12
55	1	4	22	5	12	12.6196	115	0	110	1	239	1
56	7	3	16	20	12	13.1834	115	0	110	1	197	3
57	4	2	20	20	22	12.7173	115	0	110	1	229	3
58	4	3	20	13	11	12.9419	115	0	110	1	208	12
59	6	4	22	15	12	13.0023	115	0	239	1	197	3
60	4	3	25	15	2	12.6136	115	0	239	1	229	3
61	4	3	25	13	11	13.1103	115	0	239	1	208	12
62	3	4	20	8	15	12.6072	115	0	197	3	229	3
63	7	2	20	7	11	12.9384	115	0	197	3	208	12
64	2	3	20	4	11	12.6558	115	0	229	3	208	12
65	8	5	28	16	17	12.7067	49	1	69	1	103	1
66	2	5	30	20	22	12.8275	49	1	69	1	110	1
67	7	7	29	23	15	12.5942	49	1	69	1	239	1
68	8	6	26	15	12	12.8972	49	1	69	1	197	3
69	7	8	23	4	19	12.0928	49	1	69	1	229	3
70	8	6	23	11	29	12.2522	49	1	69	1	208	12
71	2	5	26	17	24	12.7303	49	1	103	1	110	1
72	5	6	19	12	12	12.5052	49	1	103	1	239	1
73	5	5	26	17	19	12.7183	49	1	103	1	197	3
74	8	6	26	17	22	12.7852	49	1	103	1	229	3
75	8	6	26	17	29	12.6494	49	1	103	1	208	12
76	2	8	27	9	14	12.5481	49	1	110	1	239	1
77	7	7	22	21	12	13.2757	49	1	110	1	197	3
78	7	4	15	13	14	12.1314	49	1	110	1	229	3
79	8	6	26	9	29	12.3288	49	1	110	1	208	12
80	8	8	27	16	12	13.1963	49	1	239	1	197	3
81	8	7	29	15	2	12.8117	49	1	239	1	229	3
82	8	7	28	14	11	13.1899	49	1	239	1	208	12
83	8	8	23	12	19	13.0781	49	1	197	3	229	3
84	6	8	22	12	9	12.8598	49	1	197	3	208	12
85	8	8	23	20	26	12.6295	49	1	229	3	208	12
86	2	4	20	20	17	12.8656	69	1	103	1	110	1
87	4	4	20	19	15	12.8309	69	1	103	1	239	1
88	8	2	16	17	12	12.5906	69	1	103	1	197	3
89	8	2	20	1	21	12.4212	69	1	103	1	229	3
90	4	1	20	17	11	12.6684	69	1	103	1	208	`12
91	7	4	20	13	14	12.5606	69	1	110	1	239	1
92	4	8	7	13	10	12.6766	69	1	110	1	197	3

Continued on next page

Table 14.6 *(continued)*

Rule #	Logic Code	)/(Code	Cutoff Values Series 1	Series 2	Series 3	Fitness	Series Number and Differencing Interval 1 #	Diff.	2 #	Diff.	3 #	Diff.
93	7	3	20	22	23	12.6158	69	1	110	1	229	3
94	7	2	20	13	14	12.7929	69	1	110	1	208	12
95	6	8	18	14	12	13.1308	69	1	239	1	197	3
96	8	3	13	15	3	12.5319	69	1	239	1	229	3
97	7	2	20	10	11	12.8100	69	1	239	1	208	12
98	1	3	20	7	31	12.4944	69	1	197	3	229	3
99	4	1	20	21	11	12.6508	69	1	197	3	208	12
100	4	1	20	30	11	12.6661	69	1	229	3	208	12
101	5	4	23	17	9	12.7523	103	1	110	1	239	1
102	2	2	17	19	12	13.1428	103	1	110	1	197	3
103	7	8	20	13	16	12.3294	103	1	110	1	229	3
104	8	1	17	2	11	12.5545	103	1	110	1	208	12
105	6	8	16	15	12	13.2561	103	1	239	1	197	3
106	6	2	22	15	7	12.6936	103	1	239	1	229	3
107	6	2	27	14	12	12.9947	103	1	239	1	208	12
108	2	4	17	12	10	12.4581	103	1	197	3	229	3
109	2	3	17	12	19	12.7366	103	1	197	3	208	12
110	2	3	17	17	17	12.6393	103	1	229	3	208	12
111	6	4	18	15	12	13.8619	110	1	239	1	197	3
112	6	2	7	15	6	12.5899	110	1	239	1	229	3
113	4	7	7	12	9	13.0278	110	1	239	1	208	12
114	2	7	13	12	18	12.7856	110	1	197	3	229	3
115	4	5	13	16	9	12.6274	110	1	197	3	208	12
116	4	7	13	11	9	12.3257	110	1	229	3	208	12
117	2	7	15	14	31	13.0638	239	1	197	3	229	3
118	8	8	14	14	29	12.9308	239	1	197	3	208	12
119	8	5	14	2	11	13.2857	239	1	229	3	208	12
120	8	8	14	20	30	12.0782	197	3	229	3	208	12

outperformed both the buy-and-hold strategy and the good rule portfolio. For the entire 1988–1991 holdout period, the bad rule portfolio averaged a 0.19 percent loss, which was better than the buy-and-hold result but worse than the good rule portfolio. Therefore, the bad rules did better than the good rules in 1989 but worse thereafter. Six of the rules continued to perform poorly over the entire period, averaging annual double-digit losses.

We will be better able to draw conclusions about developing timing rules for individual stocks after we have examined all four under scrutiny in this chapter. However, one concern already seems evident. If we examine Figures 14.1 and 14.2 for the good rule portfolios, paying particular attention to the period prior to January 1989, it appears that a disturbing change in the underlying relationships had occurred. Both graphs show peaks prior to 1989. These are always easy to

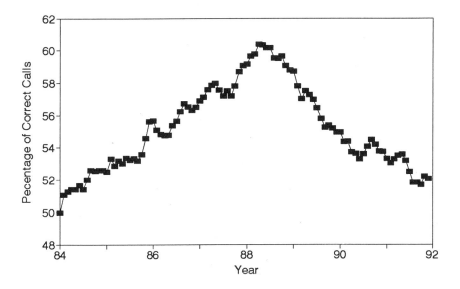

FIGURE 14.1 Percentage of Correct Calls (IBM—Good Rules) 1984–1991

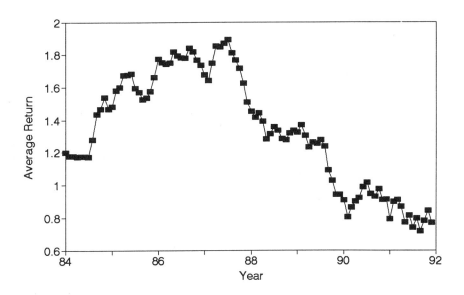

FIGURE 14.2 Average Return (IBM—Good Rules) 1984–1991

Table 14.7 Performance Summary: Good Rules—IBM Stock

Rule #	Fitness	1984–1988 Period		1989		1989–1991 Period	
		% Correct	Average Return	% Correct	Average Return	% Correct	Average Return
1	1.6309	61.67	12.12	50.00	−16.50	50.00	−2.53
2	1.4434	60.00	20.62	50.00	−9.70	52.78	5.49
3	1.4420	58.33	17.30	50.00	−9.70	55.56	5.70
4	1.6110	53.33	7.10	58.33	8.40	52.78	7.26
5	1.5993	53.33	7.10	58.33	8.40	52.78	7.26
6	1.7703	53.33	7.10	58.33	8.40	52.78	7.26
7	1.4034	60.00	15.04	58.33	−4.00	38.89	−4.50
8	1.4069	48.33	6.45	41.67	−19.40	44.44	−5.01
9	1.3450	55.00	8.14	50.00	−2.30	44.44	0.89
10	1.6981	51.67	6.41	41.67	−17.20	41.67	−6.78
11	1.6736	63.33	16.04	50.00	−6.40	50.00	1.70
12	1.6973	65.00	16.90	41.67	−3.10	50.00	2.98
13	1.8669	55.00	8.11	58.33	8.40	50.00	3.54
14	1.3395	66.67	18.49	41.67	−8.30	41.67	−1.21
15	1.7799	63.33	19.66	41.67	−15.30	47.22	−2.92
16	1.4316	60.00	19.21	50.00	−9.70	52.78	5.49
17	1.6922	58.33	12.96	50.00	1.10	50.00	4.10
18	1.5663	50.00	2.89	58.33	8.40	52.78	3.73
19	1.3994	58.33	18.04	50.00	−15.90	44.44	−0.70
20	1.5409	58.33	16.71	50.00	−9.70	50.00	0.79
21	1.5217	60.00	20.62	50.00	−9.70	52.78	5.49
22	1.6914	56.67	6.36	50.00	1.10	58.33	11.58
23	1.7330	63.33	13.32	50.00	1.60	52.78	9.22
24	1.5590	53.33	7.10	58.33	8.40	52.78	7.26
25	1.4772	58.33	16.81	50.00	−9.70	50.00	−0.84
26	1.5212	58.33	21.41	50.00	−9.20	50.00	−0.57
27	1.5599	58.33	17.28	16.67	−19.90	38.89	−5.61
28	1.8538	53.33	9.70	41.67	−1.00	47.22	1.70
29	1.5685	65.00	22.79	25.00	−18.20	38.89	−7.60
30	1.6952	65.00	22.25	16.67	−19.90	44.44	−2.01
31	1.7113	55.00	14.92	58.33	8.40	58.33	11.36
32	1.6308	60.00	22.02	58.33	7.80	63.89	16.00
33	1.6460	60.00	22.02	58.33	7.80	63.89	16.00
34	1.4105	60.00	16.13	50.00	−7.60	44.44	−5.83
35	1.4878	51.67	13.06	50.00	−4.40	52.78	4.43
36	1.4194	63.33	18.82	41.67	−14.00	52.78	0.30
37	1.4254	66.67	22.56	41.67	−21.10	44.44	−1.15
38	1.7290	53.33	8.75	41.67	−17.20	44.44	−2.39
39	1.6408	60.00	19.92	41.67	−8.30	50.00	4.74
40	1.6390	66.67	22.56	41.67	−21.10	41.67	−4.57
41	1.8498	55.00	8.11	58.33	8.40	50.00	3.54
42	1.6811	65.00	22.44	41.67	−21.10	44.44	−1.01
43	1.6551	58.33	15.69	33.33	−24.40	47.22	−1.97
44	1.3830	53.33	13.89	41.67	−19.40	47.22	−0.37
45	1.6170	53.33	8.63	66.67	12.50	55.56	7.23
46	1.5513	53.33	7.10	58.33	8.40	52.78	7.26

Continued on next page

Table 14.7 *(continued)*

Rule #	Fitness	1984–1988 Period		1989		1989–1991 Period	
		% Correct	Average Return	% Correct	Average Return	% Correct	Average Return
47	1.5412	53.33	7.10	58.33	8.40	52.78	7.26
48	1.4421	60.00	18.29	50.00	−15.90	47.22	0.99
49	1.2387	60.00	18.29	50.00	−15.90	47.22	0.99
50	1.6493	56.67	4.01	50.00	6.10	52.78	10.47
51	1.7267	51.67	−0.51	58.33	8.40	55.56	11.01
52	1.5944	53.33	7.10	58.33	8.40	52.78	7.26
53	1.3662	60.00	10.06	58.33	−14.10	55.56	3.82
54	1.3791	56.67	20.38	41.67	−19.00	44.44	−3.20
55	1.7932	68.33	23.71	41.67	−12.80	44.44	−0.57
56	1.7317	61.67	18.48	16.67	−19.90	41.67	−2.64
57	1.5681	63.33	21.64	16.67	−19.90	41.67	−2.64
58	1.5918	63.33	21.64	16.67	−19.90	38.89	−4.28
59	1.7213	53.33	15.49	58.33	8.40	63.89	13.34
60	1.5923	56.67	20.58	50.00	4.00	58.33	12.00
61	1.5921	58.33	21.13	58.33	7.80	61.11	16.03
62	1.5573	51.67	12.61	50.00	−4.40	50.00	2.28
63	1.3863	53.33	15.47	50.00	−4.40	55.56	5.49
64	1.4900	60.00	20.12	50.00	−15.90	52.78	0.70
65	1.7290	61.67	19.43	33.33	−24.40	44.44	−2.46
66	1.5908	53.33	7.10	58.33	8.40	52.78	7.26
67	1.7110	58.33	15.02	50.00	−9.90	44.44	−1.45
68	1.8431	53.33	7.10	58.33	8.40	52.78	7.26
69	1.6657	63.33	22.19	41.67	−21.10	41.67	−5.57
70	1.6934	63.33	15.36	33.33	−23.30	50.00	−0.60
71	1.7247	68.33	19.79	50.00	−11.70	44.44	−2.32
72	1.7396	58.33	8.86	33.33	−11.70	47.22	4.25
73	1.9270	53.33	7.10	58.33	8.40	52.78	7.26
74	1.7136	70.00	26.22	50.00	−11.70	41.67	−5.61
75	1.7913	65.00	25.69	50.00	−9.20	47.22	0.40
76	1.6876	66.67	23.41	33.33	−16.50	47.22	−0.87
77	1.8555	58.33	17.28	16.67	−19.90	41.67	−5.12
78	1.6012	66.67	23.41	33.33	−16.50	47.22	−0.87
79	1.6748	58.33	13.30	25.00	−27.10	41.67	−8.98
80	1.8716	55.00	13.59	58.33	8.40	52.78	7.17
81	1.6436	61.67	23.01	50.00	1.10	61.11	12.98
82	1.8421	65.00	15.85	41.67	−15.40	41.67	−6.71
83	1.8442	68.33	23.64	41.67	−3.10	44.44	1.51
84	1.8871	70.00	24.46	41.67	−3.10	44.44	0.63
85	1.7280	58.33	13.30	33.33	−24.40	44.44	−7.87
86	1.6493	53.33	0.94	58.33	8.40	55.56	11.25
87	1.5117	51.67	3.30	58.33	8.40	58.33	14.60
88	1.5591	56.67	13.08	50.00	4.60	55.56	12.87
89	1.3567	48.33	13.37	66.67	4.60	58.33	3.51
90	1.3561	53.33	18.78	50.00	−15.90	47.22	−2.71
91	1.6152	63.33	21.64	16.67	−19.90	41.67	−2.64
92	1.7619	61.67	18.48	16.67	−19.90	38.89	−3.81

Continued on next page

Table 14.7 *(continued)*

Rule #	Fitness	1984–1988 Period		1989		1989–1991 Period	
		% Correct	Average Return	% Correct	Average Return	% Correct	Average Return
93	1.6711	68.33	21.65	58.33	−3.60	50.00	5.22
94	1.6890	63.33	21.64	16.67	−19.90	41.67	−2.64
95	1.6640	51.67	12.77	58.33	8.40	58.33	11.23
96	1.6272	58.33	21.13	58.33	7.80	61.11	16.03
97	1.5980	60.00	21.33	58.33	7.80	63.89	14.37
98	1.5910	51.67	12.61	50.00	−4.40	50.00	2.28
99	1.5579	56.67	19.31	50.00	−4.40	55.56	7.98
100	1.4415	58.33	19.85	41.67	−19.40	50.00	−0.70
101	1.5896	63.33	21.64	25.00	−18.20	44.44	−1.97
102	1.8283	58.33	19.18	16.67	−21.10	38.89	−3.81
103	1.6178	63.33	22.55	25.00	−15.80	41.67	−1.73
104	1.6491	60.00	17.99	33.33	−9.80	44.44	2.91
105	1.7860	58.33	18.28	50.00	1.60	50.00	6.18
106	1.6626	58.33	21.37	50.00	4.00	58.33	12.00
107	1.6082	60.00	22.50	41.67	−0.40	47.22	0.17
108	1.5928	51.67	13.06	50.00	−4.40	52.78	4.43
109	1.6058	53.33	19.59	50.00	−3.90	55.56	5.73
110	1.5017	53.33	18.78	41.67	−14.80	47.22	−2.60
111	1.8142	55.00	14.92	58.33	8.40	55.56	9.25
112	1.6606	66.67	23.15	16.67	−19.90	44.44	−0.60
113	1.6986	63.33	21.64	16.67	−19.90	41.67	−2.64
114	1.7905	65.00	23.82	41.67	−3.10	50.00	6.15
115	1.8576	55.00	15.91	41.67	−10.30	52.78	3.42
116	1.6399	58.33	21.14	41.67	−15.30	52.78	−0.91
117	1.7650	60.00	23.15	58.33	7.80	58.33	9.94
118	1.7047	51.67	15.44	50.00	−4.40	52.78	3.51
119	1.6692	55.00	20.71	50.00	−9.70	58.33	1.15
120	1.3524	60.00	18.62	50.00	−4.40	55.56	0.03

spot with hindsight, but people using this rule portfolio in early 1989 might have had reason to feel a bit skittish about its continued effectiveness. Examination of the corresponding graphs for the bad rule portfolio indicate similar changes in the underlying relationships. Good seems to be getting worse, and bad seems to be getting better. Before placing any bets on these rule portfolios in 1989, users probably would have wanted to carefully analyze the changes that seemed to be taking shape.

TIMING RULES FOR MOBIL

The good and bad rule portfolios for Mobil are shown in Tables 14.9 and 14.10, respectively. Rule 37 in Table 14.9 performed best over the holdout period, generating a 19.81 percent annual return. This rule says that a good time to invest in

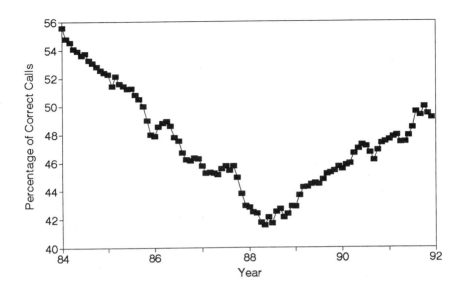

FIGURE 14.3 Percentage of Correct Calls (IBM—Bad Rules) 1984–1991

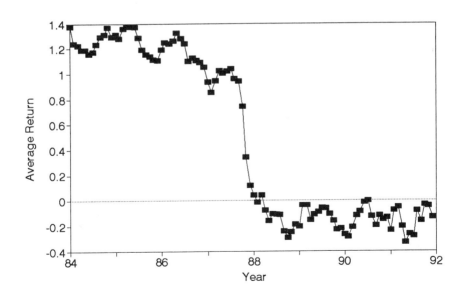

FIGURE 14.4 Average Return (IBM—Bad Rules) 1984–1991

Table 14.8 Performance Summary: Bad Rules—IBM Stock

Rule #	Fitness	1984–1988 Period		1989		1989–1991 Period	
		% Correct	Average Return	% Correct	Average Return	% Correct	Average Return
1	12.8915	46.67	0.57	50.00	−8.00	44.44	−5.53
2	12.4683	40.00	−6.38	50.00	3.90	52.78	−0.03
3	12.4723	40.00	−6.38	50.00	3.90	52.78	−0.03
4	12.6619	38.33	−5.82	50.00	2.30	47.22	−4.43
5	13.0814	46.67	3.40	41.67	−19.40	47.22	−5.87
6	1.25345	50.00	0.83	50.00	3.90	47.22	−3.06
7	12.8358	46.67	0.57	41.67	−19.40	44.44	−7.17
8	12.6073	48.33	2.38	58.33	6.80	44.44	−3.59
9	12.5230	48.33	5.37	50.00	−2.30	47.22	1.93
10	12.6694	43.33	−1.46	50.00	−5.90	55.56	2.79
11	12.5562	38.33	−4.53	58.33	−4.70	52.78	−0.03
12	13.1418	45.00	2.42	50.00	−13.60	50.00	−3.81
13	12.7391	45.00	2.42	41.67	−19.40	50.00	−2.50
14	12.9750	38.33	−4.53	58.33	−4.70	52.78	−0.03
15	13.1108	35.00	−2.75	58.33	3.20	61.11	7.49
16	12.4465	41.67	−6.18	50.00	3.90	50.00	−3.06
17	12.8269	41.67	−6.18	50.00	3.90	52.78	−0.03
18	13.1248	51.67	3.07	50.00	−9.80	55.56	1.25
19	12.5127	41.67	−6.18	50.00	3.90	50.00	−3.06
20	12.4212	45.00	0.98	50.00	−8.00	47.22	−2.95
21	12.9227	40.00	−8.20	50.00	−3.30	47.22	−4.28
22	12.3573	46.67	−6.75	58.33	7.80	55.56	7.52
23	13.0558	48.33	11.30	50.00	−15.90	50.00	−4.50
24	12.7959	48.33	−1.44	50.00	0.50	58.33	8.07
25	12.6731	48.33	0.30	58.33	7.80	58.33	465
26	12.3573	46.67	−6.75	58.33	7.80	55.56	7.52
27	13.1939	41.67	−5.57	83.33	9.00	55.56	3.20
28	12.6766	46.67	1.57	58.33	−11.80	52.78	−0.74
29	12.6634	41.67	−5.57	83.33	9.00	55.56	3.20
30	12.5367	51.67	9.65	50.00	1.10	55.56	7.66
31	13.4191	46.67	−4.48	41.67	−21.10	50.00	−2.11
32	13.0529	41.67	−9.00	50.00	−15.40	55.56	−0.37
33	13.3422	41.67	−3.29	41.67	−19.00	44.44	−9.55
34	12.5821	48.33	−2.04	50.00	−8.70	47.22	−3.34
35	12.1416	48.33	−2.04	50.00	−8.70	47.22	−3.34
36	12.4245	46.67	1.96	50.00	−10.70	44.44	−8.78
37	12.1450	35.00	−9.62	58.33	10.70	58.33	5.79
38	12.6830	41.67	−1.98	41.67	−7.20	55.56	0.89
39	12.8495	43.33	−4.95	58.33	10.70	52.78	3.82
40	12.7844	30.00	−9.83	50.00	−1.10	61.11	6.77
41	12.8972	45.00	2.42	41.67	−19.40	50.00	−2.50
42	12.6485	33.33	−7.51	50.00	−1.10	55.56	2.12
43	12.7935	40.00	−6.38	50.00	3.90	52.78	−0.03
44	12.2736	46.67	−2.77	58.33	8.40	52.78	1.35
45	12.4475	41.67	−6.18	50.00	3.90	52.78	−0.03
46	12.4611	36.67	−4.32	41.67	−10.40	50.00	−1.97

Continued on next page

Table 14.8 *(continued)*

Rule #	Fitness	1984–1988 Period		1989		1989–1991 Period	
		% Correct	Average Return	% Correct	Average Return	% Correct	Average Return
47	12.2891	46.67	0.57	41.67	− 19.40	44.44	− 7.17
48	12.5165	46.67	0.57	41.67	− 19.40	44.44	− 7.17
49	12.7649	41.67	− 6.18	50.00	3.90	52.78	− 0.03
50	12.4986	40.00	− 6.38	50.00	3.90	52.78	− 0.03
51	12.4853	40.00	− 4.17	41.67	− 9.00	52.78	− 3.52
52	12.5906	46.67	3.40	41.67	− 19.40	47.22	− 5.87
53	12.2462	40.00	− 6.38	50.00	3.90	52.78	− 0.03
54	12.6057	40.00	− 6.38	50.00	3.90	58.33	4.46
55	12.6196	40.00	− 7.29	66.67	9.80	61.11	5.67
56	13.1834	46.67	− 2.22	75.00	13.00	55.56	9.39
57	12.7173	31.67	− 10.08	58.33	0.20	55.56	− 0.77
58	12.9419	43.33	− 4.06	41.67	− 1.00	50.00	− 1.63
59	13.0023	41.67	− 7.61	33.33	− 24.40	41.67	− 11.29
60	12.6136	41.67	− 9.00	58.33	− 5.30	50.00	1.64
61	13.1103	45.00	0.16	50.00	− 9.80	47.22	− 6.59
62	12.6072	41.67	− 5.77	50.00	3.90	52.78	1.38
63	12.9384	48.33	0.18	50.00	− 4.40	50.00	− 0.81
64	12.6558	46.67	− 1.42	50.00	− 4.10	47.22	− 5.98
65	12.7067	38.33	− 7.26	66.67	15.50	55.56	3.51
66	12.8275	36.67	− 9.41	58.33	10.70	55.56	2.12
67	12.5942	43.33	− 1.70	41.67	− 9.00	55.56	3.01
68	12.8972	46.67	3.40	41.67	− 19.40	47.22	− 5.87
69	12.0928	46.67	5.73	50.00	− 15.90	50.00	− 1.35
70	12.2522	36.67	− 1.57	66.67	5.40	55.56	5.22
71	12.7303	38.33	− 11.79	66.67	14.90	58.33	9.83
72	12.5052	38.33	− 2.75	58.33	− 4.70	58.33	3.13
73	12.7183	46.67	− 6.75	58.33	7.80	55.56	7.52
74	12.7852	43.33	− 5.52	41.67	− 6.40	50.00	3.13
75	12.6494	36.67	− 11.86	50.00	8.50	50.00	6.79
76	12.5481	41.67	− 5.57	83.33	9.00	58.33	6.44
77	13.2757	41.67	− 3.52	75.00	13.00	52.78	8.07
78	12.1314	41.67	− 5.57	83.33	9.00	58.33	6.44
79	12.3288	41.67	− 0.48	66.67	11.80	55.56	5.91
80	13.1963	45.00	− 3.63	41.67	− 19.40	44.44	− 7.60
81	12.8117	38.33	− 10.63	58.33	− 9.90	50.00	0.00
82	13.1899	38.33	− 4.48	50.00	− 13.60	44.44	− 6.52
83	13.0781	30.00	− 11.04	58.33	− 9.90	55.56	− 0.54
84	12.8598	43.33	− 3.87	58.33	− 2.60	52.78	0.66
85	12.6295	31.67	− 4.22	58.33	3.20	50.00	3.66
86	12.8656	43.33	− 2.64	16.67	− 24.90	36.11	− 11.38
87	12.8309	48.33	11.30	50.00	− 15.90	44.44	− 8.22
88	12.5906	46.67	3.40	41.67	− 19.40	47.22	− 5.87
89	12.4212	46.67	− 1.72	25.00	− 19.50	38.89	− 9.31
90	12.6684	56.67	− 6.75	50.00	3.90	55.56	6.59
91	12.5606	38.33	− 8.88	83.33	9.00	61.11	6.97
92	12.6766	46.67	1.57	58.33	− 11.80	52.78	− 0.74

Continued on next page

Table 14.8 (continued)

Rule #	Fitness	1984–1988 Period		1989		1989–1991 Period	
		% Correct	Average Return	% Correct	Average Return	% Correct	Average Return
93	12.6158	38.33	−7.23	50.00	3.90	50.00	2.91
94	12.7929	40.00	−9.18	58.33	8.40	52.78	0.60
95	13.1308	43.33	−4.53	41.67	−19.40	41.67	−8.70
96	12.5319	41.67	−9.00	50.00	−15.40	50.00	−4.35
97	12.8100	36.67	−9.03	50.00	3.90	41.67	−5.20
98	12.4944	41.67	−7.42	50.00	3.90	52.78	3.23
99	12.6508	46.67	4.35	50.00	−4.40	55.56	3.23
100	12.6661	48.33	−1.23	50.00	−4.10	44.44	−7.91
101	12.7523	38.33	−5.37	58.33	−5.20	55.56	4.86
102	13.1428	46.67	−5.44	75.00	12.40	55.56	6.56
103	12.3294	43.33	−4.25	83.33	9.00	55.56	2.34
104	12.5545	51.67	−0.81	41.67	−1.60	52.78	5.58
105	13.2561	45.00	−2.28	50.00	−15.90	38.89	−10.45
106	12.6936	43.33	−7.15	50.00	−15.40	47.22	−2.11
107	12.9947	41.67	−5.57	41.67	−19.00	38.89	−10.08
108	12.4581	46.67	−7.40	50.00	−9.20	44.44	−4.54
109	12.7366	46.67	−7.40	58.33	−0.30	47.22	0.33
110	12.6393	46.67	−6.75	58.33	7.80	55.56	7.52
111	13.8619	45.00	−5.62	33.33	−24.40	44.44	−6.63
112	12.5899	41.67	−9.00	50.00	−15.40	50.00	−0.40
113	13.0278	46.67	−1.06	50.00	−13.60	55.56	1.64
114	12.7856	35.00	−10.57	75.00	6.70	55.56	2.98
115	12.6274	43.33	0.50	58.33	−1.80	52.78	3.57
116	12.3257	43.33	−3.59	66.67	−2.00	55.56	−1.80
117	13.0638	40.00	−11.11	50.00	−15.40	50.00	−0.91
118	12.9308	41.67	−10.26	41.67	−19.00	38.89	−10.33
119	13.2857	51.67	−2.70	41.67	−19.00	36.11	−13.11
120	12.0782	45.00	−3.77	66.67	−3.30	41.67	−7.71

Mobil is when (the one-month change in employee hours is not in the upper portion of its range *and* the one-month change in M1 money supply is not in the lower third of its range) *or* the one-month change in German stock prices is not in the lower half of its range.

The patterns in the rule relationships for Mobil are perhaps even more unstable than those for IBM. Figures 14.5 and 14.6 show the percentage of correct calls and the average return for the good rule portfolio. The percentage of correct calls climbed through most of 1984–85, reached a small plateau, declined in 1986–87, rose sharply, peaked in 1988, and then declined steadily. Average returns achieved an uneasy plateau during the 1987–1988 period and then began an unsteady downtrend in 1989. Once again, anyone using these rules in early 1989 would probably have felt some trepidation because the relationships appeared to be tenuous and uncertain.

Table 14.9 Good Rules—Mobil Stock

Rule #	Logic Code	)/(Code	Cutoff Values			Fitness	Series Number and Differencing Interval					
			Series 1	Series 2	Series 3		1 #	Diff.	2 #	Diff.	3 #	Diff.
1	4	2	17	27	18	2.3094	16	1	46	1	106	1
2	7	2	17	15	21	1.5553	16	1	46	1	209	1
3	4	1	17	28	15	1.7951	16	1	46	1	210	1
4	2	3	8	7	20	1.9370	16	1	46	1	46	3
5	7	3	17	29	18	1.8579	16	1	46	1	92	3
6	7	1	15	29	14	2.2673	16	1	46	1	197	3
7	3	1	17	27	15	1.7115	16	1	46	1	208	3
8	2	3	7	8	15	1.9097	16	1	46	1	150	12
9	5	4	17	18	0	2.0774	16	1	106	1	209	1
10	6	4	16	15	0	2.2701	16	1	106	1	210	1
11	8	3	17	18	1	2.0774	16	1	106	1	46	3
12	8	3	16	15	6	2.2701	16	1	106	1	92	3
13	4	3	31	15	8	2.1281	16	1	106	1	197	3
14	8	3	16	15	1	2.2701	16	1	106	1	208	3
15	8	3	2	15	10	2.3943	16	1	106	1	150	12
16	8	1	16	21	17	1.7293	16	1	209	1	210	1
17	2	1	3	27	20	1.9269	16	1	209	1	46	3
18	2	2	16	27	18	1.8914	16	1	209	1	92	3
19	8	1	15	1	11	1.8219	16	1	209	1	197	3
20	3	3	17	26	23	1.6337	16	1	209	1	208	3
21	2	1	12	29	15	1.9470	16	1	209	1	150	12
22	4	1	16	20	20	1.8348	16	1	210	1	46	3
23	6	1	16	18	19	1.6927	16	1	210	1	92	3
24	8	1	15	18	11	1.9135	16	1	210	1	197	3
25	2	2	17	22	25	1.8123	16	1	210	1	208	3
26	4	1	15	20	15	1.9335	16	1	210	1	150	12
27	2	2	16	20	18	2.1795	16	1	46	3	92	3
28	2	1	15	20	14	2.1735	16	1	46	3	197	3
29	6	1	17	20	22	1.8830	16	1	46	3	208	3
30	2	1	9	20	15	2.0661	16	1	46	3	150	12
31	2	1	15	24	11	1.9177	16	1	92	3	197	3
32	2	1	17	23	21	1.5533	16	1	92	3	208	3
33	7	1	5	31	15	2.0035	16	1	92	3	150	12
34	2	1	15	11	28	1.8406	16	1	197	3	208	3
35	5	1	15	12	15	2.2902	16	1	197	3	150	12
36	2	1	2	31	15	1.8999	16	1	208	3	150	12
37	4	3	28	12	19	1.9013	46	1	106	1	209	1
38	6	4	20	15	19	2.0571	46	1	106	1	210	1
39	3	7	11	18	20	1.9849	46	1	106	1	46	3
40	3	7	6	15	12	2.1359	46	1	106	1	92	3
41	3	7	9	15	8	2.2174	46	1	106	1	197	3
42	8	3	20	15	15	2.0857	46	1	106	1	208	3
43	5	3	21	15	16	2.2507	46	1	106	1	150	12
44	4	1	28	25	18	1.8446	46	1	209	1	210	1
45	7	1	29	27	11	1.8186	46	1	209	1	46	3
46	4	2	29	25	25	1.8172	46	1	209	1	92	3

Continued on next page

Table 14.9 (continued)

Rule #	Logic Code	)/(Code	Cutoff Values			Fitness	Series Number and Differencing Interval					
			Series 1	Series 2	Series 3		1 #	Diff.	2 #	Diff.	3 #	Diff.
47	1	1	29	27	14	2.3477	46	1	209	1	197	3
48	7	1	28	27	15	1.8442	46	1	209	1	208	3
49	6	1	28	17	15	2.0207	46	1	209	1	150	12
50	3	5	10	12	20	1.9370	46	1	210	1	46	3
51	7	1	29	20	14	1.6953	46	1	210	1	92	3
52	3	1	29	18	12	2.3098	46	1	210	1	197	3
53	4	2	29	22	27	1.8070	46	1	210	1	208	3
54	6	1	28	15	15	2.0790	46	1	210	1	150	12
55	3	5	11	20	13	1.8668	46	1	46	3	92	3
56	3	3	29	30	14	2.1966	46	1	46	3	197	3
57	3	5	8	20	6	1.9370	46	1	46	3	208	3
58	4	3	26	17	11	1.9142	46	1	46	3	150	12
59	3	3	29	29	14	2.2002	46	1	92	3	197	3
60	7	1	28	24	16	1.6126	46	1	92	3	208	3
61	5	1	19	24	15	1.8918	46	1	92	3	150	12
62	3	1	29	14	12	2.2183	46	1	197	3	208	3
63	7	1	26	14	11	2.2991	46	1	197	3	150	12
64	6	5	10	11	15	1.9097	46	1	208	3	150	12
65	2	7	15	0	18	1.9102	106	1	209	1	210	1
66	2	5	15	23	20	2.3065	106	1	209	1	46	3
67	8	5	15	18	12	2.1321	106	1	209	1	92	3
68	4	7	15	4	8	2.1281	106	1	209	1	197	3
69	7	5	15	27	19	1.9868	106	1	209	1	208	3
70	8	5	15	19	10	2.3846	106	1	209	1	150	12
71	2	5	15	20	20	2.2314	106	1	210	1	46	3
72	8	5	15	15	4	2.1951	106	1	210	1	92	3
73	6	5	12	18	14	2.1566	106	1	210	1	197	3
74	8	6	15	18	27	1.9657	106	1	210	1	208	3
75	4	1	31	17	15	1.9192	106	1	210	1	150	12
76	8	5	15	8	12	2.1771	106	1	46	3	92	3
77	2	5	18	21	10	2.2754	106	1	46	3	197	3
78	5	5	15	20	29	2.1229	106	1	46	3	208	3
79	7	5	9	20	11	2.0857	106	1	46	3	150	12
80	5	5	15	7	13	2.2185	106	1	92	3	197	3
81	8	5	15	12	12	2.1643	106	1	92	3	208	3
82	4	7	15	10	9	2.2498	106	1	92	3	150	12
83	6	7	15	8	20	2.2421	106	1	197	3	208	3
84	5	5	18	12	15	2.2571	106	1	197	3	150	12
85	6	5	4	12	15	2.1181	106	1	208	3	150	12
86	6	5	15	18	20	1.8584	209	1	210	1	46	3
87	8	1	19	18	6	1.6992	209	1	210	1	92	3
88	6	1	25	18	11	2.0415	209	1	210	1	197	3
89	4	2	24	21	28	1.4646	209	1	210	1	208	3
90	8	1	19	17	12	1.9478	209	1	210	1	150	12
91	6	3	9	20	4	1.7955	209	1	46	3	92	3
92	5	1	11	20	14	2.1474	209	1	46	3	197	3

Continued on next page

Table 14.9 *(continued)*

Rule #	Logic Code	>/< Code	Cutoff Values			Fitness	Series Number and Differencing Interval					
			Series 1	Series 2	Series 3		1 #	Diff.	2 #	Diff.	3 #	Diff.
93	4	1	27	20	11	1.9269	209	1	46	3	208	3
94	7	2	19	2	14	1.9329	209	1	46	3	150	12
95	1	1	25	26	11	1.9947	209	1	92	3	197	3
96	3	3	27	18	19	1.7502	209	1	92	3	208	3
97	2	1	19	28	14	2.0182	209	1	92	3	150	12
98	7	3	25	11	24	2.0662	209	1	197	3	208	3
99	2	1	19	14	15	2.2884	209	1	197	3	150	12
100	3	1	29	2	15	1.9470	209	1	208	3	150	12
101	8	1	18	20	4	1.8267	210	1	46	3	92	3
102	2	1	18	20	14	2.3589	210	1	46	3	197	3
103	2	2	14	20	16	1.8796	210	1	46	3	208	3
104	7	2	17	2	15	1.9207	210	1	46	3	150	12
105	2	1	18	24	11	1.9615	210	1	92	3	197	3
106	2	1	18	10	20	1.5400	210	1	92	3	208	3
107	7	1	14	30	15	2.0035	210	1	92	3	150	12
108	6	3	19	11	13	1.8511	210	1	197	3	208	3
109	2	1	18	11	16	2.3405	210	1	197	3	150	12
110	7	1	17	28	15	1.9251	210	1	208	3	150	12
111	3	1	20	12	14	2.1021	46	3	92	3	197	3
112	4	3	20	18	15	1.8730	46	3	92	3	208	3
113	3	1	20	12	18	1.9890	46	3	92	3	150	12
114	4	1	20	14	12	2.1706	46	3	197	3	208	3
115	1	5	6	12	15	2.1672	46	3	197	3	150	12
116	6	1	20	13	18	2.0800	46	3	208	3	150	12
117	3	1	24	11	17	1.8562	92	3	197	3	208	3
118	5	1	5	12	15	2.1672	92	3	197	3	150	12
119	3	1	29	12	15	2.0035	92	3	208	3	150	12
120	6	1	14	3	15	2.2813	197	3	208	3	150	12

Looking at Figure 14.7, the bad rule portfolio looks attractive. The percentage of correct calls declined quite steadily over the 1984–1988 period, but by the end of 1989, the trend had reversed. Of course, users in early 1989 could not have easily foreseen this reversal. However, the average return graph, Figure 14.8, does show a disturbing pattern. The return rose quickly over most of the 1986–1987 period and then dropped sharply. We need to remember that our fitness measure tries to project average return based on the 1984–1988 pattern. Given the violent ups and downs in the relationship, we might feel uneasy about the fitness measure in this case.

The user who held back from investing based on these qualitative concerns would have made the correct decision. The bad rule portfolio actually outper-formed the good rule portfolio during 1989 and over the entire 1989–1991 holdout

Table 14.10 Bad Rules—Mobil Stock

Rule #	Logic Code	)/(Code	Cutoff Values			Fitness	Series Number and Differencing Interval					
			Series 1	Series 2	Series 3		1 #	Diff.	2 #	Diff.	3 #	Diff.
1	4	7	3	26	5	12.7830	16	1	46	1	106	1
2	5	8	23	26	17	12.4985	16	1	46	1	209	1
3	5	8	25	26	6	12.4852	16	1	46	1	210	1
4	3	7	11	26	8	12.2525	16	1	46	1	46	3
5	4	8	6	26	31	12.2320	16	1	46	1	92	3
6	7	8	22	19	9	12.1373	16	1	46	1	197	3
7	5	8	25	26	10	12.4852	16	1	46	1	208	3
8	4	8	11	26	23	12.4082	16	1	46	1	150	12
9	4	6	16	15	27	11.8426	16	1	106	1	209	1
10	7	7	16	15	23	11.9133	16	1	106	1	210	1
11	3	6	17	4	19	11.9104	16	1	106	1	46	3
12	1	6	10	15	13	12.6729	16	1	106	1	92	3
13	3	6	17	16	16	11.8859	16	1	106	1	197	3
14	1	6	3	15	21	11.9762	16	1	106	1	208	3
15	6	7	10	5	15	12.3694	16	1	106	1	150	12
16	5	6	17	22	18	11.6360	16	1	209	1	210	1
17	6	6	7	27	12	11.4862	16	1	209	1	46	3
18	7	8	21	18	19	11.5617	16	1	209	1	92	3
19	8	8	21	25	10	11.3497	16	1	209	1	197	3
20	6	4	20	27	21	12.4714	16	1	209	1	208	3
21	3	8	6	27	22	11.6512	16	1	209	1	150	12
22	7	4	14	18	20	11.4220	16	1	210	1	46	3
23	1	4	20	17	13	11.8535	16	1	210	1	92	3
24	1	7	17	15	18	11.3993	16	1	210	1	197	3
25	1	6	17	27	21	11.7379	16	1	210	1	208	3
26	1	8	17	19	11	11.8861	16	1	210	1	150	12
27	3	7	17	20	18	12.2558	16	1	46	3	92	3
28	5	4	20	20	10	11.6684	16	1	46	3	197	3
29	4	8	16	24	21	12.0691	16	1	46	3	208	3
30	4	8	17	20	22	12.0996	16	1	46	3	150	12
31	2	8	21	13	10	11.6310	16	1	92	3	197	3
32	5	4	1	13	21	11.7156	16	1	92	3	208	3
33	2	8	25	13	19	11.7051	16	1	92	3	150	12
34	5	4	20	12	21	12.0181	16	1	197	3	208	3
35	6	8	2	12	15	11.8381	16	1	197	3	150	12
36	5	8	25	15	15	11.4763	16	1	208	3	150	12
37	1	6	20	23	2	12.6894	46	1	106	1	209	1
38	1	6	20	22	17	12.7283	46	1	106	1	210	1
39	2	6	26	5	4	12.6358	46	1	106	1	46	3
40	1	6	19	22	13	13.4683	46	1	106	1	92	3
41	5	6	26	5	6	12.7641	46	1	106	1	197	3
42	1	6	20	23	9	12.7009	46	1	106	1	208	3
43	8	6	26	5	19	12.9005	46	1	106	1	150	12
44	3	8	26	23	19	12.0115	46	1	209	1	210	1
45	2	7	26	27	21	12.7465	46	1	209	1	46	3
46	6	8	26	27	11	12.7614	46	1	209	1	92	3

Continued on next page

Table 14.10 *(continued)*

Rule #	Logic Code	⟩/⟨ Code	Cutoff Values			Fitness	Series Number and Differencing Interval					
			Series 1	Series 2	Series 3		1		2		3	
							#	Diff.	#	Diff.	#	Diff.
47	6	8	26	27	7	12.8637	46	1	209	1	197	3
48	1	8	19	17	21	12.6926	46	1	209	1	208	3
49	4	8	26	14	23	12.4082	46	1	209	1	150	12
50	3	7	20	18	15	12.4439	46	1	210	1	46	3
51	1	8	19	17	13	13.3965	46	1	210	1	92	3
52	3	8	20	18	17	12.3309	46	1	210	1	197	3
53	7	8	27	8	24	12.2123	46	1	210	1	208	3
54	7	8	26	10	23	12.4082	46	1	210	1	150	12
55	2	6	26	30	29	11.9429	46	1	46	3	92	3
56	6	8	16	20	14	12.1106	46	1	46	3	197	3
57	2	8	26	19	22	12.6251	46	1	46	3	208	3
58	4	8	21	18	24	12.3442	46	1	46	3	150	12
59	3	8	19	13	22	12.2867	46	1	92	3	197	3
60	3	8	19	23	21	12.7187	46	1	92	3	208	3
61	1	8	19	13	6	12.5879	46	1	92	3	150	12
62	5	8	26	22	10	12.2578	46	1	197	3	208	3
63	4	8	19	9	19	12.3290	46	1	197	3	150	12
64	7	8	26	12	24	12.4082	46	1	208	3	150	12
65	6	4	12	29	19	11.7244	106	1	209	1	210	1
66	1	4	16	23	15	11.7411	106	1	209	1	46	3
67	1	4	15	17	13	12.6371	106	1	209	1	92	3 .
68	8	4	4	27	22	11.7473	106	1	209	1	197	3
69	6	4	15	27	21	12.3965	106	1	209	1	208	3
70	7	4	8	19	13	12.5128	106	1	209	1	150	12
71	2	4	5	18	20	12.0713	106	1	210	1	46	3
72	1	4	15	15	13	12.7468	106	1	210	1	92	3
73	4	4	15	17	17	11.8497	106	1	210	1	197	3
74	3	4	15	27	21	12.0691	106	1	210	1	208	3
75	7	4	5	8	15	12.3694	106	1	210	1	150	12
76	1	4	15	15	13	12.5520	106	1	46	3	92	3
77	1	3	15	12	17	11.7421	106	1	46	3	197	3
78	6	4	16	24	21	12.6040	106	1	46	3	208	3
79	8	4	5	20	19	12.4374	106	1	46	3	150	12
80	7	4	15	13	17	12.7983	106	1	92	3	197	3
81	1	4	16	13	13	12.3720	106	1	92	3	208	3
82	7	4	11	13	15	12.4346	106	1	92	3	150	12
83	5	4	16	17	21	12.4073	106	1	197	3	208	3
84	2	4	5	9	15	12.3626	106	1	197	3	150	12
85	7	4	5	14	15	12.5617	106	1	208	3	150	12
86	5	8	25	22	18	11.9159	209	1	210	1	46	3
87	1	8	18	15	13	11.7964	209	1	210	1	92	3
88	7	8	24	17	9	11.3249	209	1	210	1	197	3
89	3	6	17	10	21	11.5690	209	1	210	1	208	3
90	7	8	27	16	22	11.6512	209	1	210	1	150	12
91	1	8	19	17	19	11.8439	209	1	46	3	92	3
92	4	8	4	20	14	11.7831	209	1	46	3	197	3

Continued on next page

Table 14.10 (continued)

Rule #	Logic Code	)/(Code	Cutoff Values			Fitness	Series Number and Differencing Interval					
			Series 1	Series 2	Series 3		1 #	Diff.	2 #	Diff.	3 #	Diff.
93	3	8	17	23	21	12.2756	209	1	46	3	208	3
94	3	6	19	16	13	12.0441	209	1	46	3	150	12
95	4	8	19	20	14	11.5380	209	1	92	3	197	3
96	1	8	19	13	21	11.9784	209	1	92	3	208	3
97	5	4	14	13	15	11.3491	209	1	92	3	150	12
98	4	6	27	11	21	11.6364	209	1	197	3	208	3
99	8	8	25	11	16	11.8925	209	1	197	3	150	12
100	4	8	18	21	18	12.1898	209	1	208	3	150	12
101	7	8	21	20	22	11.7514	210	1	46	3	92	3
102	4	8	18	20	14	11.8717	210	1	46	3	197	3
103	1	2	27	24	21	12.0113	210	1	46	3	208	3
104	4	8	22	18	19	12.2283	210	1	46	3	150	12
105	7	8	22	13	11	11.7623	210	1	92	3	197	3
106	7	8	27	11	21	11.6019	210	1	92	3	208	3
107	1	8	17	13	15	11.8102	210	1	92	3	150	12
108	4	4	21	10	22	11.9226	210	1	197	3	208	3
109	6	8	13	12	15	11.8381	210	1	197	3	150	12
110	1	8	17	13	15	11.5626	210	1	208	3	150	12
111	5	6	25	22	10	11.5113	46	3	92	3	197	3
112	2	8	29	19	22	11.7265	46	3	92	3	208	3
113	7	8	20	13	19	12.0951	46	3	92	3	150	12
114	8	8	24	22	21	12.2209	46	3	197	3	208	3
115	4	8	15	11	17	12.1758	46	3	197	3	150	12
116	8	8	31	21	18	12.1938	46	3	208	3	150	12
117	1	8	12	3	21	11.7215	92	3	197	3	208	3
118	3	8	13	11	17	12.4430	92	3	197	3	150	12
119	7	6	19	22	9	11.5521	92	3	208	3	150	12
120	4	8	12	21	16	12.1956	197	3	208	3	150	12

period, and both portfolios underperformed a buy-and-hold Mobil strategy that earned 44.4 percent in 1989 and averaged 19.8 percent annually over the entire period. The bad rule portfolio beat the good rule portfolio in 1989, with increases of 28.8 percent and 18.0 percent, respectively. Over the entire period, the bad rule portfolio averaged 15.18 percent versus 8.55 percent for the good rule portfolio.

The detailed results are shown in Tables 14.11 and 14.12. None of the good rules beats the buy-and-hold alternative. However, a dramatic reversal occurred; 32 of the 120 bad rules actually beat the buy-and-hold strategy over the 1988–1991 period. The best of the group had an average annual return of 32.2 percent. Clearly, good became bad and vice versa.

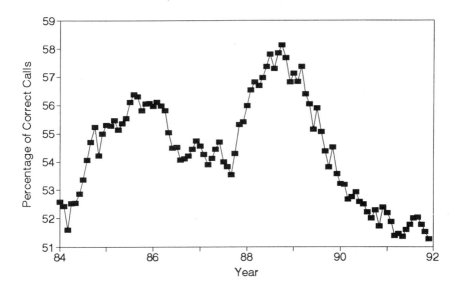

FIGURE 14.5   Percentage of Correct Calls (Mobil—Good Rules) 1984–1991

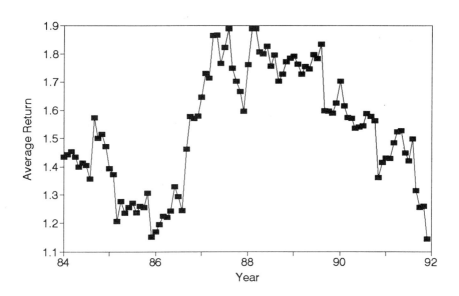

FIGURE 14.6   Average Return (Mobil—Good Rules) 1984–1991

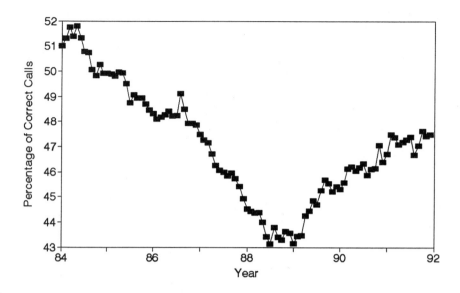

FIGURE 14.7   Percentage of Correct Calls (Mobil—Bad Rules) 1984–1991

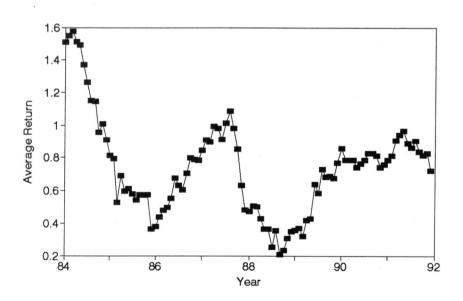

FIGURE 14.8   Average Return (Mobil—Bad Rules) 1984–1991

Table 14.11 Performance Summary: Good Rules—Mobil Stock

Rule #	Fitness	1984–1988 Period		1989		1989–1991 Period	
		% Correct	Average Return	% Correct	Average Return	% Correct	Average Return
1	2.3094	58.33	16.16	66.67	33.70	55.56	16.08
2	1.5553	61.67	25.17	58.33	26.10	44.44	6.88
3	1.7951	63.33	22.09	33.33	13.80	44.44	7.03
4	1.9370	56.67	27.15	50.00	21.30	50.00	12.95
5	1.8579	66.67	25.27	50.00	21.30	50.00	12.00
6	2.2673	51.67	12.62	25.00	11.70	41.67	7.89
7	1.7115	60.00	23.76	33.33	10.50	44.44	4.25
8	1.9097	50.00	14.57	25.00	11.70	44.44	7.03
9	2.0774	68.33	31.73	41.67	18.30	41.67	2.98
10	2.2701	66.67	33.79	25.00	15.80	27.78	−0.94
11	2.0774	68.33	31.73	41.67	18.30	41.67	2.98
12	2.2701	66.67	31.45	41.67	24.20	30.56	0.89
13	2.1281	63.33	25.30	50.00	21.70	38.89	4.65
14	2.2701	66.67	33.79	25.00	15.80	27.78	−0.94
15	2.3943	66.67	30.22	58.33	30.30	41.67	6.00
16	1.7293	58.33	21.70	41.67	22.70	44.44	9.47
17	1.9269	48.33	11.93	33.33	14.60	50.00	10.27
18	1.8914	66.67	24.09	75.00	34.60	52.78	14.65
19	1.8219	50.00	10.96	33.33	16.00	36.11	3.45
20	1.6337	58.33	18.95	25.00	8.40	36.11	1.77
21	1.9470	45.00	12.22	25.00	8.40	44.44	4.95
22	1.8348	58.33	20.08	41.67	16.80	38.89	3.57
23	1.6927	58.33	19.08	33.33	14.60	38.89	2.91
24	1.9135	58.33	15.82	41.67	22.70	38.89	4.56
25	1.8123	61.67	21.04	41.67	18.30	41.67	3.85
26	1.9335	53.33	18.36	25.00	8.40	36.11	1.83
27	2.1795	56.67	23.26	33.33	14.60	41.67	5.76
28	2.1735	50.00	11.39	25.00	15.80	44.44	12.53
29	1.8830	61.67	29.42	50.00	29.40	47.22	15.00
30	2.0661	48.33	14.96	25.00	9.90	52.78	12.16
31	1.9177	51.67	16.04	33.33	16.00	36.11	3.45
32	1.5533	53.33	16.67	66.67	38.40	50.00	13.00
33	2.0035	48.33	18.00	25.00	8.40	47.22	6.21
34	1.8406	55.00	24.16	50.00	26.20	47.22	8.91
35	2.2902	55.00	22.14	50.00	26.20	47.22	12.08
36	1.8999	48.33	12.96	25.00	8.40	44.44	8.38
37	1.9013	55.00	14.29	75.00	44.40	55.56	19.81
38	2.0571	60.00	27.00	16.67	8.20	33.33	2.03
39	1.9849	56.67	17.01	75.00	44.40	55.56	17.13
40	2.1359	65.00	16.90	58.33	30.30	47.22	10.30
41	2.2174	63.33	25.30	50.00	21.70	41.67	5.16
42	2.0857	56.67	17.01	75.00	44.40	55.56	19.81
43	2.2507	58.33	21.93	50.00	21.30	52.78	14.60
44	1.8446	66.67	31.20	58.33	22.40	52.78	10.63
45	1.8186	73.33	35.28	58.33	22.20	52.78	12.43
46	1.8172	63.33	25.35	58.33	31.10	50.00	16.00

Continued on next page

Table 14.11 (continued)

Rule #	Fitness	1984–1988 Period		1989		1989–1991 Period	
		% Correct	Average Return	% Correct	Average Return	% Correct	Average Return
47	2.3477	45.00	9.64	25.00	8.40	44.44	4.95
48	1.8442	73.33	34.90	50.00	17.00	52.78	12.79
49	2.0207	46.67	15.58	25.00	8.40	47.22	5.61
50	1.9370	58.33	20.08	41.67	16.80	44.44	4.43
51	1.6953	63.33 ·	27.67	41.67	16.80	38.89	3.57
52	2.3098	55.00	17.79	33.33	14.60	44.44	4.22
53	1.8070	61.67	32.93	58.33	22.30	50.00	13.00
54	2.0790	50.00	16.96	25.00	8.40	38.89	2.19
55	1.8668	61.67	32.13	50.00	29.40	47.22	12.43
56	2.1966	43.33	7.51	16.67	8.20	52.78	16.96
57	1.9370	61.67	32.13	50.00	29.40	47.22	12.43
58	1.9142	55.00	23.01	25.00	6.50	38.89	11.55
59	2.2002	43.33	10.88	25.00	8.40	47.22	9.36
60	1.6126	61.67	19.76	50.00	25.60	47.22	14.34
61	1.8918	45.00	12.00	25.00	8.40	50.00	9.61
62	2.2183	68.33	31.99	50.00	22.50	47.22	11.47
63	2.2991	58.33	25.32	66.67	34.90	55.56	16.57
64	1.9097	48.33	12.96	25.00	8.40	44.44	8.38
65	1.9102	60.00	30.42	16.67	8.20	36.11	0.46
66	2.3065	61.67	26.29	25.00	14.40	41.67	5.16
67	2.1321	60.00	30.42	16.67	8.20	36.11	0.46
68	2.1281	60.00	27.00	16.67	8.20	33.33	2.03
69	1.9868	63.33	32.77	25.00	8.40	44.44	3.07
70	2.3846	60.00	30.42	16.67	8.20	38.89	1.93
71	2.2314	68.33	31.94	33.33	16.60	2778	−0.70
72	2.1951	63.33	31.35	16.67	8.20	27.78	−2.78
73	2.1566	55.00	17.79	33.33	14.60	41.7	3.29
74	1.9657	65.00	30.91	25.00	14.30	30.56	0.27
75	1.9192	53.33	17.70	33.33	14.60	44.44	4.25
76	2.1771	60.00	27.00	16.67	8.20	41.67	10.00
77	2.2754	56.67	23.54	25.00	8.40	47.22	12.48
78	2.1229	73.33	40.77	50.00	29.40	47.22	15.00
79	2.0857	55.00	30.14	25.00	14.90	44.44	15.10
80	2.2185	45.00	12.00	25.00	8.40	44.44	7.26
81	2.1643	61.67	32.81	16.67	8.20	33.33	2.03
82	2.2498	61.67	32.81	16.67	8.20	33.33	2.03
83	2.2421	46.67	16.45	33.33	16.20	38.89	5.91
84	2.2571	58.33	23.16	50.00	26.20	50.00	13.11
85	2.1181	48.33	12.96	25.00	8.40	44.44	8.38
86	1.8584	58.33	20.08	41.67	16.80	38.89	3.57
87	1.6992	55.00	20.65	33.33	14.60	44.44	4.80
88	2.0415	55.00	17.79	33.33	14.60	41.67	3.29
89	1.4646	65.00	25.21	41.67	19.60	41.67	6.35
90	1.9478	53.33	20.56	33.33	14.60	47.22	5.76
91	1.7955	63.33	35.26	50.00	29.40	47.22	15.00
92	2.1474	43.33	7.51	16.67	8.20	52.78	16.96

Continued on next page

Table 14.11 *(continued)*

Rule #	Fitness	1984–1988 Period % Correct	1984–1988 Period Average Return	1989 % Correct	1989 Average Return	1989–1991 Period % Correct	1989–1991 Period Average Return
93	1.9269	65.00	34.64	50.00	20.60	52.78	13.73
94	1.9329	46.67	15.58	16.67	8.20	52.78	14.45
95	1.9947	45.00	12.00	25.00	8.40	44.44	7.26
96	1.7502	66.67	26.27	75.00	34.60	58.33	16.10
97	2.0182	48.33	20.87	25.00	8.40	52.78	9.25
98	2.0662	55.00	23.99	50.00	26.20	52.78	12.98
99	2.2884	60.00	22.40	66.67	34.90	52.78	12.66
100	1.9470	48.33	12.96	25.00	8.40	44.44	8.38
101	1.8267	68.33	36.13	50.00	29.40	47.22	15.00
102	2.3589	55.00	18.24	25.00	14.40	41.67	10.60
103	1.8796	58.33	32.00	41.67	21.70	38.89	6.27
104	1.9207	55.00	19.92	33.33	16.20	50.00	11.55
105	1.9615	56.67	23.17	33.33	14.60	41.67	3.29
106	1.5400	56.67	23.17	33.33	14.60	41.67	3.29
107	2.0035	50.00	21.71	25.00	8.40	44.44	4.43
108	1.8511	55.00	24.06	50.00	26.20	52.78	10.60
109	2.3405	55.00	23.88	50.00	26.20	50.00	9.61
110	1.9251	53.33	17.70	33.33	14.60	41.67	4.31
111	2.1021	45.00	12.00	25.00	8.40	47.22	9.36
112	1.8730	58.33	28.11	25.00	11.30	44.44	14.01
113	1.9890	48.33	15.51	50.00	26.00	52.78	10.55
114	2.1706	60.00	23.95	58.33	32.40	50.00	14.78
115	2.1672	55.00	22.14	50.00	26.20	50.00	13.11
116	2.0800	53.33	19.47	25.00	8.40	36.11	4.07
117	1.8562	56.67	16.45	66.67	32.40	52.78	13.00
118	2.1672	55.00	22.14	50.00	26.20	50.00	13.11
119	2.0035	48.33	12.96	25.00	8.40	44.44	8.38
120	2.2813	48.33	12.96	25.00	8.40	44.44	7.55

TIMING RULES FOR MCDONALD'S

The good and bad rule portfolios for McDonald's can be seen in Tables 14.13 and 14.14. The best rule for McDonald's, rule 117, earned an annual rate of 24.83 percent over the holdout period. This rule is unusual because it involves two different change intervals for the same series; it says to invest in McDonald's when the 12-month change in the coincident index change is in the lower third of its range, *and* the 1-month change in the coincident index change is in the lower half of its range, *and* the 3-month change in industrial production is in the lower half of its range. The "coincident index change" is the change over a 3-month span, so the first two components of the rule relate to changes in the acceleration of the coincident index. When the rate of change in the coincident index is fairly low, which would occur near peaks and troughs of the business

Table 14.12 Performance Summary: Bad Rules—Mobil Stock

Rule #	Fitness	1984–1988 Period		1989		1989–1991 Period	
		% Correct	Average Return	% Correct	Average Return	% Correct	Average Return
1	12.7830	36.67	− 3.20	58.33	28.40	50.00	10.11
2	12.4985	36.67	− 3.24	50.00	28.20	52.78	12.64
3	12.4852	36.67	− 4.82	58.33	28.40	52.78	9.03
4	12.2525	36.67	− 3.20	58.33	28.40	52.78	11.52
5	12.2320	36.67	− 3.20	58.33	28.40	52.78	9.03
6	12.1373	43.33	4.26	50.00	29.00	47.22	13.13
7	12.4852	36.67	− 4.82	58.33	28.40	52.78	9.03
8	12.4082	36.67	0.14	50.00	28.20	47.22	9.25
9	11.8426	36.67	− 4.08	75.00	35.20	72.22	29.74
10	11.9133	33.33	− 6.33	75.00	35.20	72.22	29.74
11	11.9104	46.67	12.80	41.67	20.10	50.00	10.08
12	12.6729	35.00	6.20	33.33	14.60	50.00	13.13
13	11.8859	38.33	3.52	58.33	32.30	58.33	23.75
14	11.9762	43.33	7.10	25.00	8.40	44.44	7.26
15	12.3694	60.00	22.00	33.33	19.90	38.89	5.58
16	11.6360	45.00	− 0.42	58.33	32.30	52.78	20.76
17	11.4862	33.33	− 0.75	25.00	16.30	44.44	11.74
18	11.5617	53.33	8.42	75.00	44.40	50.00	19.93
19	11.3497	55.00	14.29	75.00	44.40	58.33	23.64
20	12.4714	40.00	2.37	41.67	27.60	44.44	11.60
21	11.6512	45.00	10.48	66.67	36.60	58.33	20.28
22	11.4220	43.33	4.78	58.33	34.00	58.33	23.64
23	11.8535	46.67	6.62	41.67	18.90	41.67	8.86
24	11.3993	45.00	7.67	33.33	14.60	44.44	7.72
25	11.7379	36.67	0.73	50.00	25.20	63.89	22.09
26	11.8861	36.67	1.02	50.00	25.20	58.33	22.05
27	12.2558	38.33	0.63	58.33	34.00	55.56	21.85
28	11.6684	46.67	5.39	58.33	28.50	44.44	5.91
29	12.0691	40.00	0.46	50.00	20.90	52.78	11.76
30	12.0996	38.33	− 3.18	50.00	20.90	52.78	11.76
31	11.6310	55.00	11.89	75.00	44.40	55.56	19.81
32	11.7156	48.33	10.43	41.67	21.10	52.78	16.69
33	11.7051	45.00	1.53	41.67	21.50	41.67	13.73
34	12.0181	43.33	7.10	16.67	8.20	38.89	6.97
35	11.8381	45.00	2.60	50.00	24.00	50.00	13.63
36	11.4763	51.67	10.93	75.00	44.00	55.56	18.57
37	12.6894	40.00	− 3.31	41.67	25.20	47.22	10.11
38	12.7283	40.00	9.02	25.00	8.40	47.22	7.49
39	12.6358	41.67	− 0.77	58.33	28.40	52.78	9.03
40	13.4683	40.00	12.15	25.00	14.40	41.67	6.68
41	12.7641	38.33	− 0.90	50.00	24.60	52.78	8.91
42	12.7009	36.67	− 3.61	33.33	19.40	47.22	9.36
43	12.9005	50.00	8.21	66.67	38.10	52.78	10.52
44	12.0115	36.67	− 3.20	58.33	28.40	52.78	9.03
45	12.7465	38.33	− 0.90	58.33	28.40	52.78	9.03
46	12.7614	30.00	− 9.24	58.33	37.80	50.00	12.11

Continued on next page

Table 14.12 *(continued)*

Rule #	Fitness	1984–1988 Period		1989		1989–1991 Period	
		% Correct	Average Return	% Correct	Average Return	% Correct	Average Return
47	12.8637	30.00	− 9.24	58.33	37.80	50.00	12.11
48	12.6926	38.33	3.00	41.67	22.00	47.22	11.76
49	12.4082	41.67	− 0.46	66.67	36.60	52.78	16.72
50	12.4439	40.00	0.18	41.67	22.00	44.44	9.03
51	13.3965	35.00	− 2.37	41.67	22.00	47.22	13.88
52	12.3309	36.67	− 5.52	41.67	22.00	50.00	11.98
53	12.2123	41.67	− 1.93	58.33	32.10	47.22	9.78
54	12.4082	43.33	− 0.51	58.33	32.10	55.56	13.60
55	11.9429	38.33	− 0.90	58.33	28.40	52.78	9.03
56	12.1106	53.33	14.34	83.33	40.50	50.00	11.23
57	12.6251	41.67	0.50	66.67	30.90	52.78	8.83
58	12.3442	36.67	− 6.38	58.33	24.70	52.78	10.93
59	12.2867	41.67	− 0.30	50.00	29.00	47.22	13.13
60	12.7187	45.00	8.32	41.67	21.10	55.56	16.20
61	12.5879	41.67	− 0.30	50.00	29.00	47.22	13.13
62	12.2578	41.67	0.40	33.33	11.70	44.44	7.38
63	12.3290	45.00	− 2.70	33.33	20.10	41.67	13.78
64	12.4082	33.33	− 6.02	58.33	30.20	50.00	9.59
65	11.7244	43.33	− 5.95	66.67	30.50	52.78	18.95
66	11.7411	40.00	1.31	75.00	36.90	61.11	21.01
67	12.6371	40.00	− 3.91	83.33	44.70	63.89	27.92
68	11.7473	45.00	10.48	66.67	36.60	58.33	20.28
69	12.3965	35.00	− 2.55	66.67	36.60	55.56	22.94
70	12.5128	53.33	8.42	75.00	44.40	50.00	19.93
71	12.0713	45.00	4.48	58.33	34.00	61.11	24.05
72	12.7468	36.67	− 4.61	83.33	44.70	72.22	32.19
73	11.8497	46.67	6.47	66.67	36.60	55.56	23.27
74	12.0691	33.33	− 3.87	66.67	34.30	72.22	29.45
75	12.3694	50.00	7.14	75.00	44.40	61.11	25.74
76	12.5520	40.00	− 1.34	75.00	42.40	47.22	11.33
77	11.7421	43.33	7.10	50.00	24.20	50.00	11.31
78	12.6040	38.33	− 1.78	50.00	20.90	52.78	11.76
79	12.4374	45.00	3.37	66.67	34.10	55.56	13.65
80	12.7983	56.67	13.15	75.00	44.40	55.56	20.71
81	12.3720	43.33	− 2.41	83.33	44.70	63.89	22.43
82	12.4346	55.00	11.89	75.00	44.40	52.78	19.56
83	12.4073	43.33	7.10	16.67	8.20	38.89	6.97
84	12.3626	43.33	1.15	33.33	16.00	41.67	8.80
85	12.5617	51.67	10.93	75.00	44.40	55.56	18.57
86	11.9159	38.33	− 0.75	41.67	27.90	50.00	18.52
87	11.7964	50.00	4.60	75.00	44.40	58.33	24.95
88	11.3249	46.67	6.47	66.67	36.60	55.56	23.27
89	11.5690	43.33	2.20	58.33	34.00	63.89	24.40
90	11.6512	40.00	− 0.20	41.67	27.90	50.00	15.78
91	11.8439	43.33	− 1.68	50.00	20.90	50.00	9.83
92	11.7831	56.67	16.55	83.33	44.70	47.22	9.86

Continued on next page

Table 14.12 *(continued)*

Rule #	Fitness	1984–1988 Period		1989		1989–1991 Period	
		% Correct	Average Return	% Correct	Average Return	% Correct	Average Return
93	12.2756	40.00	−1.65	50.00	20.90	52.78	11.76
94	12.0441	53.33	8.42	75.00	44.40	50.00	19.93
95	11.5380	55.00	11.89	75.00	44.40	52.78	17.49
96	11.9784	46.67	5.71	41.67	21.10	50.00	15.95
97	11.3491	55.00	11.89	75.00	44.40	50.00	17.25
98	11.6364	36.67	5.37	16.67	8.20	38.89	7.95
99	11.8925	45.00	1.06	50.00	24.00	47.22	13.75
100	12.1898	45.00	10.14	75.00	44.40	66.67	24.50
101	11.7514	35.00	−5.67	50.00	20.90	52.78	11.76
102	11.8717	56.67	16.55	83.33	44.70	47.22	9.86
103	12.0113	38.33	3.83	33.33	13.60	47.22	8.97
104	12.2283	43.33	2.69	41.67	15.90	47.22	8.26
105	11.7623	55.00	11.89	75.00	44.40	55.56	19.81
106	11.6019	48.33	10.06	33.33	16.00	47.22	14.09
107	11.8102	45.00	1.81	66.67	36.60	52.78	20.92
108	11.9226	48.33	8.59	33.33	10.50	38.89	3.57
109	11.8381	45.00	2.60	50.00	24.00	50.00	13.63
110	11.5626	46.67	6.47	66.67	36.60	58.33	23.20
111	11.5113	48.33	8.49	75.00	44.40	50.00	14.27
112	11.7265	48.33	6.85	25.00	8.40	50.00	12.45
113	12.0951	43.33	−0.55	33.33	15.60	38.89	11.87
114	12.2209	46.67	3.75	25.00	10.30	41.67	8.15
115	12.1758	46.67	0.69	50.00	24.00	41.67	9.94
116	12.1938	43.33	6.56	75.00	44.40	66.67	24.50
117	11.7215	43.33	7.10	16.67	8.20	38.89	6.97
118	12.4430	48.33	2.20	50.00	24.00	47.22	13.29
119	11.5521	33.33	−2.24	33.33	13.40	52.78	14.19
120	12.1956	51.67	10.93	75.00	44.40	61.11	23.49

cycle, and industrial production is slowing, then it is a good time to buy McDonald's stock. This rule seems to say that McDonald's is a good stock to own as the business cycle reaches a trough and starts climbing. Patterns in the McDonald's rule portfolios are more stable than those of IBM and Mobil. As shown in Figure 14.9, the average return shows a fairly stable increase over the 1984–1987 period, reaching a semistable plateau over the 1987–1990 period, after which time it began a rapid decline. Figure 14.10 illustrates that the percentage of correct calls climbed smoothly until mid–1988, when it began a minor downtrend. The drop took on greater speed after 1990. A user trying to assess the situation at the beginning of 1989 would have noticed that although the percentage of correct calls had its ups and downs, the average return looked fairly good. The behavior after 1989 showed a reversal in the effectiveness of the good rule port-

Table 14.13 Good Rules—McDonald's Stocks

Rule #	Logic Code	>/< Code	Cutoff Values			Fitness	Series Number and Differencing Interval					
			Series 1	Series 2	Series 3		1 #	Diff.	2 #	Diff.	3 #	Diff.
1	4	7	20	21	16	2.5989	234	3	228	1	229	3
2	2	7	24	13	25	2.4995	234	3	228	1	193	3
3	6	8	9	22	11	2.5991	234	3	228	1	61	0
4	4	7	21	21	12	2.6237	234	3	228	1	239	1
5	3	7	8	21	19	2.5736	234	3	228	1	225	12
6	2	5	14	28	17	2.3800	234	3	228	1	225	1
7	7	6	21	14	18	2.5020	234	3	228	1	71	3
8	6	6	10	21	25	2.5764	234	3	228	1	190	1
9	3	5	9	19	10	2.5825	234	3	229	3	193	3
10	6	7	13	15	11	2.7019	234	3	229	3	61	0
11	3	5	8	17	12	2.5666	234	3	229	3	239	1
12	6	5	14	16	17	2.5540	234	3	229	3	225	12
13	2	5	19	15	31	2.5060	234	3	229	3	225	1
14	8	5	14	16	1	2.4569	234	3	229	3	71	3
15	5	5	14	16	27	2.7003	234	3	229	3	190	1
16	2	6	19	24	9	2.4165	234	3	193	3	61	0
17	4	5	21	20	12	2.5384	234	3	193	3	239	1
18	3	5	9	17	18	2.5818	234	3	193	3	225	12
19	7	5	21	23	27	2.5619	234	3	193	3	225	1
20	7	1	27	24	17	2.2666	234	3	193	3	71	3
21	7	5	25	24	27	2.6112	234	3	193	3	190	1
22	4	5	19	10	12	2.5362	234	3	61	0	239	1
23	2	7	21	9	22	2.3994	234	3	61	0	225	12
24	4	7	13	11	16	2.6513	234	3	61	0	225	1
25	6	6	21	9	30	2.2846	234	3	61	0	71	3
26	6	6	9	22	25	2.3656	234	3	61	0	190	1
27	6	7	20	12	6	2.4773	234	3	239	1	225	12
28	8	5	31	12	16	2.6020	234	3	239	1	225	1
29	1	5	9	14	31	2.4596	234	3	239	1	71	3
30	2	5	21	12	27	2.6540	234	3	239	1	190	1
31	2	5	20	13	27	2.4290	234	3	225	12	225	1
32	4	5	12	17	10	2.3463	234	3	225	12	71	3
33	5	5	14	11	27	2.4276	234	3	225	12	190	1
34	8	5	21	14	18	2.4220	234	3	225	1	71	3
35	5	5	14	17	27	2.5872	234	3	225	1	190	1
36	6	5	21	18	31	2.3670	234	3	71	3	190	1
37	5	5	13	16	25	2.5359	228	1	229	3	193	3
38	6	7	14	16	11	2.7950	228	1	229	3	61	0
39	6	5	11	15	12	2.7110	228	1	229	3	239	1
40	6	5	14	15	17	2.6082	228	1	229	3	225	12
41	2	5	21	18	28	2.6134	228	1	229	3	225	1
42	6	7	21	16	0	2.5238	228	1	229	3	71	3
43	7	5	12	19	14	2.4963	228	1	229	3	190	1
44	3	6	14	21	18	2.5612	228	1	193	3	61	0
45	2	5	21	22	14	2.8596	228	1	193	3	239	1
46	2	5	21	24	20	2.6053	228	1	193	3	225	12

Continued on next page

Table 14.13 *(continued)*

Rule #	Logic Code	⟩/⟨ Code	Cutoff Values			Fitness	Series Number and Differencing Interval					
			Series 1	Series 2	Series 3		1 #	Diff.	2 #	Diff.	3 #	Diff.
47	2	5	21	23	27	2.6793	228	1	193	3	225	1
48	3	5	13	23	15	2.5236	228	1	193	3	71	3
49	4	5	14	23	14	2.5938	228	1	193	3	190	1
50	5	7	22	11	20	2.5594	228	1	61	0	239	1
51	3	7	14	12	19	2.4803	228	1	61	0	225	12
52	2	7	21	11	29	2.6620	228	1	61	0	225	1
53	3	7	13	9	24	2.5202	228	1	61	0	71	3
54	2	7	21	9	22	2.6305	228	1	61	0	190	1
55	8	5	21	12	10	2.6813	228	1	239	1	225	12
56	7	7	14	12	24	2.5969	228	1	239	1	225	1
57	8	5	24	12	3	2.6430	228	1	239	1	71	3
58	2	5	21	12	23	2.9016	228	1	239	1	190	1
59	2	5	21	17	27	2.5251	228	1	225	12	225	1
60	2	5	21	11	30	2.3568	228	1	225	12	71	3
61	2	5	21	18	22	2.5297	228	1	225	12	190	1
62	7	5	19	27	23	2.5811	228	1	225	1	71	3
63	6	5	7	17	25	2.3984	228	1	225	1	190	1
64	1	5	9	30	27	2.4985	228	1	71	3	190	1
65	2	1	16	18	19	2.5846	229	3	193	3	61	0
66	7	1	15	24	14	2.6918	229	3	193	3	239	1
67	8	1	16	18	1	2.5237	229	3	193	3	225	12
68	5	1	11	22	29	2.6200	229	3	193	3	225	1
69	6	3	15	18	10	2.5691	229	3	193	3	71	3
70	5	1	12	24	27	2.5480	229	3	193	3	190	1
71	8	3	15	24	12	2.5436	229	3	61	0	239	1
72	6	2	15	11	25	2.3356	229	3	61	0	225	12
73	2	3	16	11	29	2.6269	229	3	61	0	225	1
74	2	4	19	9	21	2.3547	229	3	61	0	71	3
75	2	3	15	9	21	2.5911	229	3	61	0	190	1
76	2	5	26	12	29	2.5153	229	3	239	1	225	12
77	5	1	17	12	28	2.5887	229	3	239	1	225	1
78	6	3	17	12	12	2.5396	229	3	239	1	71	3
79	2	1	16	12	21	2.7903	229	3	239	1	190	1
80	5	1	17	17	29	2.4377	229	3	225	12	225	1
81	8	1	17	13	18	2.4563	229	3	225	12	71	3
82	2	3	18	12	16	2.3922	229	3	225	12	190	1
83	8	1	17	17	13	2.4111	229	3	225	1	71	3
84	7	1	17	29	17	2.5204	229	3	225	1	190	1
85	7	1	18	31	21	2.5605	229	3	71	3	190	1
86	1	3	25	0	15	2.5740	193	3	61	0	239	1
87	8	3	24	19	10	2.3131	193	3	61	0	225	12
88	6	2	23	18	27	2.5388	193	3	61	0	225	1
89	3	4	24	3	12	2.3213	193	3	61	0	71	3
90	1	1	24	30	27	2.5257	193	3	61	0	190	1
91	7	1	22	16	11	2.5922	193	3	239	1	225	12
92	4	1	24	13	11	2.7656	193	3	239	1	225	1

Continued on next page

Table 14.13 *(continued)*

Rule #	Logic Code	⟩/⟨ Code	Cutoff Values				Series Number and Differencing Interval					
			Series 1	Series 2	Series 3	Fitness	1 #	Diff.	2 #	Diff.	3 #	Diff.
93	4	1	25	15	1	2.5740	193	3	239	1	71	3
94	7	1	24	15	14	2.6236	193	3	239	1	190	1
95	5	1	23	11	28	2.6373	193	3	225	12	225	1
96	8	1	19	13	13	2.3646	193	3	225	12	71	3
97	5	1	24	11	25	2.5860	193	3	225	12	190	1
98	4	1	24	27	3	2.4838	193	3	225	1	71	3
99	6	1	24	13	25	2.6454	193	3	225	1	190	1
100	5	1	24	3	27	2.5646	193	3	71	3	190	1
101	3	5	2	12	11	2.5029	61	0	239	1	225	12
102	4	5	11	13	14	2.5942	61	0	239	1	225	1
103	6	7	10	12	21	2.4343	61	0	239	1	71	3
104	2	5	21	12	25	2.5662	61	0	239	1	190	1
105	5	7	4	22	28	2.4113	61	0	225	12	225	1
106	2	6	12	16	11	2.2252	61	0	225	12	71	3
107	3	5	2	14	16	2.4327	61	0	225	12	190	1
108	2	6	11	19	14	2.4609	61	0	225	1	71	3
109	1	5	4	29	27	2.5394	61	0	225	1	190	1
110	6	5	9	17	21	2.3602	61	0	71	3	190	1
111	4	1	12	17	16	2.5961	239	1	225	12	225	1
112	3	2	12	31	21	2.4190	239	1	225	12	71	3
113	5	1	12	10	26	2.6134	239	1	225	12	190	1
114	2	2	12	16	11	2.5081	239	1	225	1	71	3
115	6	1	12	16	25	2.7613	239	1	225	1	190	1
116	1	3	12	2	25	2.5264	239	1	71	3	190	1
117	8	1	13	16	18	2.4737	225	12	225	1	71	3
118	7	1	17	27	16	2.5210	225	12	225	1	190	1
119	5	5	31	25	25	2.2188	225	12	71	3	190	1
120	7	1	15	30	22	2.3444	225	1	71	3	190	1

folio, as evinced by sharp declines in both the average return and percentage of correct calls.

The graphs for the bad rule portfolio are shown in Figures 14.11 and 14.12. Both graphs show a smooth decline followed by a slight flattening out in 1988. At the beginning of 1989, the patterns looked attractive; subsequently, average returns stabilized and an uptrend in the percentage of correct calls occurred.

In 1989, the good rule portfolio substantially outperformed the bad rule portfolio, earning 33.2 percent versus the latter's 23.9 percent. For the entire 1988–1991 period, both portfolios performed about equally, meaning that after 1990 the good rules got worse and the bad rules got better. McDonald's did extremely well in 1989. A buy-and-hold strategy would have earned 44.9 percent. For the entire 1988–1991 period, the buy-and-hold average annual return was 17.7 percent.

Table 14.14 Bad Rules—McDonald's Stock

Rule #	Logic Code	$\rangle/\langle$ Code	Cutoff Values			Fitness	Series Number and Differencing Interval					
			Series 1	Series 2	Series 3		1 #	Diff.	2 #	Diff.	3 #	Diff.
1	3	4	14	23	16	12.7173	234	3	228	1	229	3
2	4	1	14	19	7	12.3952	234	3	228	1	193	3
3	4	1	12	15	5	13.2306	234	3	228	1	61	0
4	2	2	10	23	12	12.9674	234	3	228	1	239	1
5	3	2	28	13	15	12.9050	234	3	228	1	225	12
6	5	4	14	28	15	13.0661	234	3	228	1	225	1
7	3	2	14	16	16	12.5090	234	3	228	1	71	3
8	5	4	15	31	6	12.3596	234	3	228	1	190	1
9	6	4	14	31	15	12.7756	234	3	229	3	193	3
10	7	2	13	15	11	13.0597	234	3	229	3	61	0
11	4	4	13	17	12	13.3773	234	3	229	3	239	1
12	4	4	14	16	22	13.5199	234	3	229	3	225	12
13	5	4	14	21	15	13.2184	234	3	229	3	225	1
14	2	3	15	22	30	12.5236	234	3	229	3	71	3
15	7	4	14	15	24	13.2583	234	3	229	3	190	1
16	2	1	11	27	5	13.1044	234	3	193	3	61	0
17	4	4	12	20	12	13.4743	234	3	193	3	239	1
18	5	2	15	10	10	12.9319	234	3	193	3	225	12
19	6	4	14	31	15	12.7534	234	3	193	3	225	1
20	4	4	13	18	22	12.7387	234	3	193	3	71	3
21	4	4	14	10	25	12.9331	234	3	193	3	190	1
22	5	1	11	5	22	13.2166	234	3	61	0	239	1
23	2	2	11	5	6	13.1747	234	3	61	0	225	12
24	5	2	13	5	15	13.2436	234	3	61	0	225	1
25	2	2	11	5	16	13.4615	234	3	61	0	71	3
26	5	2	10	5	10	13.2771	234	3	61	0	190	1
27	4	2	10	25	14	13.0343	234	3	239	1	225	12
28	5	4	11	12	14	13.3413	234	3	239	1	225	1
29	2	4	12	11	18	13.4521	234	3	239	1	71	3
30	5	4	10	12	7	13.1432	234	3	239	1	190	1
31	5	4	11	14	13	13.2515	234	3	225	12	225	1
32	4	4	12	4	22	12.8547	234	3	225	12	71	3
33	4	4	14	10	27	13.1716	234	3	225	12	190	1
34	2	4	13	17	18	12.9234	234	3	225	1	71	3
35	7	4	15	15	25	13.5613	234	3	225	1	190	1
36	4	4	15	10	25	13.0820	234	3	71	3	190	1
37	6	4	14	19	16	12.8855	228	1	229	3	193	3
38	4	3	13	15	5	13.1479	228	1	229	3	61	0
39	6	4	23	29	12	12.9432	228	1	229	3	239	1
40	4	4	13	7	15	12.9282	228	1	229	3	225	12
41	2	4	14	19	20	12.5179	228	1	229	3	225	1
42	7	4	15	15	20	12.6427	228	1	229	3	71	3
43	8	4	13	19	27	12.7018	228	1	229	3	190	1
44	2	1	14	27	6	12.8976	228	1	193	3	61	0
45	4	4	20	27	12	13.1083	228	1	193	3	239	1
46	8	4	6	24	16	12.9852	228	1	193	3	225	12

Continued on next page

Table 14.14 *(continued)*

Rule #	Logic Code	>/< Code	Cutoff Values			Fitness	Series Number and Differencing Interval					
			Series 1	Series 2	Series 3		1		2		3	
							#	Diff.	#	Diff.	#	Diff.
47	4	4	30	21	28	12.7944	228	1	193	3	225	1
48	4	4	13	15	20	12.4852	228	1	193	3	71	3
49	8	4	13	22	25	12.7193	228	1	193	3	190	1
50	5	1	14	5	22	12.9738	228	1	61	0	239	1
51	5	2	15	5	9	13.2912	228	1	61	0	225	12
52	2	2	14	11	19	13.4421	228	1	61	0	225	1
53	8	1	14	4	3	12.9320	228	1	61	0	71	3
54	5	2	13	4	10	13.0996	228	1	61	0	190	1
55	2	4	13	0	16	12.7144	228	1	239	1	225	12
56	7	4	15	12	19	12.9046	228	1	239	1	225	1
57	7	4	17	10	18	13.1039	228	1	239	1	71	3
58	5	4	9	12	7	12.6681	228	1	239	1	190	1
59	7	4	15	9	19	12.7298	228	1	225	12	225	1
60	5	4	14	15	10	13.1588	228	1	225	12	71	3
61	6	4	13	16	10	13.0150	228	1	225	12	190	1
62	7	4	14	15	20	12.6979	228	1	225	1	71	3
63	8	4	14	31	25	12.4003	228	1	225	1	190	1
64	8	4	13	25	25	12.8290	228	1	71	3	190	1
65	8	7	19	24	5	12.6865	229	3	193	3	61	0
66	8	8	22	22	12	13.0223	229	3	193	3	239	1
67	5	8	19	21	10	12.8018	229	3	193	3	225	12
68	5	8	29	21	15	12.6996	229	3	193	3	225	1
69	4	8	9	21	20	12.6882	229	3	193	3	71	3
70	3	8	15	21	22	12.3509	229	3	193	3	190	1
71	4	2	8	9	12	12.6645	229	3	61	0	239	1
72	5	6	15	5	6	12.4500	229	3	61	0	225	12
73	6	7	14	4	21	12.9649	229	3	61	0	225	1
74	5	6	18	5	12	12.4170	229	3	61	0	71	3
75	5	6	16	5	13	12.2028	229	3	61	0	190	1
76	4	8	7	12	18	12.7734	229	3	239	1	225	12
77	5	8	22	12	14	12.8730	229	3	239	1	225	1
78	7	6	10	12	15	12.6049	229	3	239	1	71	3
79	1	8	7	12	6	12.6138	229	3	239	1	190	1
80	5	8	16	19	19	12.7881	229	3	225	12	225	1
81	6	8	17	22	23	12.2805	229	3	225	12	71	3
82	1	8	16	10	13	12.4075	229	3	225	12	190	1
83	7	4	8	17	18	12.5344	229	3	225	1	71	3
84	3	8	15	22	22	12.8637	229	3	225	1	190	1
85	3	8	17	23	21	12.4444	229	3	71	3	190	1
86	2	6	24	19	12	12.9959	193	3	61	0	239	1
87	2	6	24	12	17	12.8308	193	3	61	0	225	12
88	5	6	21	4	15	12.7303	193	3	61	0	225	1
89	5	2	3	8	15	12.1143	193	3	61	0	71	3
90	2	6	24	5	9	12.7433	193	3	61	0	190	1
91	8	8	24	17	23	13.0745	193	3	239	1	225	12
92	4	8	21	3	25	12.5709	193	3	239	1	225	1

Continued on next page

Table 14.14 *(continued)*

Rule #	Logic Code	⟩/⟨ Code	Cutoff Values			Fitness	Series Number and Differencing Interval					
			Series 1	Series 2	Series 3		1 #	Diff.	2 #	Diff.	3 #	Diff.
93	6	8	22	12	15	13.1835	193	3	239	1	71	3
94	2	8	22	12	9	13.0582	193	3	239	1	190	1
95	5	8	21	14	15	13.0225	193	3	225	12	225	1
96	5	8	23	15	16	12.7698	193	3	225	12	71	3
97	6	8	24	17	9	12.6649	193	3	225	12	190	1
98	6	8	22	27	16	12.7097	193	3	225	1	71	3
99	8	8	22	27	25	12.8960	193	3	225	1	190	1
100	5	8	21	20	7	12.2153	193	3	71	3	190	1
101	4	4	18	12	18	12.9283	61	0	239	1	225	12
102	7	3	4	22	26	12.6923	61	0	239	1	225	1
103	6	4	5	12	16	12.8247	61	0	239	1	71	3
104	7	4	18	12	18	12.6000	61	0	239	1	190	1
105	7	4	5	8	26	12.7912	61	0	225	12	225	1
106	5	4	7	22	15	12.3956	61	0	225	12	71	3
107	7	4	5	9	22	12.5347	61	0	225	12	190	1
108	5	2	7	2	15	12.1143	61	0	225	1	71	3
109	5	4	4	25	10	12.7412	61	0	225	1	190	1
110	7	4	7	15	21	12.7578	61	0	71	3	190	1
111	5	8	12	17	14	13.2708	239	1	225	12	225	1
112	2	8	12	18	14	12.8414	239	1	225	12	71	3
113	6	8	12	18	8	12.9350	239	1	225	12	190	1
114	7	8	12	14	22	13.0131	239	1	225	1	71	3
115	1	8	12	11	7	12.9566	239	1	225	1	190	1
116	5	6	12	3	10	12.7519	239	1	71	3	190	1
117	3	8	13	23	18	12.9070	225	12	225	1	71	3
118	3	8	10	25	22	12.3352	225	12	225	1	190	1
119	2	8	18	18	21	12.3286	225	12	71	3	190	1
120	6	8	25	20	9	12.2920	225	1	71	3	190	1

Tables 14.15 and 14.16 show the detailed results for both portfolios. Fifteen of the good rules outperformed the buy-and-hold alternative over the entire 1988–1991 holdout period. Thirty of the bad rules outperformed the buy-and-hold strategy over that same period, which illustrates the dramatic reversal in the effectiveness of the two rule portfolios. Once again we see that users must be alert to changes in the underlying structure of the relationships. For McDonald's, the good rules continued to outperform the bad rules in 1989, but this situation reversed later. The main condition needed for money-making with timing strategies is consistency. Reversals can be tolerated if they lead to another trend. We will have more to say about this in Chapter 15.

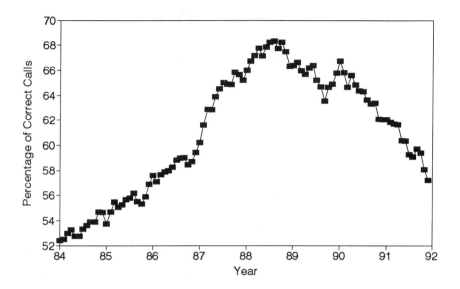

FIGURE 14.9 Percentage of Correct Calls (McDonald's—Good Rules) 1984–1991

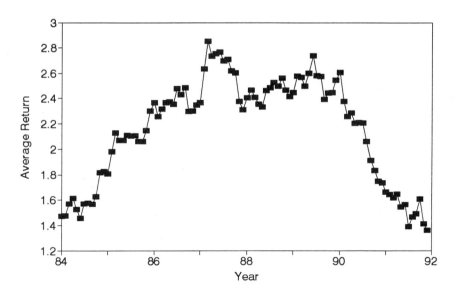

FIGURE 14.10 Average Return (McDonald's—Good Rules) 1984–1991

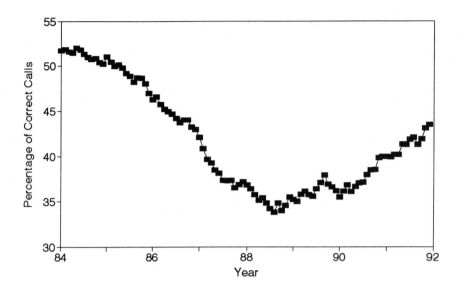

FIGURE 14.11   Percentage of Correct Calls (McDonald's—Bad Rules) 1984–1991

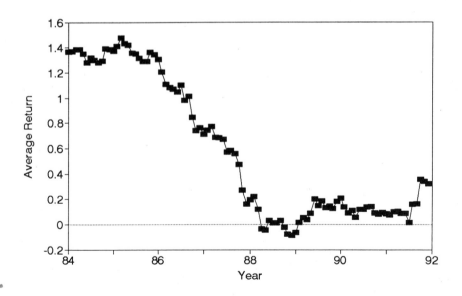

FIGURE 14.12   Average Return (McDonald's—Bad Rules) 1984–1991

Table 14.15 Performance Summary: Good Rules—McDonald's Stock

Rule #	Fitness	1984–1988 Period		1989		1989–1991 Period	
		% Correct	Average Return	% Correct	Average Return	% Correct	Average Return
1	2.5989	350.00	14.45	58.33	33.70	44.44	12.79
2	2.4995	66.67	27.70	358.33	29.60	58.33	15.51
3	2.5991	65.00	28.95	66.67	37.10	58.33	16.74
4	2.6237	50.00	12.37	41.67	24.10	38.89	11.68
5	2.5736	66.67	27.81	75.00	44.90	58.33	16.74
6	2.3800	55.00	22.57	75.00	53.30	50.00	18.78
7	2.5020	63.33	26.58	50.00	23.20	52.78	14.95
8	2.5764	63.33	28.68	66.67	43.30	58.33	20.48
9	2.5825	70.00	37.68	75.00	44.90	58.33	12.92
10	2.7019	68.33	31.71	66.67	43.30	55.56	17.45
11	2.5666	65.00	31.46	75.00	44.90	58.33	11.49
12	2.5540	66.67	32.73	66.67	43.30	55.56	9.28
13	2.5060	68.33	38.29	66.67	43.30	58.33	17.33
14	2.4569	70.00	40.06	66.67	43.30	52.78	13.39
15	2.7003	70.00	40.06	66.67	43.30	55.56	13.81
16	2.4165	66.67	32.86	75.00	50.50	52.78	16.05
17	2.5384	58.33	17.89	16.67	0.90	41.67	2.66
18	2.5818	66.67	25.43	25.00	1.30	50.00	9.72
19	2.5619	66.67	30.69	41.67	12.70	41.67	2.76
20	2.2666	65.00	30.09	58.33	28.80	44.44	4.74
21	2.6112	68.33	31.79	58.33	28.80	44.44	4.74
22	2.5362	38.33	0.77	41.67	15.10	52.78	9.45
23	2.3994	66.67	32.64	75.00	44.90	55.56	16.67
24	2.6513	60.00	25.05	75.00	44.90	61.11	20.51
25	2.2846	65.00	32.25	75.00	44.90	52.78	17.69
26	2.3656	61.67	27.92	75.00	44.90	52.78	17.69
27	2.4773	71.67	38.02	41.67	27.80	44.44	12.92
28	2.6020	63.33	26.19	58.33	31.30	50.00	13.93
29	2.4596	66.67	33.31	41.67	19.80	47.22	10.85
30	2.6540	70.00	37.39	41.67	27.80	44.44	12.92
31	2.4290	71.67	34.89	66.67	36.20	55.56	21.94
32	2.3463	73.33	40.31	75.00	44.90	55.56	16.74
33	2.4276	66.67	37.20	75.00	44.90	52.78	15.35
34	2.4220	63.33	29.41	41.67	25.50	44.44	12.06
35	2.5872	70.00	40.23	41.67	25.50	47.22	12.79
36	2.3670	63.33	31.13	58.33	34.80	47.22	11.25
37	2.5359	68.33	31.01	75.00	44.90	66.67	22.72
38	2.7950	68.33	31.01	75.00	44.90	61.11	20.87
39	2.7110	61.67	30.81	58.33	33.40	55.56	15.98
40	2.6082	66.67	32.73	75.00	44.90	61.11	13.57
41	2.6134	70.00	35.28	75.00	44.90	52.78	10.77
42	2.5238	70.00	37.51	66.67	43.30	55.56	12.66
43	2.4963	75.00	40.47	66.67	37.10	61.11	15.80
44	2.5612	66.67	28.87	58.33	29.80	61.11	20.23
45	2.8596	63.33	26.87	25.00	11.60	50.00	13.99
46	2.6053	73.33	34.93	41.67	15.40	58.33	16.74

Continued on next page

Table 14.15 *(continued)*

| Rule # | Fitness | 1984–1988 Period | | 1989 | | 1989–1991 Period | |
		% Correct	Average Return	% Correct	Average Return	% Correct	Average Return
47	2.6793	68.33	33.31	58.33	28.80	52.78	15.51
48	2.5236	75.00	36.16	25.00	1.00	44.44	0.46
49	2.5938	73.33	34.93	25.00	1.00	47.22	2.69
50	2.5594	70.00	32.86	75.00	48.40	58.33	14.06
51	2.4803	66.67	28.87	58.33	29.80	61.11	20.23
52	2.6620	71.67	34.50	75.00	48.40	55.56	17.61
53	2.5202	66.67	28.87	58.33	29.80	61.11	20.23
54	2.6305	65.00	31.90	75.00	44.90	55.56	16.67
55	2.6813	73.33	40.20	41.67	26.10	44.44	12.43
56	2.5969	70.00	38.24	33.33	17.60	52.78	12.24
57	2.6430	73.33	40.20	50.00	29.40	44.44	9.97
58	2.9016	73.33	40.20	41.67	26.10	44.44	12.43
59	2.5251	65.00	29.58	75.00	44.90	55.56	19.11
60	2.3568	68.33	34.79	66.67	34.40	58.33	21.60
61	2.5297	65.00	29.13	75.00	44.90	52.78	17.69
62	2.5811	58.33	25.41	58.33	35.80	44.44	11.60
63	2.3984	58.33	27.38	50.00	28.50	47.22	11.15
64	2.4985	63.33	31.47	66.67	37.10	55.56	15.10
65	2.5846	75.00	38.80	66.67	34.80	58.33	17.01
66	2.6918	66.67	33.97	41.67	18.60	50.00	10.87
67	2.5237	75.00	38.80	66.67	34.80	58.33	17.01
68	2.6200	70.00	34.15	41.67	12.70	52.78	9.81
69	2.5691	71.67	38.00	66.67	34.80	55.56	16.96
70	2.5480	68.33	32.64	58.33	28.80	47.22	8.26
71	2.5436	50.00	16.25	58.33	33.40	50.00	20.87
72	2.3356	71.67	35.70	75.00	44.90	52.78	17.69
73	2.6269	71.67	35.70	75.00	44.90	58.33	17.03
74	2.3547	66.67	31.21	75.00	44.90	52.78	17.69
75	2.5911	61.67	30.36	75.00	44.90	61.11	17.93
76	2.5153	68.33	36.12	33.33	17.60	41.67	6.12
77	2.5887	68.33	35.79	75.00	44.90	50.00	10.90
78	2.5396	68.33	35.79	75.00	44.90	50.00	10.90
79	2.7903	70.00	39.53	66.67	43.30	47.22	10.49
80	2.4377	65.00	30.24	75.00	44.90	55.56	19.11
81	2.4563	63.33	27.63	75.00	44.90	52.78	17.69
82	2.3922	66.67	33.36	75.00	44.90	52.78	8.83
83	2.4111	70.00	35.17	75.00	44.90	55.56	10.25
84	2.5204	71.67	38.90	66.67	37.20	52.78	8.26
85	2.5605	60.00	28.55	75.00	44.90	52.78	12.37
86	2.5740	53.33	15.33	66.67	28.30	61.11	13.47
87	2.3131	61.67	22.99	58.33	28.80	47.22	10.36
88	2.5388	66.67	30.69	41.67	12.70	41.67	5.55
89	2.3213	68.33	31.79	58.33	28.80	44.44	4.74
90	2.5257	68.33	31.79	58.33	28.80	52.78	3.66
91	2.5922	68.33	33.97	41.67	18.40	41.67	3.17
92	2.7656	66.67	33.90	25.00	12.70	36.11	1.51

Continued on next page

Table 14.15 *(continued)*

Rule #	Fitness	1984–1988 Period		1989		1989–1991 Period	
		% Correct	Average Return	% Correct	Average Return	% Correct	Average Return
93	2.5740	73.33	37.77	66.67	42.20	50.00	12.00
94	2.6236	65.00	28.24	66.67	42.20	52.78	17.01
95	2.6373	68.33	32.11	58.33	26.30	47.22	10.85
96	2.3646	68.33	32.69	66.67	36.20	50.00	13.68
97	2.5860	70.00	33.27	66.67	34.40	47.22	10.33
98	2.4838	70.00	36.51	50.00	22.00	47.22	3.35
99	2.6454	68.33	36.88	41.67	20.70	44.44	4.16
100	2.5646	66.67	30.91	58.33	28.80	50.00	6.35
101	2.5029	68.33	36.12	33.33	17.60	38.89	3.82
102	2.5942	63.33	28.16	41.67	19.80	44.44	10.52
103	2.4343	66.67	35.50	33.33	17.60	36.11	3.79
104	2.5662	68.33	37.38	33.33	17.60	41.67	12.06
105	2.4113	61.67	28.93	75.00	44.90	52.78	17.69
106	2.2252	63.33	29.47	66.67	45.00	50.00	17.74
107	2.4327	65.00	31.83	75.00	44.90	52.78	14.50
108	2.4609	66.67	30.27	75.00	48.40	52.78	18.64
109	2.5394	65.00	35.19	66.67	37.20	55.56	16.13
110	2.3602	60.00	29.18	66.67	36.20	50.00	10.11
111	2.5961	65.00	30.45	75.00	44.90	52.78	14.50
112	2.4190	68.33	36.12	33.33	17.60	38.89	3.82
113	2.6134	70.00	38.20	66.67	29.70	47.22	6.88
114	2.5081	66.67	36.08	33.33	16.40	36.11	2.06
115	2.7613	68.33	38.04	33.33	16.40	38.89	2.34
116	2.5264	65.00	34.49	33.33	17.60	47.22	7.78
117	2.4737	70.00	32.76	75.00	44.90	58.33	24.83
118	2.5210	70.00	37.96	66.67	37.20	58.33	17.54
119	2.2188	56.67	24.42	75.00	44.90	55.56	16.91
120	2.3444	63.33	31.64	75.00	44.90	50.00	11.12

TIMING RULES FOR CONSOLIDATED EDISON

The good and bad rule portfolios for Consolidated Edison are shown in Tables 14.17 and 14.18. The best rule for Consolidated Edison, Rule 89, averaged 21.12 percent annually over the test period. It says to invest in Consolidated Edison when (the 3-month change in labor cost is not in the lower third of its range *and* the 3-month change in industrial production is in the upper half of its range) *or* the 3-month change in the diffusion index of lagging indicators is in the upper half of its range. This rule seems to point towards a "peak of the business cycle" strategy. If labor costs and industrial production are up, then the business cycle is near a peak. When the diffusion index of lagging indicators is up, the business cycle is probably in or just past its peak. It seems logical that Consolidated Edison might do better in this phase of the business cycle.

Table 14.16 Performance Summary: Bad Rules—McDonald's Stock

Rule #	Fitness	1984–1988 Period		1989		1989–1991 Period	
		% Correct	Average Return	% Correct	Average Return	% Correct	Average Return
1	12.7173	46.67	4.61	25.00	2.40	52.78	10.08
2	12.3952	35.00	−5.74	50.00	14.10	50.00	10.38
3	13.2306	33.33	−1.74	25.00	8.40	38.89	4.77
4	12.9674	41.67	5.63	66.67	32.10	58.33	16.84
5	12.9050	48.33	14.42	66.67	38.90	52.78	17.54
6	13.0661	58.33	13.03	33.33	3.50	58.33	14.93
7	12.5090	38.33	−3.18	50.00	14.10	52.78	11.44
8	12.3596	46.67	5.63	41.67	7.90	50.00	7.38
9	12.7756	31.67	−8.45	33.33	9.50	47.22	11.33
10	13.0597	31.67	−2.68	33.33	9.50	44.44	7.49
11	13.3773	46.67	6.50	75.00	43.70	50.00	12.53
12	13.5199	26.67	−9.74	33.33	9.50	41.67	9.67
13	13.2184	28.33	−9.71	33.33	9.50	44.44	14.09
14	12.5236	35.00	−4.53	50.00	14.10	47.22	9.78
15	13.2583	30.00	−8.77	33.33	9.50	41.67	9.67
16	13.1044	38.33	0.16	33.33	9.50	41.67	4.77
17	13.4743	55.00	17.97	75.00	51.60	55.56	20.35
18	12.8319	38.33	−3.18	58.33	23.60	50.00	8.12
19	12.7534	35.00	−3.70	66.67	33.20	52.78	10.87
20	12.7387	30.00	−4.41	58.33	39.30	44.44	15.90
21	12.9331	35.00	−2.86	66.67	33.20	52.78	13.47
22	13.2166	33.33	−6.73	33.33	9.50	50.00	7.64
23	13.1747	36.67	−0.40	33.33	9.50	41.67	4.77
24	13.2436	36.67	0.67	25.00	8.40	38.89	4.77
25	13.4615	36.67	−0.40	33.33	9.50	41.67	4.77
26	13.2771	38.33	1.46	33.33	9.50	41.67	4.77
27	13.0343	31.67	−4.44	66.67	32.40	52.78	11.76
28	13.3413	36.67	0.00	58.33	31.00	55.56	14.22
29	13.4521	31.67	−1.10	25.00	1.10	36.11	0.30
30	13.1432	33.33	−4.95	66.67	33.50	55.56	18.57
31	13.2515	35.00	−3.50	33.33	15.20	52.78	15.03
32	12.8547	26.67	−5.52	25.00	1.10	41.67	4.68
33	13.1716	31.67	−7.40	33.33	13.00	52.78	14.95
34	12.9234	38.33	−0.08	66.67	33.80	55.56	11.71
35	13.5613	31.67	−8.09	66.67	30.50	55.56	13.52
36	13.0820	40.00	−3.91	50.00	14.10	52.78	12.58
37	12.8855	25.00	−8.77	25.00	8.40	36.11	7.03
38	13.1479	33.33	−1.21	25.00	8.40	38.89	4.43
39	12.9432	38.33	−0.73	75.00	39.60	52.78	13.16
40	12.9282	40.00	−0.40	58.33	31.30	44.44	9.45
41	12.5179	31.67	−1.91	41.67	20.90	36.11	7.61
42	12.6427	31.67	−3.02	25.00	8.40	36.11	7.03
43	12.7018	26.67	−7.26	41.67	20.90	36.11	7.61
44	12.8976	35.00	0.02	41.67	20.90	38.89	5.01
45	13.1083	55.00	17.97	75.00	51.60	55.56	20.35
46	12.9852	41.67	7.16	83.33	56.60	58.33	19.14

Continued on next page

Table 14.16 *(continued)*

Rule #	Fitness	1984–1988 Period		1989		1989–1991 Period	
		% Correct	Average Return	% Correct	Average Return	% Correct	Average Return
47	12.7944	28.33	− 3.29	66.67	47.10	47.22	18.00
48	12.4852	28.33	− 1.02	75.00	55.40	47.22	19.98
49	12.7193	26.67	− 5.62	75.00	55.40	50.00	22.63
50	12.9738	30.00	− 6.86	41.67	20.90	44.44	5.55
51	13.2912	36.67	3.49	50.00	26.10	38.89	5.13
52	13.4421	33.33	− 0.55	41.67	20.90	38.89	5.01
53	12.9320	30.00	− 6.86	41.67	20.90	38.89	5.01
54	13.0996	33.33	0.42	41.67	20.90	38.89	5.01
55	12.7144	30.00	− 3.04	58.33	33.50	41.67	6.30
56	12.9046	31.67	− 0.81	41.67	20.90	50.00	11.20
57	13.1039	30.00	− 0.42	58.33	27.50	50.00	8.66
58	12.6681	31.67	− 5.37	66.67	33.50	58.33	21.24
59	12.7298	26.67	− 7.86	50.00	26.10	52.78	12.24
60	13.1588	28.33	− 7.64	25.00	8.40	44.44	9.67
61	13.0150	28.33	− 7.64	25.00	8.40	44.44	9.67
62	12.6979	36.67	− 1.63	66.67	41.60	58.33	15.43
63	12.4003	36.67	− 0.63	50.00	22.20	41.67	5.37
64	12.8290	33.33	− 4.34	41.67	20.90	33.33	3.42
65	12.6865	26.67	− 5.92	41.67	21.90	50.00	21.10
66	13.0223	55.00	17.97	75.00	51.60	55.56	22.54
67	12.8018	26.67	− 4.61	66.67	47.10	41.67	17.35
68	12.6996	30.00	− 2.09	66.67	47.10	47.22	18.00
69	12.6882	31.67	1.79	75.00	55.40	50.00	20.21
70	12.3509	30.00	− 6.02	33.33	16.50	44.44	12.66
71	12.6645	61.67	27.19	58.33	36.40	47.22	15.35
72	12.4500	40.00	3.71	41.67	17.70	44.44	8.86
73	12.9649	41.67	0.71	25.00	8.40	38.89	7.06
74	12.4170	45.00	9.20	25.00	8.40	44.44	16.79
75	12.2028	43.33	6.58	33.33	16.50	41.67	12.90
76	12.7734	31.67	− 5.84	66.67	33.50	61.11	19.58
77	12.8730	36.67	0.00	58.33	31.00	55.56	14.22
78	12.6049	30.00	− 6.99	66.67	33.50	61.11	21.60
79	12.6138	31.67	− 5.84	66.67	33.50	61.11	19.58
80	12.7881	36.67	0.42	25.00	8.40	47.22	7.26
81	12.2805	38.33	3.99	25.00	8.40	47.22	7.26
82	12.4075	33.33	− 3.50	25.00	8.40	41.67	4.83
83	12.5344	38.33	0.14	75.00	45.00	61.11	16.84
84	12.8637	33.33	− 4.13	41.67	17.70	52.78	12.24
85	12.4444	36.67	− 2.30	25.00	8.40	47.22	12.35
86	12.9959	51.67	15.61	58.33	36.40	61.11	24.53
87	12.8308	31.67	− 2.75	41.67	21.90	55.56	20.53
88	12.7303	38.33	4.66	33.33	16.50	36.11	9.20
89	12.1143	43.33	7.10	25.00	8.40	47.22	7.26
90	12.7433	31.67	− 2.75	41.67	21.90	55.56	20.53
91	13.0745	26.67	− 7.13	41.67	21.90	55.56	22.96
92	12.5709	28.33	− 3.06	66.67	47.10	52.78	21.98

Continued on next page

Table 14.16 *(continued)*

Rule #	Fitness	1984–1988 Period		1989		1989–1991 Period	
		% Correct	Average Return	% Correct	Average Return	% Correct	Average Return
93	13.1835	31.67	− 5.84	66.67	33.50	61.11	21.60
94	13.0582	28.33	− 7.51	83.33	49.70	58.33	26.29
95	13.0225	38.33	− 0.34	25.00	8.40	47.22	10.25
96	12.7698	36.67	− 1.21	25.00	8.40	47.22	10.25
97	12.6649	28.33	− 5.97	41.67	21.90	52.78	14.65
98	12.7097	30.00	− 7.51	58.33	38.30	52.78	20.21
99	12.8960	33.33	− 4.61	75.00	48.60	52.78	23.53
100	12.2153	30.00	− 3.08	66.67	47.10	50.00	22.87
101	12.9283	31.67	− 6.70	66.67	33.50	58.33	14.95
102	12.6923	40.00	0.30	25.00	8.40	47.22	7.26
103	12.8247	31.67	− 5.84	66.67	33.50	61.11	21.60
104	12.6000	31.67	− 6.70	66.67	33.50	58.33	14.95
105	12.7912	38.33	− 0.59	25.00	8.40	47.22	7.26
106	12.3956	35.00	− 2.86	25.00	8.40	47.22	7.26
107	12.5347	35.00	− 2.61	25.00	8.40	47.22	7.26
108	12.1143	38.33	− 1.55	25.00	8.40	47.22	7.26
109	12.7412	36.67	− 5.14	41.67	15.60	50.00	11.49
110	12.7578	41.67	− 0.53	33.33	15.20	50.00	14.67
111	13.2708	33.33	− 2.88	33.33	15.20	52.78	15.03
112	12.8414	30.00	− 6.26	66.67	33.50	61.11	21.60
113	12.9350	31.67	− 6.23	58.33	29.00	58.33	18.21
114	13.0131	30.00	− 3.73	83.33	54.10	66.67	26.20
115	12.9566	26.67	− 7.89	66.67	33.50	61.11	21.60
116	12.7519	33.33	− 5.34	66.67	33.50	61.11	19.58
117	12.9070	30.00	− 3.47	25.00	8.40	41.67	1.12
118	12.3352	36.67	− 1.38	33.33	16.90	47.22	7.46
119	12.3286	40.00	− 0.59	33.33	15.20	50.00	14.67
120	12.2920	40.00	− 4.46	50.00	23.00	52.78	16.96

Utility stocks tend to be stable. E. E. Peters's results (1991) bear this out, with a cycle length for Consolidated Edison of 90 months. The percentage of correct calls and average return graphs for the good rule portfolio are shown in Figures 14.13 and 14.14. Both are quite stable in comparison to the other three stocks. The percentage of correct calls rose sharply to a plateau that lasted throughout most of the 1986–1989 period. After 1990, the good rule portfolio experienced a sharp decline in accuracy, but despite periods of change, the transitions were smooth. The average return graph displays a similar pattern but without a wide plateau; it peaked in 1987 and then enters a gradual decline. Going into 1989, this pattern of decline in average return was somewhat worrisome, but the percentage of correct calls was still high and had only dipped slightly.

Turning to the graphs for the bad rule portfolio, we see similar, stable patterns. Figure 14.15 shows the percentage correct calls smoothly declining and then

Table 14.17 Good Rules—Consolidated Edison Stock

Rule #	Logic Code	)/(Code	Cutoff Values			Fitness	Series Number and Differencing Interval					
			Series 1	Series 2	Series 3		**1**		**2**		**3**	
							#	Diff.	#	Diff.	#	Diff.
1	4	5	17	16	19	2.3091	57	0	5	1	23	3
2	5	8	23	20	9	2.5520	57	0	5	1	61	3
3	6	5	23	16	20	2.1066	57	0	5	1	71	3
4	8	5	25	14	23	2.0475	57	0	5	1	77	3
5	8	6	29	14	20	2.3581	57	0	5	1	173	3
6	8	5	29	14	18	2.2270	57	0	5	1	229	3
7	4	6	7	18	20	2.2942	57	0	5	1	234	3
8	6	6	23	20	17	2.4271	57	0	5	1	193	12
9	5	6	23	14	9	2.4802	57	0	23	3	61	3
10	8	5	29	18	11	2.2566	57	0	23	3	71	3
11	8	5	29	18	13	2.1868	57	0	23	3	77	3
12	5	2	26	19	9	2.4377	57	0	23	3	173	3
13	8	5	30	14	18	2.2436	57	0	23	3	229	3
14	8	2	17	14	21	2.4926	57	0	23	3	234	3
15	5	1	1	23	17	2.5648	57	0	23	3	193	12
16	7	8	19	9	7	2.3719	57	0	61	3	71	3
17	7	6	24	9	23	2.5084	57	0	61	3	77	3
18	2	4	4	10	10	2.4639	57	0	61	3	173	3
19	6	8	25	13	27	2.4524	57	0	61	3	229	3
20	6	8	7	13	22	2.5560	57	0	61	3	234	3
21	4	5	28	19	17	2.3974	57	0	61	3	193	12
22	7	5	23	20	22	2.1294	57	0	71	3	77	3
23	8	6	29	11	16	2.3385	57	0	71	3	173	3
24	8	1	16	11	18	2.3010	57	0	71	3	229	3
25	6	7	25	18	14	2.3364	57	0	71	3	234	3
26	4	5	27	16	17	2.4145	57	0	71	3	193	12
27	6	7	19	20	16	2.3597	57	0	77	3	173	3
28	4	7	25	27	18	2.4061	57	0	77	3	229	3
29	6	7	23	21	21	2.2670	57	0	77	3	234	3
30	2	5	28	29	17	2.5042	57	0	77	3	193	12
31	4	7	23	23	18	2.4934	57	0	173	3	229	3
32	8	4	4	20	22	2.3578	57	0	173	3	234	3
33	1	7	1	10	17	2.5119	57	0	173	3	193	12
34	6	7	7	18	21	2.6688	57	0	229	3	234	3
35	5	5	25	19	17	2.4585	57	0	229	3	193	12
36	4	7	25	12	16	2.4857	57	0	234	3	193	12
37	2	2	14	23	10	2.5134	5	1	23	3	61	3
38	5	1	16	19	27	2.2953	5	1	23	3	71	3
39	8	1	16	19	18	2.3043	5	1	23	3	77	3
40	8	2	14	14	20	2.4262	5	1	23	3	173	3
41	8	1	14	14	18	2.2485	5	1	23	3	229	3
42	6	7	11	19	22	2.4577	5	1	23	3	234	3
43	7	5	20	23	17	2.6220	5	1	23	3	193	12
44	5	4	15	9	6	2.3735	5	1	61	3	71	3
45	5	4	14	13	5	2.3716	5	1	61	3	77	3
46	4	8	5	11	20	2.3703	5	1	61	3	173	3

Continued on next page

Table 14.17 *(continued)*

Rule #	Logic Code	⟩/⟨ Code	Cutoff Values Series 1	Series 2	Series 3	Fitness	Series Number and Differencing Interval 1 #	Diff.	2 #	Diff.	3 #	Diff.
47	6	2	21	13	18	2.4438	5	1	61	3	229	3
48	6	8	13	13	21	2.5560	5	1	61	3	234	3
49	2	7	23	7	17	2.4332	5	1	61	3	193	12
50	6	1	18	18	23	2.1239	5	1	71	3	77	3
51	2	2	14	18	16	2.3717	5	1	71	3	173	3
52	8	1	16	17	18	2.3427	5	1	71	3	229	3
53	4	2	15	23	22	2.3823	5	1	71	3	234	3
54	4	7	23	12	17	2.3915	5	1	71	3	193	12
55	4	2	22	20	16	2.3283	5	1	77	3	173	3
56	7	1	14	24	18	2.2903	5	1	77	3	229	3
57	8	2	15	15	21	2.4453	5	1	77	3	234	3
58	5	1	16	29	17	2.5270	5	1	77	3	193	12
59	8	3	14	22	18	2.4509	5	1	173	3	229	3
60	2	4	15	16	9	2.5187	5	1	173	3	234	3
61	7	6	20	10	17	2.6303	5	1	173	3	193	12
62	3	2	31	18	21	2.6581	5	1	229	3	234	3
63	6	5	18	18	16	2.4566	5	1	229	3	193	12
64	8	7	23	31	17	2.3875	5	1	234	3	193	12
65	6	4	14	13	18	2.3928	23	3	61	3	71	3
66	6	4	24	13	27	2.4496	23	3	61	3	77	3
67	7	4	19	9	16	2.6215	23	3	61	3	173	3
68	8	4	11	13	27	2.5176	23	3	61	3	229	3
69	4	4	18	11	21	2.7058	23	3	61	3	234	3
70	1	3	23	10	17	2.6548	23	3	61	3	193	12
71	8	2	19	12	30	2.2651	23	3	71	3	77	3
72	2	2	19	21	15	2.3436	23	3	71	3	173	3
73	3	7	7	25	18	2.2792	23	3	71	3	229	3
74	3	2	23	15	12	2.5137	23	3	71	3	234	3
75	1	1	23	27	17	2.5970	23	3	71	3	193	12
76	7	4	14	5	20	2.3822	23	3	77	3	173	3
77	4	3	23	22	18	2.4033	23	3	77	3	229	3
78	4	2	18	21	21	2.6277	23	3	77	3	234	3
79	3	1	23	16	16	2.6083	23	3	77	3	193	12
80	4	3	27	23	18	2.4082	23	3	173	3	229	3
81	7	4	10	10	13	2.5680	23	3	173	3	234	3
82	5	3	19	16	17	2.6544	23	3	173	3	193	12
83	8	2	14	18	21	2.7065	23	3	229	3	234	3
84	6	1	23	1	17	2.5648	23	3	229	3	193	12
85	5	3	19	22	17	2.6710	23	3	234	3	193	12
86	4	7	10	7	0	2.3719	61	3	71	3	77	3
87	1	8	9	6	10	2.5193	61	3	71	3	173	3
88	7	8	13	3	27	2.4878	61	3	71	3	229	3
89	4	6	13	19	21	2.6248	61	3	71	3	234	3
90	1	7	10	4	23	2.4398	61	3	71	3	193	12
91	1	8	10	6	9	2.5084	61	3	77	3	173	3
92	4	6	13	29	27	2.5540	61	3	77	3	229	3

Continued on next page

Table 14.17 *(continued)*

Rule #	Logic Code	⟩/⟨ Code	Cutoff Values			Fitness	Series Number and Differencing Interval					
			Series 1	Series 2	Series 3		1 #	Diff.	2 #	Diff.	3 #	Diff.
93	4	6	11	23	21	2.6574	61	3	77	3	234	3
94	4	5	13	28	4	2.5618	61	3	77	3	193	12
95	7	6	14	9	15	2.5558	61	3	173	3	229	3
96	4	8	13	12	21	2.6891	61	3	173	3	234	3
97	6	6	11	20	16	2.5617	61	3	173	3	193	12
98	4	6	9	18	22	2.7409	61	3	229	3	234	3
99	4	5	11	19	5	2.6868	61	3	229	3	193	12
100	2	5	14	25	12	2.5247	61	3	234	3	193	12
101	4	6	5	20	17	2.3123	71	3	77	3	173	3
102	3	7	2	30	18	2.2575	71	3	77	3	229	3
103	6	3	28	16	13	2.3667	71	3	77	3	234	3
104	6	1	27	16	17	2.4127	71	3	77	3	193	12
105	3	7	2	23	18	2.4436	71	3	173	3	229	3
106	7	4	18	16	17	2.4421	71	3	173	3	234	3
107	4	3	18	18	17	2.4575	71	3	173	3	193	12
108	4	2	25	18	22	2.6920	71	3	229	3	234	3
109	1	5	2	29	17	2.3603	71	3	229	3	193	12
110	5	3	19	22	17	2.4498	71	3	234	3	193	12
111	4	7	19	16	18	2.4502	77	3	173	3	229	3
112	2	4	16	11	12	2.5560	77	3	173	3	234	3
113	5	3	15	10	17	2.5416	77	3	173	3	193	12
114	6	7	10	18	22	2.6581	77	3	229	3	234	3
115	5	3	29	27	17	2.4956	77	3	229	3	193	12
116	3	3	29	29	17	2.4227	77	3	234	3	193	12
117	4	6	13	18	22	2.7084	173	3	229	3	234	3
118	6	5	16	18	15	2.6405	173	3	229	3	193	12
119	3	7	10	20	17	2.5504	173	3	234	3	193	12
120	5	3	19	15	17	2.4587	229	3	234	3	193	12

bottoming out in 1988. There was a subsequent reversal, but at the bottom the percentage of correct calls was only averaging about 36 percent. This low percentage provides some cushion, as long as the change does not occur too abruptly. The pattern of average return is shown in Figure 14.16. There was little cause for concern at the beginning of 1989, and indeed the average return stayed down in the subsequent period.

The detailed performance of the two portfolios is reported in Tables 14.19. The buy-and-hold alternative would have earned 34.2 percent in 1989. The average return for the rules in the good rule portfolio was 29.4 percent for that year versus 18.2 percent for the bad rule portfolio. Despite the very high return of the buy-and-hold alternative in 1989, 52 of the 120 good rules either equalled or exceeded its performance. The same could be said for only 9 of the 120 bad

Table 14.18 Bad Rules—Consolidated Edison Stock

Rule #	Logic Code	)/(Code	Cutoff Values Series 1	Series 2	Series 3	Fitness	Series Number and Differencing Interval 1 #	Diff.	2 #	Diff.	3 #	Diff.
1	2	4	21	15	19	12.5856	57	0	5	1	23	3
2	2	3	21	13	13	12.9091	57	0	5	1	61	3
3	2	4	22	18	20	12.2878	57	0	5	1	71	3
4	3	3	28	18	13	11.8054	57	0	5	1	77	3
5	2	3	21	15	20	12.9438	57	0	5	1	173	3
6	2	4	22	14	18	12.6975	57	0	5	1	229	3
7	7	2	23	16	22	12.3274	57	0	5	1	234	3
8	4	2	13	25	17	12.5841	57	0	5	1	193	12
9	8	3	22	23	9	13.0729	57	0	23	3	61	3
10	5	4	21	19	2	12.5843	57	0	23	3	71	3
11	6	2	21	19	31	12.5683	57	0	23	3	77	3
12	5	3	27	19	21	12.8816	57	0	23	3	173	3
13	4	4	21	2	18	12.7360	57	0	23	3	229	3
14	2	3	22	19	22	12.9062	57	0	23	3	234	3
15	8	4	13	23	17	12.8520	57	0	23	3	193	12
16	6	1	23	13	27	12.8253	57	0	61	3	71	3
17	6	1	23	13	31	12.9064	57	0	61	3	77	3
18	6	1	24	13	22	13.0666	57	0	61	3	173	3
19	2	1	23	13	27	12.9148	57	0	61	3	229	3
20	6	3	21	10	3	12.9201	57	0	61	3	234	3
21	5	2	23	13	4	13.0450	57	0	61	3	193	12
22	2	3	10	20	30	12.1217	57	0	71	3	77	3
23	5	3	28	29	21	12.4384	57	0	71	3	173	3
24	2	4	21	12	18	12.7348	57	0	71	3	229	3
25	2	3	21	19	21	12.3573	57	0	71	3	234	3
26	4	2	13	23	17	12.7269	57	0	71	3	193	12
27	2	3	10	20	17	12.6311	57	0	77	3	173	3
28	7	3	22	30	18	12.8075	57	0	77	3	229	3
29	2	3	14	16	12	12.4641	57	0	77	3	234	3
30	2	4	14	16	17	12.7284	57	0	77	3	193	12
31	8	2	22	5	18	12.7490	57	0	173	3	229	3
32	2	1	22	20	22	12.6799	57	0	173	3	234	3
33	8	2	13	10	17	12.8145	57	0	173	3	193	12
34	8	3	21	18	2	12.5996	57	0	229	3	234	3
35	2	4	21	18	16	12.8301	57	0	229	3	193	12
36	7	4	18	3	17	12.7565	57	0	234	3	193	12
37	4	8	15	10	25	12.1007	5	1	23	3	61	3
38	3	8	16	19	20	12.1844	5	1	23	3	71	3
39	3	8	16	19	23	12.2300	5	1	23	3	77	3
40	7	6	18	14	16	12.1971	5	1	23	3	173	3
41	1	6	15	30	18	11.5789	5	1	23	3	229	3
42	1	7	15	14	24	12.4919	5	1	23	3	234	3
43	1	8	15	10	16	12.3578	5	1	23	3	193	12
44	5	6	21	11	2	12.0353	5	1	61	3	71	3
45	8	5	21	11	13	12.4829	5	1	61	3	77	3
46	6	5	15	4	20	12.6735	5	1	61	3	173	3

Continued on next page

Table 14.18 *(continued)*

Rule #	Logic Code	)/(Code	Series 1	Series 2	Series 3	Fitness	1 #	Diff.	2 #	Diff.	3 #	Diff.
47	8	5	21	11	7	12.0629	5	1	61	3	229	3
48	6	5	16	10	13	12.1236	5	1	61	3	234	3
49	8	8	24	20	17	12.2672	5	1	61	3	193	12
50	4	7	15	12	13	12.2906	5	1	71	3	77	3
51	5	7	15	29	20	12.6735	5	1	71	3	173	3
52	3	7	16	18	11	11.8839	5	1	71	3	229	3
53	5	5	16	10	21	12.1242	5	1	71	3	234	3
54	2	8	21	16	17	12.6746	5	1	71	3	193	12
55	1	7	15	0	20	12.6735	5	1	77	3	173	3
56	2	5	15	10	29	11.7189	5	1	77	3	229	3
57	6	5	15	13	22	12.4953	5	1	77	3	234	3
58	8	6	21	13	17	12.9549	5	1	77	3	193	12
59	7	5	15	20	6	12.7690	5	1	173	3	229	3
60	1	5	15	20	25	12.8036	5	1	173	3	234	3
61	3	6	15	17	17	12.9000	5	1	173	3	193	12
62	8	1	10	11	16	12.2832	61	3	77	3	173	3
63	2	7	21	18	21	12.4120	5	1	229	3	234	3
64	5	4	14	23	15	12.1202	61	3	77	3	229	3
65	2	8	21	6	17	12.3839	5	1	229	3	193	12
66	4	5	15	23	9	12.4776	5	1	234	3	193	12
67	2	7	22	16	12	11.9637	61	3	77	3	234	3
68	8	5	24	9	7	12.2021	23	3	61	3	71	3
69	6	7	23	9	14	12.2103	23	3	61	3	77	3
70	8	2	8	13	17	12.4842	61	3	77	3	193	12
71	6	5	14	10	17	12.3040	23	3	61	3	173	3
72	8	5	23	10	7	12.2474	23	3	61	3	229	3
73	3	2	22	10	18	11.9864	61	3	173	3	229	3
74	3	5	11	12	12	12.2130	23	3	61	3	234	3
75	8	4	6	27	17	12.4800	23	3	61	3	193	12
76	1	1	31	20	26	12.1771	61	3	173	3	234	3
77	4	7	19	16	13	12.0755	23	3	71	3	77	3
78	5	7	14	19	20	12.3123	23	3	71	3	173	3
79	8	6	25	15	21	12.3729	61	3	173	3	193	12
80	2	4	6	14	15	11.8631	23	3	71	3	229	3
81	2	7	23	14	12	12.3469	23	3	71	3	234	3
82	2	4	11	19	3	11.9757	61	3	229	3	234	3
83	7	8	23	15	17	12.3648	23	3	71	3	193	12
84	6	5	14	13	20	12.6202	23	3	77	3	173	3
85	2	3	11	19	27	11.9068	61	3	229	3	193	12
86	5	6	19	12	3	12.0688	23	3	77	3	229	3
87	6	5	14	13	23	12.4730	23	3	77	3	234	3
88	4	1	13	21	10	12.3698	61	3	234	3	193	12
89	8	2	6	13	17	12.6546	23	3	77	3	193	12
90	5	2	5	20	3	11.8076	23	3	173	3	229	3
91	1	7	11	14	20	12.0382	71	3	77	3	173	3
92	1	5	14	20	23	12.5683	23	3	173	3	234	3

Continued on next page

Table 14.18 *(continued)*

Rule #	Logic Code	)/(Code	Cutoff Values			Fitness	Series Number and Differencing Interval					
			Series 1	Series 2	Series 3		1 #	Diff.	2 #	Diff.	3 #	Diff.
93	8	2	5	15	21	12.5265	23	3	173	3	193	12
94	8	6	20	13	18	12.1392	71	3	77	3	229	3
95	1	7	12	16	22	12.2200	23	3	229	3	234	3
96	2	4	6	0	17	12.2252	23	3	229	3	193	12
97	6	5	16	10	12	11.8780	71	3	77	3	234	3
98	1	6	14	23	6	12.2513	23	3	234	3	193	12
99	4	3	13	6	13	11.9723	61	3	71	3	77	3
100	3	8	15	24	17	12.3600	71	3	77	3	193	12
101	2	3	10	12	17	12.0745	61	3	71	3	173	3
102	6	3	13	7	18	11.9826	61	3	71	3	229	3
103	7	5	14	20	7	12.0757	71	3	173	3	229	3
104	2	3	13	19	26	12.1577	61	3	71	3	234	3
105	2	8	26	16	17	12.4117	61	3	71	3	193	12
106	7	5	27	20	26	12.1096	71	3	173	3	234	3
107	6	7	16	16	17	12.4730	71	3	173	3	193	12
108	3	5	20	21	16	11.5527	71	3	229	3	234	3
109	3	6	15	8	17	12.1207	71	3	229	3	193	12
110	1	6	16	30	17	12.1516	71	3	234	3	193	12
111	5	2	13	20	4	11.8761	77	3	173	3	229	3
112	2	1	13	20	26	12.4802	77	3	173	3	234	3
113	4	6	20	15	17	12.6100	77	3	173	3	193	12
114	5	3	13	18	21	12.4880	77	3	229	3	234	3
115	4	6	24	27	17	12.1669	77	3	229	3	193	12
116	2	4	13	3	17	12.4918	77	3	234	3	193	12
117	2	3	15	18	19	12.3269	173	3	229	3	234	3
118	2	4	16	10	17	12.3431	173	3	229	3	193	12
119	1	2	20	25	6	12.2171	173	3	234	3	193	12
120	7	3	9	25	17	11.9510	229	3	234	3	193	12

rules, emphasizing the fact that the GA procedure is indeed identifying rules that differ strongly in their performance characteristics.

HEDGE PORTFOLIO RESULTS

The results of our hedge portfolio test for IBM are summarized in Table 14.21. Initially the hedge portfolio performs poorly. IBM's stock had a −19.42 percent return in 1989. Both the long and short portfolio outperformed the buy-and-hold strategy for that year, with the short portfolio performing better. Over the entire holdout period, the long portfolio had a 9.40 percent return, compared to a buy-and-loss of 16.61 percent and a short portfolio loss of 0.28 percent. Therefore, the cumulative return for the hedge portfolio is 8.08 percent at the end of the period.

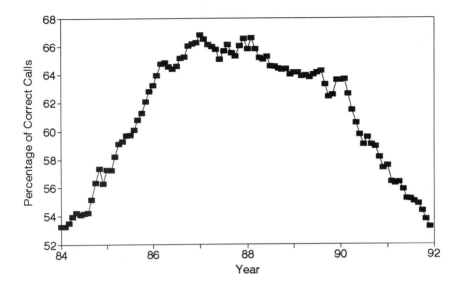

FIGURE 14.13   Percentage of Correct Calls (Consolidated Edison—Good Rules) 1984–1991

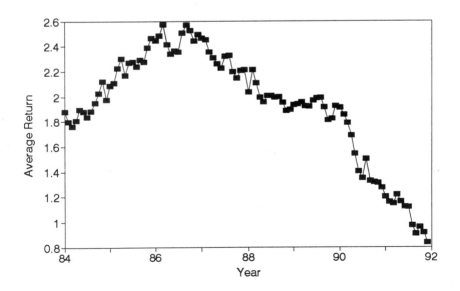

FIGURE 14.14   Average Return (Consolidated Edison—Good Rules) 1984–1991

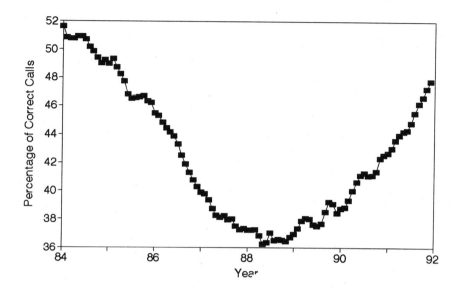

FIGURE 14.15 Percentage of Correct Calls (Consolidated Edison—Bad Rules)
1984–1991

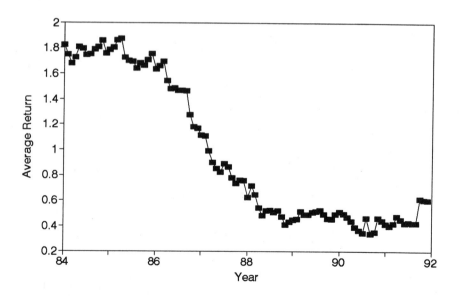

FIGURE 14.16 Average Return (Consolidated Edison—Bad Rules) 1984–1991

Table 14.19 Performance Summary: Good Rules—Consolidated Edison Stock

Rule #	Fitness	1984–1988 Period		1989		1989–1991 Period	
		% Correct	Average Return	% Correct	Average Return	% Correct	Average Return
1	2.3091	55.00	17.84	66.67	27.00	55.56	11.98
2	2.5520	61.67	23.21	83.33	39.50	52.78	11.39
3	2.1066	58.33	20.94	75.00	36.30	58.33	14.57
4	2.0475	60.00	21.24	75.00	34.20	62.78	12.48
5	2.3581	66.67	24.97	50.00	13.40	52.78	6.06
6	2.2270	65.00	24.26	58.33	21.40	52.78	10.27
7	1.2942	70.00	28.22	50.00	18.50	44.44	6.77
8	2.4271	66.67	25.20	41.67	11.10	38.89	0.07
9	2.4802	53.33	17.95	75.00	34.20	58.33	12.35
10	2.2566	73.33	30.62	58.33	30.50	52.78	14.70
11	2.1868	73.33	30.62	58.33	30.50	52.78	14.70
12	2.4377	55.00	19.95	58.33	27.60	55.56	18.97
13	2.2436	71.67	30.30	58.33	30.50	52.78	14.70
14	2.4926	51.67	19.61	33.33	8.30	50.00	5.49
15	2.5648	65.00	24.82	50.00	24.30	50.00	12.87
16	2.3719	73.33	31.57	75.00	35.00	55.56	15.53
17	2.5084	73.33	31.57	75.00	35.00	58.33	14.95
18	2.4639	73.33	31.57	75.00	35.00	52.78	11.74
19	2.4524	73.33	33.58	83.33	40.30	55.56	12.35
20	2.5560	73.33	33.58	83.33	40.30	55.56	12.35
21	2.3974	50.00	9.20	41.67	15.70	52.78	13.52
22	2.1294	71.67	27.91	66.67	30.80	47.22	9.81
23	2.3385	50.00	17.14	66.67	20.00	55.56	13.37
24	2.3010	66.67	27.61	50.00	22.80	47.22	10.85
25	2.3364	75.00	28.87	75.00	34.20	50.00	10.74
26	2.4145	60.00	22.56	50.00	24.40	50.00	11.49
27	2.3597	61.67	22.96	75.00	34.20	50.00	10.74
28	2.4061	63.33	19.90	75.00	42.40	58.33	13.63
29	2.2670	65.00	25.59	75.00	34.20	47.22	7.09
30	2.5042	68.33	23.02	75.00	37.10	52.78	10.90
31	2.4934	50.00	17.77	58.33	27.30	50.00	14.32
32	2.3578	63.33	26.25	33.33	13.30	47.22	10.71
33	2.5119	38.33	6.17	50.00	18.20	58.33	11.66
34	2.6688	61.67	28.14	75.00	34.20	55.56	14.50
35	2.4585	65.00	25.47	75.00	34.20	50.00	7.35
36	2.4857	65.00	22.59	66.67	31.80	50.00	5.19
37	2.5134	63.33	23.04	66.67	32.20	58.33	14.01
38	2.2953	71.67	30.51	58.33	28.80	55.56	18.64
39	2.3043	73.33	31.43	58.33	28.80	55.56	18.64
40	2.4262	56.67	22.16	41.67	11.10	47.22	4.92
41	2.2485	70.00	30.46	66.67	33.80	58.33	17.81
42	2.4577	60.00	24.28	66.67	29.50	55.56	13.50
43	2.6220	68.33	27.80	50.00	24.30	44.44	8.21
44	2.3735	73.33	31.57	83.33	38.50	58.33	16.52
45	2.3716	75.00	34.56	83.33	38.50	58.33	12.56
46	2.3703	73.33	32.60	83.33	40.30	58.33	16.69

Continued on next page

Table 14.19 *(continued)*

Rule #	Fitness	1984–1988 Period		1989		1989–1991 Period	
		% Correct	Average Return	% Correct	Average Return	% Correct	Average Return
47	2.4438	68.33	25.56	75.00	34.20	52.78	14.93
48	2.5560	73.33	33.58	83.33	40.30	55.56	12.35
49	2.4332	58.33	9.98	41.67	15.70	50.00	15.20
50	2.1239	73.33	29.17	58.33	28.80	50.00	10.14
51	2.3717	58.33	21.74	50.00	17.30	55.56	12.92
52	2.3427	73.33	30.80	66.67	32.20	55.56	15.28
53	2.3823	53.33	18.31	33.33	10.00	52.78	7.23
54	2.3915	58.33	22.49	58.33	26.30	52.78	11.66
55	2.3283	56.67	20.59	75.00	34.20	52.78	12.66
56	2.2903	70.00	25.52	75.00	40.60	66.67	19.77
57	2.4453	63.33	22.93	50.00	19.20	55.56	15.30
58	2.5270	55.00	16.64	50.00	26.40	44.44	7.92
59	2.4509	58.33	22.29	75.00	34.20	58.33	15.38
60	2.5187	78.33	31.77	33.33	14.40	41.67	7.09
61	2.6303	51.67	13.09	41.67	14.60	50.00	9.33
62	2.6581	61.67	28.14	66.67	32.20	50.00	13.50
63	2.4566	68.33	33.27	75.00	34.20	47.22	9.45
64	2.3875	48.33	12.64	50.00	26.30	47.22	6.30
65	2.3928	73.33	33.58	83.33	40.30	55.56	12.35
66	2.4496	73.33	33.58	83.33	40.30	55.56	12.35
67	2.6215	73.33	34.48	58.33	26.70	52.78	14.67
68	2.5176	75.00	34.52	75.00	36.00	55.56	12.11
69	2.7058	73.33	32.95	75.00	36.80	61.11	18.45
70	2.6548	63.33	18.78	25.00	9.10	44.44	7.69
71	2.2651	71.67	30.88	41.67	19.70	47.22	10.52
72	2.3436	68.33	27.47	75.00	35.90	58.33	20.18
73	2.2792	58.33	25.46	50.00	22.80	55.56	9.70
74	2.5137	71.67	27.75	50.00	22.80	47.22	11.95
75	2.5970	61.67	23.01	50.00	24.40	50.00	11.49
76	2.3822	58.33	23.47	33.33	7.20	58.33	12.79
77	2.4033	65.00	23.58	75.00	42.40	61.11	14.73
78	2.6277	66.67	26.96	66.67	29.50	61.11	20.51
79	2.6083	56.67	17.28	50.00	26.40	44.44	7.92
80	2.4082	48.33	16.41	58.33	27.30	50.00	14.32
81	2.5680	73.33	26.97	58.33	27.70	50.00	12.50
82	2.6544	41.67	8.58	50.00	22.00	58.33	16.57
83	2.7065	63.33	28.44	75.00	34.20	58.33	15.46
84	2.5648	63.33	24.52	50.00	22.80	41.7	4.19
85	2.6710	55.00	17.15	33.33	21.20	41.67	6.62
86	2.3719	73.33	31.57	75.00	35.00	55.56	13.21
87	2.5193	71.67	26.17	75.00	35.00	55.56	18.40
88	2.4878	70.00	31.49	83.33	40.30	61.11	13.24
89	2.6248	61.67	27.15	83.33	41.70	66.67	21.12
90	2.4398	75.00	31.91	75.00	35.00	50.00	8.72
91	2.5084	73.33	31.57	75.00	35.00	50.00	9.45
92	2.5540	71.67	33.23	83.33	40.30	55.56	12.35

Continued on next page

Table 14.19 *(continued)*

Rule #	Fitness	1984–1988 Period		1989		1989–1991 Period	
		% Correct	Average Return	% Correct	Average Return	% Correct	Average Return
93	2.6574	63.33	26.33	91.67	43.90	61.11	18.02
94	2.5618	73.33	35.32	83.33	40.30	55.56	12.35
95	2.5558	73.33	30.98	75.00	38.20	55.56	9.83
96	2.6891	75.00	32.64	66.67	32.70	55.56	12.21
97	2.5617	63.33	27.84	66.67	27.90	52.78	10.06
98	2.7409	65.00	28.70	75.00	35.00	52.78	11.23
99	2.6868	78.33	37.43	83.33	40.30	47.22	8.18
100	2.5247	66.67	22.80	66.67	28.90	47.22	7.06
101	2.3123	60.00	21.54	75.00	34.20	58.33	16.86
102	2.2575	58.33	18.97	75.00	42.40	55.56	13.19
103	2.3667	63.33	23.47	75.00	34.20	52.78	14.93
104	2.4127	55.00	16.64	50.00	26.40	44.44	7.92
105	2.4436	48.33	16.41	58.33	27.30	50.00	14.32
106	2.4421	71.67	27.35	41.67	18.90	44.44	10.06
107	2.4575	58.33	22.06	58.33	24.70	58.33	14.85
108	2.6920	65.00	28.69	75.00	34.20	52.78	11.01
109	2.3603	65.00	25.47	75.00	34.20	47.22	6.94
110	2.4498	53.33	16.21	33.33	21.20	47.22	5.67
111	2.4502	46.67	13.35	58.33	20.80	50.00	12.32
112	2.5560	71.67	24.90	66.67	36.30	52.78	12.24
113	2.5416	40.00	6.72	58.33	26.10	58.33	10.47
114	2.6581	61.67	28.14	75.00	34.20	52.78	11.01
115	2.4956	63.33	25.16	75.00	34.20	50.00	7.35
116	2.4227	45.00	11.82	50.00	26.30	44.44	3.66
117	2.7084	66.67	27.34	58.33	27.70	55.56	11.44
118	2.6405	68.33	33.27	75.00	34.20	47.22	9.45
119	2.5504	68.33	24.82	66.67	29.70	61.11	14.98
120	2.4587	53.33	15.19	50.00	26.30	44.44	3.35

These results contain both good and bad news. The good news is that the long portfolio outperformed the buy-and-hold alternative and that the cumulative return on the hedge portfolio at the end of the test period was positive. The bad news is that the hedge portfolio started off with poor initial performance. It appears that the rule relationships in the test period have changed from what they were over the rule-building period, which may be due to the short cycle time for IBM as reported by E. E. Peters in his chaos research; the returns on IBM stock may be undergoing fundamental shifts every 18 months on average; this may point to the need for caution when using our approach to build trading rules for stocks with short cycle times. However, as we pointed out earlier, the percentage of correct calls and average return graphs for both rule portfolios displayed warning signs at the time of the test period. For example. Figure 14.1 shows the percentage of correct calls for the good rules peaking in early 1988, but the

Table 14.20   Performance Summary: Bad Rules—Consolidated Edison Stock

Rule #	Fitness	1984–1988 Period		1989		1989–1991 Period	
		% Correct	Average Return	% Correct	Average Return	% Correct	Average Return
1	12.5856	43.33	10.37	33.33	14.50	50.00	15.30
2	12.9091	36.67	5.76	25.00	8.40	55.56	14.95
3	12.2878	45.00	9.94	25.00	6.70	44.44	8.91
4	11.8054	31.67	4.41	50.00	20.40	61.11	16.96
5	12.9438	30.00	1.36	66.67	34.40	66.67	27.45
6	12.6974	38.33	5.53	50.00	20.80	52.78	17.28
7	12.3274	38.33	7.97	58.33	30.30	55.56	16.13
8	12.5841	41.67	9.15	58.33	28.90	55.56	15.58
9	13.0729	35.00	6.82	50.00	18.50	55.56	13.91
10	12.5843	25.00	−1.34	50.00	17.00	58.33	13.57
11	12.5683	25.00	−1.34	50.00	17.00	58.33	13.57
12	12.8816	45.00	8.36	41.67	21.00	47.22	16.81
13	12.7360	28.33	−0.20	50.00	17.00	61.11	17.45
14	12.9062	38.33	3.75	25.00	7.00	50.00	13.70
15	12.8520	35.00	4.28	50.00	17.00	52.78	12.27
16	12.8253	23.33	−3.89	16.67	3.70	55.56	13.68
17	12.9064	23.33	−3.89	16.67	3.70	50.00	11.76
18	13.0666	25.00	−2.88	25.00	10.70	55.56	16.13
19	12.9148	23.33	−3.89	16.67	3.70	52.78	14.24
20	12.9201	23.33	−2.30	25.00	7.80	58.33	18.64
21	13.0450	28.33	−3.04	16.67	3.70	52.78	14.24
22	12.1217	30.00	2.24	33.33	11.20	52.78	14.60
23	12.4384	50.00	15.00	41.67	20.60	41.67	9.47
24	12.7348	33.33	2.00	50.00	18.50	55.56	14.65
25	12.3573	41.67	6.67	33.33	10.10	52.78	12.00
26	12.7269	40.00	6.22	50.00	17.00	52.78	13.65
27	12.6311	40.00	7.10	25.00	8.40	44.44	9.11
28	12.8075	41.67	9.41	25.00	2.10	50.00	12.98
29	12.4641	40.00	7.10	25.00	8.40	44.44	9.72
30	12.7284	45.00	11.60	50.00	15.10	55.56	16.59
31	12.7490	63.33	22.69	41.67	18.90	58.33	18.95
32	12.6799	33.33	1.81	66.67	28.40	52.78	13.63
33	12.8145	61.67	22.60	50.00	23.10	47.22	14.06
34	12.5996	30.00	−2.41	25.00	8.40	55.56	15.78
35	12.8301	30.00	−2.41	25.00	8.40	55.56	15.78
36	12.7565	53.33	16.10	50.00	15.20	61.11	20.99
37	12.1007	33.33	4.11	75.00	35.70	55.56	15.85
38	12.1844	26.67	−0.96	41.67	12.90	44.44	4.25
39	12.2300	26.67	−0.96	41.67	12.90	44.44	4.25
40	12.1971	33.33	2.64	66.67	33.00	52.78	13.73
41	11.5789	30.00	−0.77	41.67	12.90	47.22	7.81
42	12.4919	38.33	5.16	66.67	34.40	50.00	14.04
43	12.3578	31.67	2.66	41.67	12.90	41.67	7.61
44	12.0353	33.33	−1.40	25.00	5.30	41.67	11.44
45	12.4829	33.33	−1.31	25.00	5.30	41.67	12.06
46	12.6735	40.00	4.24	50.00	27.90	50.00	12.87

Continued on next page

Table 14.20 (continued)

Rule #	Fitness	1984–1988 Period		1989		1989–1991 Period	
		% Correct	Average Return	% Correct	Average Return	% Correct	Average Return
47	12.0629	31.67	−1.61	25.00	5.30	41.67	11.44
48	12.1236	25.00	−3.27	25.00	7.80	50.00	11.09
49	12.2672	51.67	20.55	66.67	27.70	52.78	9.89
50	12.2906	46.67	13.70	66.67	29.60	55.56	17.01
51	12.6735	50.00	11.35	66.67	32.30	47.22	15.38
52	11.8839	31.67	3.08	33.33	10.10	44.44	6.06
53	12.1242	50.00	13.70	66.67	32.30	50.00	14.01
54	12.6746	43.33	5.63	50.00	17.00	47.22	13.13
55	12.6735	43.33	6.41	58.33	30.30	41.67	11.01
56	11.7189	38.33	5.35	66.67	32.30	52.78	15.65
57	12.4953	43.33	6.20	75.00	34.70	52.78	15.95
58	12.9549	56.67	11.62	58.33	17.20	55.56	16.64
59	12.7690	25.00	−2.75	58.33	22.30	50.00	12.19
60	12.8036	25.00	−2.75	66.67	27.10	52.78	14.29
61	12.9000	38.33	5.35	66.67	32.30	50.00	15.78
62	12.4120	40.00	1.57	33.33	10.10	41.67	9.42
63	12.3839	38.33	4.04	33.33	10.10	47.22	16.37
64	12.4776	33.33	1.49	58.33	28.90	41.67	11.90
65	12.2021	23.33	−2.48	41.67	14.80	50.00	9.36
66	12.2103	25.00	−2.28	33.33	13.10	47.22	8.80
67	12.3040	30.00	−2.61	50.00	20.20	50.00	13.16
68	12.2474	21.67	−3.99	41.67	14.80	52.78	13.08
69	12.2130	26.67	−1.80	25.00	7.00	47.22	10.44
70	12.4800	5167	20.86	58.33	25.80	44.44	8.58
71	12.0755	38.33	10.18	75.00	36.40	66.67	16.47
72	12.3123	48.33	11.39	75.00	37.80	47.22	11.98
73	11.8631	43.33	7.48	50.00	17.00	47.22	15.25
74	12.3469	28.33	1.91	50.00	18.50	52.78	10.49
75	12.3648	38.33	5.82	50.00	17.00	50.00	10.96
76	12.6202	41.67	5.44	75.00	38.10	52.78	13.00
77	12.0688	28.33	−0.08	50.00	17.00	52.78	8.52
78	12.4730	43.33	8.23	83.33	40.30	61.11	19.63
79	12.6546	45.00	11.00	58.33	17.20	55.56	16.64
80	11.8076	38.33	3.90	66.67	28.40	55.56	12.87
81	12.5683	26.67	−2.88	66.67	28.40	50.00	12.82
82	12.5265	48.33	18.86	58.33	24.80	52.78	15.55
83	12.2200	38.33	5.53	41.67	10.90	47.22	12.98
84	12.2252	35.00	3.19	25.00	8.40	44.44	14.60
85	12.2513	30.00	0.22	75.00	37.80	50.00	13.42
86	11.9723	38.33	8.83	33.33	16.40	55.56	15.05
87	12.0745	43.33	8.21	41.67	13.70	44.44	9.59
88	11.9826	30.00	1.53	33.33	11.20	50.00	11.17
89	12.1577	28.33	−2.44	25.00	5.30	41.67	7.29
90	12.4117	40.00	6.22	50.00	17.00	47.22	11.52
91	12.2832	43.33	8.35	50.00	25.70	47.22	11.39
92	12.1202	31.67	−0.79	33.33	10.20	50.00	14.50

Continued on next page

Table 14.20 *(continued)*

Rule #	Fitness	1984–1988 Period		1989		1989–1991 Period	
		% Correct	Average Return	% Correct	Average Return	% Correct	Average Return
93	11.9637	41.67	9.17	33.33	9.20	44.44	7.46
94	12.4842	45.00	11.60	58.33	17.20	63.89	18.69
95	11.9864	56.67	19.03	41.67	22.10	50.00	12.85
96	12.1771	36.67	3.10	66.67	28.40	52.78	11.20
97	12.3729	46.67	18.63	58.33	24.80	50.00	13.11
98	11.9757	21.67	− 5.29	16.67	3.70	52.78	14.34
99	11.9068	21.67	− 5.29	16.67	3.70	52.78	14.34
100	12.3698	25.00	− 1.34	25.00	5.30	47.22	7.89
101	12.0382	55.00	14.44	50.00	26.60	33.33	4.43
102	12.1392	41.67	9.64	33.33	4.00	50.00	12.74
103	11.8780	40.00	7.10	25.00	8.40	47.22	9.50
104	12.3600	38.33	5.69	50.00	17.00	55.56	18.76
105	12.0757	35.00	1.02	58.33	20.30	44.44	10.55
106	12.1096	36.67	3.10	66.67	28.40	55.56	13.68
107	12.4730	33.33	5.44	66.67	26.70	55.56	13.70
108	11.5527	31.67	3.00	33.33	11.20	47.22	8.18
109	12.1207	28.33	− 1.42	25.00	8.40	50.00	15.85
110	12.1516	43.33	9.69	41.67	16.70	58.33	17.76
111	11.8761	38.33	3.90	75.00	30.70	58.33	15.08
112	12.4802	36.67	3.10	75.00	30.70	55.56	14.29
113	12.6100	53.33	19.36	50.00	20.70	52.78	15.51
114	12.4880	38.33	1.59	33.33	10.30	50.00	10.96
115	12.1669	35.00	3.78	25.00	8.40	50.00	15.25
116	12.4918	55.00	17.45	50.00	15.20	61.11	20.78
117	12.3269	35.00	2.42	50.00	16.90	52.78	12.58
118	12.3431	36.67	6.84	58.33	22.30	58.33	15.90
119	12.2171	33.33	2.00	66.67	28.40	52.78	14.22
120	11.9510	46.67	8.88	50.00	15.20	58.33	21.35

average return, as shown in Figure 14.2, appears to have peaked even earlier. Warning signs of this type should be carefully investigated before investing.

The cycle time for Mobil is 36 months, but the problems with the hedge portfolio are severe. The cumulative return, as seen in Table 14.22, goes from bad to worse. The good and bad rule portfolios seem to have reversed their roles in the test period. Again, the comments about warning signs in the percentage of correct calls and average return graphs are applicable. Both rule portfolios show some erratic behavior during the rule-building period.

The results for McDonald's are much better. The numbers are recapped in Table 14.23 and graphically displayed in Figure 14.17. The cumulative return for the hedge portfolio is 8.23 percent by the end of 1989. The hedge portfolio did reasonably well in most months but got clobbered in July and August of 1990. In spite of a loss exceeding 19 percent for these two months, however, the hedge

Table 14.21 Hedge Portfolio Results—IBM

| | | Cumulative Return | | | Hedge Portfolio | |
| | | Buy and | Long | Short | | Cumulative |
Year	Month	Hold	Portfolio	Portfolio	Return	Return
1989	1	7.18	3.09	3.87	−0.77	−0.77
	2	0.59	−1.39	2.51	−3.04	−3.82
	3	−9.65	−3.76	−2.64	2.62	−1.19
	4	−5.62	−1.75	0.22	−0.85	−2.05
	5	−8.24	−2.28	−1.01	0.68	−1.36
	6	−6.36	−1.16	0.38	−0.26	−1.62
	7	−3.74	0.35	2.12	−0.19	−1.81
	8	−0.95	2.16	4.05	−0.09	−1.90
	9	−7.62	−1.20	1.46	−0.80	−2.70
	10	−15.23	−5.22	−1.92	−0.74	−3.45
	11	−16.42	−5.76	−2.09	−0.40	−3.85
	12	−19.42	−7.06	−4.09	0.66	−3.18
1990	1	−15.56	−4.94	−1.49	−0.42	−3.61
	2	−10.03	−1.93	2.95	−1.35	−4.95
	3	−8.08	−0.88	4.67	−0.60	−5.55
	4	−5.60	0.49	6.89	−0.74	−6.29
	5	4.97	6.54	13.05	0.26	−6.02
	6	2.79	6.13	12.30	0.27	−5.75
	7	−2.46	4.96	8.73	2.07	−3.68
	8	−9.82	2.14	3.14	2.46	−1.22
	9	−5.83	4.67	6.22	−0.51	−1.73
	10	−6.72	4.60	6.26	−0.11	−1.84
	11	1.66	11.72	10.07	3.22	1.39
	12	1.10	11.55	10.20	−0.27	1.12
1991	1	13.41	17.76	19.75	−3.11	−1.99
	2	16.27	19.17	22.23	−0.87	−2.86
	3	2.84	16.84	11.66	6.69	3.84
	4	−6.98	12.45	4.84	2.35	6.19
	5	−3.06	15.12	7.59	−0.25	5.94
	6	−11.28	9.88	3.09	−0.37	5.57
	7	−7.52	12.07	6.50	−1.31	4.26
	8	−10.40	11.51	3.68	2.15	6.40
	9	−4.16	13.72	10.18	−4.29	2.12
	10	−9.13	12.33	6.57	2.06	4.18
	11	−13.33	10.24	3.11	1.38	5.55
	12	−16.61	9.40	−0.28	2.53	8.08

portfolio finished the test period slightly in the black. Again, users must be alert to possible changes in the underlying relationships. Frequent updating of the rule base might improve the performance.

The Consolidated Edison hedge portfolio results are shown in Table 14.24. The hedge portfolio finished 1989 in good shape but then experienced declining performance. The long portfolio beat the short portfolio by about 10 percent in

Table 14.22   Hedge Portfolio Results—Mobil

		Cumulative Return			Hedge Portfolio	
Year	Month	Buy and Hold	Long Portfolio	Short Portfolio	Return	Cumulative Return
1989	1	7.65	2.56	5.76	−3.20	−3.20
	2	3.75	1.67	4.31	0.49	−2.70
	3	9.02	3.32	8.58	−2.46	−5.16
	4	12.92	4.61	11.64	−1.57	−6.73
	5	16.03	6.06	13.62	−0.39	−7.13
	6	11.25	6.00	10.91	2.33	−4.79
	7	15.47	7.56	14.03	−1.34	−6.13
	8	25.11	9.99	19.50	−2.54	−8.67
	9	27.96	11.19	21.13	−0.29	−8.96
	10	28.58	11.86	21.82	0.04	−8.91
	11	35.79	13.87	25.56	−1.27	−10.18
	12	44.44	17.90	28.73	1.01	−9.17
1990	1	37.87	14.90	26.28	−0.64	−9.81
	2	43.98	16.33	30.94	−2.44	−12.26
	3	43.40	16.55	31.19	0.00	−12.26
	4	40.49	15.75	30.22	0.05	−12.21
	5	48.31	18.23	33.97	−0.73	−12.95
	6	45.64	18.40	32.73	1.07	−11.87
	7	55.61	21.94	36.49	0.15	−11.72
	8	52.34	21.12	35.85	−0.21	−11.93
	9	49.95	20.64	35.44	−0.09	−12.02
	10	37.37	13.53	34.11	−4.91	−16.93
	11	42.20	17.02	35.24	2.24	−14.69
	12	40.08	16.24	35.20	−0.64	−15.34
1991	1	38.81	16.22	35.27	−0.07	−15.41
	2	54.09	20.35	43.40	−2.46	−17.87
	3	57.76	22.31	44.82	0.65	−17.22
	4	67.54	24.47	50.52	−2.17	−19.39
	5	63.08	23.49	48.67	0.44	−18.95
	6	59.05	22.37	47.72	−0.26	−19.21
	7	69.41	26.84	51.33	1.20	−18.01
	8	71.29	28.00	52.49	0.15	−17.86
	9	70.66	28.08	52.67	−0.06	−17.92
	10	77.98	29.73	55.83	−0.77	−18.69
	11	64.04	24.46	49.18	0.21	−18.49
	12	71.96	27.61	52.01	0.63	−17.86

1989. The GA seems to have done well in identifying two rule portfolios with sharply different return characteristics. However, this difference disappears over time.

In summary, the hedge portfolio results are intriguing. If the findings reported in Peters's 1991 article are correct, then it may be difficult to build rule portfolios that continue their behavioral trends for stocks with shorter cycle times. If the

Table 14.23 Hedge Portfolio Results—McDonald's

| Year | Month | Cumulative Return | | | Hedge Portfolio | |
		Buy and Hold	Long Portfolio	Short Portfolio	Return	Cumulative Return
1989	1	8.06	7.12	2.55	**4.57**	**4.57**
	2	5.23	4.46	2.99	**−2.91**	**1.66**
	3	7.06	5.94	4.22	**0.22**	**1.88**
	4	14.61	11.78	7.08	**2.76**	**4.65**
	5	24.56	18.02	11.51	**1.45**	**6.10**
	6	22.21	16.14	11.80	**−1.86**	**4.24**
	7	30.07	21.50	15.46	**1.34**	**5.58**
	8	20.99	14.97	14.02	**−4.12**	**1.46**
	9	24.64	17.73	15.65	**0.96**	**2.42**
	10	29.87	22.33	16.98	**2.76**	**5.18**
	11	38.06	27.81	21.02	**1.03**	**6.21**
	12	44.87	32.97	23.46	**2.02**	**8.23**
1990	1	37.02	28.88	21.02	**−1.10**	**7.13**
	2	32.59	25.08	20.87	**−2.82**	**4.31**
	3	33.64	26.05	21.67	**0.11**	**4.42**
	4	27.33	22.83	19.11	**−0.45**	**3.97**
	5	46.13	34.33	25.23	**4.22**	**8.19**
	6	49.80	37.45	26.21	**1.54**	**9.73**
	7	32.40	23.18	24.61	**−9.12**	**0.61**
	8	18.00	10.84	24.60	**−10.00**	**−9.39**
	9	10.05	6.02	21.69	**−2.02**	**−11.41**
	10	6.88	3.75	21.79	**−2.23**	**−13.63**
	11	19.42	14.87	24.87	**8.19**	**−5.44**
	12	23.66	18.75	26.11	**2.38**	**−3.05**
91	1	20.99	16.61	25.92	**−1.65**	**−4.71**
	2	34.28	27.88	29.17	**7.09**	**.38**
	3	47.88	39.49	31.40	**7.35**	**9.73**
	4	42.56	39.49	31.56	**−3.37**	**6.36**
	5	49.33	45.52	32.69	**3.46**	**9.82**
	6	40.28	38.67	29.74	**−2.48**	**7.33**
	7	39.72	38.70	29.71	**0.04**	**7.38**
	8	39.59	39.04	29.80	**0.18**	**7.55**
	9	49.72	43.46	36.42	**−1.93**	**5.63**
	10	48.66	42.74	36.64	**−0.66**	**4.97**
	11	44.25	39.54	35.68	**−1.54**	**3.43**
	12	63.01	49.76	44.90	**0.53**	**3.96**

underlying relationships get scrambled periodically, then rules built from past patterns will lose their effectiveness when the scrambling occurs. Our findings are roughly consistent with this idea. The hedge portfolios for McDonald's and Consolidated Edison performed well in 1989, but the Mobil and IBM hedge portfolios performed poorly. McDonald's and Consolidated Edison have longer cycle times than both Mobil and IBM.

Table 14.24   Hedge Portfolio Results—Consolidated Edison

		Cumulative Return			Hedge Portfolio	
Year	Month	Buy and Hold	Long Portfolio	Short Portfolio	Return	Cumulative Return
1989	1	1.33	1.10	0.88	0.22	0.22
	2	−1.89	−0.74	0.13	−1.07	−0.85
	3	0.30	0.87	1.79	−0.04	−0.89
	4	3.59	2.93	3.73	0.13	−0.76
	5	9.55	7.32	6.53	1.57	0.81
	6	13.21	10.08	8.66	0.57	1.38
	7	19.32	15.16	11.25	2.23	3.61
	8	15.66	12.87	10.80	−1.59	2.03
	9	12.85	11.46	10.02	−0.54	1.49
	10	15.66	13.95	11.20	1.16	2.65
	11	25.01	21.75	14.43	3.94	6.59
	12	34.22	29.35	18.03	3.10	9.69
1990	1	25.56	22.60	16.90	−4.27	5.42
	2	23.65	21.25	16.47	−0.73	4.69
	3	21.87	19.99	16.21	−0.81	3.87
	4	11.33	11.66	14.20	−5.21	−1.34
	5	11.73	12.22	14.77	0.01	−1.34
	6	12.30	12.84	15.41	−0.01	−1.34
	7	19.47	18.54	18.17	2.66	1.32
	8	6.11	9.38	12.54	−2.96	−1.64
	9	2.45	7.38	11.47	−0.88	−2.52
	10	14.06	12.97	20.53	−2.93	−5.45
	11	14.42	13.43	21.07	−0.04	−5.49
	12	17.56	16.32	22.79	1.12	−4.36
1991	1	16.91	15.91	22.65	−0.23	−4.59
	2	21.71	19.80	25.65	0.91	−3.69
	3	30.59	26.89	31.65	1.14	−2.54
	4	24.91	22.66	29.14	−1.42	−3.97
	5	25.34	23.13	29.66	−0.02	−3.99
	6	27.31	24.78	31.01	0.30	−3.69
	7	31.20	27.90	33.53	0.58	−3.11
	8	33.60	29.81	35.18	0.26	−2.85
	9	33.60	30.09	35.45	0.01	−2.84
	10	35.55	31.28	36.95	−0.19	−3.04
	11	39.31	33.59	39.28	0.06	−2.98
	12	53.39	41.14	46.92	0.16	−2.81

CONCLUSIONS

There are some definite lessons contained in our test results for individual stocks. We suggest the following:

1.   The percentage of correct calls and average return graphs should be carefully examined. It appears that rule portfolios display definite trends in

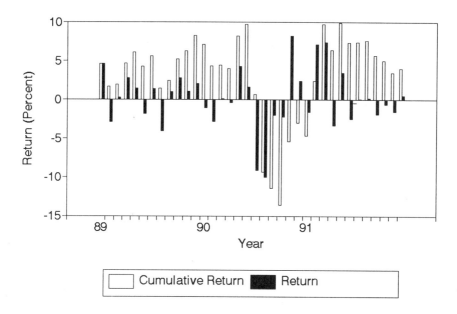

FIGURE 14.17   Hedge Portfolio—McDonald's

behavior. The user should watch carefully to see that good rule portfolios have not peaked, starting to trend downward, and that bad rule portfolios have not bottomed out.
2. Stocks with longer cycle times are probably better candidates for timing rules. Point 1 above is even more critical for stocks with shorter cycle times.
3. The rule base needs periodic updating. The effectiveness of our rule portfolios diminished markedly after 12 months. Frequent, perhaps even monthly, updating might greatly improve performance.
4. There may be some valuable clues contained in the specific rules. Rule 117 for McDonald's, as we discussed earlier, seems to suggest that McDonald's should be purchased near the trough of the business cycle. Serious examination of the content of the specific rules might reveal significant insights into the behavior of the associated stock.

In summary, the results show promise but need additional refinement. There are many possible variations to our basic approach, and that is the main topic of the next chapter.

15

Modifying the Search Procedure

In this chapter, we discuss possible modifications to our basic approach. When you start experimenting with GAs, you will face similar issues. There are always countless variations to any chosen approach, and it is virtually certain that you will not find the Holy Grail of investments with your first efforts. Everyone seems to be in search of an ever-elusive, unchanging money-making scheme, but because markets are always changing, modifications are an ongoing necessity. This chapter is meant to be suggestive, to help stimulate your thinking about variations that you might try with your own research. We use our approach as the basis for discussing many different methodological variations and continue this line of thought in the next chapter, where we outline specific alternative applications.

REFINEMENTS TO OUR METHODOLOGY

We have devoted very little effort to the refinement of our GA procedures, having chosen instead to focus more effort on the methodology of problem representation, performance calculation, and testing. The GA version we have used is simple and straightforward, and refinements to our basic approach might lead to significant improvements in the results.

We have opted for fairly rapid convergence in our GA procedure, which risks missing more attractive solutions. One of the principal tools for slowing convergence is the selection, or ranking, procedure. The one we employed is fairly heavy handed; replacing the bottom performers with additional copies of the top performers eventually forces a uniform population. If the search keeps failing to produce better performers, then the population continues to receive more copies of the same best performer. A different selection procedure, such as roulette wheel selection, would extend the search time and possibly find more attractive (based on historical performance) solutions. This would be a simple refinement.

In Chapters 12–14, our method involved making one GA run for each of 120 different three-variable combinations—in other words, only one GA trial was performed for each of the 120 variable combinations. GAs start from a random initial population. Particularly with rapid convergence, different starting points can lead to different solutions, so multiple trials may be necessary to find the optimal solution. One simple modification would be to increase the number of trials per variable combination. Let's say we were to run ten trials per combination. We could then use the best result from each of the ten trials per combination and investigate the performance of this 120-rule collection, or we could use all 1,200 rules. Another possibility would be to use the best 50 of the 1,200 rules, which would ignore at least 70 of the 120 combinations. Again, this would be a simple refinement.

It's also possible that the search for the variable cutoff parameters is at present too exact. We split the historical range of data values into a partition with 32 segments, which permits a fairly exact fixing of the best parameter values. If the partition were reduced to 16 segments, for example, one bit per variable would be freed up in the string representation; because we have used three variables, this would liberate three bits. This would greatly reduce the search space, leading to more rapid run times. Or the additional bits could be used to somehow refine the problem representation.

We discussed some interesting twists on the basic genetic operators, crossover and mutation, in Chapter 9. It might be possible to use some different genetic operators to improve the performance of our GA. Additionally, there might be alternative approaches to the problem representation that might be more effective.

TIME-FRAME

We have chosen to focus on monthly trading rules. As we demonstrated in Chapter 10, the potential gains from accurate monthly timing decisions are highly attractive; however, quarterly timing decisions might be easier to make than monthly decisions. The stock market is noisy, with many influences converging at any one point in time. Psychological or technical factors may overshadow fundamentals, especially with a shorter investment time window, but in the long run, fundamentals are more likely to have impact. Therefore, quarterly decisions might dampen the impact of noise. It may be easier to determine good quarters to be in the market than good months.

The advantage—and possibly the disadvantage—of monthly decisions is that there are more historical observations to examine. To explain what we mean by this, consider annual timing decisions. Assume that you are going to decide whether or not you should stay in equities or Treasury bills for the entire year. Further consider the situation faced by an investor trying to make this decision on January 1 for each of the past 20 years. Twenty historical observations are not that many. In addition, do the conditions faced by investors under the Ford administration reveal valuable insight into how this decision should be made today? Many would say no. Quarterly decisions might strike a better balance between the noise inherent in monthly variations and the need for relevant historical data to construct and test timing rules.

VARIABLE SELECTION

When employing a large data base of potential variables, one of the most challenging aspects is the method of variable selection; with over 150 macroeconomic variables to choose from, the task is daunting. We chose to run regressions individually on the various time series against historical returns and then focused on a group of ten variables having the highest individual correlations. We then looked at three variable combinations within this group of ten. One problem with this approach is that it ignores correlations among the ten variables in the selected set. If all of them are highly correlated, then there may be little incremental value when a group of three is selected for further investigation. It might be fruitful to attempt to make the three variable groupings as orthogonal as possible, which could be done via several different methods.

Other approaches to variable selection are possible. Staying with three variable combinations, it would be possible to allow the GA to randomly select three variables and then optimize the parameters for that grouping. The GA could be run repeatedly in an extensive search for highly attractive combinations; doing so would place no a priori restrictions on the possible variable combinations. The main reason we chose not to do this was calculation time. By narrowing our variable set and doing some preprocessing of certain data, we were able to keep our entire dataset in RAM, thus increasing execution speed.

Another approach would be to analyze variable combinations more carefully using economic theory and the results of previous research. Economic ''experts'' would probably have some opinions about which sets of variables might be more likely to have a logical connection. A GA approach could even be married to an expert system approach. For example, the computer could randomly select three variables and then use an expert system rulebase to determine whether or not the chosen combination was worth exploring further. If it was deemed attractive, then the GA could take over.

PERFORMANCE CALCULATION

Earlier we emphasized the importance of the fitness (or performance) calculation. GAs are very good at optimizing what you tell them to optimize. If the performance calculation is poorly structured, then the end results will be disappointing. There are a myriad of possibilities for performance calculations in investment applications.

We chose a predicted moving average return as the fitness measure. This presumes that positive trends in moving average performance are likely to persist. There are, of course, many other possible approaches. A simple modification would be to merely focus on the trend in percentage of correct calls. If the rule's predictive correctness is increasing, then it should lead to profitable trading decisions.

However, there are some drawbacks to focusing solely on either return or percentage of correct calls. If a rule is right 60 percent of the time about whether to be in stocks or T-bills but correctly calls only those months in which there is a small difference between the two returns and incorrectly calls many months in which there is a large difference, then the rule is not profitable. Alternatively, if the rule seems to generate good returns but makes correct calls only about 50 percent of the time, it may just be a lucky rule with no meaningful content.

A combination fitness criteria might be better. One simple solution would be to multiply the return measure by the percentage of correct calls, thus penalizing high-return strategies that have a lower percentage of correct calls. This measure, or something similar, might provide a better balance in the tension between return and forecasting accuracy.

Another issue concerns the robustness of the cutoff value parameters in the trading rules. A potential concern is knife-edge points in the historical data. Let's say that a cutoff value of 22 is what the GA identifies as the best setting related to the first variable in the rule. Due to unusual patterns in the historical data used in the rule-building, it might be that a cutoff value of 21 or 23 does extremely poorly—in other words, the sensitivity to the particular cutoff value is quite high. However, it is probably desirable to develop rules that seem to work reasonably well over a range of cutoff values. The user probably wants to feel that the rules are reasonably robust with respect to cutoff values.

One solution to this problem is to let the fitness calculation be a weighted average result around a particular cutoff value. So when the rule says "use 22 as the cutoff value for the first series," the fitness calculation might calculate a return measure using 21, 22, and 23 as the cutoff values for the first series and then combine the results into an average. This would "center" the calculation on the value of 22 but would adjust for the possibility of extreme sensitivity around the center value. This might lead to final parameter settings that are more robust.

DATA ISSUES

We have probably been overly conservative in our lag settings. In cases where the series are sometimes released two and sometimes three months late, we have used the greater figure. We have also assumed that the monthly holding period begins at the beginning of the month. If certain series are always released in the second week of the month, it might be possible to add more precision to the timing of the rules by keying them to holding periods that begin right after the information is released.

There are many other series that could be investigated. First, we have not used every series maintained by the Department of Commerce. Second, the Federal Reserve Board maintains monthly time series data for many series that are not in the Department of Commerce Bulletin Board data base; these data might be particularly helpful in developing bond market trading rules. Third, other sources maintain macroeconomic time series data that could be useful. Fourth, time series data related to particular industries might have predictive value. This would be especially true for company-specific trading rules. For example, new car sales data might be useful in developing trading rules for General Motors stock. Finally, additional market-oriented time series might prove useful. Continuing with the GM example, Ford and Chrysler stock returns might be combined with industry and macroeconomic data to formulate a GM trading rule.

RULES FOR INDIVIDUAL STOCKS

Timing trading rules for individual stocks can be extremely lucrative. Market indexes represent an average performance. Remember that averages bring both the extreme good and the extreme bad back into line; some stocks do far better than average, some do far worse. Individual stock returns, in most cases, will experience wider fluctuations than will market index returns. This creates the potential for big-money trading rules.

Industry forces are usually important factors in individual stock returns, so industry data may need to be combined with macroeconomic data, as described in the previous section, to develop good trading rules. In addition, the returns on the stock of competitors may be important to investors making decisions about an individual stock. Our recommendation for building individual stock market timing rules would be to utilize macroeconomic data, industry data, and stock return data of companies in the same industry.

Another way to approach the direction of an aggregate index is through the collection of individual stocks that comprise the index. For example, a timing rule for trading contracts that are closely correlated with the movement of the Dow Jones Industrial Average could be based on 30 trading rules for the 30 stocks that make up the average. There are many possible methods for aggregating the signals from 30 rules into a composite signal; the simplest would be to let each of the 30 rules have one vote. For example, if 20 of the 30 rules predict that those stocks will outperform Treasury bills in the upcoming period, then maybe it is a safe bet that the index as a whole will outperform Treasury Bills.

OTHER SECURITIES

The basic methodology we have presented could easily be applied in other markets. For example, we could use it to develop rules for timing in the gold or silver markets, and these rules might be used for trading in either the spot, futures, or options markets. We could, for example, develop trading rules for gold mining stocks. Similarly, we could develop rules for trading oil, orange juice, or oats; we could use various international variables to develop rules for trading marks, yen, or francs.

Options present additional challenges and opportunities. The difficulty is that to make big money with options, you have to be right about the direction, timing, and magnitude of price movements. In Chapter 12, we tried to make simple calls about whether or not stocks would outperform Treasury bills in the upcoming month. We did not try to forecast the magnitude of the differential in performance or to pinpoint the precise timing of price movements.

One approach to dealing with forecasting the magnitude of price changes could be to structure the fitness calculation so as to more heavily reward correct predictions of large price changes. Essentially the rule would try to predict whether a large change was imminent or not. If a large upward movement in prices seemed likely, then it might be a good time to buy call options.

Digressing slightly, rules that focus on large changes could also add value to our basic approach. Avoiding major downturns and catching major upswings is essential for highly lucrative market timing. These signals might be combined with the kinds of signals we discussed in Chapters 12–14. Let's say that your basic set of rules pointed towards being ''in'' stocks. If, at the same time, your ''large swing'' rules pointed to a major upturn, then the investor might want to leverage up investment in that month. If correct, this approach could greatly augment returns.

QUANTIFYING OUR BINARY INDICTOR

In our formulation, we merely produce a signal that says to be in one asset or the other. However, there is additional information contained within our rules that could be used. For example, let's say we have a rule, X, that we will simplify to make our point. Rule X says (if series 1 is greater than 18 *and* series 2 is greater than 18) *and* series 3 is greater than 18, then invest in the S&P 500. Now compare two different situations, A and B. At time A, all three series have a value of 19. At time B, all three series have a value of 30. In both situations, the rule says to invest in the S&P 500. However, if this was the rule, wouldn't you feel more confident about the rule at time B than at time A? The condition is strongly satisfied at time B but only marginally satisfied at time A.

There are distance-type measures that could be calculated for our binary (either/or) rules. These measures would provide a quantitative measure of how close we are to the *boundary point* of the rule. The boundary point is based on the accumulation of the cutoff values from each of the rule's components. If we were near the cutoff values on all three components of the rules, as in situation A, then the distance measure would be small. In situation B, the distance measure would be much greater. There are various methods that we might use to compute such a measure.

We could use the distance measures in computing a weighted average signal. Let's say we develop a portfolio of 120 trading rules as was done in Chapters 12–14. In our work, we effectively weighted each rule equally when we examined the performance of the entire set of 120 rules; we did not give any one rule extra emphasis. The distance-type measure we have described above could be used as a weighting measure. Consider again rule X and situations A and B, described above. Let's say that all 120 rules have cutoff values of 18 for each component but involve different series combinations. Now compare two points in time. In the first, all 120 of the rules are giving us a signal to invest in the S&P 500, but all 120 are in a situation like situation A, where each rule is barely giving us the signal to invest in stocks. In the second, all 120 rules are in the B situation. We would probably feel better about investing in the market in the second of these cases. By weighting the individual rule signals based on the strength of their signals, we could develop a measure that mirrors this qualitative distinction.

CLASSIFIER SYSTEMS

In Chapter 9, we described some of the basic features of classifier systems. As we stated, the philosophy behind using classifier systems differs from that of using straight GAs. The objective is to develop a set of coadapted rules, not a single best rule.

A search for attractive market timing rules might be better accomplished via classifier systems. The structure of the rules used in Chapters 12–14 could be modified substantially along these lines. As a highly simplified example, consider the following six-bit rule structure:

Bit Position	Macroeconomic Condition
1	Rapidly rising T-bill rates
2	Rapidly rising prices
3	High capacity utilization
4	Upward-sloping term structure
5	Rapidly rising stock prices
6	Buy stocks

With this structure, a rule such as 1##110, would mean that with stock prices already high, increasing T-bill rates, and the prospect of higher interest rates (as evinced by the upward-sloping term structure), it might be a good time to avoid stocks and stick to T-bills.

The classifier system approach might then lead to a set of rules that, as a group, would cover a wide range of macroeconomic conditions. Different rules would fire under different conditions. This approach sounds well worth further investigation.

16

Other Trading Applications and Conclusions

The use of GAs for business applications is still in its infancy; their use in finance and investments has only recently begun. In this chapter, we will suggest other GA applications and describe the efforts of other researchers.

STOCK SELECTION USING FUNDAMENTAL ANALYSIS

We have focused on market timing rather than stock selection in our tests, but we have thought some about how GAs might be used to facilitate stock selection from a fundamentalist perspective. Much of portfolio management revolves around selection criteria. What are the criteria that should be used to select stocks to buy? And what are the selling criteria? GAs might be used to explore large numbers of different possibilities. A few of the many fundamental variables that could be used are price/earnings ratio, sales growth, earnings growth, debt ratio, asset turnover, and profit margin. For example, consider this selection rule: If (sales growth over the past three years has been greater than 75 percent *or* earnings growth over the past five years has been greater than 100 percent) *and* debt is less than 10 percent of total assets, then buy the stock. Hopefully you can see the strong parallels between this general rule structure and those that we tested in Chapters 12 through 14. There are three variables, three cutoff values, greater than/less than conditions, and a logical relationship between the rule components. A GA could be used to refine the parameters for rules with this general structure.

Another approach would be to simplify the binary coding of the various stock characteristics and examine complex combinations of stock-screening criteria. For example, one bit position might relate to an acceptably low debt level. If the bit is set to a 1, then the stock must have an acceptably low debt level: if the value is 0, then the debt level is unimportant. The user would have to define what is meant by "acceptably low."

For example, the bit positions might be defined as follows:

Bit Position	Stock Characteristic
1	Low debt level
2	Rapid sales growth
3	Consistent sales growth
4	Rapid earnings growth
5	Low P/E ratio
6	Low Price/Book value ratio
7	Low number of shares outstanding
8	Low institutional ownership
9	High profit margin
10	High asset turnover
11	High dividend yield
12	High relative strength (compared to market)
13	High relative strength (compared to industry)
14	High beta
15	High forecasted earnings
16	Large increase in trading volume
17	Improving profit margins
18	Improving debt position
19	Improving asset turnover
20	High return on equity
21	Increasing return on equity

This bit representation will accommodate over 2.1 million possible stock screening criteria. A genetic algorithm search could be used to find the optimal or near optimal screening combination.

The data requirements would be high but well within the reach of today's systems. There are commercially available data bases in CD-ROM form, for example, that could contain the data necessary to compute the above conditions for thousands of stocks over many years.

The fitness calculation would be moderately complex. Let's walk through how the GA might calculate fitness in a search for the best screening criteria to use for annual portfolio rebalancing. Consider one string in the population that consists of some combination of 21 0s and 1s. This string could then be translated into a particular stock-screening scheme using the above list of stock characteristics by bit position. A very simple example would be a string with 1s only in positions 1, 5, and 10. This rule would say: Choose stocks that have low debt, a low P/E, and high asset turnover.

Let's further assume that we decide to use the 20-year period from 1974 to 1993 to test this screening criteria. The algorithm would first search through all the stocks as of, say, January 1974 to see which stocks met the selection criteria. We could then form a hypothetical, equally weighted portfolio of these stocks, assuming a $1 million initial investment. Using the January 1975 data, we would then reexamine all stocks and hold only those that met the criteria. Many stocks would probably be sold, and many new ones would be purchased. The algorithm would continue through this process until January 1993, at which point we would liquidate the hypothetical portfolio. The fitness measure for this particular string would be the resulting terminal wealth.

This process would be repeated for every string in the population; these would compete generation by generation in a survival-of-the-fittest contest until the population converged. The resulting final string would then represent the optimal or near optimal screening criteria.

There are three extremely important points to note about this example. First, notice the number of required computations. It is extremely high, but using genetic algorithms is within reach using today's technology. This type of search would have been impossible in the past. Second, consider the power of the finding. It would represent possibly the single best screening criteria out of over 2 million possible combinations. Portfolio managers have been debating for years about how to select stocks. This search would show quantitatively which criteria has been the best. Third, think about the market impact of this type of computational power. Traders of the future will have information vastly superior to any information available to previous generations.

The comments we made about a classifier system approach are also applicable in this example. A classifier system could be used to develop a set of portfolio management rules, which could even be linked to market timing. The market timing portions of the rules might be encoded along the lines presented at the end of Chapter 15, with the stock selection rules constructed along the lines presented in this section.

The potential power of such approaches boggles the mind. The hardware technology of today's trading systems are light-years ahead of those in the past; now the software technology is about to reach into new dimensions never before seen. For those who get there first, how large will the profits be?

STOCK SELECTION USING TECHNICAL ANALYSIS

Because we are more favorably inclined toward fundamental approaches, we have not spent as much time thinking about technical applications. However, we do have a few thoughts on the matter.

Many technical approaches look for various patterns in prices, trading volumes, or both. The problem is this: Which patterns indicate attractive buying opportunities and which signal that it is time to sell? The task of the GA might then be to find the best group of buying patterns out of a multitude of possibilities.

The fitness calculation could be the return earned by a strategy that employed a given group of patterns as buy signals. The trick to using a GA in this case would be to devise a method for representing a multitude of possible patterns and their groupings. We refer interested readers to the GA applications concerning pattern recognition. Previous research along these lines might provide valuable insight into creative methods for attacking this problem.

USING CLASSIFIER SYSTEMS TO BUILD A TRADING SYSTEM

The cover story of the May 1993 issue of *Futures* magazine, a general introduction to genetic algorithms, described experiments being conducted at the Sante Fe Institute by John Holland and others. Because Holland is the founding father of genetic algorithms, his participation might be cause for concern by other traders.

The group of researchers at the Sante Fe Institute has been performing computer simulation experiments using classifier systems. A simulated market contains stocks that periodically declare dividends, giving rise to a fundamental stock value. Simulated traders pursue various strategies for trading; some are based on fundamentals, while others are based on technical signals. Using a classifier system approach, rules employed by the population of simulated traders gradually evolve over time.

Their experiments have yielded some interesting results and conclusions. First, prices do not always revolve around fundamental values. Technical patterns can develop and persist for significant periods of time. Second, supertraders do emerge, and the rules they use are usually either very simple or highly complex— not in between. Third, the character of the market changes over time. Strategies that work well in one time period may perform poorly in later time periods. The potential of such research efforts is hard to overestimate.

THE NEED FOR A COMPREHENSIVE SYSTEM

The number of possible variations to our basic approach in Chapters 12 through 14 is unlimited. The data requirements for our tests were significant, but there are many other possible data sources that could also be included. Literally thousands and thousands of tests could be conducted using our basic procedure. This points to the need for a higher level of organization.

Anyone who is seriously interested in using GAs to develop a trading system should give serious thought about how to organize such an effort. This is far from a trivial issue, but it is often ignored in practice. Many investment organizations spend too much time on the content of their research efforts and too little time on the process. The major questions to be answered are as follows:

1. How will the databases be organized and maintained?

2. How many people will be involved? Who will provide overall guidance concerning the research effort? Who will generate creative insights?

3. How will tests be conducted? Will they be done one by one with subsequent tests being determined by the results of preceding tests, or will there be a master plan that guides a battery of tests?

4. What are the hardware requirements? Will the programs be run on dedicated machines or in a shared environment? Will tests be run during peak hours or conducted at other times?

5. How will the software be developed and modified? What testing procedures will be used to validate the results?

6. How will attractive rules be market tested? What are the criteria for determining that a given rule is not working or is beginning to fail?

7. How will sensitive, proprietary results be disseminated throughout the organization?

FINAL CONCLUSIONS

We hope we have accomplished what we set out to do, which was to offer practical guidance concerning how GAs might be used to develop attractive trading strategies. We do not pretend to have specific guidance about how to beat the market using GAs, but we feel that approaches along the lines we have suggested warrant considerable additional investigation. Most readers will probably modify our ideas and suggestions to fit their own trading theories and operating constraints. We wish you success in your own GA endeavors.

Now is a good time to repeat some of the assertions we made in Chapter 1. The best trading ideas of today are being developed by computers. The competing logics are computer developed, and the battle is being waged at computer, not human, speed. Skirmishes last seconds, battles last minutes, and entire wars are fought in a week. Those who ignore chaos theory, neural networks, and genetic algorithms may be writing their own prescription for extinction.

In a different vein, we hope you have been captivated by the possibilities offered by GAs. The more that we have worked with GAs, the more we have marvelled at the beauty, simplicity, and extreme power, inherent in natural genetic processes. Life is truly an incredible and wonderful gift.

Glossary

Allele: The value of a gene, such as "blue" in a gene representing eye color. In genetic algorithms, the value of a given bit position would be analogous to an allele.

Bias: A quantitative measure of the degree of convergence in a population of strings. Bias varies between 50 and 100 percent. When all strings in the population are identical for all string positions, then bias equals 100 percent.

Binary representation: The encoding of a potential problem solution into a binary string, which is a sequence of 0s and 1s. Problem characteristics, or parameters, are encoded as binary sequences in certain string positions.

Chromosome: A grouping of genes that contains some of the genetic coding of a biological organism. With genetic algorithms, the strings are similar to chromosomes.

Classifier System: A learning system that tries to develop a set of coadapted rules that perform well in the given environment. Rules bid against each other in an auction-like process for the right to perform actions. Genetic algorithms are used as part of the procedure to allow the classifier system to develop better rules.

Convergence: Increasing uniformity in a population of strings. Initially, the population of strings might be constructed using a random number generator, leading to a diverse population. However, as the population undergoes genetic operations, strings tend to become more similar. Eventually all strings in the population may be identical.

Crossover: A genetic operation that involves the exchange of genetic information between two strings; it is one of the main genetic algorithm operators. There are many different types of crossover that can be performed. The simplest, single-point crossover, involves randomly cutting two strings at the same randomly determined string position and then swapping the two tail portions. Crossover extends the search for new solutions in far-reaching directions.

Fitness/performance: A quantitative measure that indicates the quality of the solution associated with a particular string. The genetic algorithm searches for the string, or strings, that have the highest level of fitness. These strings would then correspond to an optimal, or near optimal, problem solution.

Gene: A component of a chromosome that encodes some feature, such as eye color, in a biological organism. In genetic algorithms, a given bit position in a string would correspond to a gene in a chromosome.

Genetic Algorithm: A software procedure patterned after genetics and evolution. Genetic algorithms are designed to efficiently search for optimal or near optimal solutions to large complex problems. The population gradually evolves through survival-of-the-fittest competition by means of genetic operations such as selection, crossover, and mutation.

Genetic Operators: Operations performed on the population of strings in a genetic algorithm. The two principal operators are crossover and mutation.

Implicit Parallelism: Simultaneous search across multiple dimensions of the search space. The property of implicit parallelism is what makes the genetic algorithm search so powerful. Genetic algorithm strings simultaneously explore multiple regions of the search space.

Mutation: A genetic operation that alters one character in a particular string position. For example, a 0 in a string could be altered to a 1, or vice versa, through mutation. Mutation usually occurs with very low frequency. It is one of the main genetic algorithm operators.

Schema, schemata (pl.): A template that describes the pattern of groups of strings with similarities in certain string positions.

Selection: Choosing which members of the population will be allowed to contribute offspring to the generation of children. Genetic algorithms use various selection methods, but all weight selection towards more highly fit parents. Weaker members of the population are not as likely to reproduce.

String: A linear grouping of symbols analogous to a chromosome in a natural system. For example, 010100 is an example of a six-bit binary string.

Bibliography

GENETIC ALGORITHMS

Baker, J. E. "Reducing Bias and Inefficiency in the Selection Algorithm." In *Genetic Algorithms and Their Applications: Proceedings of the Second International Conference on Genetic Algorithms*, edited by J. J. Greffenstette. Hillsdale, N. J.: Lawrence Erlbaum Associates, 1987.

Bauer, R. J., and G. E. Liepins. "Genetic Algorithms and Computerized Trading Strategies." In *Expert Systems in Finance,* edited by D. E. O'Leary and P. R. Watkins. Amsterdam, The Netherlands: Elsevier Science Publishers, 1992.

Belew, R. K., and L. B. Booker, eds. *Proceedings of the Fourth International Conference on Genetic Algorithms.* San Mateo, CA: Morgan Kaufmann Publishers, 1991.

Bennett, K., Ferris, M. C., and Y. E. Ioannidis. "A Genetic Algorithm for Database Query Optimization." In *Proceedings of the Fourth International Conference on Genetic Algorithms. See* Belew and Booker 1991.

Bethke, A. D. *Genetic Algorithms as Function Optimizers.* Ph.D. diss. University of Michigan, 1980. University Microfilms No. 8106101.

Bramlette, M. F., and E. E. Bouchard. "Genetic Algorithms in Parametric Design of Aircraft." In *Handbook of Genetic Algorithms,* edited by L. Davis. New York: Van Nostrand Reinhold, 1991.

Bramlette, M. F., and R. Cusic. "A Comparative Evaluation of Search Methods Applied to Parametric Design of Aircraft." In *Proceedings of the Third International Conference on Genetic Algorithms*, edited by J. D. Schaffer. San Mateo, CA: Morgan Kaufmann Publishers, 1989.

Burke, G. "Good Trading a Matter of Breeding?" *Futures*, 22, no. 5 (May 1993:pp. 26–29).

Caldwell, C., and V. S. Johnston. "Tracking a Criminal Suspect Through 'Face-Space' with a Genetic Algorithm." In *Proceedings of the Fourth International Conference on Genetic Algorithms. See* Belew and Booker 1991.

Cleveland, G. A., and S. F. Smith. "Using Genetic Algorithms to Schedule Flow Shop Releases." In *Proceedings of the Third International Conference on Genetic Algorithms. See* Bramlette and Cusic 1989.

Coombs, S., and L. Davis. "Genetic Algorithms and Communication Link Speed Design: Constraints and Operators." In *Genetic Algorithms and Their Applications. See* Baker 1987.

Davis, L. "Adapting Operator Probabilities in Genetic Algorithms." In *Proceedings of the Third International Conference on Genetic Algorithms, See* Bramlette and Cusic 1989.

———. "Job Shop Scheduling with Genetic Algorithms." In *Proceedings of an International Conference on Genetic Algorithms and Their Applications,* edited by J. J. Greffenstette. Hillsdale, N. J.: Lawrence Erlbaum Associates, 1985.

———, ed. *Handbook of Genetic Algorithms.* New York: Van Nostrand Reinhold, 1991.

Davis, L., and S. Coombs. "Genetic Algorithms and Communication Link Speed Design: Theoretical Considerations." In *Genetic Algorithms and Their Applications. See* Baker 1987.

———. "Optimizing Network Link Sizes with Genetic Algorithms." Conference on Computer Simulation and Modelling, Tuscon, Arizona, 1987.

De Jong, K. *An Analysis of the Behavior of a Class of Genetic Adaptive Systems.* Ph.D. diss., University of Michigan 1975. University Microfilms No. 76-9381.

de la Maza, M. "A SEAGUL Visits the Race Track." In *Proceedings of the Third International Conference on Genetic Algorithms. See* Bramlette and Cusic 1989.

Eldredge, N. *The Miner's Canary.* New York: Prentice Hall, 1991.

Fitzpatrick, J. M., Grefenstette, J. J., and D. Van Gucht. "Image Registration by Genetic Search." In *Proceedings of IEEE Southeast Conference,* 1984; and 460–64.

Gabbert, P. S., Brown, D. E., Huntley, C. L., Markowicz, B. P., and D. E. Sappington. "A System for Learning Routes and Schedules with Genetic Algorithms." In *Proceedings of the Fourth International Conference on Genetic Algorithms. See* Belew and Booker 1991.

Goldberg, D. E. *Computer-Aided Gas Pipeline Operation Using Genetic Algorithms and Rule Learning.* Ph.D. diss., University of Michigan, 1983. University Microfilms No. 8402282.

———. *Genetic Algorithms in Search, Optimization, and Machine Learning.* Reading, MA: Addison-Wesley, 1989.

———. "Sizing Populations for Serial and Parallel Genetic Algorithms." *Proceedings of the Third International Conference on Genetic Algorithms, See* Bramlette and Cusic 1989.

———. "Zen and the Art of Genetic Algorithms." In *Proceedings of the Third International Conference on Genetic Algorithms. See* Bramlette and Cusic 1989.

Goldberg, D. E., and K. Deb, "A Comparative Analysis of Selection Schemes Used in Genetic Algorithms," In *Foundations of Genetic Algorithms,* edited by G. J. E. Rawlins. San Mateo, CA: Morgan Kaufmann, 1991.

Goldberg, D. E., and A. L. Thomas. "Genetic Algorithms: A Bibliography 1962–86." TCGA Report No. 86001. Tuscaloosa: University of Alabama, The Clearinghouse for Genetic Algorithms, 1986.

Grefenstette, J. J., ed. *Proceedings of an International Conference on Genetic Algorithms and Their Applicatons. See* Davis 1985.

———. *Genetic Algorithms and Their Applicatons. See* Baker 1987.

Grefenstette, J. J., and J. M. Fitzpatrick. "Genetic Search with Approximate Function Evaluations." In *Proceedings of an International Conference on Genetic Algorithms and Their Applications. See* Davis 1985.

Holland, J. H. *Adaptation in Natural and Artificial Systems.* Ann Arbor, MI: The University of Michigan, 1975.

——. "Escaping Brittleness: The Possibilities of General-Purpose Learning Algorithms Applied to Parallel Rule-Based Systems." In *Machine Learning: Volume II,* edited by Ryszard Michalski, Jaime Carbonell, and Tom Mitchell, 593–623. Los Altos, CA: Morgan Kaufman, 1986.

——. "Genetic Algorithms and the Optimal Allocation of Trials." *SIAM Journal of Computing* 2 (1973): 88–105.

Holland, J. H., J. S. Reitman. "Cognitive Systems Based on Adaptive Algorithms." In *Pattern-Directed Inference Systems,* edited by Donald Waterman and Frederick Hayes-Roth. New York: Academic Press, 1978, pp. 313–329.

Horner, A. and D. E. Goldberg. "Genetic Algorithms and Computer-Assisted Music Composition." In *Proceedings of the Fourth International Conference on Genetic Algorithms. See* Belew and Booker 1991.

Karr, C. L. "Design of an Adaptive Fuzzy Logic Controller Using a Genetic Algorithm." In *Proceedings of the Fourth International Conference on Genetic Algorithms. See* Belew and Booker 1991.

Kuchinski, M. J. "Battle Management Systems Control Rule Optimization Using Artificial Intelligence." Technical Report No. NSWC MP 84-329. Dalgren, VA: Naval Surface Weapons Center, 1985.

Lucasius, C. B., and G. Kateman. "Application of Genetic Algorithms in Chemometrics" In *Proceedings of the Third International Conference on Genetic Algorithms. See* Bramlette and Cusic 1989.

Nakano, R., and T. Yamada. "Conventional Genetic Algorithm for Job Shop Problems." In *Proceedings of the Fourth International Conference on Genetic Algorithms. See* Belew and Booker 1991.

Nordvik, J., and J. Renders. "Genetic Algorithms and Their Potential for Use in Process Control: A Case Study." In *Proceedings of the Fourth International Conference on Genetic Algorithms. See* Belew and Booker 1991.

Powell, D. J. Tong, S. S., and M. M. Skolnick. "EnGENEous Domain Independent, Machine Learning for Design Optimization." In *Proceedings of the Fourth International Conference on Genetic Algorithms. See* Belew and Booker 1991.

Rawlins, G. J. E., ed. *Foundations of Genetic Algorithms.* San Mateo, CA: Morgan Kaufmann Publishers, 1991.

Schaffer, J. D., ed. *Proceedings of the Third International Conference on Genetic Algorithms. See* Bramlette and Cusic 1989.

Smith, S. F. *A Learning System Based on Genetic Adaptive Algorithms.* Ph.D. diss., University of Pittsburgh, 1980. University Microfilms No. 8112638.

Syswerda, G., and J. Palmucci. "The Application of Genetic Algorithms to Resource Scheduling." In *Proceedings of the Fourth International Conference on Genetic Algorithms. See* Belew and Booker 1991.

Whitley, D. "The GENITOR Algorithm and Selection Pressure: Why Rank-Based Allocation of Reproductive Trials is Best." In *Proceedings of the Third International Conference on Genetic Algorithms. See* Bramlette and Cusic 1989.

Wilson, S. W., and D. E. Goldberg. "A Critical Review of Classifier Systems." *Proceedings of the Third International Conference on Genetic Algorithms. See* Bramlette and Cusic 1989.

MARKET TIMING AND INVESTING

Barach, R. *Mindtraps.* Homewood, IL: Dow Jones-Irwin, 1988.

Beebower, G. L., and A. P. Varikooty. "Measuring Market Timing Strategies." *Financial Analysis Journal* 47, no. 6 (November/December 1991): 78–84.

Clarke, R. G., Fitzgerald, M. T., Berent, P., and M. Statman. "Market Timing with Imperfect Information." *Financial Analysts Journal* 45, no. 6 (November/December 1989): 27–36.

Droms, W. G. "Market Timing as an Investment Policy." *Financial Analysts Journal* 45, no. 1 (January/February 1989): 73–77.

Fuller, R. J., and J. L. Kling. "Is the Stock Market Predictable?" *Journal of Portfolio Management* 16, no. 4 (Summer 1990): 28–36.

Hardy, D. C. "Market Timing and International Diversification." *Journal of Portfolio Management* 16, no. 4 (Summer 1990): 23–27.

Ibbotson Associates, Inc. *Stocks, Bonds, Bills, and Inflation 1992 Yearbook.* Chicago, Ill., 1983–1992.

Jeffrey, R. "The Folly of Stock Market Timing." *Harvard Business Review* (July/August 1984): 689–706.

Kester, G. W. "Market Timing with Small Versus Large-Firm Stocks: Potential Gains and Required Predictive Ability." *Financial Analysts Journal* 46, no. 5 (September/October 1990): 63–69.

Kleiman, R. T., and A. P. Sahu. "An Empirical Investigation of the Timing Abilities of Insurance Company Investment Managers." *Mid-Atlantic Journal of Business* (May 1989): 1–12.

Murphy, J. J. *Intermarket Technical Analysis.* New York: John Wiley & Sons, 1991.

Phillips, D. and J. Lee. "Differentiating Tactical Asset Allocation from Market Timing." *Financial Analysts Journal* 45, no. 2 (March/April 1989): 14–16.

Pink, G. H. "Market Timing by Canadian Bond Funds." *Journal of Business Administration* 18, no. 1 (1988/1989): 165–182.

Sharpe, W. F. "Likely Gains from Market Timing." *Financial Analysts Journal* 31, no. 2 (March/April 1975), 60–69.

Shilling, G. A. "Market Timing: Better than a Buy-and-Hold Strategy." *Financial Analysts Journal* 48, no. 2 (March/April 1992): 46–50.

Sinclair, N. A., "Market Timing Ability of Pooled Superannuation Funds: January 1981 to December 1987." *Accounting and Finance* 30 (May 1990): 51–65.

Slovic, P. "Analyzing the Expert Judge: A Descriptive Study of a Stockbroker's Decision Processes." *Journal of Applied Psychology* 53 (1969): 255–63.

Slovic, P., Fleissner D., and W. S. Bauman. "Analyzing the Use of Information in Investment Decision Making: A Methodological Proposal." *Journal of Business* 45 (1972): 283–301.

Soros, G. *The Alchemy of Finance.* New York: Simon and Schuster, 1987.

Sy, W. "Market Timing: Is it a Folly?" *Journal of Portfolio Management* 16, no. 4 (Summer 1990): 11–16.

Weigel, E. J. "The Performance of Tactical Asset Allocation," *Financial Analysts Journal* 47, no. 5 (September/October 1991): 63–70.

CHAOS THEORY

Bahlmann, T. "The Learning Organization in a Turbulent Environment." *Human Systems Management*, Netherlands edition, 9 (1990): 249–56.

Barnsley, M. *Fractals Everywhere*. San Diego, CA: Academic Press, 1988.

Berge, P., Pomeau, P., and C. Vidal. *Order Within Chaos*. Paris, France: Hermann and John Wiley & Sons, 1984.

Blank, S. C. "Chaos in Future Markets? A Nonlinear Dynamical Analysis." *Journal of Futures Markets*, 11 (December 1991), 711–28.

Cartwright, T. J. "Planning and Chaos Theory." *Journal of the American Planning Association* 57 (Winter 1991): 44–56.

Eisenhardt, K. M., and C. B. Schoonhoven. "Organizational Growth: Linking Founding Team, Strategy, Environment, and Growth Among U.S. Semiconductor Ventures, 1978–1988." *Administrative Science Quarterly* 35 (September 1990): 504–29.

Feder, J. *Fractals*. New York: Plenum Press, 1988.

Gleick, J. *Chaos: Making a New Science*. New York: Viking Press, 1988.

Hurst, H. E. "Long Term Storage Capacity of Reservoirs." *Transactions of the American Society of Civil Engineers* 116 (1951): 770–808.

Larrain, M. "Testing Chaos and Nonlinearities in T-Bill Rates." *Financial Analysts Journal* 47 (September/October 1991): 51–62.

Mandelbrot, B. B. *The Fractal Geometry of Nature*. New York: W. H. Freeman, 1982.

———. *Fractals*. San Francisco, CA: W. H. Freeman and Company, 1977.

Peters, E. E. "Fractal Structure in the Capital Markets." *Financial Analysts Journal* 45 (July/August 1989): 32–37.

———. *Chaos and Order in the Capital Markets*. New York: John Wiley & Sons, 1991.

———. " A Chaotic Attractor for the S&P 500." *Financial Analysts Journal* 47 (March/April 1991): 55–62.

Priesmeyer, R. H. *Organizations and Chaos*. Westport, CT: Quorum Books, 1992.

Priesmeyer, R. H., and K. Baik. "Discovering the Patterns of Chaos." *Planning Review* 17, no. 6 (1989): 14–21, 47.

Priesmeyer, R. H., and J. Davis. "Chaos Theory: A Tool for Predicting the Unpredictable." *Journal of Business Forecasting* 10 (Fall 1991), 22–28.

Rappa, M. A., and K. Debackere. "Technological Communitites and the Diffusion of Knowledge." *R & D Management* (July 1992): 209–20.

Ruelle, D. *Chance and Chaos*. Princeton, NJ: Princeton University, 1991.

Ruelle, D., and F. Takens. "On the Nature of Turbulence." *Communications on Mathematical Physics* 20 (1971): 167–92; and 23 (1971), 343–44.

Smilor, R. W., and H. R. Feeser. "Chaos and the Entrepreneurial Process: Patterns and Policy Implications for Technology Entrepreneurship." *Journal of Business Venturing* 6 (May 1991): 165–72.

"Technical Analysis: Tilting at Chaos." *Economist,* 15 August 1992, 70.

Vaga, T. "The Coherent Market Hypothesis." *Financial Anaylsts Journal* 46 (November/December 1990): 36–49.

NEURAL NETWORKS

Alexander, M., "Pentagon Funds Peacetime Projects." *Computerworld*, 11 February 1991, 20.

Arend, M., "New Automated 'Experts' Ready for Lenders." *ABA Banking Journal* (January 1992): 61–62.

Beaverstock M., and K. Wolchina. "Neural Network Helps G-P Ashdown Mill Improve Brownstock Washer Operation." *Pulp & Paper* (September 1992): 134–36.

Berardinis, L. "Mechatronics: The Key to Man-Made Miracles." *Machine Design,* 24 September 1992, 30–31.

Burke, G., "Neural Networks: Brainy Way to Trade?" *Futures* (August 1992): 34–36.

Coats, P. K., and L. F. Fant. "A Neural Network Approach to Forecasting Financial Distress." *Journal of Business Forecasting* 10 (Winter 1991–1992): 9–12.

DeSilets, L., Golden, B., Wang, Q., and R. Kumar. "Predicting Salinity in the Chesapeake Bay Using Backpropogation." *Computers & Operations Research* 19 (April/May 1992): 277–85.

Gianturco, M. "The Eye Is a Computer." *Forbes,* 12 November 1990, 326–30.

Gregory, P. "Just Think—A Computer with Brains." *British Telecom World*, U.K. edition (September 1989): 68–70.

Gross, N. "A Japanese 'Flop' That Became a Launching Pad." *Business Week,* 8 June 1992, 103.

Hansen, J. V., McDonald, J. B., and J. D. Stice. "Artificial Intelligence and Generalized Qualitative-Response Models: An Empirical Test on Two Audit Decision-Making Domains." *Decision Sciences* 23 (May/June 1992): 708–23.

Inglesby, J. "No Clowning Around, Neural Networks Can Help Manufacturing." *Manufacturing Systems* 6 (October 1988): 26–31.

Johnstone, B. "The Thinking Man's Computer." *Far Eastern Economic Review* (Hong Kong edition), 21 September 1989, 79.

Judge, P. "Researching Neural Systems." *Systems International* U.K. edition (July/August 1989): 23–26.

Jurik M., "Going Fishing with a Neural Network." *Futures* 21 (September 1992): 38–42.

———. "Trading Techniques: The Care and Feeding of a Neural Network." *Futures* 21 (October 1992): 40–44.

Kehoe, B. "EAF Controller Passes Intelligence Test." *Iron Age* 8 (March 1992): 28–29.

King, E. "Modeling Made Easier." *Target Marketing* 15 (September 1992): 30.

Kornel, A. "Investing in R & D Prowess." *Computerworld,* 13 August 1990, 28–29.

Kurita, S. "Expanding Neural Marketplace Challenges Japanese Engineers." *Electronic Business,* 18 September 1989, 79–80.

Looi, C. "Neural Network Methods in Combinatorial Optimization." *Computers & Operations Research* 19 (April/May 1992): 191–208.

Mendelsohn, L., and J. Stein. "Fundamental Analysis Meets the Neural Network." *Futures* 20 (September 1991): 22–24.

Nash, J. "The Many Tongues of Computers." *Computerworld,* 18 February 1991, 20.

Nash, K. S. "Bank Enlists Neural Net to Fight Fraud." *Computerworld,* 23 December 1991/2 January 1992, 53, 55.

Natraj, N. D. "OCR Integrated with Imaging Systems: Reducing Data Entry Costs." *IMC Journal* 26 (January/February 1990), 11–15.

Nelson, M. M., and W. T. Illingworth. *A Practical Guide to Neural Nets.* Reading, MA: Addison-Wesley, 1991.

Noaker, P. M. "Smart Sensing on the Factory Floor." *Production* 100 (Decmeber 1988): 42–48.

Osborne, D. A. "Neural Networks Provide More Accurate Reservoir Permeability." *Oil & Gas Journal* 90, 28 September 1992, 80–83.

Patrick, K. L. "Neural Network Keeps BSW Filtrate Solids at Maximum, Uniform Levels." *Pulp & Paper* 65 (March 1991): 55–58.

Port, O. "Adding Eagle Eyes to Those Lightning-Fast Computers." *Business Week*, 31 December 1990/7 January 1991, 60B.

Rappa, M., and K. Debackere. "Technological Communities and the Diffusion of Knowledge." *R&D Management* 22 (July 1992): 209–20.

Relihan, W. J., III. "The Yield-Management Approach to Hotel-Room Pricing." *Cornell Hotel & Restaurant Administration Quarterly* 30 (May 1989): 40–45.

Rochester, J. B. "New Business Uses for Neurocomputing." *I/S Analyzer* 28 (Feb 1990): 1–12.

Rolfe, J. E. "Finding Cancer Cells and Mapping the Human Brain." *Inform* 6 (January 1992): 28–29.

Rosenbaum, A. "Siemens Restructures R&D to Be Closer to End Markets." *Electronic Business*, 20 March 1989, 60, 62.

Salchenberger, L. M., Cinar, M. E., and N. A. Lash. "Neural Networks: A New Tool for Predicting Thrift Failures." *Decision Science* 23 (July/August 1992): 899–916.

Schantz, H. F. "OCR Recognition Systems: High-Speed Reading of Hand-Printed Forms." *Information Systems Management* 9 (Fall 1992): 68–69.

Sriram, R. S. "Emerging Technologies: Implications for Internal Auditors." *Internal Auditing*, 7 (Spring 1992): 78–83.

Stewart, J. "Can Neurocomputing Live Up to Its Promise?" *Credit Card Management* 4 (1991): 74–79.

Sun, Y. and C. Tsai. "Segmentation of Echocardiograms Using a Neural Network." *Microprocessing & Microprogramming* 35 (September 1992): 791–98.

Tam, K. Y., and M. Y. Kiang. "Managerial Applications of Neural Networks: The Case of Bank Failure Predictions." *Management Science* 38 (July 1992): 926–47.

Vaithyanathan, S., and J. P. Ignizio. "A Stochastic Neural Network for Resource Constrained Scheduling." *Computers & Operations Research* 19 (April/May 1992): 241–54.

Welles, E. O. "Anatomy of a Start-Up: Decisions, Decisions." *Inc.* 12 (August 1990): 80–90.

Williamson, M. "Going Beyond AI." *CIO* 5 (January 1992): 62–65.

Wong, F. S., Wang, P. Z., Goh, T. H., and B. K. Quek. "Fuzzy Neural Systems for Stock Selection." *Financial Analysts Journal* 48 (January/February 1992): 47–52.

Index